God's Soldiers

Adventure, Politics, Intrigue, and Power

A History of the Jesuits

JONATHAN WRIGHT

DOUBLEDAY

New York   London   Toronto   Sydney   Auckland

PUBLISHED BY DOUBLEDAY
a division of Random House, Inc.

DOUBLEDAY and the portrayal of an anchor with a dolphin are registered trademarks of
Random House, Inc.

Book design by Claire Vaccaro

Library of Congress Cataloging-in-Publication Data
Wright, Jonathan.
God's soldiers : adventure, politics, intrigue, and power : a history of the Jesuits /
Jonathan Wright.—1st ed.
p. cm.
Includes bibliographical references (p. 303) and index.
1. Jesuits—History. I. Title.
BX3706.3.W75 2004
271.53—dc22
2003062714

ISBN 0-385-50078-5

PRINTED IN THE UNITED STATES OF AMERICA

May 2004

First Edition

1 3 5 7 9 10 8 6 4 2

For my mother, Audrey,
and my brother, Andrew

Contents

Contents

God's Soldiers

INTRODUCTION

The Afterlife of Francis Xavier

. . . the Jesuits. The name alone will be enough to alarm a certain class of readers; and therefore, in order to tranquilise them, I will say that I do not here undertake to write an apology for the Jesuits. . . . But it is impossible to call to mind the religious institutions, the religious, political and literary history of Europe during the last three centuries, without meeting the Jesuits at every step: we cannot travel in the most distant countries, traverse unknown seas, visit the most remote lands, or penetrate the most frightful deserts without finding everywhere under our feet some memorials of the Jesuits.

Jaime Balmes, Protestantism and Catholicity Compared, *1849*[1]

There have been bad, unscrupulous, ambitious, foolish Jesuits—especially foolish ones, and a Jesuit fool is much the same as any other sort of fool—but if we seek the spirit of the Society of Jesus we are absolutely justified in returning to its great army of canonised or beatified saints and martyrs who were the living embodiment of its rules and constitutions.

James Brodrick, S.J., 1934[2]

In 1554, so the story goes, a Portuguese noblewoman bit the fifth toe off the right foot of Francis Xavier's corpse.[3] It was an act of profound, if somewhat gruesome, piety: Xavier's much-traveled toe was a holy relic well worth having. A founding member and the first great missionary of the Society of Jesus, Xavier had made a remarkable journey through life, preaching and baptizing across India, the Spice Islands, and Japan, tending to lepers and clashing with Buddhists, mocking strange customs and harvesting souls. He had rung a bell through Goan streets to entice potential catechumens, watched his converts smash and trample on the idols of the faith they had only recently cast off, won toleration from a mighty Japanese daimyo by flattering him with chic European gifts of spectacles, mirrors, and a three-muzzle musket.[4] For the most part, he had basked in an infectious optimism; on occasion, weary, ill, and homesick, he had bordered on despair.

Though barely twelve years old when Francis Xavier died, the Society of Jesus was already emerging as the most vibrant, most provocative religious order the Catholic Church had yet produced. It would soon stake its claim as a potent force in the classroom, pulpit, and confessional, in the laboratory and the observatory, in the salon and the academy, in the loftiest bastions of political power; but Xavier's outlandish evangelical career had been the first truly great Jesuit success story. His posthumous journey through history—a journey of mutilation, sainthood, and memory—would be more extraordinary still.

Xavier's body had arrived back in Goa on March 16, 1554, fifteen months after his lonely death on the island of Sancian, off the Chinese mainland, some ninety miles west of Macao. Since being captured in 1510 by Admiral Afonso de Albuquerque in spectacular if typically ruthless fashion—"a great deed, well fought and well finished" (though the thousands of slaughtered residents might have disagreed)—Goa had emerged as the hub of Portuguese interests in Asia, ideally placed between the key economic areas of Gujarat and Malabar, a stronghold from which to dominate the northern reaches of the Arabian Sea.[5]

Franciscans had been here since 1518, a bishopric was established in 1534, an archdiocese in 1557, and in 1556 the city would become home to the first European printing press in Asia. When Xavier first arrived, in May 1542, after a thirteen-month sea voyage from Lisbon, Goa struck him as "a city worth seeing," a real cause for celebration when a person considered that "Christ's name flourishes so well in such distant lands, among so many unbelievers."[6]

This was an overly optimistic, and decidedly arrogant, remark, but an easy enough judgment for the thirty-six-year-old Spaniard to rush to when confronted with a city—Nova Roma as it would be known—in which Hindu temples and Moslem mosques had been efficiently razed to the ground. With perhaps sixty thousand inhabitants by 1580, Goa would never be huge by Indian standards—Delhi, Lahore, and Agra all boasted populations of around half a million in 1600—but it was nonetheless impressive to Western eyes. By century's end Rome and Lisbon were both home to something like a hundred thousand souls, while Madrid had a population roughly the same size as Goa's.

And besides, the city, home to fifty-five Jesuits (priests, brothers, and novices) by 1555, was always more important not for its demographic prowess but for its symbolic, captivating power.[7] Goa was the place where, in often brutal ways, Europe presumed to teach Asia how to serve the Christian God.

Over the next decades and centuries, scores of Jesuits, so often obliged to follow in the wake of imperial incursion, would eagerly make the journey from Lisbon to Goa: a journey, according to the Jesuit Alessandro Valignano in 1574 (and he knew from personal experience), which was "without any doubt the greatest and most arduous of any that are known in the world."[8] Those Jesuits who, en route to India, managed to survive the rounding of the Cape or a spell in Mozambique ("the sepulchre of the Portuguese") knew themselves to be, and were fiercely proud of being, in the shadow of Xavier, the man who would be declared a saint in 1622, the endlessly eulogized blazer of their evangelical trail.

This heroic status was already well in evidence when the ship carrying Xavier's body reached Goa on March 16. We are told that, by viceregal command, every church bell in the city rang, and all the cannon in the city's forts were fired. And then, almost inevitably, the miracle talk began. On the seventeenth, an examination of the corpse was carried out, and the reports spoke of fleshiness, still-oozing blood, and not the slightest whiff of decay. Nor, the doctors were keen to stress, was there any evidence of embalming.[9] Rumors of such astounding incorruptibility began to spread, and the Catholic world began to clamor for its share of Xavier's prodigious remains.

In 1614, the superior general of the Jesuits, Claudio Acquaviva, had the lower part of Xavier's right arm cut off and shipped to Rome—a mission almost ruined when Dutch pirates tried to capture the vessel transporting the precious limb. Five years later the rest of Xavier's right arm was divided in three, one part each for the Jesuit communities in Macao, Cochin, and Malacca. In the coming years Xavier's internal organs would be removed so that they might be scattered around the world as relics, and by the eighteenth century, Xavier water, in which relics or medals of the saint had been immersed, had become a popular central European cure for fevers, lame feet, and bad eyesight. This was a useful accompaniment to Loyola water, made wonderful by relics of the Society's founder and first superior general, Ignatius Loyola, which was prized as an excellent way to wipe out plagues of caterpillars.[10]

Not that the potency of physical relics was the be-all and end-all of the Xavier magic. In eighteenth-century Bavaria a picture of the saint, hung on a cattle shed door, was claimed to have deterred the devil from spreading cow-killing diseases.[11] Charles Albanel, writing from North America in 1669, re-called the time when his "whole head [was] extremely swollen, and my face covered with pustules like those of smallpox. . . . My lips became as if dead, and my eyes extremely afflicted with an inflammation." Shortness of breath and a "severe earache . . . together with a furious toothache" rendered the priest in even greater need of any intercession that might be available; but then "I vowed a novena to St. Francis Xavier, and at the same time I was cured."[12]

Naturally, to a sharp-eyed Protestant, something like the mathematics of the relic industry was always too good a polemical opportunity to miss. According to the calculations of the Elizabethan bishop of Durham, James Pilkington: "If the relics, as arms, heads, legs, scalp, hair, teeth, etc. were to-gether in one place that are said to be worshipped in many, some should have two or three heads, more legs and arms than a horse could carry."[13] It was surely bizarre, John Calvin had suggested, that the "superabundant" St. Matthias had bequeathed his entire body to churches in Toulouse, Rome, and Trier, or that the faithful could pay homage to complete corpses of St. Sebastian either in Rome, Soissons, Narbonne, or Poligny, failing which there were always the two extra heads or the four extra arms scattered around France and Italy.[14]

But to a Catholic audience in the crucible of reformation, Calvin's witty sniping (and Calvin was amply possessed of wit when he so chose) could only ever be a blunted weapon. As the Jesuit Louis Richeome explained in 1605, it was a telltale mark of the heretic to dismiss all pious things rather than em-brace them. It was precisely such issues as the bewildering power of saints that served as shibboleths, separating (by Rome's account) the heretics bound for eternal oblivion from the faithful destined, assuming they behaved them-selves, for a somewhat jollier afterlife.

"A natural light founded upon divine law," Richeome continued, led every Catholic toward the sacred duty of honoring the memory and bodily residue of saints. Of course, as Rome had sternly declared back in 1563, "the celebration of saints and the visitation of relics" should never be "perverted into revellings and drunkenness" by overzealous devotees, and huge efforts would be made in Goa down the centuries to prevent visitors from making away with saintly souvenirs.[15] But Xavier's incorruptibility was always treasured as a sign of divine approval, the counterpoint to what God inflicted upon the sinful and the reprobate: Jezebel, it was well to remember, had been devoured by dogs, her carcass left "as dung upon the face of the field." All mortal men decay, but some mortal men decay more disgustingly than others. The corpse of Martin Luther, Richeome was delighted to point out, had quickly begun to give off "an odour so nasty and abominable" that it threatened to spread disease, much as the "stench of his infernal heresy had infected the skies over parts of Europe."[16] All very different from the long-dead Xavier apparently encountered by Joseph Simon Bayard in 1694. "The saint's hair is black, a little curly and still fresh," he reported from Goa; "the eyes are black, vibrant and sweet," as penetrating as the eyes of a man still breathing. The beard was still good and thick, the limbs still flexible; the cheeks had a vermilion hue, the tongue was red and moist.[17] Signs that God had blessed the Jesuit enterprise were rarely more spectacular.

JUST FOUR YEARS after Bayard's visit, the body of Francis Xavier was placed in a baroque mausoleum of marble and bronze, the gift of one of the saint's greatest fans, Grand Duke Cosimo III of Tuscany, and the lavishly unsubtle masterwork of Giovanni Battista Foggini. Shipped from Europe in 1698, it still surrounds the saint with delicate murals and altars gleaming with red jasper. A cohort of alabaster cherubim stand guard around a silver casket, forged earlier in the century in the workshops of Goan craftsmen, its Italiante columns and delicate Indian filigree framing a panorama of thirty-two panels depicting Xavier's mission and magic: Xavier preaching and baptizing; his humble willingness to suck poison from a patient's ulcer; and the Catholic world's most famous crab, which obligingly returned Xavier's crucifix after he had lost it at sea.

Here was an exercise in mythmaking, a blend of fierce devotion and sumptuous, boisterous propaganda. It would, of course, be hard for those outside the Catholic faith, and for some within, to credit all the magic and the relics and the miracles. And they count for only half the story, having nothing much to do with Xavier's linguistic shortcomings in distant lands, his damaging preference for epic adventuring over administrative duty, his bred-in-the-bone European prejudice when confronted with the strangeness of Asia. But this was how Jesuits chose to honor their first, perhaps most favored saint, the man they chose to sum them up.

And by 1698, after a century and a half of extraordinary progress, unexpected challenges, and endless, bilious criticism (sometimes deserved, other times not), the Society of Jesus had learned a valuable lesson—a lesson that would not be forgotten as the coming decades and centuries piled up: to be grateful for all the help its saints could provide.

Whether loved or loathed, the Society of Jesus could never be ignored. It would disrupt the certainties and hierarchies of the Catholic Church, transform the intellectual, cultural, and devotional landscapes of Europe, and meddle in successive controversies of reformation, empire building, enlightenment, and revolution. The contest to adjudicate its history was always going to be hard fought.

In such a struggle—a struggle for historical reputation, to possess the past—a hero like Xavier, sanitized and incorruptible, was an anchor to be depended upon. After all, he had been there at the very beginning, at the future order's embryonic moment on Montmartre in 1534. He had been, as Jesuits would so often strive to be, a priest in and of the world, not cloistered away but confronting the sin and clutter of workaday Christian life. The enemies might snarl—and sometimes the enemies would have every right to snarl—but the Jesuits would always have their model and their icon.

For close on five centuries, Jesuits have maintained a turbulent, influential presence in world history—and not simply as evangelists, theologians, or priestly intermediaries. They have been urbane courtiers in Paris, Peking, and Prague, telling kings when to marry, when and how to go to war, serving as astronomers to Chinese emperors or as chaplains to Japanese armies invading Korea. As might be expected, they have dispensed sacraments and homilies, and they have provided educations to men as various as Voltaire, Castro, Hitchcock, and Joyce. But they have also been sheep farmers in Quito, hacienda owners in Mexico, wine growers in Australia, and plantation owners in the antebellum United States. The Society would flourish in the worlds of letters, the arts, music, and science, theorizing about dance, disease, and the laws of electricity and optics. Jesuits would grapple with the challenges of Copernicus, Descartes, and Newton, and thirty-five craters on the surface of the moon would be named for Jesuit scientists.

Jesuit missionaries would provide Europe with accounts of unknown cultures, with reports of new rivers, new stars, new animals, plants, and drugs—from camellias to ginseng to quinine—and a dazzling array of exciting commodities in between. Jesuit missionaries would locate the source of the Blue Nile, find land routes from Muscovy to China, and chart large stretches of the Oronoco, Amazon, and Mississippi Rivers. They would bring snuff, and the works of Aesop and Galileo, to Peking, coffee to Venezuela, and Kepler's laws of planetary motion to Indian astronomy.

Such success (alongside no few transgressions) has often bred resentment—the sort of resentment that made the cosseting of Xavier's memory all the more urgent. Jesuits have never lacked enemies willing to depict them as king-killers, poisoners, or practitioners of the black arts. By Catholics and non-Catholics alike, they have been painted as purveyors of absurdly laxist moral advice, as sexual deviants, as avaricious scoundrels setting up secret gold mines and duping rich widows out of their inheritances. Self-styled champions of intellectual freedom have routinely characterized Jesuits as mindless automatons, unthinkingly loyal to their superiors. For those opposed to Roman influence they have been the pope's myrmidons, the sworn enemies of secular authority. While few have doubted the skill and verve of the Society of Jesus—its prowess in self-publicity, its ability to generate unique theologies and spiritualities, to train up, organize, and motivate its vast and versatile workforce—some have wondered whether such virtuosity was a blessing or a blight.

Reformation Protestants, eighteenth-century philosophers, and nineteenth-century liberals have turned against them. They have infuriated John

Donne, Blaise Pascal, Thomas Jefferson, and Napoleon, and if they have sought to guard, define, and cherish their reputation—not least by doting on their saints and martyrs—others have tried to wrest it from their control.

IN THE MIDDLE of 1679 a group of five Jesuits came "limping along toward Heaven's gate." With priestly confidence they announced to St. Peter that "we have . . . recommendations to thee from the Vicar of Christ and thy successor at Rome." St. Peter, who seems intent on flaunting his Protestant credentials from the outset, replies, "I know of no Vicar nor any successor that Christ or I have in any such place. What is his name?" he asks, remembering the simpler days of Galilee. "Is he a fisherman?" A suspicious St. Peter next asks the Jesuits the cause of their deaths and is scandalized to hear that they have just been executed for trying to kill the king of England: these Jesuits, it would seem, are the infamous popish plotters.

Undeterred, the Jesuits insist that there was no sin attached to their attempted regicide since the king is a heretic, and besides, the pope had issued bulls which fully justified their actions. St. Peter, apparently unaware of such Catholic terminology, is puzzled. "Tell me not of your bulls nor your bears; there are no such beasts admitted here—Heaven is no bear garden, I assure you, nor no Roman amphitheatre."

Sensing that their prospects of eternal happiness are waning, the Jesuits offer their trump card—surely heaven is packed with earlier Jesuits who would gladly offer testimonials. "We have several acquaintances that would own us, if thou wouldst be but pleased to call them forth." Names as illustrious as Ignatius Loyola and Francis Xavier are proudly invoked, but St. Peter remains unimpressed. However, in the interests of fair play, and realizing that the roster of the damned and saved must certainly contain a lot of names, "St. Peter, unwilling to trust to his own memory, called to the Angel Gabriel and desired him to look over the register." But Gabriel only confirms the complete absence of any Jesuits in heaven.

St. Peter's patience is now at an end. He offers a final insult to Roman Catholic doctrine—those who offer devotions to the Virgin Mary are "like so many hoarse Smithfield ballad-singers" and they would be better served keeping their breath to cool their porridge—and orders the Jesuits to leave, threatening that otherwise he would "be forced to call forth Martin Luther, and then you know what will become of you." Finally, after further debate, each of the Jesuits is sentenced to "a hundred stripes apiece upon the back" and incarceration in "a smoking hole" in hell for 60 million years. The message is clear: heaven is a place where Jesuits can expect the roughest justice.[18]

Such tales, so vividly conjured up in one of the countless anti-Jesuit tracts of Stuart England, rather overlook the fact that the Society of Jesus had nothing whatsoever to do with any popish plot against King Charles II. But this hardly matters. They represent the mythologizing counterblast to the mythologizing of Francis Xavier. "Survey heaven itself, and all the heavenly host"— so another seventeenth-century critic of the Society advised—"look well into all the ports and coasts of it . . . you shall not find there (upon my word) one Jesuit or one papist. For none shall stand in Mount Sion with the lamb that have received the mark of the Beast, or belong to Antichrist."[19]

A Jesuit saint, whatever the harlot of the seven hills might say, was a contradiction in terms. Jesuits did not go to heaven; they went directly to hell, and if opportunity arose, there was surely justice in ridding the world of their earthly residue. As when, at the suppression of the order in 1773, "the relics of saints were plucked out of the gold or silver in which they had been enclosed, and thrown together promiscuously into a basket while the precious metal was carried off with care."[20] Or when, six decades later, anticlerical crowds attacked the Jesuits' main college in Madrid, killed fourteen of the residents, and took the bones of saints from reliquaries and ground them to dust.[21]

IT HAS SO often seemed necessary to take sides over the Society of Jesus because it has counted for so much, not merely witnessing but molding the history of five centuries and as many continents. Though not created as some Catholic antidote to Luther, it would quickly emerge as the champion of counterreformation, harassing heretics and emboldening the faithful. In its missionary arenas—spread out in the Americas from Canada to Brazil, in Africa and Asia from the Congo to the Philippines—it would forge inventive strategies for saving souls and grapple with the legacy of slavery and colonialism. In the eighteenth century, its troubled encounter with the nostrums of enlightenment would lead to a fraught, absurd decade of name-calling, national banishments, and worldwide suppression. In the modern era, the era of the isms, it would confront the deeds and legacies of Marx, Darwin, Freud, and Hitler, and seek to redefine the Catholic Church.

Of course, both the hagiographies and the black legends are hopelessly misleading. There have been good Jesuits and bad Jesuits, otherworldly innocents and ambitious political schemers. Some have joined the Society to serve Christ, others to advance their careers. It was not unknown for Jesuit administrators in colonial Peru to develop unseemly, opulent tastes in carriages, wine, and cigars. But neither was it unknown for Jesuits to grow addicted to the most extravagant mortifications, as when the Polish priest Martin Costens chose to wear an iron crown that he tightened with pins, or when the preacher and missionary Paolo Segneri developed a penchant for mixing ash into his food.

Jesuits, so one eighteenth-century historian revealed, had a habit of seeing themselves as "celestial ministers," the heirs, no doubt, of Francis Xavier. Their enemies insisted on thinking of them as "infernal spirits," the heirs, presumably, of the regicidal Tyburn traitors. "This double view," the historian admitted, left him confused, putting him "in mind of a picture I have seen representing an angel [in which], when turning up the bottom of it, a cloven foot appears."[22] There has never been a single Jesuit history, no one Jesuit ethos that easily invites general praise or general blame. But the myth and the countermyth, the competing caricatures of Jesuits as priestly thugs and Jesuits as saintly heroes, the ways in which Jesuits have moved in and out of fashion, represent the marrow of the Society's story.

1

"NEW ATHLETES TO COMBAT GOD'S ENEMIES"[1]

Jesuits and Reformations

. . . this sect, which was . . . only recently established by the Roman pontiff for the specific purpose of destroying the Churches that embrace the pure teaching of the Gospel.

Martin Chemnitz, Examination of the Council of Trent, *1565*[2]

It may be said with truth, that this order alone has contributed more than all the other orders together to confirm the wavering nations in the faith of Rome, to support the tottering authority of the high pontiff, to check the progress of the Reformation, and to make amends for the losses their holiness had sustained in Europe, by propagating the gospel, and with it a blind submission to the Holy See, among the African, American and Indian infidels.

Archibald Bower, History of the Popes, *1766*[3]

In any case, although the Society of Jesus would have had a much different history, it would have come into being even if the Reformation had not happened, and it cannot be defined primarily in relationship to it.

John O'Malley, S.J., The First Jesuits, *1993*[4]

1527

E arly in the fog-smothered morning of May 6, 1527, troops of Charles V's imperial army began their clumsy assault on Rome. The feeble, neglected defenses of the city were breached with embarrassing ease, and the soldiers, undisciplined, unpaid, grumbling about months of pestilence and hunger, embarked upon a spree of looting, vandalism, and fleshy excess. Very quickly, reliable, sober reports of workshop smashing, iconoclasm, and theft merged with the more gruesome stories of torture, dismemberment, and serial rape. Across Europe, for generations to come, tales would be told of entire hospitals and orphanages being emptied, their helpless inmates drowned in the blood-gorged waters of the Tiber.

Charles, Habsburg ruler of Germany, Spain, and the Netherlands, was quick to deny all responsibility for his renegade forces. The Italian Wars, the dynastic struggles inaugurated by a French king's crossing of the Alps in 1494, had once more flaunted their uncanny talent for blighting southern Europe.

The sack of Rome sent monks and artists scurrying, and it convulsed the Western imagination. Not until the grotesque Parisian carnage of the St. Bartholomew's Day Massacre, four decades later—when hundreds of French Protestants lost their lives—would Europe be quite so scandalized, quite so shaken. The events of May 1527 were really about dynastic politics and disgruntled, leaderless troops. Religious animosity played its part—shrines were desecrated, cardinals were threatened, and one especially zealous participant brandished a golden rope with which he intended to hang the pope—but Spanish Catholics had contributed to the mayhem just as eagerly as German Lutherans.

What truly mattered, though, was the symbolism. Rome, the place that stood for papal plenitude, for Italian Renaissance grandeur, for the Roman Catholic Church, had, as one onlooker put it, become a cadaver of a city. The Venetian ambassador suggested that not even hell itself could offer so miserable a vista. In 1527, a decade on from the first stirrings of reformation, there was still much hope that schism might be averted and schismatics reconciled. But the sight of a ruined, ransacked Rome, of a pope hidden away in the Castel Sant'Angelo, was an eloquent reminder of how much had changed since Martin Luther's Wittenberg revolution, since the iconoclasm of Ulrich Zwingli's Zurich, since the withering assault on Catholic dogmas, rituals, and certainties had begun. Anarchic weeks that can best be blamed on the quarrels of supremely Catholic kings had managed to sum up Christendom's newly found frailty.

And at this bleakest of moments, Ignatius Loyola, the Jesuits' future founder and first superior general, was about to arrive in Salamanca, as part of his search for a belated education. Within a few decades his place in the Catholic pantheon would be secure, and at his death a viceroy of Sicily could confidently announce that "after so many battles and victories he has taken up his rightful place in heaven alongside Dominic and Francis."[5] In the mission fields of seventeenth-century Canada, pregnant women, having struggled in labor for twenty-four hours, would have Ignatian relics applied to their stomachs and babies would apparently rush into the world; a man with a burning fever would be urged to invoke Loyola's name, and in an instant he would be rendered as "cool as a fish."[6]

But in the summer of 1527, the heirs of St. Dominic had not been so sure of Loyola's credentials. Rather, they had invited him to a meal at their San Esteban convent, questioned him about his suspect brand of spirituality, and consigned him to twenty-two days in prison. Throughout its history, the Society of Jesus would enjoy similar encounters with the machinery of

Catholic orthodoxy, whether the Inquisition or the papal Index. It was the kind of setback to which Loyola, incarcerated for six weeks at Alcalá a year earlier, was growing accustomed.

For the man who would soon be likened to David—providentially sent to combat Luther's Goliath, to help the Catholic world recover from indignities such as the sack of Rome—these were inauspicious beginnings: an early sign that there was to be nothing easy or inevitable about the Jesuits' contribution to the defense and renovation of the Roman Catholic Church.

Loyola

When Loyola died, at Rome, in 1556, his autopsy revealed a body wasted by disease. Renaldo Colombo, holder of the chair of anatomy at Padua University, reported, "I extracted almost innumerable gallstones of various colours that I found in the kidney, the lungs, the liver and the portal vein."[7] There was a distinct lack of Xavierian incorruptibility. For years, Loyola had been a part-time patient, often made worse by inept medical advice: one doctor even prescribed that he be shut indoors during the summer months and be given nothing to drink but strong wine—hardly the most suitable regimen for a man prone to stomachaches and systemically weakened by extreme austerities and mortifications earlier in life.[8] But at least Loyola had suffered one worthwhile injury, back in May 1521, when it was definitively proven that a cannonball shot to the legs could do much for a person's hopes of sainthood.

The facts of Loyola's early life are not easy to excavate. Any account inevitably relies on his so-called autobiography, dictated late in life to his close friend Luís Gonçalves da Camara, a work that was always destined, first and foremost, to be an inspirational exercise in rousing admiration among future members of the Society of Jesus.[9] But basic facts there are. Born in 1491 at the castle of Loyola in northern Spain, close to Azpeitia in the province of

Guipúzcoa, Iñigo López de Loyola was destined for a typical courtier's life, entering the service of Juan Velázquez de Cuéllar at Arévalo at the age of thirteen and, by his own admission, quickly developing a taste for brawling and for unseemly encounters with women.

In 1517, military duty under Antonio Manrique de Lara, viceroy of Navarre, beckoned, and it was four years later, when Loyola was facing French troops at the battle for Pamplona, that the fabled cannonballs entered the historical record. His right leg was shattered and his left badly injured. While recuperating back at home, it seems that Loyola was deprived of his favorite chivalric literature and had to make do with reading Ludolph of Saxony's *Life of Christ* and the saint-filled *Golden Legend* of Jacopo de Voragine. And that, so we are told, is when the extraordinary transformation began. Loyola apparently discerned something enviable in the heroic lives of the saints, a sort of spiritual chivalry, and he determined to emulate it. Or as a caustic account from Enlightenment France would have it, the "Spanish gentlemen . . . having had his brain heated by romances of chivalry and afterwards by books of devotion, took it into his head to be the Don Quixote of the Virgin."[10]

Loyola's account of the next few years is replete with epochal, stirring moments. A night spent before the Black Madonna at the Benedictine monastery in Montserrat prompted Loyola to exchange his robe and sword for a pilgrim's staff and the rough cloak and sandals of a beggar. A spell at Manresa saw him begging, praying, fasting, and flagellating, allowing his hair and fingernails to grow to uncommon length, being treated to visions, and working on his *Spiritual Exercises*. The *Exercises*, on which Loyola continued to work over the coming decades, would emerge as the lodestone of a distinctive Ignatian spirituality—arguably one of the most impressive, enduring Jesuit contributions to the Roman Catholic tradition. Over the next five centuries, Loyola's spiritual vision—optimistic, rooted in notions of magnanimity and fraternity—would lead Catholics through prayer and meditation, allowing them to examine their consciences, convincing them that their God was in all things and that it was entirely possible for them to discern the specific will of their Creator in their individual lives.

By 1523 Loyola was visiting the holy sites of Jerusalem, but when it became clear that the city was far too dangerous for an extended stay, he opted to return to Europe in pursuit of a university education. After two years at Barcelona, taking Latin classes with children, Loyola moved on to the lecture halls of Alcalá in 1526 and Salamanca in 1527, the university towns where his preaching and theologizing (reminiscent to some minds of the outlawed *alumbrado* movement) first attracted unwelcome attention.[11] Released by the Dominicans of Salamanca without prejudice (although they urged him to remain silent on certain theological issues), Loyola rode a donkey to Barcelona and decided to cross over into France. Friends warned him that given the political climate, he risked a hostile reception, telling him that Frenchmen were currently roasting Spaniards on spits, but, undeterred, he left for Paris on foot, arriving on February 2, 1528.[12]

Over the next six years Loyola studied, begged for alms, lost money to unscrupulous countrymen, and lived in something very close to destitution. But then, in the summer and autumn of 1534, Paris witnessed two events—one intensely private, the other all too public—that would help transform the religious landscape of Western Europe.

At sixty days' distance, the whole Jesuit experiment began and the Protestant Reformation revealed, as spectacularly as ever before, just how disruptive it could be. Neither incident caused, or even really influenced, the other, but for those who would later insist on portraying the Jesuits as the fated champions of Catholic renewal, the timing was exquisite. It was certainly a more portentous coincidence than the year 1527 had been able to provide.

1534

On the morning of October 18, 1534, Parisians woke up to find dozens of placards posted around their city. A bitter attack had been launched on "the horrible, great and insufferable abuses of the papal mass," on the risible notion that the body of Jesus Christ could somehow be concealed within a morsel of bread. The hocus-pocus—*Hoc est corpus meum*—of transubstantiation was denounced as a grotesque human invention, a way for the dissolute cabal of magician priests to devalue the magnificence and sufficiency of Christ's sacrifice on Calvary, a tactic to trap a gullible laity in false and hazardous security. Through their tricks at the altar, clerics were certainly winning power and prestige; they had been doing so for centuries, but only at the cost of peoples' eternal souls. To the guardians of Roman Catholic orthodoxy, already reeling from seventeen years of Protestant posturing and incursion, the placards were a blasphemy too far.

Copies of the protesters' manifesto were found also in Blois, Tournon, and Rouen, and legend has it that Francis I, enjoying a weekend at his château at Amboise, discovered one of the broadsides on the door of his bedchamber. The French establishment was launched into a vengeful rage that would trigger weeks of persecution, lynching, and execution. A shoemaker's son and a wealthy draper were among the first Parisian victims. One unfortunate Flemish merchant fell foul of mistaken identity, being pursued to his death by a mob chanting that if he was a German, his murder would likely gain them indulgences.[13]

Francis (Renaissance monarch par excellence, who had created lectureships in Hebrew and Greek out of which the forward-thinking Collège de France would emerge) made the uneasy transition from enlightened humanist to lighter of autos-da-fé. By the following January, Francis was leading a religious procession through the capital, torch in hand, shrines and relics proudly on display, leading to high mass at Notre Dame. Lest anyone be unsure of what was at stake, the bishop of Paris carried the Blessed Sacrament in a canopy held aloft by the king's three sons and the duc de Vendôme. Later the same day, six Protestants were burned to death in front of the cathedral, and Francis boldly declared that if it transpired that any of his children were stained by heresy, he would light their funeral pyres with his own hands.

Throughout the period of the Reformation, there would be rows about salvation, about the impenetrable decrees of predestination, about how, and

by whom, the Bible ought to be interpreted; but there would be no more potent shibboleth than the theology of the real presence—the transformations of
wine to blood and bread to body and all the symbolism and ritual that surrounded them. To Calvinists, the "peevish, popish, prattling, private mass"
had forgotten that the sacrament was really a memorial of Christ, who, when
one thought about it, was supposed to be at God's right hand, not to-ing and
fro-ing between heaven and earth. Protestants across Europe sometimes lost
all patience when "a stinking sodomite or a wicked whoremonger . . . dressed
in his fool's coat and standing at an altar" launched into his transubstantiating
nonsense, making a God out of that which "not many days past was corn in
the ploughman's barn."[14] When William Gardiner was forced to endure such
a spectacle in Portugal in 1552, he felt obliged to "snatch away the cake from
the priest and tread it under his feet." A decade earlier, John Ellis had found
himself before the Archdeacon's Court at Colchester, accused of feeding the
communion wafer to his dog.[15]

Not that Catholics regarded Protestant innovation and denial of the real
presence with any less disdain. In 1570, Elizabeth Milner of Clapham removed
"the sacramental bread from her mouth and spewed forth the wine," doubtless
conscious that, as one Catholic authority advised, it would be better "to eat so
much ratsbane than that polluted bread and to drink so much dragon's gall or
viper's blood than that sacrilegious wine" of the lackluster Protestant communion.[16]

Such battle lines were drawn during the so-called Affair of the Placards,
and in the very same year and city, Ignatius Loyola embarked upon the spiritual pilgrimage that would culminate in a religious order as determined as any
other to sustain the awe and dignity of the Roman Catholic Eucharist. It was
a coincidence. Loyola and his friends, at least in what survives of their testimony, seem hardly to have noticed the gathering theological storm. But for
sixteenth-century Catholics, under siege and confident that theirs was an as-
siduous, interventionist Creator, it was very hard to believe in coincidences.
As Gregory XIII (the sixteenth-century pope who, more than any other,
prized the Jesuits) told a member of the Society in 1581, "there is in this day
no single instrument raised up by God against heretics greater than your holy

order. It came into the world at the very moment when the new errors began to spread abroad."[17]

※

THE TASK OF launching the Jesuits upon the Roman Catholic world would fall to Alessandro Farnese, Pope Paul III—addicted, as was any self-respecting Renaissance pope, to nepotism, lavish banquets, and the arts, though also capable of appointing brilliant men to the College of Cardinals.[18] The Society of Jesus would achieve official recognition only with that pope's bull *Regimini militantis ecclesiae,* in September 1540, but a crucial step toward this fateful moment had been taken a full six years earlier.

By Saturday, August 15, 1534, two months before the Affair of the Placards, Paris had already witnessed its share of Reformation havoc. Statues of the Virgin had been attacked, heretics had been jailed and killed, scandal had ensued when a leading light of the University of Paris, Nicholas Cop, had dared to lecture in alarmingly reformist-leaning ways. Only a few weeks earlier, the university district had been warmed by a half dozen bonfires kindled by the works of proscribed authors, the "devil of Wittenberg" among them. And it was from their austere lodgings in this same district that, early in the morning of the feast of the Assumption of Mary, seven friends, Loyola and Francis Xavier among them, set out across the city. Emerging through one of the bulky gates in Charles V's great stone wall, they began their ascent of Montmartre, and assembled at a chapel dedicated to Paris's patron St. Denis.

The seven friends, their ages ranging from nineteen to forty-three, exchanged solemn vows of poverty, and a simple mass was celebrated by Peter Faber, formerly a shepherd boy in Savoy but the only one of the friends who had as yet been ordained. The official recognition of the Jesuits was still six years off; there was as yet no explicit desire to create a new religious order; but this, unequivocally, was a founding moment. Simon Rodriguez, who had been there, looked back four decades later and confessed that in the midst of his recollections, a new devotion arose in his heart, filling him with what he described as wonderment beyond belief.[19]

After finishing their studies in Paris, the friends aimed to travel to Jerusalem to help with the conversion of the infidel. If this proved impossible, they pledged to visit Rome and offer themselves to the vicar of Christ so that he might use them in whatever way he thought most useful to the glory of God and the good of souls.[20] Given what would happen in October, given everything that had happened since Luther's revolt in 1517, it might seem that the vicar of Christ would have welcomed all the assistance he could get. In the years to come, once John Calvin had published his legalistic *Institutes of the Christian Religion* and launched a fresh assault on Catholic minds and territories, the need would only grow.

LOYOLA, DEGREE IN hand, left Paris, and after a spell at home in Spain (intended to bolster his precarious health), he moved to Venice at the end of December 1535. His companions (now ten in number) would join him thirteen months later, though not before Loyola had endured another tussle with the Inquisition. An advance party was dispatched to Rome in the spring of 1537, and Pope Paul III offered up both permission and funds for the proposed pilgrimage to Jerusalem. Delays followed—military action in the Adriatic made travel all but impossible—and over the coming months members of the future Society, now ordained, spent time praying and preaching across Italy. In November 1537, Peter Faber, Diego Laínez, and Loyola embarked for Rome, and in a chapel at La Storta, God seems to have appeared in a vision, promising Ignatius that he would be favorable to him in the Eternal City.

After another successful audience with the pope, Rome began to emerge as the center of the companions' preaching and teaching apostolates. Allies— not least Cardinal Gasparo Contarini—were cultivated and led through Loyola's spiritual exercises, and by mid-1539 it had become clear that the longed-for journey to Jerusalem would have to be abandoned. Over the coming months, an intense lobbying campaign was begun, and following the Society's canonical approval in 1540, Loyola was duly appointed as the Jesuits' first superior general a year later.

Not that everyone in Rome was delighted. Loyola's form of spirituality was still frowned upon in some quarters, and for reasons legal and political, some cardinals had responded with either hostility or ambivalence to the prospect of a brand-new religious order.[21] But if there was no shortage of birth pangs and suspicions, this would prove remarkably easy for future generations to overlook. Given the timing, it would always be tempting to suppose that the Society of Jesus had been created by a grateful Catholic Church in direct response to the incursions of Luther and Calvin—created to win back the souls snatched in Europe and to locate new souls in Asia, Africa, and the Americas to balance the spiritual books.

The nineteenth-century Protestant theologian Theodor Griesinger, for one, would happily cite a lavishly diabolical account of the Jesuits' origins:

> *The devil sat in hell and doubled himself up with pain, because the monk Luther was courageous enough to encroach on the round world and to upset the order of things. . . . "By my grandmother, he has taken up a position and will rob hell if I do not oppose him by a greater power. And who will help me in this severe exigency when the world threatens to depart from its course?" Thus howled Satan, and flogged his brain in such a way, as to make his black forehead the colour of blood. At this juncture the serpent approached him . . . and whispered softly a couple of words into his ear. The devil lost not a syllable in his immoral thoughts. Up he sprang, and his swollen breast was relieved, and his eye shone again with pleasure and lust. Nine months after that a woman gave birth to a youngster whose name was Don Inigo de Loyola.[22]*

Most Catholics saw nothing of the devil in the birth of the Jesuits, but their explanation of the Society's origins was often strikingly similar. Shortly after the death of Elizabeth I, a monarch he had never failed to irritate, the

Jesuit Robert Persons found himself "at this present somewhat disoccupied through want of health, and retired into a solitary place not far from Naples, to seek the benefit of a more moderate air." He took a moment to meditate on the origins of the Society of Jesus and decided that it had been "properly stirred up by God to oppose itself against infidelity and heresy," a task it had accomplished "with wonderful velocity not only into most parts of Europe but into Asia . . . Africa and the Indies."[23] Two centuries on, a French Catholic would recall how Protestantism had emerged "like a vast fire, threatening to devour everything," spreading carnage and spoilation, provoking licentiousness and revolt. And then, Ignatius Loyola had arrived with "an inspiration of Providence that it is impossible to ignore."[24]

Persons was partly in the right—as things fell out, opposing heresy was precisely the way many Jesuits would come to spend their careers. But back in 1540, Loyola and his first companions were not especially interested in leading the charge of counterreformation. They did not see the upheaval of the previous two decades in hard-and-fast doctrinal terms but, rather, as a symptoms of widespread spiritual malaise and moral crisis. They aimed at spiritual renewal, at purifying souls, at correcting ignorance of doctrine, expunging sin and superstition; and the spirituality they espoused was not envisaged as some counterblast to Protestant heresy: it was firmly rooted in the medieval *devotia moderna* tradition.

Over the next decades, much time would be spent preaching to and catechizing Spanish and Italian flocks who were under no immediate threat of Protestant infection but who, to Jesuit eyes, *did* require lessons in the difference between virtue and vice, who did need to learn that gambling and bullfighting were not appropriate recreations for good Christian folk. If you happened to be a Jesuit in Spain it was highly unlikely that you would express the slightest interest in heading off to Germany to grapple with heretics.

The new Society efficiently set about organizing its ranks and hierarchies, securing patronage, enticing and training up recruits. A rapidly expanding membership, quite diverse in social background and national origin, began to establish a presence in pulpits and classrooms across Europe and in the mission fields of Asia and the Americas. Just as they had taken on the humble duties of caring for syphilis patients and burying bodies in 1530s Venice, so now many Jesuits focused their ministry on prisoners, prostitutes, and orphans, counseling female religious communities, responding when needed to outbreaks of plague.

What the Society was set up to achieve would inevitably influence the texture of its history, and trampling down the heresiarchs of Geneva and Wittenberg had simply not been part of Loyola's plan, not in 1534 and not in 1540. Many Jesuits would carve out careers in which the conflict with Protestantism only ever served as a backdrop. But as well as missioning in lands where no one had so much as heard of Martin Luther, alongside its manifold contributions to Catholic spirituality, education, the sciences, and the arts, the Society of Jesus would certainly not avoid entanglement in the confessional struggles of sixteenth-century Europe.

The 1540 "Formula of the Institute," a manifesto that formed the basis of the Society's foundation bull, talked of the "propagation of the faith" as a key Jesuit obligation. By 1550 this phrase had become the "*defense* and propagation of the faith."[25] There was a world of meaning in this new word "defense." Confronting the type of threat to the church symbolized by the sack of Rome and embodied in the Affair of the Placards very quickly became the Society's business. It would also serve as one of the chief sources of Jesuit pride and self-identity.

Members of the Society would not always fare particularly well in their dealings with Satan and his cohorts. Famously, having sought to exorcize Jeanne des Anges at Loudun during the 1630s, the Jesuit mystic Jean-Joseph Surin lapsed into a melancholy so debilitating that he had to be hospitalized. Happily, there were more productive encounters. In mid-seventeenth-century Poland, for instance, a Calvinist noblewoman announced that she was possessed by a demon. In desperation, her family asked the rector of the local Jesuit college to attempt an exorcism. Aware of what was most likely to offend a satanic presence, the rector touched the woman with Ignatian relics and the devil announced that he was suitably tormented. Next, the devil was offered a copy of John Calvin's *Institutes,* and much to the embarrassment of the onlooking Calvinist family, the devil gratefully accepted it. The Jesuit then offered the *Institutes* once more, but this time with an Ignatian relic concealed inside. At this point the devil gave up the fight and left the possessed woman, who, of course, then abandoned all faith in the Protestant heresy and embraced Catholicism.[26] Jesuits confounding Calvinists and their demonic allies: this sort of confessional tussle was no part of Loyola's initial vision, but circumstances ensured that it would be an essential part of his legacy.

Reformation

The Reformation was many things: an erudite (some said recondite) but always boisterous discussion about how mankind might hope to be saved, about the kind of church, the kinds of sacraments and ministers, best suited to make that salvation possible. The Reformation was a culmination of medieval thoughts and trends. It was also, for better or worse, a place where new things started and where, in baffling ways, enduring social certainties—sex and gender, class and family, order and dissent—were muddled even further. And the Reformation was vicious, provoking religious enemies to spit at each other in the street, or dig up the dead in order to burn their corpses, and much, much worse besides.

Quite which church was capable of the most elaborate cruelties was a matter for debate among contemporaries. The ambition of one Protestant, writing in 1599, was that the "very babes and sucklings" might behold the Catholics' "abominations and spit at their villainous practises." The leaders of a church so addicted to killing, torturing, and tormenting its enemies were surely like nothing so much as "wasps, horse-flies and hornets," like the insects which, when confronted with sheep, "first bite away their wool, after that their skin, and lastly do suck their blood, to which they are wondrously addicted."[27]

The Jesuit Edmund Campion, who would be executed in 1581 after a clandestine mission to England, saw things rather differently, mocking those

Protestant "men in the world which drink blood as easily as beasts do water . . . and because the earth does not open up and presently swallow them
down . . . think all is well."[28] Both the Protestant and Campion were exaggerating, but both were right in ascribing vileness to their opponents; both were
wrong in pretending that those opponents had a monopoly on such unsavory,
if theologically sanctioned, kinds of behavior.

Although some people managed to live through the sixteenth and seventeenth centuries without ever having to face difficult religious decisions, many
were not so lucky. They were expected to hate and avoid their confessional adversaries, and made to endure tormenting crises of conscience: crises involving a choice between the tenets of theological correctness and other, not
ignoble, duties to family, friends, and community, not to mention their own
health, wealth, and happiness.

But the real world of the Reformation was also about those people who refused to live by the theologians' rules and who carved out compromises and
solutions of their own. Reformation was about people who resented the tone
of it all, who were annoyed that "religion is strangely metamorphosed into
snarling," and that "a generation of tautological tongue men" had "brought
too much gall to the pulpit and such store of wormwood to the press, that hath
drowned too many of us in the gall of bitterness."[29] Above all the Reformation
was about confusion: the fact that not everyone could quite see the obvious-
ness of the choices put before him.

And if people were being prevented from living quiet lives in noisy times,
if they were being urged to snap out of their confusion, who was responsible?
One seventeenth-century onlooker had a suggestion: surely it was those most
zealous and uncompromising figures at opposite ends of the religious spectrum, the Calvinists of Geneva and the Jesuits of Rome, each as unflinching
as the other, "tail-tied together with firebrands between them."[30]

Protestantism, according to James Brooks, preaching in 1553, was the
"filthy sink" from which had emerged "all these tragedies which hath raged
well nigh over all Christendom, out of the which hath raked of late so many
stinking, filthy, contagious heresies."[31] Heresy was fever to be cooled, excrement to be evacuated, humoral imbalance to be righted. The Jesuits, as the

rhetoric often went on to say, were the spiritual physicians, dispensing the antidotes, the counterpoison, the purgative, the cauterizing agent, disabusing and disheartening Protestants and healing wayward Catholics. And as contemporary medical theory insisted, the best doctors always appreciated the full range of remedies and procedures—some gentle, others violent—at their disposal.

⁂

BY MOST STANDARDS, the later career of Thomas Cottam, graduate of the English College at Douai and the Jesuits' Sant'Andrea novitiate in Rome, was something of a debacle. When he arrived at Dover in 1580 (and if bad health had not precluded it, he would much rather have been arriving somewhere on the Indian subcontinent), the port officials were expecting him. A spy had made his acquaintance in Lyons and dutifully informed the English ambassador in Paris, who, in turn, had let his employers know that another Jesuit was planning a mission to bolster the morale of England's benighted Catholic community. Cottam actually succeeded in shaking off his pursuers but only by placing a fellow Catholic in jeopardy, and so, in service to conscience, he gave himself up. After spells of incarceration in the Tower and Marshalsea Prison, where he was treated to the delights of the rack and the "scavenger's daughter," Cottam was convicted of high treason on November 20, 1581.

Having watched three diocesan priests perish before his eyes—their innards ripped out and their limbs chopped off—Cottam was hanged on May 30, 1582. Astutely, those presiding over his execution threw his mutilated body into vats of boiling water, thus preventing any sympathetic bystanders from collecting the martyr's relics.[32]

Elizabethan England was a perilous place for any member of the Society of Jesus. Suspected (and not always undeservedly) as political agitators, the "rabble of vagrant friars," reduced to traveling around England in disguise and under false names, would bear the brunt of anti-Catholic legislation. A

dozen other Jesuit missionaries would perish before 1603, and though numerically modest, and for all the rows and rifts it provoked within the Catholic
community, the Jesuit presence in England was always capable of scandaliz-
ing Protestant magistrates and edifying wavering Catholics.

Robert Southwell, who joined Cottam on the roster of martyrs in 1595—
his body quartered and displayed on London's four city gates—gave particular attention to rescuing his own father from the perils of conformity. "With
young Tobias," he wrote, "I have travelled far, and brought home a freight of
spiritual substance to enrich you, and medicinable receipts against your ghostly
maladies." Southwell acknowledged the frailties of his aged father—"Your
strength languishes, your senses become impaired, your body droops"—but
there was still time to repair "the ruinous cottage of your faith." Being a
Catholic at heart, attending Protestant services under sufferance, was not
enough, and nor was counting on the prospect of a deathbed repentance.

"Why then," Southwell implored, "do you not, at least, devote the small
remnant and surplus of these your latter days in seeking to make an atonement
with God and in freeing your conscience from the corruption that, by your
treason and fall, has crept into it?" Having been "too long an alien in the tab-
ernacles of sinners," having "strayed too far from the folds of God's church,"
he still had hope of making amends. All that was needed was to "henceforth
be more fearful of hell than of persecution, and more eager of heaven than of
worldly repose."[33]

Though never as pitilessly or as universally persecuted as triumphalist histories tried to make out, many Elizabethan Catholics felt obliged to temporize
and dissimulate in their spiritual lives. Faced with the onerous burdens (both
fiscal and social) of principled resistance, they either conformed to the
Protestant church settlement in every detail or desperately sought out strategies and compromises that allowed them to serve both their consciences and
the law of the land.

Catholics attended their parish churches but stuffed their ears with wool
when ministers started to preach; they joined in with prayers but refused to defile themselves with the wretched Protestant communion, surreptitiously reading their illegal breviaries during services. It was just such gestures of partial

conformity that Jesuit missionaries like Robert Southwell sought to eradicate once they began arriving in the realm during the 1580s. Those who indulged in any form of spiritual duplicity were warned that they risked both infection from heresy and the terrible consequences of a guilty conscience. Such behavior merely sapped the morale of their already timorous fellow Catholics.[34]

IN SEMINARIES ACROSS Europe, the Society of Jesus would train priests (Jesuits and non-Jesuits alike) destined for careers on the front lines of counterreformation; their duty, as laid down in 1552, to "search out the hidden venom of heretical doctrine and to refute it, and then to replant the uprooted trunk of the tree of faith."[35] Many of the first Jesuit missionary initiatives in England, Bohemia, France, Hungary, Germany, and Poland sought to take the battle directly to the Protestant enemy, to win back souls from Lutheranism and Calvinism and shore up the resolve of those Catholics most immediately at risk of falling into schism.

Heroic deaths such as those of Campion, Cottam, and Southwell certainly helped such a cause. As Robert Persons remarked of the deaths of his fellow Jesuit missionaries, "Not though the lives of those men had been lengthened out to the hundredth year could they have done such good to their cause as has been effected by their brief but glorious death agony. . . . Many who had been timid before have come to stand out with intrepidity and constancy; some have joined the Catholic Church; a countless multitude have begun to have their doubts of the soundness of the opposite cause."[36] And it was with obvious satisfaction— along with a dose of propagandist exaggeration—that a visitor to the Society's English College in Rome during the 1590s offered this analysis of the recruits: "So eager are they to shed their blood for Christ that this forms the constant topic of their conversation . . . many would shorten the time of their studies to be free to rush into the fray . . . when the news is brought from England of some fresh outbreak of heretical rage and cruelty, it enkindles the desire to undergo in their turn the like afflictions and tortures."[37]

Not that self-sacrifice or virulent denunciations of Protestant beliefs were the only weapons in a missionary's arsenal. As one French Jesuit explained in 1555: "I would prefer that they [the preachers] spend their time instructing the people in what they must know, and inculcate virtue and correct vice. When it is absolutely necessary to speak of heresy, one should simply tell the Christian what he is to believe without telling him what the heretics say."[38] Giving aberrant ideas a platform was the most dangerous of policies.

Only in areas where Protestants were in a dominant majority was it really necessary to attack reformed ideas head-on, and even here Jesuits should "uncover the frauds [and] the blindness" with "charity and with deep felt pain."[39] In his Society-wide instructions for preachers, the Jesuits' third superior general, Francis Borgia, duke of Gandía, suggested that it was usually enough to dwell on good Catholic doctrines and habits, such as clerical celibacy, the intercessory power of the Blessed Virgin Mary, and good works.

What Protestants insulted, Jesuits promoted. Calvinists mocked the Blessed Sacrament—the consecrated bread reserved outside the celebration of the Eucharist; Jesuits displayed it to the faithful in forty-hour rituals, lighting it, during one such spectacle at their mother church, the Gesù, in Rome, with twenty-three hundred lamps and five hundred candles.[40] Protestants grumbled about the Catholic obsession with saints; Jesuits made sure that students at their schools prayed before images of their impeccably holy predecessors whenever they entered their classrooms.[41] Images, as Jesuits advised Neapolitan painters in the late sixteenth century, which always had to portray saints with suitable decency.[42] And saints, if you happened to be a member of another Jesuit-sponsored confraternity, at Lecce, during the same period, who were involved in an unusually devout monthly lottery: each member randomly drawing a printed card which bore the name of the saint who was to serve as his guide and advocate for the month ahead.[43]

Jesuits knew how to score a rhetorical point, and they did not always shy away from insulting their Protestant adversaries—routinely blaming them for the onset of plague, for instance.[44] But many of them also shared the early-modern conviction that religious faith was often best inculcated through cautious persuasion and that lustily denouncing Protestant audiences was likely to be counterproductive. The career of Peter Faber, a story of years of polite, measured engagement with what he felt sure was religious error, sums up this tendency.

But such restraint (and there were many instances of more forthright encounter) was a strategic maneuver, not a sign of budding ecumenism. To a man, and this is one of the few generalizations about the order that can be sustained, Jesuits wanted to destroy Protestantism as quickly and as efficiently as possible. Someone like Peter Canisius—who preached through central and eastern Europe in the middle of the sixteenth century, producing catechisms, establishing or helping to establish eighteen colleges, winning hordes of Bavarian souls back to Rome—was (and still is) a Jesuit hero: after Boniface, he is regarded as the second apostle of Germany.[45]

There were key battles to be fought, and Jesuits were often present when the ruptures between Catholicism and heresy were closely defined. At the Council of Trent, the series of meetings held between 1545 and 1563 to revitalize Catholic life and denounce heretical abuses, the Jesuit Diego Laínez was instrumental in ensuring the church's rejection of Protestant predestinarian ideas (a move that was far from inevitable). Jesuits were also involved in some of the most high-profile conversions and reconversions of the sixteenth and seventeenth centuries, including such publicity coups as winning back Landgrave Frederick of Hesse and Queen Christina of Sweden, for which goal Francesco Malines and Paolo Casati, professors of theology and mathematics, would travel to Stockholm in 1652 under false names and passports.[46]

Even education could, on occasion, emerge as a bona fide Reformation battleground. It was no coincidence that Jesuit schools were established in Toulouse and Lyons during the 1560s in the immediate aftermath of violent attacks on local Protestant communities: having massacred four thousand Protestants, the Catholic population of Toulouse would happily turn to the Jesuits to revitalize the educational dimension of its social infrastructure.[47]

In 1568, at the Society's college in Cologne, the largest Jesuit community north of the Alps, the students performed a play in which hell was portrayed not as the home of tyrannicidal Jesuits but, quite to the contrary, as the inevitable destination of Martin Luther, Calvin, and their rebellious band of squabbling Protestant followers. In act two, an angel appears and laments the sad condition of the church, but he is soon cheered by the arrival of St. Michael. The saint advises courage and promises better times ahead. There are already encouraging signs in Germany, France, Spain, and Italy, he explains: the church is being revitalized, despite the best efforts of Protestantism, by the dedication of those who are teaching Catholic children in new and better ways, and by that he means the Jesuits.[48]

When they secured political influence, Jesuits were no less combative, regularly counseling unflinching hostility toward rival Protestant powers. It was surely appropriate, the Jesuit Henry Fitzsimon suggested, that the twelve largest cannon at the battle for Prague in 1620, during the Thirty Years' War, were named for the twelve apostles and that, when victory arrived, those citizens of Prague who wanted to reveal their true Catholic colors kissed the soutanes of Jesuit chaplains. This was the same Henry Fitzsimon who had "elected to militate under the Jesuits' banner because they did most impugn the impiety of the heretics."[49] It was a war in which many of the key Catholic players—Ferdinand of Bohemia, the generals Wallenstein and Tilly—were Jesuit educated, and throughout the conflict Jesuits regularly dispensed decidedly hawkish advice. Adam Contzen tried to convince Maximilian of Bavaria to forge a treaty with France in 1629, while William Lamormaini constantly advised against making any peace settlement with the Protestant foe. At the very end of the war, in 1648, it was a Jesuit, George Plachý, who along with some of his students strove to hold the Charles Bridge in Prague against the advancing Protestant Swedish troops.[50]

HISTORIANS SQUABBLE OVER whether Catholicism was renewed, reformed, revived, reshaped, or re-whatevered in the century after Trent. They wonder whether it was countering the Protestant Reformation or indulging in a Catholic reformation of its own, with roots stretching much further back in time than the rebellions of Luther and Calvin, and with objectives, made urgent by a century of unparalleled political, social, demographic, and economic disruption, that were far more complex and various than simply reacting to the Protestant challenge.[51] It was doing all of these things, of course: adoring saints and sacraments was about articulating long-cherished Catholic spirituality *and* it was about rebutting Protestant innovation. Jesuits avidly endorsed both campaigns.

There must surely have been satisfaction in hearing a Protestant grumble in 1641 that "it is well known . . . that the Jesuits (the pope's best and dearest sons) have not yet troubled the world a hundred and twenty years . . . [but] what service they have done their master the pope, all men guess, wise men know, and all nations in Christendom feel to their pain, more or less."[52] As William Crashaw continued just two years later, Luther and Calvin had made the "Romish Church . . . that scarlet whore" feel old, exhausted, and impotent: she had realized that "in this latter age her cup of abominations was almost drunk up and emptied even to the dregs." But then, in the autumn of 1540, the Jesuits had made their entrance, flying like locusts "out of the bottomless pit, to repair the ruins of the Romish state and to fill her golden cup up with a new supply of spiritual fornications."[53] If Protestants were quite that cross, the Society must have been doing something right.

Jesuits would encounter hostility within the Catholic fraternity too. Within a few decades of the Society's inception, two clashing orthodoxies had already begun to compete for the attention of the faithful. One was rooted in the manifest achievements and sacrifices of Jesuit missionaries and theologians; the other was born of the resentment and insecurity provoked by a religious order that had been far too successful, far too quickly, for some Catholic tastes.

1593–1594: Catholic Misgivings

James Salès was shot in the back in the afternoon of February 7, 1593, in the city of Aubenas, in the Cévennes region of France. In Calvinist eyes, the theological crime of this Jesuit priest was as unforgivable as any that might be imagined: he had refused to abjure belief in transubstantiation. Born in the Auvergne in 1556, Salès's Jesuit training led to a university career at Pont-à-Mousson and, later, Tournon. He regularly made preaching missions to nearby towns, and his sermons at Metz proved so impressive that local Huguenots felt obliged to turn up and heckle him.

In 1592, his reputation secured an invitation to preach the Advent sermons at Aubenas, a city long fragmented by confessional bickering. After touring other towns in the region, Salès heard that tension between Catholics and Calvinists was escalating, and he returned to Aubenas early the next year. On February 5, while trying to win round a Protestant family, he began to fear that violence and sacrilege might be about to erupt in the city. Salès rushed to the nearby church to rescue the Blessed Sacrament before it could be profaned by the crowd.

The next day, Salès and his companion, the lay brother William Saultemouche, were hauled before Calvinist ministers and a lengthy interrogation began. Subjects as pivotal as the nature of salvation, the role of free will, and the various sacraments of the Catholic Church were discussed, but the Calvinists' efforts were centered on forcing Salès to denounce the real presence. By the next day it had become clear that the priest would not succumb. He was taken outside and shot. When Saultemouche declared that he wished to die alongside him, he was stabbed accordingly. Huguenots dismissed them as idolaters; Catholics called them heroes who had died in defense of a cornerstone of their faith, the very cornerstone that had been insulted in Paris back in October 1534.

The Society would always cherish those of its members who died at the hands of Protestant aggression: men like Thomas Cottam, or men like Melchior Grodziecki and Stephan Pongrácz, a Transylvanian and a Silesian, who, after failing to renounce their faith before Calvinist troops in Košice in 1619, were beaten, stabbed, mutilated, and beheaded, their corpses going unburied for six months afterward. They represented precisely the sort of endeavor that Catholic audiences craved and that the Society of Jesus was never slow to advertise.

And yet, less than two years after the clinical martyrdom of Salès and Saultemouche, and only a few hundred miles to the northwest, other Catholics were seizing upon a scandal in the murky world of Parisian politics to promote a radically different vision of what the Society of Jesus truly represented.

※

ON DECEMBER 27, 1594, Henry IV of France paid a visit to his mistress Gabrielle d'Estrées at the Hôtel de Schomberg, close by the Louvre. Unfortunately, Jean Châtel, the twenty-year-old son of Parisian clothiers, deranged by musings about sin and eternal punishment (a common sixteenth-century ailment), was there as well, and he intended to kill the king. Châtel aimed his knife at the monarch's throat but missed, managing only to cut his lip and break one of his teeth. It was just the opportunity the enemies of the Society of Jesus, none more vehement than the University and Parlement of Paris, were waiting for.

Under interrogation, Châtel was endlessly invited to implicate Jesuits in his crime: had he not studied at one of the Society's schools? Had not the Jesuit Jean Guéret been his teacher for two years? Surely members of the Society had encouraged him to kill a monarch only recently received into the Catholic Church for such patently political reasons, just as they had supposedly inspired Jacques Clément to kill Henry III in 1589, and just as they would supposedly inspire François Ravaillac to assassinate Henry IV in 1610. Châtel admitted to no such thing, but this did not prevent a raid on the Jesuits' College de Clermont and Maison St. Louis in search of damning evidence. Châtel, upon conviction, was pulled limb from limb by four horses. Guéret was banished from France. Jean Guignard, the librarian at Clermont, among whose papers antimonarchist sentiments were in fact found in abundance, was hanged in January 1595 on the Place de Grève.[54]

It is almost entirely certain that the Jesuits had nothing directly to do with Châtel's crime. Yes, some within the order were far from happy with Henry

IV and politicked and criticized accordingly. This was, beyond doubt, an era in which certain French Jesuits sullied their hands with the factionalism and intrigues of political life—although it was a tendency that the Society's leadership in Rome frowned upon and sought to eliminate. Yes, the papers in Guignard's library were deeply suggestive of that particular Jesuit's approval of an attempt to remove Henry from the throne—but Châtel had never seen these papers.

Such nuance was of little interest to the Jesuits' Parisian enemies, however. Furious with Jesuit intrusions on the French educational, political, and devotional scene (all real enough), they found it useful to paint the Society en masse as a tool of Spanish interests—had they not been founded by a Spaniard not averse to fighting against French troops?—and as willing to countenance (as a matter of policy) the murder of inconvenient monarchs. Shortly ahead of Guignard's execution, a *plaidoyer* was brought before the Parlement ordering all Jesuits out of Paris in three days and out of France in a fortnight.

Although this order was enacted only within the Paris Parlement's jurisdiction, it would not be until 1603 that Jesuits, who now realized that much of their energies would be taken up by efforts at self-justification,[55] were officially readmitted to the realm. A pyramid erected on the site of Châtel's demolished house bore a Latin inscription which joined the would-be assassin with the Jesuits who had supposedly inspired him, in a single indictment.[56] Abhor Châtel, Paris was warned, and beware the Jesuits who beguiled his youth and destroyed his reason.

IT WAS PERHAPS IRONIC that Paris, the place where the Jesuit adventure had begun, was the setting for one of the more outlandish examples of sixteenth-century Jesuit baiting. But it was hardly a localized phenomenon. Members of other religious orders (supplanted or challenged by Jesuits in their roles as confessors and missionaries), secular priests (annoyed that Jesuits were blithely portraying themselves as the best hope Christendom had in the battle against Protestantism), displaced educators, and politicians wary of anything that reminded them of Roman influence would all grumble about the Society of Jesus from time to time.

The Catholic Church faced a conundrum: the fact that the Jesuits had been such a spectacular success was the very reason why many Catholics began to question their motives. The choice was between the Society of Jesus, redoubtable champion of counterreformation, supposedly encapsulated by the martyrdom of James Salès, and the Society of Jesus portrayed by some Catholic commentators as arrogant, grasping, and disruptive—made up of men who, according to one story from seventeenth-century France, refused to join in the daily round of church ritual because "the pride of [their] hearts will not suffer them to go in procession with the meaner orders."[57]

In September 1621, Robert Bellarmine, Jesuit and reluctant cardinal (a man who could have been pope), died at Rome. His muddled reputation does an excellent job of summing up this schizophrenic Catholic attitude toward Loyola's new Society.

Bellarmine had written eloquently about the art of dying well—an art that obsessed early-modern Europeans like few others—but from the outset, it was his posthumous career as miracle maker and saintly intercessor that seemed uppermost in many people's minds. Francis Xavier, who had arrived at Goa in the very year of Bellarmine's birth, was not, it seems, the only Jesuit able to inspire gruesome acts of devotion.

If we are to believe one contemporary account, "many were present with towels, handkerchiefs, sponges and other linen to save the blood and preserve it for relics." Although one of his physicians "in lieu of reward, cut away a little piece of the hinder part of his skull," his three medical colleagues were "already provided for" since, earlier in the course of the cardinal's sickness, they had secured a supply of the blood obtained by bloodletting and leeching. Once on display, Bellarmine's corpse had apparently needed bodyguards to prevent the crowds from kissing and mauling his face, "permitting them only his hands and feet." Nonetheless, some individuals managed to make away with pieces of his miter, tassels from his cardinal's hat, and the skirts of his vestments. It was a wise and pious kind of theft since, only a short while after his death, cloth that had merely touched the cardinal's body was reported to be capable of healing broken bones.[58]

Here, then, was the Society of Jesus being cherished and adored. Bellarmine may not have faced the perils of persecution and martyrdom like Cottam, Salès, or Southwell, but he had still done as much as any of his contemporaries in the battle against the heirs of Luther and Calvin. Back in 1588—an excellent year, with armadas and such, for insulting Catholics—William Whitaker had remembered how, with the onset of reformation, "the clear and cheerful lustre of the gospel had illuminated with its rays some portions of the Christian world," and the "black, deadly, baneful and tedious night of popish superstition" had seemingly been vanquished. But then, "on a sudden," the Jesuits "sprang up to obscure with pestilential vapours, and ravish ... from our view, this light so hateful to themselves." And "amongst these locusts," so Whitaker calculated, none had done quite so much mischief as "Robert Bellarmine, a native of Italy." Bellarmine looked very much like "an invincible champion, as one with whom none of our men would dare to engage, whom nobody can answer, and whom, if anyone should hope to conquer, they would regard him as an utter madman."[59]

In print, in the pulpit, as theology professor in Rome, Bellarmine had molded a sophisticated, expansive defense of Catholic doctrine and ritual. The fact that he had done so with politeness, resisting the insulting ad hominem attacks so fashionable among his peers, hardly lessened his reputation as, to borrow the phrase of one Protestant critic writing in 1652, "the grand-master of controversies."[60]

But there was more to Bellarmine than this, aspects of his reputation that were rather more unsettling. An enviable reputation for generosity, holiness, and austerity melded with the fact that his theorizing about the temporal power of the pope (his right to intervene in secular affairs) had offended a good many Catholics, Jesuits among them, and almost earned him a place on the Index of Forbidden Books.[61] He had been embroiled in the cosmological chaos of the Galileo affair, he had irritated English Catholics through his pamphlet war with James I, he had infuriated Venetian Catholics by criticizing their attitude toward papal authority. He had even managed to sum up the unwholesome Jesuit habit of getting involved in the political struggles of sixteenth-century France. Having made it through an ambush en route to the city, he and his Jesuit retinue survived the siege of Paris in 1590 only by virtue of a horse's haunch given them to eat by the Spanish ambassador; much of the city's population had been reduced to a diet of cats and dogs.

It would always be possible for Catholics to tailor their selections from this extraordinary career. Supporters of his reputation would pursue the canonization of Robert Bellarmine for more than three centuries: it took three centuries because others did not see the saint in him. But what Bellarmine's life and legacy make abundantly clear is that there had been much, much more to the Jesuits' first century than the plaudit-winning business of countering reformation. In the worlds of education, science, politics, and global evangelism, an innovative, ambitious multinational organization, of which the prolific Bellarmine was surely the quintessence, had made spectacular advances. As we are about to see, it was precisely this vigor and versatility that managed to delight and disrupt the Catholic world in roughly equal measure.

2

"ONE WORLD IS NOT ENOUGH"

The First Jesuit Century

Should anyone be unwilling to set down aught save the good, then let him call his book, not History, but Select History. . . . To wish to persuade the world that our Society never was touched by a breath of scandal, would be . . . extravagance of pride, seeing that there were scandals among the Apostles and first deacons. . . . All history, sacred or secular, has the same tale of imperfection to tell, so why should we want our history to be something special?

Francesco Sacchini, S.J., 1590[1]

I think it is perhaps desirable, in dealing with a matter of this kind, to point out to you at once exactly what a Jesuit is.

Hugo Young, acting for Bernard Vaughan, S.J.,
in the Jesuit Libel Case of 1902[2]

Mandelslo in Goa

The setting was spectacular—"the pleasantest prospect in the world, as well towards the sea as on the land side." The food was exemplary—"the meat was brought in little dishes of porcelain, to every man his own dish, and this for several courses both of flesh and fish all excellently well dressed." And the wine was some of the best Johann Albrecht von Mandelslo had ever tasted. Mandelslo, a German in Asia, a Saxon from Mecklenburg more specifically, had experienced a great deal over the previous two years: the account of his travels talks of parrots, cormorants, twenty-foot crocodiles, and bats as big as crows, of Hindu widows being burned alive, of leopards and bulls fighting near Agra. But Goa, which is where he found himself in January 1639, the place where Francis Xavier, or most of him, lay at rest, impressed him every bit as much—"one of the noblest and greatest of those [cities] the Portuguese are masters of in any part of the Indies"—and the Jesuits' college, which is where he enjoyed his lavish meal, impressed him most of all. The high-vaulted dining room, he concluded, was "so richly furnished as might become . . . a very noble house."

His hosts had much to lament: two days after dinner at the New College of St. Paul they talked sadly (though, perhaps, with a sense of pride) of the recent persecutions endured by their brethren in Japan, "where the emperor had made use of the most exquisite torments [that] could be invented," and from whose shores Portuguese merchants and companions of the Society of Jesus were now wholly excluded. But however harrowing the Japanese death toll must have been, there was something to celebrate as well.

The Society of Jesus was about to turn one hundred years old, and the Jesuits of Goa were more than happy to put on a show for their visitor:

> *Persons . . . came in, bringing along with them some pieces of a broken pillar, some garlands of diverse flowers wherewith they adorned the pillar after they had, after several turnings, absolutely set it together, all performed with observance of music. At the upper end of this pillar came out a flower made like a tulip which opened itself while they danced, till at last came out of it an image of the Blessed Virgin with her child in her arms and the pillar itself opened in several places to cast out perfumed waters like a fountain . . . by that invention they represented the pains they had taken in planting among the pagans and Mohammedans of those parts the Church of God whereof our saviour is the only pillar or cornerstone.*[3]

The Goan Jesuits were at the center of a missionary enterprise which, in less than a hundred years, had spread out across the Americas, from the Great Lakes to Paraguay, through Africa and Asia, from Ethiopia to Vietnam. This startling advance was, in turn, only the most glamorous aspect of a staggering, though hardly untroubled, century of growth and achievement.

When the *Imago primi saeculi*, a timely compendium of Jesuit ideals and exploits, was published at Antwerp in 1640, critics accused the Society of hubris, and some cautious voices from within the order itself expressed misgivings about the boastful tone of the work.[4] But what made the *Imago* such an adept propagandist flourish was the fact that it was based on an irrefutable reality: that for the young Society of Jesus (as one illustration in the *Imago* put it) *unus non sufficit orbis*—one world was not enough.

BY THE TIME Mandelslo arrived in Goa, the hierarchies and regions of the Jesuit order were for the most part well established, although new mission fields would continue to open up down the years. A superior general, installed for life by a general congregation, was to be the only elected figure in the Society, regional leaders being appointed from above rather than chosen locally. This general ("general" as in "complete" or "universal," not as in "military officer": a distinction the Jesuits' enemies, eager to portray the Society as a military machine, were inclined to ignore) ruled over regional "assistancies," with each of these divided up into smaller "provinces," all of which, in accordance with Loyola's wishes and commandments, were to remain in regular written contact with Jesuit headquarters in Rome and, whenever possible, with one another.[5]

If, during the first decades after 1540, there were those in the Society not particularly well versed in just what it meant to be a Jesuit (and these were, after all, early days), they could count on guidance and instruction not only by dint of the mammoth letter-writing efforts of Loyola and his dynamic secretary, Juan Polanco, but also through face-to-face meetings with Jerónimo Nadal, who, as the Society's official European visitor, traveled tirelessly through Spain, Italy, Portugal, and beyond. There was an energetic campaign to establish what the Society's constitutions, printed in their Latin version in 1558–59, termed a union of hearts.[6]

An alternative route toward such union was provided by Loyola's *Spiritual Exercises*, papally sanctioned and in print since 1548, and by an order of 1608, to be revisited once a year by every Jesuit. To be guided through these exercises— a course of meditation, prayer, and rigorous examination of conscience— turned out to be not only a popular, if daunting, recreation among Europe's laity (Catholic soldiers, Catholic painters, and even a few Protestants) but also an effective way of enticing recruits into a career as a Jesuit.

The Society had long had its ways, unusually lengthy and rigorous, of training its membership—which had expanded from just short of a thousand at Loyola's death, in 1556, to 15,544 seventy years later. Dismissals had sometimes proved necessary—Xavier himself had found time to sack an individual who did not care to run the risks associated with an evangelical sojourn in the

Spice Islands—and there had been those like Edward Thorne, "carried away by the evil tendencies of the time," who had embarked upon a career in the Society not "because he was moved by the good life or inspired by faith, but simply to escape poverty."[7] But few doubted that to become a Jesuit was an exacting business, hardly to be entered into lightly. Someone like Thomas Stapleton was forced to admit that joining the Society of Jesus was very much a young man's game. In 1585, aged fifty, after an eminent theological career, he presented himself to the Jesuits of Douai and spent two years under their tutelage, only to decide that the Society "suited neither [his] temperament nor [his] habits of a lifetime" and "that at [his] age to embrace the religious life was not really feasible."[8]

The Society's founding documents were replete with advice about who might best enjoy the privilege of becoming a Jesuit. Naturally, anyone who was married, or subscribed to erroneous religious opinions, or suffered from mental instability was ruled out, and unless absolute reformation of character had taken place, a person guilty of homicide or otherwise "publicly infamous because of enormous sin" was unlikely to have a Jesuit future ahead of him. It was important that a candidate be asked whether "he has any stomach trouble or headaches or trouble from some other bodily malfunction" since a Jesuit's life could well turn out to be physically demanding; and as well as concerns about "a lack of bodily integrity, illness and weakness," there were doubts about individuals possessed of "notable ugliness." "Persons who have notable disfigurements or defects, such as hunchbacks and other deformities, whether they be natural or accidental such as from wounds and the like," were at a disadvantage because such "obstacles to the priesthood . . . do not help towards the edification of neighbours."

However, such physical encumbrances could be confidently ignored if a candidate with exceptional talents presented himself. The guiding principle to be observed by those in charge of Jesuit admissions was that "the greater the number of natural and infused gifts someone has from God our Lord which are useful for what the Society aims at . . . and the more experience the candidate has in the use of these gifts, the more suitable will he be for reception into the Society." Wealth and social status, it was averred (though this was not always heeded), simply did not matter; qualities such as spiritual vigor, an affection for the Society, a good memory, and a pleasing manner of speech most certainly did.[9]

In the Jesuit scheme of formation as it eventually emerged, a two-year novitiate—of probation and spiritual instruction—was followed by the moment at which the three simple, perpetual vows of chastity, poverty, and obedience were taken. At this time a decision was made as to whether an individual was destined to become a brother or a scholastic (intended for the priesthood—although express dispensation would always be required if, at a later date, a Jesuit aspired to any ecclesiastical dignity such as a cardinal's hat). For the scholastic, years of study in philosophy (three years as a rule) and theology (usually four years) lay ahead, interrupted by the "regency," usually taken up with teaching duties. Finally, the period of "tertianship" would arrive, during which an individual revisited more spiritual concerns, and spent time making the *Spiritual Exercises* in full. At this point, the three vows of poverty, chastity, and obedience were repeated, and it was decided whether the now fully formed Jesuit was to become a spiritual coadjutor or a "professed" Jesuit, who had the honor of taking the additional, fourth vow, of obedience to the pope as regards missions. It was from the elite, relatively small body of the professed that superiors were chosen.

Those who were chosen to be brothers, or temporal coadjutors, accounted for something like a quarter of the membership. This group—which, the constitutions meanly suggested, ought to be content with the equivalent role of the Bible's Martha in the Society—worked as gardeners, builders, and cooks, but also included within their number eminent architects such as Pieter Huyssens and Andrea Pozzo, an explorer like Bento de Goes (the first Jesuit to find a land route between India and China, via Lahore and Kabul), and the much-doted-upon Alphonsus Rodriguez, a lowly porter at the Society's college at Palma, Majorca, whose exemplary and deeply spiritual life would be held up for admiration by generations of Jesuits, even securing him canonization in 1888.

"Ways of Proceeding"

Structure, of course, was much easier to pin down than ethos, and contemporaries struggled, as historians struggle still, to define a Jesuit mentality. To many observers, it seemed as though the Society was developing a unique spirituality and a specifically Jesuit way of teaching and preaching: a taste not only for lonely contemplation but for the role of the senses in devotion and the place of elegant rhetoric in the persuasive work of Christian instruction.

There was talk of a Jesuit worldview: a determination not to be shut up in the cloister but to be involved in the rush and bustle of the whole of Catholic life. Jesuits, in contrast to other, suburb-dwelling orders, often deliberately tried to establish their churches and communities close to a city's busiest thoroughfares. In the words of one contemporary Protestant critic, the most troubling thing about Loyola's scoundrels was that they had "left the shade of ancient sloth and inactivity, in which the other monks had grown grey," and "come forth to engage in toils."[10] It seemed to some as if Jesuits were not quite regular clergy—like those monks who lived in cloistered communities and chanted matins, lauds, and vespers together—and not quite members of the secular clergy, such as parish priests.

Some saw dynamism in this; others, such as the Society's early critic Etienne Pasquier, claimed that it produced a "hermaphrodite" species of clerics, lacking even a distinctive dress code, conforming instead to the style of priests in whatever place they found themselves: men not to be trusted.[11] To John Donne, Jesuits were "as eunuchs," men who seemed to have lost their "apprehension and capacity of worldly estates" but who retained "the lust, and itch, and concupiscence, to be conversant therein."[12] John Donne, as we will see, despised the Society of Jesus.

The Council of Trent had been keen, especially in light of Luther's democratizing priesthood of all believers, to elevate and isolate the clergy: to set priests apart, to insist on their special cassocks and sacramental role, to train them more effectively, to make sure they had appropriately stocked libraries, to wean them away from the pleasures of hunting. And Jesuits were not necessarily antithetical to such trends. But Loyola's spirituality—the conviction that God was in all, and all was in God—meant that, as Jerónimo Nadal put it, "the world is our house."[13] Jesuits seemed determined to occupy (to borrow the terms of one recent historian) both social and religious space.[14]

It was never quite that simple, however, and if many Jesuits were intent on being in and of the world, others, most notably the Society's third superior general, Francis Borgia, duke of Gandía, militated for a more meditative, monkish Jesuit identity, advocating traditional clerical dress and, in addition to regular examinations of conscience, an hour of private prayer each day.[15] Throughout the Society's first century there would be talk of a spiritual malaise, of a need to rediscover the Jesuits' inner religious world and restore the delicate Ignatian balance between action and contemplation.

What is more, although Ignatian spirituality was broadly, sometimes supremely, optimistic—eager to grasp and console the totality of early-modern Christian life—it hardly lacked its pessimistic emphases, the suspicion of fleshiness and worldliness without which any kind of early-modern spirituality would be unrecognizable. Anyone who had progressed through the first week of the *Spiritual Exercises* would have learned an enormous amount about the lineaments of sin, as would the crowds across Europe addressed by those Jesuit missionaries who opted to brandish skulls as a none-too-subtle reminder of the baleful consequences of immorality.[16]

WHAT CAN BE said with certainty is that the century-old Society was emerging as one of Europe's most influential organizations. Although plans to establish a sister order for the Society were quickly abandoned, a number of female religious groups drew inspiration from the Jesuit experiment: Mary Ward's uncloistered order of English Sisters would be widely referred to as

Jesuitesses up to their suppression in 1630. One Habsburg princess, Juana of Austria, even achieved the rare distinction of becoming a "female Jesuit" in 1554, secretly admitted under the pseudonym Mateo Sánchez.

The Jesuits were famous and they were glamorous, able to inspire the most extraordinary devotion within a family such as the Acostas of Medina del Campo. As well as producing a son, José, who was perhaps the most accomplished Jesuit missionary to Latin America in the early-modern period, the family included four other sons who joined the Society; a father, Antonio, who regularly contributed land and money to Jesuit building and educational projects; and a mother, Ana, who repeatedly asked the Society's authorities if she, her husband, and her daughter Juana might be buried in the Jesuit church in Valladolid or, failing that, in the Jesuit church nearest to wherever in the world they happened to die.[17]

The Society could inspire carnival as well. In 1622, when Francis Xavier and Ignatius Loyola became the first Jesuits to be canonized, the Society could count on the population of Antwerp, that deeply Catholic place, that snub-nosed riposte to über-Calvinist Amsterdam, to decorate the city with flowers and tapestries, and to set up makeshift theaters in which episodes in the lives of the saints were reenacted. It could count on the congregations, guilds, and students of the city, in the heart of the most thriving of the Society's provinces, to stage an elaborate procession, the highlights of which were the floats bearing effigies of the saints, the float of Xavier preceded by catechumens clothed in the manner of the disparate peoples he had sought to convert.[18]

It could also rely on no less an artistic talent than Peter Paul Rubens to paint celebratory altarpieces for its Antwerp church—the same Rubens, it should be noted, who belonged to a Jesuit lay sodality, who also found time to provide sketches for an adoring life of Loyola and engravings for the influential treatise on optics by the Jesuit François d'Aguilon: putti studying the eye of Cyclops, putti being instructed in binocular vision.[19] D'Aguilon himself was just one example of the burgeoning Jesuit contribution to science (in mathematics, geometry, astronomy, and much else besides), while Rubens reflected the flourishing artistic interest in the Society. Caravaggio had fumed when refused the chance to paint an altarpiece for the Gesù, the Jesuits' Roman church, the same church to which Francesco Borromini, master of the Italian baroque, would leave five hundred scudi in his will.

※

BUT WHAT, BEYOND patronage and putti, did the Jesuits do? By the mid–seventeenth century they had a virtual monopoly in the role of confessor to the likes of the kings of France and the dukes of Bavaria, and although it was not part of their original brief, they were now a dominant force in the education of the Catholic world. This development, which inevitably meant setting up permanent educational establishments, rather diluted the concept of itinerant ministry so dear to Loyola and his earliest collaborators. But it also made the Society truly revolutionary: it became the first religious order of the Catholic Church to adopt formal education as a significant ministry.

The Society trained not only its own recruits but a sizable portion of the secular clergy of Europe. Colleges dedicated to training, among others, German, Hungarian, Greek, and English priests were placed in Jesuit hands, and it would soon become clear that locating an archbishop of Vienna not educated by the Society would be a fool's errand. In 1621, the first Jesuit-trained pope, Gregory XV, took possession of the papal tiara.

And then there were the children (Catholic and even, on occasion, Protestant) who were taught in a worldwide network of schools and colleges, expanding from humble beginnings in Spain, at Gandía in 1546 and in Sicily at Messina in 1547 (the first institution primarily intended for non-Jesuit pupils, or "externs"), at an average rate of six new institutions a year by the end of the sixteenth century. Leaders of the Society had grown accustomed to turning down many of the requests to establish schools that came flooding in, and by 1600 there were fifty-six institutions in Italy and Sicily alone, seventy-seven in Spain and its overseas empire. In France, where Jesuits were teaching as many as forty thousand students by 1630, figures as eminent as Descartes, Corneille, Bossuet, and Molière would receive a Jesuit education, and although some of these men would be far from kind to their former teachers, those taught in Jesuit schools would also manage to provide the Society with more than half its novices.

Jesuit education, that much discussed phenomenon—damned by many, though praised by, among others, Francis Bacon and Arthur Conan Doyle— was neither as unique nor as regimented as is sometimes thought, and the success and popularity of the schools and colleges can all too easily be overstated. In some places it had taken a while for local elites to be convinced of the value of Jesuit instruction;[20] rival educators routinely put up stern resistance to the Society's incursions, and it is clear that the schools had their share of mediocre teachers. In a venue such as Speyer, there had been concern during the 1560s that the establishment of a Jesuit college in the city was the most likely way to undermine the relatively peaceful modus vivendi established by local Catholics and Protestants.[21] But despite such setbacks, by the time the final version of the *Ratio studiorum*, or plan of studies, was produced in 1599, the Society had taken charge of a distinctive and influential pedagogical system.[22]

In the Jesuit educational structure, lower schools, usually entered by boys at nine or ten, offered instruction, usually over five or six years, in grammar (three years of Greek and Latin), humanities (one year, including study of Cicero, Virgil, Horace, and the histories of Livy, Caesar, and Sallust), and rhetoric. Some schools—often referred to as academies—also offered two further years of study in philosophy and moral theology. Much emphasis was placed on the so-called *modus parisiensis*, an educational philosophy that (with rather more novelty than a modern audience might realize) favored structuring classes according to ability, would not allow progress to the next level until existing material had been mastered, and skillfully employed disputations, exercises, and drill-learning techniques.

Classes, taught by teachers who demanded no salary (quite a selling point in the contemporary educational marketplace), were often large (sometimes to an unwieldy degree), closely disciplined, thriving on emulation and competition, and often composed of pupils from across the social spectrum. Loyola's insistence (not always heeded) that pupils have at least a rudimentary knowledge of Latin before embarking upon their studies clearly excluded large swathes of Europe's illiterate population, and some institutions—the Collegium Nobilium in Parma and La Flèche in France, for instance—did emerge as favored haunts of the nobility, but the fact that Jesuit education was almost always free made for a relatively impressive social mix.

Beyond these schools were full-fledged universities offering degrees in philosophy (Aristotelian logic, physics, and metaphysics) and theology (grounded in a revised form of Thomism: a scholasticism conscious of humanist criticism). An institution such as the Collegio Romano, founded in 1551 and home to teachers as eminent as Christopher Clavius, Francis Toledo, and Juan Mariana, was a competitive rival to Rome's Sapienza and as reputable an educational institution as Catholic Europe possessed.

Jesuit schools, although we should be wary of generalizations, sought to combine the educational advances of humanism—which included a reverence for classical culture—with the duty to produce pious members of Christian society.[23] Students were obliged to examine their consciences, develop an interior spirituality, and attend mass every bit as much as they were expected to read Cicero or hone their skills in Latin metrics and prosody. In this decidedly Christian-humanist way, the Society set about training students to be good Christians and virtuous citizens, but it also strove to produce eloquent, elegant members of the secular world.

Jesuits wrote about the art of courtly wisdom; they sometimes employed dance masters in their schools to cultivate refined gesture and posture; and the popularity of dramatic productions and staged disputations amply testified to the importance afforded to rhetorical proficiency.[24] There was a rejection of Machiavellian pessimism—Machiavelli was the sort of person to be burned in effigy, which is just what Jesuits did at Ingolstadt in 1555—and a confidence that a person could be eminently devout at the same time as being a successful politician or lawyer.[25]

BEYOND ITS COLLEGES and pulpits, the two true engine rooms of Jesuit activity, the Society extended its moral, usually well-intentioned grasp through a network of lay sodalities and confraternities (most importantly the Marian congregations, instigated by Jean Leunis from 1563 onward), encouraging members to examine their consciences, spreading certain kinds of devotion, gaining friends in high places, certainly, but also coopting elites into pastoral work intended to benefit those on society's margins.[26]

Within this network there were rivalries and snobberies—confraternities could all too easily become a pawn in local political and economic power games—but the Jesuit congregations (not, admittedly, to everyone's taste) were destined to emerge as an important and enduring focus of the spiritual life of the European Catholic laity. On occasion, they could even find themselves on the front line of the confessional battle, growing up at an unusually urgent rate in areas recently despoiled by iconoclasts, or urging their members to monitor local bookshops, keeping an eye out for any heretical wares.

And radiating outward from the towns were the Jesuits' rural missions, not only into areas infected by the Protestant heresy but throughout Catholic Europe, from Brittany to southern Spain, from Italy to Poland, preaching, erecting crosses, healing feuds, offering confession and communion, even supplying food and clothing. Historians differ, as historians will, as to what these missions, also featuring Capuchins in large numbers, set out to achieve: were they aimed at expunging pagan survivalism, or at revitalizing corrupt but recognizably Christian populations? Levels of success are also difficult to gauge: the classically Tridentine notion of imposing boundaries of belief, specific ritual, forms, and moralities was confronted with the fact that rural communities had a habit of sustaining their own, deeply felt religious sensibilities, with which missionaries often had to seek compromise.

What manifestly did characterize such missions was a rich diversity of evangelical tactics, geared to local circumstances and tastes: from Silvestro Landini's Savonarolaesque bonfires of the vanities in Corsica to the lavishly theatrical and emotional mission tours in Italy with their terrifying penitential processions. By the late seventeenth century and throughout the eighteenth, rural missionaries such as Julien Maunoir in Brittany, Paolo Segneri in Italy, and Pedro de Calatayud in Spain would be among the most celebrated members of the Society; and by turning to a figure like Jean François Régis, there was even a chance to find common cause between the Society's efforts back in Europe and its missioning across the Atlantic Ocean.[27]

Régis, hero of the rural missions in seventeenth-century France, died in 1640 and did not achieve beatification until 1716 or canonization until 1737, but a popular cult grew up around him almost immediately, and it was a growth the Society of Jesus was happy to promote.[28] If, back in the south of France, Régis's memory, pieces of his soutane, and earth from his tomb were quickly praised for healing ulcers, reforming sinners, and multiplying grain, so, on the cusp between the seventeenth and eighteenth centuries, he would emerge in New France as the most efficacious of heavenly allies, saving priests trapped by ice or at risk of drowning. When Jacques Gravier headed down the Mississippi in 1700, "a small piece of Father Francis Regis's hat, which one of our servants gave me," proved to be "the most infallible remedy that I know for curing all kinds of fevers." A few years later, local neophytes with access to a picture of Régis were reported as being "in ecstasies" as they passed "the hand several times over the face of the saint."[29]

OVER THE SOCIETY'S first century there had, of course, been problems. As we have seen, fellow educators, national politicians, bishops, and parish clergy had sometime resented Jesuit success. As Muzio Vitelleschi, the Society's sixth superior general, pointed out in 1620, those Jesuits addicted to hyperbole when describing their companions ought to realize that "the religious of other orders, and strangers in general, do not look upon our Society with the same eyes as we do."[30]

Nor had all sixteenth-century popes been quite as enthusiastic as Paul III about the novelty and verve of the new Society of Jesus. In 1555, the deeply anti-Spanish Paul IV sent troops to search for arms in the Society's professed house in Rome and undertook an examination of the Jesuits' constitutions that reduced the tenure of the superior general from life to three years, and removed the Jesuits' controversial exemption from reciting divine office in common. This was overturned by the next pope, Pius IV, but papal attacks on Jesuit innovation were destined to continue. Pius V removed the divine office exemption again in 1568, though Gregory XII once more restored it four years later. Sixtus V, along with many Catholics, disliked the arrogance and audacity of the Jesuits' name—the Society of *Jesus*—and but for his timely death in 1590, the Society would have been required to adopt a new, less provocative title.[31]

Wilier members of the Society had sometimes seen the potential folly in blowing their trumpets too loudly (or too inappropriately), or in having others do so on their behalf. In the fraught Parisian political atmosphere of 1626, when the Society's rivals were ready to pounce on the slightest instance of Jesuit pride, a sermon by Jean-Pierre Camus, bishop of Belley, and an ardent Jesuitophile, was so adoring of the Jesuits, calling the recently departed Pierre Coton a saint five or six times, and so heavily critical of those who opposed the Society, that the Jesuit François Garasse had to admit that it had "more passion and vehemence than we would have wanted."[32]

It is also easy to exaggerate the new Society's appeal. Jesuits may have secured their fair share of patronage (although in the early years it was an uphill struggle), but work on their mother church, the Roman Gesù, drew to a halt in 1589 once funds from the Farnese family dried up, and was not completed until well into the next century.[33] While it is true that the Society rarely lacked applicants for membership, there were many parents who took drastic steps to prevent their sons from entering Jesuit ranks: the father of Pompeio Capuano locked his son in a closet when he expressed a desire to join the Society.

Most worrying of all, there had been demoralizing internal squabbles. These sometimes came in surprising guises, such as the mini rebellions of two of the original founders of the Society, Simon Rodriguez and Nicholas Bobadilla. At the death of Loyola in 1556, Bobadilla, earlier banished from the Empire because of his stout opposition to concessions being offered to Protestant congregations, proved unhappy with the way the Society had been organized and suggested that the governance of the order should devolve to all of the original companions.

During the interim between Loyola's death and the election of his successor, Diego Laínez, Bobadilla and his ally Ponce Cogordan found a receptive audience in Paul IV, a pope with particular grudges against Loyola, and set about describing the Society in the most unflattering terms—as a dictatorship in need of reform, governed by labyrinthine constitutions; as a body that had ambitions to resettle in Spain, well away from papal influence.

Rodriguez, another critic of the emerging orthodoxy that the Society had been the single-handed masterwork of Ignatius Loyola (a flawed orthodoxy, it should be said), proved to be an infuriatingly headstrong provincial of Portugal. With the support of the Portuguese king, he resisted Loyola's attempts to bring him into line, continuing to rule in a muddled, arbitrary fashion, promoting excessive fasting and flagellation and, according to some reports, encouraging a bizarre practice whereby Jesuits went to their rooms to meditate about death in front of corpses. Those with an eye for irony must have noted that these two men, whose activities caused the Society such great embarrassment, might have been in a less than ideal position from which to rouse rabble had they been dispatched, as was originally intended, on the Asian mission which ultimately fell to Francis Xavier.[34]

But for consistent irritation nothing could compete with the Spanish branch of the Society, located in a country that has always wanted to develop its own particular brand of Catholicism. Many Spanish Jesuits clearly resented the Rome-centered nature of the order, pleading for more autonomy and fuming at the election of the first non-Spanish superior general, the Belgian Everard Mercurian, in 1573. In their unsavory way they also agitated against what they perceived as the Society's lax attitude on the issue of purity of blood, finding it unconscionable that men with Moorish or Jewish ancestry might secure a career as a Jesuit. Spanish agitation, regularly stirred up by Spanish kings, was an unhappy reality of the Jesuits' first decades, and not for the last time in its history, the Society even felt compelled to make a cull of some of these Spanish "false sons," expelling them at the general congregation of 1593.

These were all ominous developments, signposts toward tensions and conflicting agendas that would cripple the Society throughout its history. National rivalries—Spanish Jesuits versus Portuguese Jesuits versus Italian Jesuits versus French Jesuits; Jesuits born in the colonies versus Jesuits from Europe—would continue to blight both the order's internal politics and its missionary efforts.

It was already becoming clear that the history of the Jesuits would be energized by a tension between the authoritarianism of the Society's hierarchy (and an early general such as Claudio Acquaviva was feverishly keen on discipline) and the individualistic instincts of the rank and file; between a need for obedience and the value of initiative in far-flung places across the globe.

SUCH DISRUPTIONS STUNG, no doubt, but all in all the sixteenth century had been a century of growth, at the end of which the Society could boast more than sixteen thousand members, 521 colleges, forty-nine seminaries, fifty-four houses of probation, and twenty-four professed houses.[35]

The Society had often displayed a talent for accomplishing transformations. Loyola, after all, had remodeled himself from a Basque nobleman fighting at the siege of Pamplona in 1521 into a devout student at the University of Paris, tutoring his roommates in his novel brand of spirituality. A generation later, Alessandro Valignano would turn his back on a restless and violent youth, slashing a woman's face with a knife at one juncture, to emerge as an influential visitor of the Asian missions, while Aloysius Gonzaga, future patron saint of the young, would metamorphose from a page at Philip II's court into a comforter of plague victims in Rome, a ministry that would cost him his own life, at age twenty-three, in 1591. So perhaps it was fitting that in those grander transformations of renewal and reaction that transfixed the Catholic world of the sixteenth and seventeenth centuries, the Society had played an equally vital part.

In some ways the Jesuits' first century was their best century. Although it would sustain a vibrant, influential presence in the affairs of the Catholic world, the Society would suffer along with the rest of Europe in the decades after 1640 from dynastic squabbles and economic crises. Already by the 1640s an alarming number of colleges were being forced to close and there would even be a temporary cessation of admissions into the order. At such a vulnerable time the Society would suffer from unhealthily frequent changes in leadership—no less than six superior generals would hold office between 1646 and 1686—and the Jesuits' most skillful opponent, Blaise Pascal, would embed a frustratingly persistent image of shameful Jesuit casuistry in the European imagination.

But if the critics would find more and more opportunities to sneer at the way the *Imago primi saeculi* had portrayed the Society as a sun illuminating the whole world, or as a towering palm tree, at least there was still the pine cone opening before a fireplace: an image intended to celebrate the triumphs of martyrdom hard won in flames.[36] There was one place that could always be counted on to provide such second baptisms by fire: the Jesuit mission field, stretched across the better part of the globe.

Whatever the disruptions of reformation, and whatever the challenges awaiting the Society of Jesus, there was one aspect of its century-old history of which it was especially proud and which still seemed to hold out enormous promise in 1640, the year after Mandelslo arrived in Goa and the year in which a priest named René Ménard sailed from France to Quebec, center of the Jesuit missionary operation in North America.

THE JOURNEY HAD begun badly, and off Dieppe the French fleet had been "as near to death as we were to the coasts of France." As the journey continued, Ménard had resorted to prayers to St. Joseph to see him safely through storms; a number of lives had been lost, and an engagement with Dutch frigates had been narrowly avoided. But at least the nuns on board, granted courage (so Ménard assumed) by God, had remained steadfast; and this was striking since, ordinarily, they would "have trembled in a boat upon the Seine." And then, on the feast of the Blessed Sacrament, a "devotion most profound and most conspicuous" had come about.

"A major altar was prepared in the chamber of our admiral" and "the whole crew erected an altar at the prow of the ship." Despite all the turbulent days that had come before, "our Lord, desiring to be adored upon this so unstable element, gave us a calm so peaceful that we could imagine ourselves floating upon a pond." Next "we formed a procession truly solemn, since every one took part in it and their piety and devotion caused them to march in fine order all around the ship. Our brother Dominique Scot, wearing a surplice, bore the cross, on either side of which marched two children each bearing a lighted torch in his hands; the nuns followed with their white wax tapers, in angelic modesty. After the priest, who carried the Blessed Sacrament, walked the admiral of the fleet, and then the whole crew." With the exception of a few hands who had communicated quite recently, the entire ship's company "feasted upon the sacred food." No doubt a sight worth seeing, as Xavier had said of Goa almost a hundred years earlier.

And then, as Ménard remembered it, and it matters little if he sank into rather purple prose for the benefit of his readership, "the cannon made the air and the waves resound with their thunder, and the angels took pleasure in hearing the praises that our hearts and our lips gave to their prince and to our sovereign king."[37]

Here was, quite literally, a Jesuit with a mission, proud of being on his way to a prestigious posting and delighted to have participated during his passage in so moving a ritual on board "a house of wood, floating at the will of the winds and the waves." As it happened, New France was soon to prove a bloody evangelical arena and a place not immune to quarrels and tension between the Society and the secular arm: Ménard himself, after working among the Nipissing, the Huron, the Iroquois, and the Ottawa, would die alone in 1661, his body never discovered, in the vicinity of Wisconsin's Black River.

But on his way to New France Ménard only had time to be delighted with the prospect of engaging in the "instruction and salvation . . . of these barbarians in [the] foremost confines of the earth." Paul Le Jeune, recently retired as superior of the mission when Ménard arrived in Canada, clearly saw room to rejoice: "The faith is extending and taking deep root among the savages," he boasted; "we are living in a golden age."

The peoples of North America would not always be as dazzled by the gold of Christian salvation—far more precious, Le Jeune insisted, than the gold of the Peruvian mines—as Catholic Frenchmen might have hoped. But whatever is thought about the Jesuit missionary enterprise, and it would have its ignominious episodes, it is impossible to doubt the fervor that underpinned it.

3

"OVER MANY VAST WORLDS OF WATER"[1]

The Jesuit Missionary Enterprise

There will be seen in the actions of one single man, a New World converted by the power of his preaching, and by that of his miracles: idolatrous kings with their dominions reduced under the obedience of the gospel; the faith flourishing in the very midst of barbarism; and the authority of the Roman Church acknowledged by nations the most remote, who were utterly unacquainted with ancient Rome.

Dominique Bouhours, S.J., The Life of Francis Xavier, *English translation,*
1688[2]

The Catholic World of a "Universal Scribbler and Rhapsodist"[3]

Toward the end of a ridiculously prolific life—a life characterized by the sort of polymathic excess of which modern scholars, trapped in their worlds of specialized, atomized knowledge, can only dream—Athanasius Kircher, a Jesuit since 1618, focused his mind on matters of the spirit.

In the early days of the church, the Roman general Eustace saw a vision of the crucifixion between the antlers of a stag and decided to embrace the novel, proscribed faith called Christianity. After enduring the savage persecutions of Hadrian, he was eventually burned alive inside a brazen bull along with his wife and two sons. On the site of St. Eustace's vision, in the Italian countryside around Marino, stood the chapel of Mentorella, and it was this chapel that Kircher, increasingly old and increasingly ill, spent much of his last years restoring. He was now, as he eloquently put it, "fully occupied in penetrating the science of the saints."[4] Though Kircher was laid to rest in the Gesù, his heart would be buried beneath the altar at Mentorella.

It is well worth stressing this devotional side to Kircher because he is so much more famous to posterity as one of the more exotic geniuses of the seventeenth century. He was a scholar who taught, among much else, mathematics, Greek, Hebrew, and Syriac; who gained an early reputation as an expert in fireworks and optical displays; who observed sunspots, offered tips to

Poussin on perspective, and, wearing his musicologist's hat, transcribed the tweets and trills of birdsong. An abiding interest in geology not only saw him being lowered into the crater of Vesuvius in 1638 but also led him into the famous Grotta del Cane near Naples—the theory being, after the fashion of miners' canaries, that if the dog died it was time for the human to escape the noxious emissions of carbon dioxide. An unparalleled facility for machine building produced contraptions as enticingly named as a mathematical organ, a botanical clock, and a magnetic oracle.

It is easy to treat Kircher—a man disliked in equal measure by Descartes and the advocates of transmutative alchemy, but who also managed to be the prized correspondent of the scientific giants and crowned heads of Europe—as somehow divided between modern-looking scientific endeavor and curious, backward-looking obscurantism. What strikes us as contradictory in Kircher—the fact that he meditated seriously on Babel and Noah's ark but also produced a book that Stephen Jay Gould considered the greatest geological treatise ever written by a scientist who also held holy orders[5]—was, in fact, part of a sophisticated, if sometimes wayward, intellectual unity: a heady blend of Renaissance hermeticism, the Aristotelian foundations of Jesuit science, and an admittedly more modern-seeming empiricism. Kircher was of his time.

He was also at the very center of his world. Kircher, though he often dreamed of China, never left Europe, a divided continent of which he had seen the very worst, fleeing from Protestant troops during the Thirty Years' War as the great Vasa king Gustavus Adolphus punctuated his military progress through Germany by seizing, and sometimes despoiling, whichever Jesuit house or college came into view. But a geographically unadventurous career was no bar to the imagination. It did not stop Kircher from sending Cosmiel and Theodidactus on an imaginary trip through the universe, conversing with the intelligent life-forms they encountered. And it did not prevent Kircher's scholarship from bearing ample testimony to the scale and success of the Jesuit effort to evangelize and explore Asia, Africa, and the Americas.

His scientific data came in from missionaries around the globe, for whose geographical, cultural, botanical, and zoological discoveries Kircher served as an able conduit. His novel, some said quirky, theories about the ancient roots of language and religion found sustenance in the reports his brethren sent in from the mission field, and the exhibits at his much-visited museum in Rome reminded the steady stream of visitors of just how far the Jesuits had traveled.

As Johann Georg Keyssler would report in 1729, Kircher's museum, "divided into several closets, might have been much better organised than it is," but there was still much to marvel at: "spoons, knives, writing instruments . . . of foreign and distant nations, particularly the Chinese"; "exotic birds and skeletons: and among these . . . one of three legs"; "corals and several other vegetables from the Mediterranean and the Red Sea"; "porcelain of Japan, China and Persia"; "several kinds of Indian fruits"; "ivory works, curiously turned"; "flour and bread made of Brazil root"; "hats and caps made of the fibres of exotic trees and leaves."[6] Even though the museum fell into escalating chaos down the years, it would remain a popular tourist trap until it was disbanded by the Italian government—not always the Jesuits' greatest friend— in 1871.

Such a world-encompassing mentality prompted Kircher to devise an *horologium catholicum*, a "world clock" that might standardize the time in Jesuit colleges around the world by means of the longitude-providing observations of Jupiter's satellites made by colleagues in Europe, India, China, Canada, Mexico, Brazil, and Peru. The same mentality makes it wholly appropriate that Kircher would collaborate with Gian Lorenzo Bernini, another artist devoted to the Society, in constructing a fountain in Rome's Piazza Navona which, topped by an Egyptian obelisk, represented four great rivers of the world—not only the familiar Danube, but the Ganges, the Nile, and the Plate. These were just the kinds of rivers Jesuits knew about.

Of what, then, did this Jesuit world, with Kircher at its center, consist? What was the reach of a century and more of Jesuit missionary endeavor? Once again, Kircher provides an answer in his stylized diagram of the

Society's provinces, the Ignatian Tree, included in his 1646 treatise, *Ars magna lucis et umbrae.*[7]

FROM A EUROPEAN center, this Ignatian Tree shows the Jesuits' Portuguese assistancy, broadly coterminous with the scope of Lusitanian imperial outreach, stretching to Africa—from Angola (where Luandan Jesuits would accrue 1,080 slaves by 1760)[8] to Congo and to Ethiopia (where a chaotic, ultimately disastrous mission at least managed to convert the emperor Susenyos to Catholicism). Across the Atlantic was Brazil—bumped into in 1500 by an off-course fleet bound for India—to which Jesuits, led by the dynamic, stuttering Manuel da Nóbrega, would travel in the company of the first Portuguese governor general, Tomé de Sousa, in 1549. Twenty-seven more Jesuit missionary parties would follow before 1604, and during the seventeenth century no less than 278 members of the Society would continue to divide their time between the Portuguese coastal settlements and the inland missions.

But in the Portuguese half of the world (a world divided between the kingdoms of Spain and Portugal according to the terms of the famous 1494 Treaty of Tordesillas), it was Asia that provided Jesuits with their most illustrious mission fields, none more fabled than India, the first destination of Francis Xavier, back in 1542. There would be not only encounters with Muslims and Hindus, but also efforts to draw the thousands of long-established Thomas Christians of the Malabar Coast into Rome's orbit. Every bit as celebrated were the missions of Roberto de Nobili in Madurai from 1606—a bold experiment in cultural assimilation—and the audacious campaigns, most notably in the person of Jerome Xavier, to convert the great Moghul emperors Akbar and Jahangir.

These potentates, commanding an empire that stretched from the Bay of Bengal to the Arabian Sea, as far as Kabul in the north, were showered with religious gifts, four-volume polyglot Bibles, and engravings by Raphael and

Dürer. Jesuits invited to the Moghul court at Fatehpur Sikri proved willing to participate in multifaith conferences, debating with representatives of the other great Indian religious traditions, and for a time there was real hope that the emperor might be won round to Christ: Akbar would hold and study devotional pictures for so long that his arms began to ache.

The missionaries were generally treated with respect and kindness—courtly chefs even took the trouble to provide their European guests with familiar-looking tarts, pies, and gravied chicken⁹—but the descendants of the great Babur, whose victory at Panipat in 1526 had inaugurated a political and cultural transformation of the subcontinent, were ultimately more interested in learning about the perspective techniques of Western painting than in pledging their allegiance to the triune—always a puzzle to Moghul minds—Christian God.

To the north and east, via the cosmopolitan entrepôt of Malacca, lay another of Xavier's spiritual vineyards, Japan—long a mysterious fixture in the European imagination. Here, the missionaries' gentle evangelical strategy, based for the most part on cautious appreciation of aspects of the empire's ancient civilization, would culminate in some of the bloodiest persecutions of the early-modern era. Dozens of Jesuit martyrs would meet their deaths by the middle of the seventeenth century, many of them native Japanese—in itself a mark of just how highly many within the Society (a body not always keen on the development of an indigenous clergy) ranked the spiritual potential of the country's inhabitants. Such death tolls would fuel one of the Catholic Church's most spectacular efforts at memorializing its missionary past, with the 1867 beatification of 205 martyrs of Japan, thirty-four Jesuits among them.

Xavier had been told that if he ever wanted to convert the Japanese, he would be well advised to make inroads among the inhabitants of Ming China: missionaries would be asked by people in Japan why, if Christianity was so wonderful a faith, had the Celestial Empire not yet embraced it? Initial Portuguese contact with China had been made in the early sixteenth century by Jorge Alvares and Tomé Pirés. A market in contraband developed, and in 1556, merchants were allowed to establish a trading post at Macao, from where they were allowed to emerge twice a year for trading fairs. When Jesuits began arriving in the 1560s they were still nominally within the Portuguese colonial orbit, but the interior mission begun in the 1580s by Michele Ruggieri and Matteo Ricci could count on little support, or interference, from the Portuguese imperial machine: a situation that was later exaggerated by the influx of rival Jesuit contingents with Spanish and French allegiance, of secular clergy, and of members of the mendicant orders.

Isolation, and an awareness of Chinese cultural self-worth, elicited an unusually flexible evangelical strategy—although there was never total agreement in Jesuit ranks about its reputability. Matteo Ricci, sporting pigtails, dressed as a Confucian scholar, and proficient in the Confucian classics, applied his considerable talents to wooing the empire's intellectual and political elites, impressing his hosts with European knowledge of mathematics, geography, and science, seeking out ways to adapt his message to the sophisticated society in which he moved.

It is sometimes forgotten that Jesuits did actually establish missions in many other areas of China,[10] but it was the enduring accommodationist strategy and pastoral of technology, continued by several generations of Jesuit astronomers, clock makers, cartographers, and artists, that has captivated historians and that, during the seventeenth and eighteenth centuries, would draw such opprobrium down upon the Society.

ACROSS THE PAPALLY sanctioned border, a few hundred miles west of the Azores, Jesuits were compelled to operate within the Spanish sphere of influence—territories which included the Philippines, reached by Jesuits in 1581; Florida, where an abortive mission in 1569 cost several Jesuit lives; and from 1567, Peru, home to the oldest Jesuit school in Latin America, and the setting for the prodigious explorations of José de Acosta. Supported by alms at first, Jesuit colleges in Peru could soon look to the income provided by an impressive network of agricultural estates. Unexpectedly, perhaps, when the sugar hacienda Vilcalvaura was purchased by the Society in 1642, the missionaries' shopping list would extend to a boiling house, a purgery, four cane presses, three cauldrons, kettles, ladles, mallets, shovels, machetes, thirty-five mules, fifty cows, and six pair of oxen.[11] Across the province, Indian labor and African slaves would help tend and cultivate cattle, wheat, and yerba maté—the famous Jesuit tea.

North of Peru lay the province of Mexico (first reached by missionaries in 1572), a place that also saw much soil go under the Jesuit plow. It was from here that missionaries like Eusebio Kino would push into present-day Arizona, New Mexico, and Lower California in the late seventeenth and early eighteenth centuries, establishing twenty-four missions, nineteen ranches, and several towns. But most talked about of all was Paraguay (including parts of modern-day Argentina, Colombia, and Peru), home to the famous "reductions," where houses, mills, shops, workshops, and orchards crowded around Spanish-style churches and where, so the theory went, the indigenous population might be protected from the grasp of slave-hungry colonists. The worth and merits of these settlements remains a matter of controversy, but with a population of 113,746 in fifty-seven villages by 1767, they would become a subject of perennial fascination for the talking heads of seventeenth- and eighteenth-century Europe.

Which whistle-stop tour leaves only New France, where, from 1611 onward, though with repeated interruptions (1613–25, 1629–32), missionaries stretched out from Acadia and the St. Lawrence River across Canada and parts of the present-day United States: to the north as far as James Bay; as far as fifteen hundred miles to the west; and seventeen hundred miles to the south, along the Mississippi all the way to Louisiana. Hardly a tribe within several hundred miles of Quebec was untouched by the Society's presence: there were missions among the Algonkin, most notably to the Montagnais of the lower St. Lawrence, whose arduous winter hunting parties, in search of moose and caribou, Jesuits were obliged to join; to the member tribes of the mighty Iroquois Confederacy, south and east of Lakes Ontario and Erie; and to the Ottawa far to the west.

But above all to the Huron, the twenty-one thousand or so people crammed into a thirty-five-by-twenty-mile area between Georgian Bay and Lake Simcoe, where, during the 1630s and 1640s, many of the most celebrated of the 115 Jesuits who traveled to New France over the course of the century would struggle with local languages, complain endlessly about smoky cabins, freezing rivers, and voracious insects, but also contribute some of the most easily eulogized figures to the Society's growing roster of martyrs.

SUCH EPIC MISSIONARY endeavor fed, enriched, and baffled the European imagination, bringing news of previously unencountered cultures and much fuller accounts of places that had captivated Western minds for centuries. In 1664, John Evelyn was clearly impressed by the contents of a ship recently arrived in London and bound for the Jesuits of Paris. The hold was stuffed with "large rhinoceros's horns; glorious vests wrought and embroidered on cloth of gold, burnished with such lovely colours that for splendour and vividness we have nothing in England that approaches it; a girdle studded with achates and rubies of great value and size . . . flowers, birds, trees (on silk) . . . divers drugs that our druggists and physicians could make nothing of."[12] Mission would dictate fashions, and it would offer new and better maps: the Jesuits Eusebio Kino and Matteo Ricci, respectively, would conclude that California and Korea were not islands. Jesuits would be the first Europeans to find a land route between India and China, among the first to cross the Himalayas.

Mission helped to shattered myths—good-bye, eventually, to Prester John and Cathay—and its reports and achievements proved an irresistible resource for any European intellectual (be he Leibniz or Montesquieu) with a pet theory about language, climate, or the noble savage. Not that Jesuit missionaries ever lacked theories of their own. José de Acosta, during his career in Peru, would meditate seriously and influentially on the causes of altitude sickness, on the reasons for the tides, on volcanoes, earthquakes, and land bridges between Asia and the American continent.

And of course, mission had its legacy. In some places it would help to introduce sheep, looms, and horses, but it was also part and parcel (though in complicated, ambiguous ways) of colonial intrusion: a fact that latter-day indigenous populations are apt to bear in mind—they smashed our temples, Indians possessed of righteous irony have been heard to say, but at least they brought the chili pepper. And there is the historiographical legacy too. Mission offers a poignant lesson in the way cultures meet—a reminder that this is always a reciprocal affair, that no one remains passive during the encounter, that all involved are capable of exploitation, of reductive, essentialist analysis of what seems new and strange, and that no one goes uninfluenced.[13]

But at heart, mission was about something more fundamental than all these enduring cultural and scholarly by-products. It came down to Christ.

Xavier's Legacy

Efforts would eventually be made to play down, indeed to jettison, the miraculous episodes of Francis Xavier's earthly career[14]—making salt water sweet, raising people from the dead, and suchlike—but in the meantime such wonders only served to bolster his posthumous status as icon and representative of the entire Jesuit missionary enterprise.

Jesuit priests in the field would grow accustomed to believing that, in a very tangible way, Xavier was their constant companion. A missionary in Canada during the seventeenth century would explain how "a thousand times the light of St. Francis Xavier passes through our minds, and has great power over us." The example of Xavier's life caused him to realize that "if the men of the world, in order to have beaver skins, cod-fish, and I know not what commodities, do not fear either the storms on the sea, or the savages on the land," then "the confusion of God's servants" would be "dreadful" if they were "afraid of these things." It almost seemed, as another Canadian missionary put it, that through his enduring presence in the minds and activities of the Jesuits of New France, "this great apostle appears to wish now, at this end of the world, to repeat what of old he abundantly accomplished at the other."[15]

Xavier's memory would directly inspire John Baptist Machado to die a martyr's death in Japan in 1617, Bruno Bruni to meet a similar fate in Ethiopia in 1640, and his fellow Jesuit Eusebio Kino, who took "Francis" as his middle name after a serious illness in 1633, to embark upon his famous missionary career, for which troubles he would end up representing Arizona in Statuary Hall in the U.S. Capitol, in Washington, described there as "explorer, historian, rancher, mission-builder and apostle to the Indians."[16]

Early-modern Catholicism was defined and energized by the missionary impulse so fully embodied and symbolized by Francis Xavier. Franciscans did it, Dominicans did it, even educated Augustinians did it. In many areas of the globe Jesuits constituted neither the first nor the most significant religious presence, but their so very well publicized activities could be construed, in ways never before imaginable in the church's history, as heeding God's decree (1 Kings 8:43) "that all people of the earth may know your name," and ample proof that God had been sincere when promising (Isaiah 43:1) that "when thou passest through the waters, I will be with thee: and through the rivers, they shall not overflow thee."

The fulfillment of such familiar missiological texts provoked debate and dissension, with the brightest university minds of the sixteenth and seventeenth centuries struggling to theorize and justify European expansionism: an effort—unattractive as it sometimes seems—which nonetheless laid the groundwork for all meditations about international relations that came afterward.

But although mission was a complicated, complicating endeavor, riddled by national rivalries and by competition between Rome and the secular arm, it at least set the Tridentine church apart, making it distinct from all those Protestants, not yet fully interested in missionary derring-do, who supposed that wide-ranging evangelical duty had ended in the days of the apostles. If Luther had not even taken the time to comment on Mark 16:15—"And he said to them, go into all the world, and preach the gospel to every creature"—then more fool him.

The missionary life, even leaving aside the obvious risks of martyrdom or drowning at sea, could be deeply unpleasant. The Bavarian Samuel Fritz, who moved up and down the Amazon in the late seventeenth and early eighteenth centuries, would endure eighteen months' house arrest when the Portuguese suspected him of being a Spanish spy. While journeying along the Maranhão River, he would succumb to "unutterable burnings" and sit out his fever in a canoe, disturbed by "the gruntings of the crocodiles that all night were roving round the village" and by rats who were so hungry they chewed on the haft of his knife.[17]

A world and a century away, Juan de Beira would spend nine years in the Spice Islands, being chased by headhunters, hiding in mountains and forests, sleeping in trees, living on roots and grasses, only to be sold for a while into slavery. By the time he regained his freedom and returned to India, he had lost his mind.[18] Pedro Paez, on his way to Ethiopia, would be captured in 1589 and spend the next fourteen years carving out a career as a galley slave. When finally released in 1603, he would head off to Africa and become the first European to set eyes upon Lake Tana, the source of the Blue Nile.

Such distressing tales did not necessarily have a deterrent effect. Many of the men who opted to be trained up as Jesuits were gratefully seduced by the prospect of a missionary life, especially if it promised to unfold somewhere as suitably distant, exotic, and perilous as China, Japan, or Canada. Eusebio Kino, although destined for a career in the Americas, is said to have rejoiced on discovering that his college room faced eastward—toward the Chinese empire he was so desperate to visit.[19]

Mission represented the most glamorous aspect of that special vow which every fully professed Jesuit had to make before God: "to go anywhere His Holiness will order, whether among the faithful or the infidels, without pleading any excuse, and without requesting any expenses for the journey, for the sake of matters pertaining to the worship of God and the welfare of the Christian religion."[20] Mission was, in a sense, the culmination of the Ignatian apostolic ideal; to be a missionary was to be the finest kind of Ignatian pilgrim.

In the early years of the Society, a majority of recruits talked rather more often about cleansing their souls and turning their backs on the manifold evils of the contemporary world than about enduring perilous sea voyages to infidel lands. However, missionary ambition, among both novices and those already well into their careers as Jesuits, became an increasingly voiced theme during the Society's first century.[21] It had been, as the great Jesuit explorer of the Mississippi, Jacques Marquette, revealed, something to dream about "from my earliest boyhood and the first light of reason."[22] Pedro Martínez felt compelled to write to his superiors in 1560 "to beg you, prostrate at your feet, to send me of your charity and by the blood of Jesus Christ to China . . . [if] your Reverence still think it is an audacious request, please attribute it to the overwhelming desire which has possessed me for this enterprise for many a year now." Instead of being posted to China, Martínez ended his days being tomahawked to death off the coast of present-day Georgia.

Juan Rogel admitted that he was undereducated and possessed of a stammer that made a preaching career more or less impossible, but he could still impress his superiors by revealing that his passion for a missionary career in Asia was founded on "a desire of suffering our Lord has sent me" and the conviction that God often "chooses the base and contemptible things of the world to confound the strong."[23] This juxtaposition of a Jesuit's sense of unworthiness and the desire to suffer as excruciatingly as possible on distant shores was to be an ever-present trope in the Society's carefully constructed missionary narrative, often expressed, in order to boast, in statements dripping with propagandist intent, but sometimes genuinely and feverishly meant.

Not that every Jesuit who headed to the new worlds was consumed by dreams of heroic endeavor. Joseph Anchieta, for instance, may have gone on to a dazzling career deciphering the languages of Latin America and composing Latin poems that praised the Blessed Virgin Mary and damned Protestantism as an infernal dragon, but he was initially dispatched to Brazil in 1553 in the hope that the gentler climate would be good for his chronic bad back. But in many cases, the zeal was real enough, and all too often it needed to be tempered.

Any number of novices petitioned, often with immoderate repetition, for glamorous postings—to China especially—only to be informed by their superiors that there were other, equally vital, tasks in Europe for which they were intellectually or physically much better suited. Did those with China fever not realize that there were plenty of "Indies" in Catholic Europe itself, places, it was suggested, where populations seemed to have forgotten how to worship, to have become inured to the conscience-biting consequences of sin, returning like dogs to their own vomit, or to have succumbed to the lure of superstition and magic?

And besides all that, there was the educational ministry for which the Society was becoming increasingly famous. One superior general, Vincenzo Carafa, observed that those novices who were so desperate to shed their blood in far distant mission fields were failing to realize that an industrious career in Europe—offering the Society some of their sweat in the classroom, as he put it—was every bit as noble a Jesuit career: a very different kind of martyrdom.[24]

It was also worth remembering, as a missionary in Canada explained, that "it is not fitting that everyone should know how agreeable it is in the sacred awe of these forests, and how much heavenly light one finds in the thick darkness of this barbarism: we would have too many persons wishing to come here."[25] There was neither the room nor the resources to support them all.

Perhaps—although trainee Jesuits could hardly be blamed for dreaming of martyrdom in Asia when the extraordinary value of such a death was constantly drummed into them during their formation. It was unlikely that any fledgling Jesuit would be wholly unaware of the agreeability of the Canadian mission field, given the Society's obsession with thrusting the edifying letters and reports of the heroes of New France onto the European public. Had they been among the students taught by Enemond Massé at the Jesuit college of La Flèche in Anjou, they would have been regaled with thrilling tales of the former missionary's adventures among the Micmac and Montagnais of Acadia between 1611 and 1613.[26] The missionary enterprise, although it never demanded the same levels of manpower as the Society's educational work (and even if recruits for certain areas were sometimes annoyingly hard to find), was vital to forging Jesuit identity.

In the confessional war of words and deeds, for instance, mission held out considerable promise. Jesuit missionaries often portrayed Europe as a peaceful, unified continent when conversing with their hosts—this was a useful way of stressing the superiority of Western civilization. For the most part, missionary success was not perceived as some crude arithmetical counterbalance to the incursions of Protestantism: winning souls in the New World to make up for those lost in the Old. But there is sometimes a sense that mission was partly energized by a desire to develop a pristine Christianity wholly unsullied by the problems blighting the faith back home in Europe.

Just as usefully, as one writer explained, stories of heroic martyrdom in Japan could serve to bolster Catholic morale in a demoralized environment like Elizabethan England and help "to drive away the darkness of heresy that overshadows some part of thy dominions . . . to open their eyes that by the light of new triumphs they may discern who be the heirs of ancient truth."[27] Sometimes, if rarely, there were opportunities to bask in moments when the doctrinal struggles of Europe seemed to be transplanted directly to foreign shores: when, it could be argued, Catholics proved themselves typically brave and Protestants proved themselves despicably cruel.

Such, at any rate, was the lesson Catholics were expected to learn from the tale of forty Jesuits (priests, brothers, and novices) who died in 1570 off the Canary Islands, en route to Brazil. French Huguenot corsairs, led by Jacques Sourie (or Sore), slaughtered the Jesuits, taking particular pleasure in tossing the leader of the group, Ignatius de Azevedo, overboard, still clutching a picture of the Virgin. Or so the story goes as told by John Sanchez, the only one of the party to survive, because the French apparently needed a cook on their homeward journey to La Rochelle.

More often, however, mission was about rhetorical upmanship. Protestants grew adept at fending off the "Where was your church before Luther?" question, but the "Why is it that only Rome is winning souls in Asia and America?" question was a telling replacement. As Antonio Possevino smugly pointed out, the Catholic Church was an ever-expanding institution, "to which the vast regions of the New World, from the rising of the sun to its setting, to say nothing of from the south to the north, add themselves every day by the abundant conversion of nations."[28] In terms of Jesuit self-fashioning, the missionary impetus put the Society's (and the church's) efforts into an unprecedented, expansionist, worldwide context.

There was something illusory in all this—the people newly introduced to Christ were often far from convinced that it was to their advantage—but in many places, it took long decades for the illusion to fade. And besides, even when things went horribly wrong, when local resistance produced martyrs more often than converts, it was still possible to discern a kind of success. Second baptisms, by blood, were awfully good for the cause.

The Uncertain Vineyard

The cause, of course, was conversion, but it did not take long for missionaries to realize that first and foremost, soutanes and Bibles notwithstanding, they were early-modern Europeans in unusual places, where it was far from clear whether the beliefs, assumptions, and accomplishments of early-modern Europe would be derided, admired, misconstrued, or simply ignored.

For all the welcomes and successes recorded in the annals of the Jesuit evangelical enterprise, the incursions of missionaries just as often provoked hostility, not least from representatives of the faiths and moralities—Buddhist bonzes in Japan, neo-Confucian scholars and Muslim astronomers in China— they were set on displacing.

When Gonçalo da Silveira traveled to Mozambique in 1560, Muslim traders and clerics condemned him as a spy and strangled him in his sleep. So far as one local religious leader was concerned in 1628, Alphonsus Rodriguez and Roch González had been far too successful in their baptizing and mission-building efforts along the River Plate, and he arranged to have them killed. Paul Le Jeune complained from New France in 1635 that a local shaman, whose reputation as healer, sage, and weather maker was under siege, liked to "have sport at my expense, [making] me write vulgar things in his language, assuring me there was nothing bad in them; then made me pronounce shameful words in the presence of the savages." Word was spread that the crosses missionaries insisted on erecting were the cause of drought, and that to look at an image of

Jesus or Mary was to risk a curse. In Huronia in 1637, locals were suggesting "that when we show them [saintly images], certain tainted influences issue therefrom which steal down into the chests of those who look at them."[29]

And even in the absence of overt animosity there was room for endless confusion and misinterpretation. Why would someone living in sixteenth-century China, a place where the punishment of crucifixion was reserved for bandits, want to worship a person who, fifteen hundred years earlier and halfway across the world, had been hung on a cross like a common criminal? Such thoughts also troubled the Moghul emperor Jahangir, who was unable to understand why, if Christians so adored Christ, they portrayed him in such a dishonorable state.[30]

Why, Chinese critics of the missions sniped, if the Jesuits' God was so kind and all-powerful, had he allowed Adam and Eve to commit a vile and original sin that was destined to pass down the generations of humanity with no hope of remission? The Huron, confronted with the idea of an eternal sin that could never be expunged, were puzzled by precisely the same question.[31] Why, others asked in similar vein, if God was all-good and omnipotent, would he have created a devil? Why, if Christianity was such a blessing, had God taken so long to expose the populations of Asia and America to its promise?

And why, if you were a Huron in New France during the seventeenth century, would you want to convert to Christianity when, on the evidence of your own eyes, to do so only seemed to bring on death? Jesuit missionaries in Canada had a penchant for baptizing individuals who were close to death, but onlookers readily discerned a causal relationship between the two events: you were baptized and then, more than likely, you died. In culture after culture there were concepts that were destined to baffle—an invisible Creator outside of nature, a noncorporeal afterlife, a monotheistic paradigm thrust upon a society that was perfectly happy with its polytheistic pantheon.

And incredulity aside, why would anyone pay too much heed to the religious ideas extolled by such strange-looking people? Missionaries in New France, struggling to master local languages, observed that the first phrases they committed to memory were invariably those they heard most often: unfortunately these tended to include "He looks like a dog" and "He has a head like a pumpkin." It took long years for men with beards (disgusting to local eyes), men who were celibate, and men who were patently useless in canoes to be trusted. A particularly vicious anti-Christian tract from seventeenth-century Japan recalled that when a European ship had first reached the empire's shores there had "emerged an unnameable creature, somewhat similar in shape to a human being, but looking rather more like a long-nosed goblin."[32] Could one really trust the ideas or the intentions of people who, so it seemed to many Japanese witnesses, had such abysmal standards of personal hygiene?

Perhaps it was safer to have a little fun at the Jesuits' expense? Aware of the troubles Europeans faced in adapting to the Asian diet, the great Japanese warrior Oda Nobunaga (a convert to Western viol and organ music, as it happens) greatly enjoyed forcing the Jesuit Luis Frois to eat a bucketful of over-ripe figs before granting him an opportunity to convince his court that Christianity represented the last word in spiritual fulfillment and eternal bliss.[33] Others treated missionaries and their paraphernalia as nothing more than trendy curiosities. In 1594 Francisco Pasio reported that many Japanese "wear rosaries of drift wood on their breasts, hang a crucifix from the shoulder or waist . . . this is done not in ridicule of the Christians but simply to show off their familiarity with the latest fashions."[34]

How was a missionary to respond to such suspicions and puzzlements: ignore them, deride them, seek to defuse them? And into the bargain, how was he to shoulder his own interpretative burden? After all, if people in China, Japan, and New France struggled to understand Jesuit missionaries, then Jesuit missionaries were every bit as dazzled by the strangeness and otherness of China, Japan, and New France.

New Year in Quebec

A t the beginning of January 1651, the Jesuits of Quebec sent one Monsieur Couillon a stone calumet (a North American peace pipe) as a

New Year's gift; Madame Couillon returned the favor by dispatching two live hens to the Jesuits' residence. Five years earlier, local Ursulines had marked the beginning of 1646 by sending the Jesuits tapers, rosaries, crucifixes, and "two handsome pies of pastry," for which generosity they received images of Ignatius Loyola and Francis Xavier, "in enamel." In that year other friends of the Society had been presented, variously, with reliquaries, a "Galilean telescope," bottles of brandy; and "the woman who washes the church's linen" was treated to a crucifix. Recurrent gifts, moving to and fro between the Christian community of Quebec, included kegs of prunes (most prized if they were from Tours), turkeys, and lemon peel. There were sometimes errors of omission as when, in 1650, "the Ursulines sent nothing," but the Jesuits quickly "sent them some flowers" and by evening a rosary and a reliquary had arrived at the Jesuits' house.

The crucial, if often troubled, relationship between the Jesuit missionaries and the governor of New France was always respected. In 1637 he sent the priests four capons and eight young pigeons, and the Jesuits provided his secretary with a musk-scented rosary. In 1650 the governor was sent two bottles of Spanish wine. When, on January 4, 1660, the Jesuits Louis Lalemant and Claude Dablon went to visit the governor, they were greeted with a salvo of musket fire, for which each of the soldiers was sent a rosary, a pot of brandy, and a pound of tobacco.

New Year in Quebec was a hugely important time. Admittedly, there were occasions when the celebrations could irritate: in 1662 the Jesuits were far from pleased when "a drummer came to give a New-Year's serenade in our corridor in honour of the bishop. We did not deem it advisable to send him away . . . perhaps it will be necessary to prevent this when Monsieur the bishop ceases to lodge with us." But more often than not noise and spectacle were entirely welcome, as when on January 1, 1657, "the cannon fired at daybreak and at the elevation of the host at high mass."

The gift giving of Quebec was part of these traditional New Year festivities, but it reveals a great deal more, not least the casual mixing of very different kinds of presents. Befitting a frontier-type community, practical things—penknives and casks of candle wax—always seemed to be welcome; befitting an aggressively Christian community, devotional items—rosaries, crosses, religious books—were always favored, symbols of cultural certainty beyond their spiritual relevance; and befitting a community of Europeans in the midst of an alien culture, unusual, native items—peace pipes, locally produced gloves—were often produced. In 1650 all the Jesuits' servants received not only a "little reliquary" but, in striking juxtaposition, pairs of "savage shoes or mittens."[35]

Gift giving in Quebec was a matter of politeness, but did it also represent a way (conscious or not) of dealing with the cultural strangeness so very apparent to isolated colonists buffeted with alarming frequency by news of death, conflict, and threatening Mohawk aggression? All at once the gifts could remind a community of its European roots—the Spanish wine and Tours prunes. They could reinforce its Christianizing objective (which was, avowedly, why it was there in the first place), but also, the use of local handicrafts perhaps represented an effort to understand, or at least exploit, the alien culture in which it found itself.

This mixture of mental needs and duties neatly sums up the confusing, anxious situation of a great many Jesuit missionaries across the globe—they were travelers and settlers facing hostile environments (the kind of people who might need a penknife), members of a religious order committed to evangelism (the kind of people who valued rosaries), and Europeans confronted with local cultures that, beyond anything else, were different and strange (people who not only gave, but on occasion had to smoke from, calumets).

Their cause depended on negotiating the harshness and strangeness contained within alien cultures, and if that could be achieved in small ways such as the multifaceted, deeply suggestive gift giving of Quebec, it was also at the root of their primary duty, replicated in every arena in which they moved: the conversion of indigenous populations—the fundamental purpose of every Jesuit-laden ship that left Portugal, Spain, and France.

How was it to be achieved? How to confront the fact that alien cultures both puzzled and were puzzled by the Jesuit missionaries? Should force, or persuasion, be privileged; should missionaries follow blithely in the wake of imperial advance, smashing temples and acting as chaplains to punitive Portuguese expeditions, or was it better to develop evangelical strategies that sought to understand, perhaps even seek an accommodation with, local beliefs and moralities? This was the toughest of dilemmas, and one that provoked endless debate within Jesuit ranks: there was never a uniform "Jesuit approach" to mission.

Some people wanted to charm China and Japan into conversion, others suggested that invasion might be a more efficient policy. Some people thought that new worlds in the Americas held out Edenesque potential, a chance to cultivate a Christianity freed from centuries of corrupt European accretions; others likened the inhabitants of these new worlds to wandering beasts who ought to be Europeanized as quickly as possible. Individual members of the Society were known to veer between gleeful optimism and the darkest pessimism when evaluating the chances of evangelical success, adopting a range of different tactics and attitudes, sometimes being repelled, sometimes being enchanted, sometimes being patient, other times preaching hellfire. But the need to decide upon a conversion strategy of one sort or another was a constant, puzzling duty, and that decision relied upon cultural analysis.

One thing Jesuits almost always did in an alien environment was *describe*. Not as modern-day ethnologists would describe, not buoyed up by paradigm and theory, but describe nonetheless. They did this because they were curious, certainly—many Jesuits were among the most able scientists of their day—but also because description was ever linked to, ever a function of, the soul saving. To describe a society (and describe everything about it) was to assess its spiritual potential, its inherent capacity to receive the gospel—the Japanese and the Tupi Indians of Brazil, it was usually and grotesquely averred, were hardly of the same caliber of human being. Jesuits had to decide whether gentle persuasion or a more forceful evangelical credo was called for. Could people be converted? How should they be converted? Did they want to be converted?

Other factors (not least the influence of the European imperial machine in a particular evangelical arena) were bound to enter the equation: gunboat evangelism was something of a dead letter in the absence of gunboats. But at the most basic level, knowing about something as seemingly trivial as the agricultural soil was part of the same process as appraising that other soil in which the true faith was to be planted. Jesuits had to try to understand (which certainly did not always imply approval) and rank the people they were trying to convert: to compare them with Europeans and with one another. This, all at once, was one of the most essentialist and horribly reductive, one of the most historically important, and one of the most intellectually sophisticated things the Society of Jesus ever did.

We in the West are still prone to looking at the rest of the world through the filters Jesuits (and their confrères) provided: the rest of the world, for better or worse, is still living with the consequences. Facts, facts, facts, so the mantra went, meant souls, souls, souls.

Mandarins and Melons: Le Comte's China

Anyone who bought a copy of Louis-Daniel Le Comte's *Memoirs and Observations* in 1697 was invited by the publisher, in a wonderfully tempting advertisement, to purchase some other, recently published wares. William Whiston's *A New Theory of the Earth* was on offer, "wherein," as the subtitle explained, "the creation of the world in six days; the universal deluge, and the general conflagration as laid down in the holy scriptures, are shown to be perfectly agreeable to reason and philosophy." Those wanting something rather less earnest were pointed toward *The French Perfumer*, which, as another extravagant title declared, taught "the several ways of extracting the odours of drugs and flowers, and making all the compositions of perfumes for powder, wash-balls, essences, oils, wax, pomatum, paste, Queen of Hungary's water, Rosa Salis, and other sweet waters." But none of this was as spectacular as the contents of Le Comte's volume, because this was about China, and the European reading public of the time, largely because of members of the Society of Jesus, could not get enough of China.

The Chinese soil was excellent for growing pears, apples, peaches, figs, and grapes. The produce, according to Le Comte, was not quite up to European standards: a result, he suggested, of the Chinese lack of Western grafting techniques. But then there were the wonderful melons, especially those "yellow within, and of a sweet sugar taste, which they eat with rind as we do an apple," or the larger watermelons, which, "though they are full of a cooling juice which tastes like sugar . . . never prove offensive and may be eaten during the greatest heat of summer without fear of surfeit." But then again there was the dreaded lychee, "as big as a nut," which was "unwholesome to eat [in] quantity, and of so hot a nature as to cause a whole man's body to break out in pimples."

Le Comte urged those who thought that Paris was a mighty city to visit Peking, although it was a shame that the Chinese could only manage to build houses that "are not proportionate, being neither well built nor high enough." The tallow in China was of a high quality, so it was strange that the country could not produce the kind of candles one might expect to find back home. The paper was the softest one could imagine, and yet bookbinding techniques lagged well behind those in Europe. And besides, what curious script was enclosed in such books. No one could question the sophistication of the Chinese language, but "these riches cost foreigners dear to come by them; and I cannot tell whether some missionaries had not better have laboured in the mines than to have applied themselves for several years to this labour."

One had to respect the skill of Chinese mariners, so adept at navigating the empire's vast, impressive network of rivers and canals. And the Chinese addiction to mathematics (they were wizards at arithmetic, even though their geometry was "superficial") and astronomy was surely admirable: "China insults us by the sumptuousness of her observatory." But why did Chinese women have such small feet? They shared many of the wiles and vanities of European women—painting their faces and committing other such outrages—but the lengths to which they went to shorten their feet "in a manner make a particular species of them." And this was just one aspect of a truly curious ideal of fashion and beauty.

How could one account for all the long fingernails? And why admire the looks of a "man big, tall and gross"? "They would have him have a broad forehead, eyes little and flat, a short nose, great ears, a mouth of a middling size." Did they know nothing of the rules of Western physiognomy? As one early modern manual could have told you, small eyes "declare that man to be covetous and a crafty beguiler," a round forehead showed him "to be mutable and a doer of injury," big ears were a sure sign that he was "simple witted," "the nose small" suggested he was "a deceiver."

There were a host of curious ideas crowding the Chinese psyche—the bizarre fables attached to mountains, for instance. But their political ideals, the basis of their political philosophy, was sound enough. A shame, therefore, that such ideals were so often abandoned, so that "avarice [and] ambition . . . bear a great stroke in all transactions. They cozen and cheat in traffic; injustice reigns in sovereign courts; intrigues busy both princes and courtiers." But then again, this was all rather familiar, and in the corridors of power at least, "they live there as we do in Europe."

So why was Le Comte telling his correspondents back in Europe—and once his memoirs hit the shelves, a much wider public—about such things? On one level he believed he was making the case for a measured, objective kind of reportage. Unfortunately, he complained in his English translator's rendering, "there is a sort of jolly people that amuse themselves with what passes daily before their eyes, and are little affected with news from remote parts of the globe." Such people dismissed all talk of foreign lands as fable.

On the other hand, there were the sensationalists "who inquire after nothing but wonders, satisfied only with what raises their admiration, they think all that's natural flat and insipid, and if they are not roused up with astonishing adventures and continual prodigies [they] drop asleep over the best penned relations." There was room for a middle ground—a place where righteous curiosity was directed at the real and tangible—and Le Comte intended to occupy it.

But Le Comte was also a Jesuit priest, and in the very same volume as these cultural observations, he wrote at great, devoted length about the progress of the Christian faith in China, the triumphs and tribulations of a mission that, at the time of writing, was less than a hundred years old. This juxtaposition is vitally important. To describe a society was the first step toward converting it.

In a way, China was easy. There was much to shrink from—Jesuits moaned endlessly about homosexuality and concubinage—but there was at least as much to admire.[36] So far as Le Comte and many other Jesuits were concerned, the empire seemed to be the most promising mission field on the face of the planet. It was a shame, he admitted, that the Chinese "looked upon themselves as a chosen elect people . . . fancied other men but as dwarfs and pitiful monsters that had been the outcasts into the extremities of the earth, as the dross off-scouring of nature," but there was no denying the sophistication of their age-old culture: stratified in ways that early-modern Europeans could appreciate, even possessed of a philosophy—Confucianism—which, if stripped of its later interpretative baggage, might just contain a worthy core.[37]

Japan was likewise both annoying and inspiring. Just as strange as China, for one thing: a place where, by one early-seventeenth-century account, the people mourned in white rather than black; where they mounted their horses to the left, not to the European right; where people showed respect by taking off their shoes instead of their hats. There were the strange drinks, like sake and tea: "Their common fare is herbs and fish and rice, of the which they also make a kind of wine, although their ordinary drink be warm water into which in feasts and banquets they put a certain powder much esteemed of them, the which is called cha." There were the chopsticks, which "after a far neater fashion than we they use to eat their meat."

And Japan's people apparently had the pride as well: though for "the most part of pregnant lively wits, of exceeding memory, of stout, courageous minds and wonderful patience in occasions of adversity," they also revealed themselves as "haughty and high-minded, very desirous of honour and estimation." A shame, indeed, that they "do condemn all other nations in the world in comparison of themselves."[38] This, coming from an early-modern European whose continent arrogantly supposed that the rest of the world deserved exposure to its faith and morality, was ironic, to say the least. But for all that, Japan, like China, struck many Jesuits as a manifestly advanced society, bursting with otherness, certainly, concealed in part behind what seemed like an impenetrable language, but possessed of an ancient history, prized and continued by educated, cultivated political and intellectual elites.

On the other hand, Francisco Cabral, superior of the Japanese mission between 1570 and 1581, believed that the Japanese, intelligent as they might well be, were also deceitful, cunning, and proud. He was adamant that not one of the empire's citizens deserved the honor of becoming a Jesuit: "If one does not cease and desist admitting Japanese into the Society . . . that will be the reason for the collapse of the Society, nay! of Christianity, in Japan!" The Japanese, he moaned, were "educated to be inscrutable": and thus a stereotype was born.[39]

Alessandro Valignano, the Jesuits' "visitor to Japan and China" between 1595 and 1606, is easily portrayed as an innovative leader of the Asian missions, a person who created seminaries for indigenous populations, the man who sent a group of Japanese youths as ambassadors to Europe, where they might be feted by crowned heads and religious leaders. But even Valignano did not constantly dote on all things Japanese and Chinese, and he was entirely capable of bile and derision from time to time. In his happier moods, however, Valignano did symbolize a growing mood within some ranks of the Society that bullying and strident evangelism were wholly inappropriate to the Chinese and Japanese missions.[40] Subtler rules of engagement were called for.

There is no better example than China.[41] Beginning with the missions of Ruggieri and Ricci, it seemed sensible to flatter the intellectual elite, becoming well versed in the sacred works of Confucius, dazzling scholars with advanced scientific knowledge, producing a map of the world far beyond the scope and imaginings of contemporary Chinese geography.[42] As Joseph Amiot would later put it: "Thus we try in the interests of our religion to gain the goodwill of the prince and to make our services so useful and necessary to him that in the end he will become more favourably inclined towards Christians and persecute less than he has done."[43]

By 1629 Jesuits, including Adam Schall von Bell (who would win control of the imperial astronomical bureau), were helping with Chinese calendar reform and correctly predicting a solar eclipse.[44] "As a star of old brought the

Magi to the adoration of the true God," Ferdinand Verbiest opined, "so the princes of the Far East through knowledge of the stars would be brought to recognise and adore the Lord of the stars," the Christian God. Verbiest would not only deepen the Jesuit contribution to Chinese astronomy but also, if reluctantly, put his military expertise at the emperor's disposal, helping to renew Peking's fortifications and designing, then blessing, German-style cannon.[45]

And the pastoral of the intellect could take on other forms. In 1689, Jean-François Gerbillon would serve as the emperor's representative at border negotiations with the Russians for the Treaty of Nerchinsk; by the early eighteenth century Jesuits such as Jean-Baptiste Régis and Joachim Bouvet were winning favor by traveling across the empire, producing maps of Peking, the Great Wall, and areas from Manchuria to the Siberian border; and their countryman Jean-Denis Attiret would be among those artists producing massive paintings memorializing the emperor's military victories. Later in the century, even after persecution of Christianity had reached epidemic levels, Michel Benoît would still be designing and building a series of decorative fountains for the imperial gardens.

It was an approach nicely summed up by Dominique Parrenin, a missionary at Peking from 1698. His chemical expertise allowed him to confound Chinese audiences with tricks involving saltpeter and explosive powders, and as he once explained to a suitably dazzled crowd, he was also "only too happy to be able to undeceive you from the religious errors which you are in," which were, he suggested, "of far greater consequence for your happiness than the ignorance of a few natural phenomena."[46]

But not everyone was enamored of Jesuit scientific genius. The native astronomers displaced by Adam Schall von Bell eagerly sought their revenge. Curious allegations, that Schall had caused the death of an empress and used his astronomical expertise to select an inauspicious day for the burial of an imperial princess, led to the pitiable sight of the seventy-two-year-old Jesuit being carried into court on a stretcher, paralyzed and mute as the result of a recent stroke. He was sentenced to death, and only the timely arrival of an earthquake and a fire at the palace—interpreted as divine displeasure at the court's verdict—managed to save the priest's life.

But these were risks worth taking. As Sabatino de Ursis, genius in hydraulics, saw things, to "work with both hands, the right in the affairs of God" and the left in the affairs of science and the intellect, offered the best, albeit painstaking route to the conversion of the Chinese.[47]

✳

WHAT REMAINED FAR from clear was whether such strategies were of value the world over. If Alessandro Valignano had a broadly positive view of what he called, with none-too-subtle racism, the white races of China and Japan, he was less adoring of Africans, a "very untalented race . . . incapable of grasping our holy religion or practising it." The people of India, meanwhile, were "born to serve rather than command"; they were "miserable and poor beyond measure . . . all of a very low standard of intelligence."[48]

But perhaps it was important not to rush to conclusions. The Chinese, according to Le Comte, had been prejudiced against outsiders because until very recently they had been exposed at any great length only to supposedly inferior peoples such as the Indians and the Tartars. He hinted that, given Jesuit activity a world away in Canada, there was a lesson to be learned here. "If at three hundred leagues distance from Quebec we found Iroquois mathematicians or learned Algonkins, that could discover to us a new philosophy, more clear, comprehensive and more perfect than ours, we should be no less blameworthy than the Chinese for preferring ourselves to that people and for having hitherto termed them barbarians."[49]

In truth, however, no Jesuit missionary was really expecting to find Iroquois mathematicians three hundred leagues from Quebec. As Paul Le Jeune, superior of the New France mission between 1632 and 1639, explained: "I do not claim here to put our savages on a level with the Chinese, Japanese and other nations perfectly civilised; but only to put them above the condition of beasts."[50] This was a mean-looking compliment—just above the beasts— and Le Jeune complained endlessly about the local people's sinfulness and addiction to sensuality; but in the context of its time, it was a compliment of sorts.

Deciding on the stature of cultures perceived as less advanced than those in Europe, China, or Japan provoked one of the fiercest debates of early-modern intellectual life. It saw the worldviews of Aristotle, Augustine, and Aquinas, varied and conflicting in their understandings of mankind's potentiality and sin, join battle, and it rippled through the Society's missions. How should a Jesuit evaluate, and by extension how should a Jesuit try to convert, the Huron in New France, or the Guaraní in Paraguay, or the pearl fishers of Cape Coromandel?

Were they to be dismissed as savages, obsessed with the sensual and material? Some missionaries would characterize them as slaves to sin, cruel and gluttonous, who swore and lied and thieved, who were creaturely, concupiscent, and proud, with little sense of shame or modesty.[51] Jesuit satisfaction would often reside in seeing the accretions of native society slip away. Joseph Anchieta was delighted that those who had been won over to Christ in Brazil had seen fit to abandon their nakedness.[52] Were they, as Pierre Biard wrote of the people he encountered in New France, like wandering animals?[53] Or perhaps it was just as valid, as another Canadian missionary believed, to see them as "well formed, strong, of good mien, endowed with natural good sense," needing "only a drop of water to make them children of God."[54]

Gabriel Lalemant insisted that they had souls "as precious in the eyes of the son of God as of the persons who will read these relations," by which he meant the sophisticated reading public back in Catholic Europe. Perhaps, as Henri Lafitau later suggested, Native Americans could reasonably be compared with the ancient European tribes on the borders of the Roman frontier, or as Le Jeune believed, to the peoples of medieval Germany and Spain before the enriching, civilizing enlightenment of Christianity descended.

The papal bull *Sublimis Deus* had averred in 1537 that they were fully human beings and fundamentally rational creatures. But were they educable, with an instinctive thirst for the faith, a primordial religious yearning, with natural virtues to be enhanced—or were they a lost cause? Ought they to be treated as children of nature—or as slaves? Perhaps nomadic and seminomadic people should not be allowed to wander. Perhaps they should be settled—as happened at Joli, on the shores of Lake Titicaca, in the reductions of

Paraguay and Bolivia, at the Montagnais settlement at St. Joseph de Sillery—in European-looking communities, sometimes replete with windmills and bakeries, where they might be trained in the arts of masonry, butchery, and carpentry as well as the awesome joys of Christ. Paul Le Jeune certainly believed that four elements were crucial in the conversions of New France: the study of native languages, the establishment of hospitals, the erection of seminaries, and above all, the enforcement of a sedentary life.[55]

Jesuits provided any number of answers to such questions (crucially, different Jesuits came up with very different answers within a single mission field), but in the final analysis, the proof of the potential was in the conversion. Jesuits in New France found enormous solace in the fact that among their neophytes there were individuals who asked for penances three times as harsh as any European was likely to desire and others who were entirely capable of leading congregations in hymn, prayer, and catechism, even offering baptism when no Western priest was in the vicinity.

A convert who was renamed Francis Xavier at his baptism during the 1630s clearly had a lot to live up to, but there was manifest delight among the missionary community when he refused to join in tribal dances or to let his daughter marry outside the Christian faith. He was eager to observe all and any fasts, relying on a diet of bread and peas, enduring the delicious aroma of stewing moose tongues, and refusing to eat elk meat even if this meant going hungry for days on end while out hunting. His story, as one Jesuit saw it, offered an opportunity to return to France and "reproach heretics and bad Christians a hundred times over by telling them that the savages observe Lent while they ate meat like dogs."[56] A good convert, Le Jeune contended, was worth any three missionaries, and this filled him with the "hope of seeing, in a few years, martyrs for the faith in these countries . . . the fervour of some of these good neophytes will deserve that favour from heaven."[57]

New worlds did begin to produce their own saints, and the Virgin even began to honor such places with visionary appearances. At the end of the sixteenth century a young catechumen in India had been mocked by a group of Muslims, and then one of his detractors had been struck on the back of the head with a brick, seemingly thrown by an invisible hand: here was the kind of divine intervention that might be expected back in Europe.[58] God, it seemed, had decided to become directly involved, and there was surely no greater commendation. He was unlikely to assist those he thought beyond the salvific pale.

THERE WERE MUCH darker moments than this, when Jesuits fell into despair, worrying that mocking, undermining, and bruising existing belief systems was just as much a waste of time as discreetly, humbly infiltrating an alien culture. Not every Jesuit in New France shared Le Jeune's outlook: not everyone agreed with Matteo Ricci. For the most part, however, Jesuit missionaries (and their careers did rather depend on it) insisted that salvation was available to all the disparate populations to which they ministered.

But a clock workshop in Peking is not the same as an artificial community on the banks of the river Uruguay, and within the wider strategy of saving savable souls, there was enormous scope for tactical diversity. The critics of the Society claimed that its legendary evangelical versatility led to two antithetical kinds of excess. Sometimes, they carped, Jesuits tried far too hard to persuade—almost going native, and tolerating unhealthy syncretisms. Sometimes, however, the Society was accused of being far too much in thrall to the powerful builders of empire, happy to rely on force, convinced, as Joseph Anchieta once put it, that nothing convinces so well as the sword and the rod of iron. Jesuits were painted as opportunists, looking for whatever horses best fitted their evangelical courses.

Both stereotypes, as is usually the case with stereotypes, are flawed. Jesuits did exploit their relationship with colonial incursion, but they also found time to criticize its worst excesses. Sometimes they sought to persuade, sometimes they relied on force. Jesuits did sometimes adopt accommodationist tactics, and not only in places such as Japan and China, but they usually did so in measured, carefully judged ways.

4

"SOMETIMES SWEETLY, SOMETIMES WITH THE SWORD"

Missionary Methods

Hah! Where? What angle of the world is this
That I can neither see the politic face
Nor with my refined nostrils taste the footsteps
Of any of my disciples, sons and heirs
As well of my designs or institutions?
I thought they'd spread over the world by this time,
Covered the earth's face and made dark the land
Like the Egyptian grasshoppers.

The character of *Ignatius Loyola in Thomas Middleton's* A Game at Chess, *1610*[1]

Age of Empires

Xavier stands on the waterfront, barefooted, black-cassocked, and haloed, behind him a calm sea, busy with ships trimming toward the horizon. He holds a crucifix in one hand, a map of eastern Asia in the other. His exotic-looking companions, merchants with their turbans and their earrings and a bag overflowing with coins, are pointing to Goa, China, and Malacca, "the richest place in the world," meeting place of monsoons, of Persians, Malays, Bengalis, and no few Portuguese. This seventeenth-century engraving seems to have it all: the faith, the promise, the stereotypical Asians, and the lucre. Across the Jesuit world, mission and profit, empire and evangelism were destined to collide.[2]

IN 1717 JOHN Lockman found himself trapped between two familiar caricatures of the Jesuit missionary.

Can we possibly figure to ourselves a more amiable being, than a man who, after enriching his mind with noblest treasures of knowledge, voluntarily quits his friends, his relations, and his native country; hazards him-

self to all the perils of the sea, and afterwards goes ashore, though scarce provided with any necessities, among a barbarous people with whose language he is utterly unacquainted; there roves in their wildest solitude, in danger every moment of falling down precipices, or into deep chasms of the earth; of being murdered by wild beasts or by the natives; and all this solely from a desire of polishing their minds, of assisting their corporal part, and of saving souls.

"Such," Lockman explained, were the Jesuits "represented by themselves and their adherents." But "on the other hand":

If we reflect on a man whose only design, in acquiring learning, is to impose upon his fellow creatures; who, under the cloak of religion and to serve a set of detestable politicians, undertakes long voyages; visits foreign regions, and there ingratiates himself with the several natives of them, in order to seize upon their riches and make them slaves in their own country, where, amid their virtuous ignorance, they enjoyed undisturbed felicity: can imagination frame a more horrid creature than this? Such is the character their antagonists give of them.[3]

A stark choice, then, between Jesuits as exemplary colonial bullies and Jesuits as unworldly soul savers and mind polishers.

IN AN IDEAL world (so passages from Proverbs and Micah suggested) it would be marvelous if "every man may sit under his own vine, and under his own fig tree, and drink the waters out of his own cistern, and running waters out of his own well." But as the Jacobean compiler of travel literature Samuel Purchas pointed out in 1613, mankind had little choice but to live with the repercussions of its first forefather's dubious decisions. If Adam "had continued in his first integrity," "mine" and "yours" would never have "proved such quarrelling pronouns," but Eve, serpent, and man's first disobedience had intervened, and among a host of doleful consequences, property and exchange had found their rightful place in the everyday world of fallen humanity. What was more, no one could really deny that there was often superfluity of this or that commodity in one place, and dearth of something else, be it wine, cloth, or labor, in the next village, county, or kingdom.

Trade of one kind or another seemed to be an inevitable fact of postlapsarian human society, and it was made that much easier, and so much more far-reaching, thanks to the highway of the oceans. And in this sea-wrapped world, Europe, with its advances in nautical science, surely had the advantage over "the Persian, the Mogul, the Abyssene, the Chinois, the Tartar [and] the Turk," who might appear mighty in their little corners of the world, but whose "greatness is like Polyphemus . . . they see at home, like purblind men, near to them, not far off with those eyes of heaven and lights of the world, the learned knowledge whereof is requisite to navigation."[4] "The extent of their kingdom is so vast," Ricci would write of the Chinese, "its borders so distant, and their utter lack of knowledge of a transmaritime world is so complete that the Chinese imagine the whole world as included in their kingdom." "The Chinese think themselves the most clever of all nations," Athanasius Kircher would reveal, "but even our schoolboys know more about latitude and longitude than they do."[5]

Unfortunately, (Purchas went on), while it was entirely fitting that Europeans should traverse the globe in search of commerce and discovery—as the good old Jacobean English did—it was surely illegitimate to abuse religion in the process, to invoke some questionable papal duty to spread Christ's message in order to justify colonial brutality and land grabbing. "The gospel," Purchas barked, "is not a sword to take away earth, but to destroy hell . . . not a hammer to break in pieces the doors of earthly kingdoms." It was nothing less than a "scandal to the gospel . . . that it should rob kings of their supremacy and pre-eminence." It was a "barbarous divinity . . . to dispossess barbarians of their inheritance, and by their want of faith to increase our fees of inheritance, as if all the world were holden of the pope in Catholic fee."[6]

And if the pope was the chief culprit, he had never wanted for secular minions. Writing in 1694, Michael Geddes reckoned it a "vain conceit . . . that the world has entertained of the zeal of the Portuguese upon account of the conversions that have been made by them in the Indies." "It was covetousness and not zeal that engaged them to make those conquests . . . the government and crown having no other aim therein but the robbing of kingdoms and cities." It was surely conspicuous that "their zeal expired so quickly in all places where it was not animated with covetousness."[7] The "illustrious shades" immortalized in the poetry of Luiz de Camões—who "levelled in the dust / The idol temples and the shrines of lust / And where erewhile foul demons were revered / To holy faith unnumbered altars reared"—were, it was suggested, hardly the Iberian norm.[8]

CALCULATING THE RELIGIOUS component of empire has always been a messy business. A tangle of motives had always, and always would, energize European overseas adventure. In ways unknown since Roman times, contact with Asia had escalated during the thirteenth and early fourteenth centuries, not only through the epic travels of the Polo brothers, but with the missions of clerics such as Giovanni da Plano Carpini (to the Mongol court at Syra Orda, near Karakorum, in 1245), William of Rubruck (1253), and Giovanni da Montecorvino (who not only reached China in 1294 but over the coming years established a fledgling diocesan structure, himself becoming archbishop of Cambaluc): these were the monkish ambassadors of kings hoping to forge military and diplomatic alliances.

Then, in all-too-rapid succession, the Ming Dynasty took over China, pandemic disease struck Europe, and a hostile Ottoman Empire made land travel to the East something of a hazardous pursuit. Asia was closed for the best part of two centuries, and if its luxury goods continued to embellish European marketplaces, this was only thanks to the intermediary efforts of Levantine merchants trading with Venetian speculators in Alexandria and

Aleppo. A few hardy land travelers continued to make it as far as India and China, but for all intents and purposes, by the time the great Iberian expansion was gathering steam, Asia had become a terra incognita. The intoxicating cocktail of travelers' florid tales and alluring ancient myths had enjoyed two centuries in which to ferment, perhaps to fester, in the European imagination.

The mythology of the East was terrifying and seductive all at once. Asia could be imagined as something monstrous, as the habitat of dog-headed men, satyrs, and amazons. It was rumored that beyond a mighty wall erected by the well-traveled Alexander the Great lay the lands of Gog and Magog, from which, so the book of Revelation foretold, the pitiless rage and destruction of the Apocalypse would be launched. But it was also a place of extraordinary promise. For the rapacious there were enticing rumors of gain. Was Ophir, the land of ivory and peacocks from which Solomon had shipped the gold for his sumptuous temple, somewhere east of Persia? Could the land described by Herodotus, where riches were so plentiful that even the ants made their anthills out of gold, be rediscovered?

Those who craved less material inspiration were also well catered for. Perhaps a traveler to the East would arrive at the miraculous island visited by Iambulus where the peaceable inhabitants conversed by imitating birds and where the sun rose so high in the sky that no shadows ever fell. The fabled St. Bernard's Island was also thought to be somewhere in Asia, home to a wondrous garden, in which the daughters of Atlas cared for trees packed with golden apples. And even better gardens were on offer. Eden itself was thought to be somewhere in the Orient, providing the source of the three great civilization-bringing rivers, the Nile, the Euphrates, and the Ganges. Medieval legend told of a party of monks who had found Eden, enjoyed what they thought were three blissful days there, only to emerge from a place where time stood still to discover that three hundred years had passed.

But Europeans were also inspired by talk of isolated Christian communities, as ancient as the legendary journeys of the apostle Thomas during the first Christian century. In 1165, a letter had done the rounds of European courts, claiming to be from Prester John, a powerful Eastern monarch ruling over a utopian Christian kingdom which traced its origins to Thomas's apostolate. It was all an elaborate hoax, and the ill-starred individual, Philip the Physician, who was dispatched to make diplomatic first contact was running a fool's errand. Nonetheless, hopes of locating Christian brethren in the East were sustained all the way through to the time when Xavier set sail for Goa in 1541.[9]

When the Portuguese began arriving in India they sometimes managed to delude themselves that the temples and icons they encountered were Christian in their essentials, that images of female Hindu deities, even though they had rather more arms than strictly necessary for the mother of Christ, represented the Blessed Virgin Mary. When Jesuits heard of celibate men who chanted liturgies and lived in poverty in monasteries, they wondered if these might not be long-lost Christian monks. As it happened, they were the Buddhists of Tibet.

Early-modern empire builders (and their initial target, wherever they might have ended up, was almost always Asia) were heirs to this hodgepodge of dreams, fears, and ambitions. Spain had sent out Magellan and Columbus and progressed from conquests in the Caribbean to the seizure of Mexico and Peru. Giovanni da Verrazano had traced the American coast from Florida to Newfoundland, introducing the notion of Nova Gallia to European maps, to be followed by Frenchmen like Jacques Cartier and Samuel de Champlain, all hoping to discover a navigable shortcut to the East through the great American landmass.

Earlier still, religious and crusading zeal, a thirst for profit, and an opportunity to find employment for chivalrous young men had all coalesced in the prodigious Portuguese advance: the seizing of Ceuta, terminus of the Saharan trade routes, in 1415; the reaching out into the Atlantic, to Madeira, the Cape Verde Islands, and the Azores; the progress made along Africa's western edge and around its southern tip, culminating, on May 27, 1498, with Vasco da Gama's casting anchor off a village eight miles north of Calicut on India's southwest coast, his ships crewed in part by criminals—in search, it was said (and this was a telling phrase), of both Christians and spices.

Some of the motives of empire are easy enough to make out: once it became clear that a ship laden with a cargo of cloves, pepper, cinnamon, or nutmeg had the potential to turn a 2,000 percent profit back in Europe, enriched nobles began gratefully to put cinnamon sticks on their coats of arms. But it is terribly difficult to assess the sincerity of conspicuously devotional acts such as Cartier's arrival at Hochelaga in Canada in 1535, where he recited John's gospel, made the sign of the cross over the sick, read to the locals about the passion of Christ, and distributed Agnus Dei medals of pewter; or Vasco Núñez de Balboa's launching into a *Te Deum* when he glimpsed the Pacific Ocean for the first time in 1513.[10] Crosses were planted wherever French, Spanish, and Portuguese explorers went, but if they were potent symbols of the Christian faith, they were also prized (not always justifiably) as navigational aids.

Crucially, empire builders often *had* to claim that religious zeal was the wellspring of their adventures. Sophisticated, scholarly discussions around issues of nationhood and empire undertaken in European, especially Spanish, universities during the early-modern period laid great stress on the inherent rights of native populations to self-determination and self-government, insisting that such people were not somehow predestined to slavery but, rather, entitled to a place in the community of nations. But this was somewhat diluted by the widespread conviction that a failure to welcome Christ justified, even demanded, invasion. Such notions led, from 1513 onward, to the bizarre Spanish tool of the *requirimiento,* whereby baffled indigenous populations, who often spoke not a word of any European language, were told with great ceremony: "We will not compel you to turn Christians. But if you do not . . . I will enter forcefully against you and I will make war everywhere and however I can."[11]

In such a climate, any conquistador worth his commission did well to wear his Christian motives on his sleeve: some were more sincere than others, and an insight from one seventeenth-century Jesuit probably serves as well as any other to sum up the tangled web of motives behind the scramble for the Americas: "The Spaniard carried hither some light of the Christian religion, together with his cruelty and avarice."[12]

BUT SAMUEL PURCHAS had another point to make: the only thing worse than imperialists doing their damage in the name of Christ was men of religion exploiting the incursions of empire to pursue their avowedly spiritual goals. Catholic missionaries, Purchas pleaded, really ought to remember that the first apostles were but "a few poor fishermen and tent-makers." They "used not assistance of other nations by confederation, nor mustered multitudes in pressed and trained bands . . . nor received supportation by subsidies, nor made invasion by force, nor obtained an unwilling conquest of bodies . . . nor divided to themselves the spoils, nor erected forts, established garrisons, imposed taxations, transplanted inhabitants." They had nothing whatever to do with "that worst baggage of armies, crying, spoiling, sacking, wounding, maiming, killing, with multiformities of cruelties, as if the nethermost hells had mustered and evaporated the most and worst of her fumes and furies into our world."[13] Jesuits, it seems, were sullied by their backers' and protectors' grimy quest for wealth and power, guilty of concealing the rape of new worlds under cover of the cross. They were betrayers, basking in the covetous shadow of seaborne empires, of an honorable apostolic tradition. Was this a fair appraisal?

THE VERVE AND audacity of the age of discovery bequeathed a host of gifts to the Jesuit missions. Most obviously, it plotted itineraries—where adventurers had made good, priests would surely follow. The link between mission and empire was always there: it could not have been otherwise. It was a matter of logistics.

Just as nineteenth-century missionaries to China often had little choice but to be ferried around by opium merchants, so the Jesuits who traveled to the new worlds did so on Portuguese and Spanish ships; they required Spanish and Portuguese royal approval to do so, and they were often reliant on (and grateful for) the funds and protection provided by secular authority. The great Francis Xavier was a papal legate but he was also under commission from the

Portuguese king, arriving in Goa on board the *Santiago* in 1542 in the company of Governor Martim Afonso de Sousa.

To fall foul of secular authority could cause untold inconvenience. During the seventeenth century, Philippe Couplet, having been unwise enough to offend the Portuguese government, had to wait eight years for passage on a ship between Goa and Lisbon. Alexander of Rhodes was foolish enough to express his support for an indigenous clergy in Vietnam, and as reward for backing such an unpopular cause, he was unable to secure a berth on any Portuguese ship and had to resort to embarking for Europe by land.

In both the Spanish and Portuguese theaters, the peculiar ecclesiastical arrangements the imperial powers had worked out with Rome meant that Jesuit soul-saving would always be influenced by more obviously secular aims and achievements. Spain and Portugal could claim the rights of navigation, conquest, and trade within their empires, but only in return for a commitment to spread the gospel, erect churches and cathedrals, and support missionary work. Rome would grow increasingly weary of Iberian independence in church matters across Asia and America, and it would try to wrest back some control through the establishment of the Congregation for the Propagation of the Faith in 1622—intended to coordinate evangelical efforts—and by the introduction of apostolic vicars (a move not always welcomed by Jesuits) later in the century.[14] But the dominance of the *patronato* and *padroado* systems, the extensive rights of ecclesiastical patronage which the Iberian kings possessed, meant that those Jesuit missionaries who headed to India, China, or Latin America were acutely aware of who really dominated the spheres of influence in which they chose to move.

Such spheres were not identical, however. If the Spanish in Latin America were intent on a wholesale recasting of the political, cultural, and religious complexion of the continent—taking over, more or less—the Portuguese in Asia only ever managed to sustain a network of coastal strongholds and dominance of the seas, with very little success or interest in influencing the political makeup of the interior. As the contemporary proverb had it, the Portuguese were like fish—extremely well suited to the ocean, more than capable of outgunning and outmaneuvering Malay and Gujarati fleets, but worse than helpless once ashore. For long years the French government simply could not afford to instigate a substantial colonizing policy in Canada, and it was left to monopoly-owning merchant companies to establish a fragile French presence; only in 1663 was New France officially designated a royal territory. When Jesuits went to Agra, or Peking, or deep into the heart of Iroquois territory, they were isolated and vulnerable.

Of course, it was often easy for Jesuits to become entangled in the business and reputation of empire, and often to their great disadvantage. Sometimes Jesuits were desperately unlucky, finding themselves in the wrong place at the wrong time. In 1549, when a Portuguese captain elected to set up a toll-booth on the island of Rameswaram to fleece pilgrims en route to a Hindu holy place, Antonio Criminali was killed by the resentful Indian mob, becoming the first Jesuit martyr in the process.[15] Sometimes Jesuits were found guilty by association. When the typhoon-pummeled *San Felipe* ran aground off the island of Shikoku in 1596, the ship's pilot foolishly boasted that missionaries had avidly served as the advance guard of Spanish military conquest around the globe. Although no part of the Society's strategy, such easy, threatening linkage between mission and imperial ambition led to the execution of three Jesuit brothers, six Franciscan friars, and seventeen neophytes at Nagasaki in February 1597.

And it was not always non-European paranoia that lost Jesuits their lives. When Sebastian Rasle made good headway among the Abenaki of present-day Maine in the early eighteenth century, the English authorities in Massachusetts decided that he represented unwelcome French influence and dispatched a party to kill him: quite how badly they mutilated his corpse is something of a historical mystery, but one version of the story has Englishmen carrying his scalp back to Boston in triumph. Such notional links between Jesuits and empire could also inspire sheer flights of fancy. Christian Priber was nothing more or less than a German utopian philosopher, happily establishing his Kingdom of Paradise at Great Tellico among the Over-Hill Cherokees during the 1730s, but so natural was it for the English to associate the Society of Jesus with their imperial rivals that, when Priber began to tread on English economic toes, it was the most obvious, if entirely inaccurate, thing in the world to suppose that he was a French Jesuit agent.[16]

There were, nonetheless, many advantages to be wrung from empire. The Jesuits skillfully exploited the awe and fear in which the European invaders were held, as well as shamelessly sweetening the pill of conversion with promises of access to European military or mercantile alliances. It was sometimes made abundantly clear that to offer support to the Jesuit mission, by allowing it to preach in your dominions or, better yet, by letting it convert you, was likely to curry favor with European soldiers and merchants. Indians in New France were well aware that French traders were much more likely to supply guns to the baptized, and in an era when trade between China and Japan was at an all-time low, it was rumored that Omura Sumitada was enticed to convert to Christianity by "stirring his hopes that the China ship [the yearly Portuguese trading vessel] would come to his harbours."[17] Chinese silks and European gold and weapons thus emerged as curious but effective evangelical tools.

Exploiting such links could go too far, and when Gaspar Coelho promised Portuguese military assistance to the Japanese Empire in its planned invasion of China, his superiors were horrified. But it was an enduring reality of imperial life, visible long before the Jesuits entered the fray, that converts could be won by flaunting the promise of association with the European powers. The entire Parava community of southern India had been willing to be baptized to gain Portuguese military help against the bullying *zamorin* of Calicut, and when the ruler of Tanor opted to be baptized, he was sure to insist that the ceremony be accompanied with as much pomp and as many Portuguese ships and men as possible, so that his neighbors might be suitably impressed by how well connected he was to the daunting European arrivistes.[18]

Ultimately, however, this was only another kind, albeit a sordid kind, of persuasion. The tougher question was whether it was acceptable to benefit from, advocate, and even participate in the more forceful interventions of the colonial powers. At Cuncolim, within the archdiocese of Goa, in the second half of the sixteenth century, it certainly looked as if it might.

ON JULY 25, 1583, five Jesuits were killed, in horrible ways, in the town of Cuncolim. Scimitars, lances, swords, and arrows provided Rudolph Acquaviva (a veteran of the Moghul mission), Peter Berno, Francis Aranha, Alphonsus Pacheco, and Anthony Francisco with a route toward beatification (achieved, by the grace of Pope Leo XIII, in 1893). The fact that no one sought to memorialize the local Christian neophytes who died alongside them has been a source of considerable resentment.

The five Jesuits, at the beginning of a tour of the Salsette mission stations, had arrived at Cuncolim to erect a cross and pick out a sight for a new church. Harmless enough, one might think. The trouble was that Salsette had had enough of Christian intrusion, an invasion in which Jesuit missionaries and Portuguese troops had marched shoulder to shoulder. Over the past two decades new Portuguese tax burdens had been imposed, punitive expeditions had smashed Hindu idols and temples, and a town such as Cuncolim, whose especially sumptuous idols and temples were at the heart of its economic well-being, had suffered enormously. This is what the five martyrs of Salsette represented, and it was not lost on the local crowds that one of the Jesuits, Peter Berno, had been in Cuncolim before, destroying a sacred anthill and slaughtering a sacred cow.

The link between Jesuit evangelism and colonial ambition was clear for all to see—and would be further highlighted by the cunning, nasty way in which the secular authorities dealt with the Jesuits' assassins.[19] Certainly, the priests who died would be lionized by the faithful: after the fashion of Francis Xavier, the right arm of Acquaviva would be dispatched to Rome in 1600 as a precious relic, the left arm following on to the Society's college in Naples nine years later. But that should not obscure the fact that Cuncolim represents a relationship between Jesuits and empire rather less innocent than service as diplomats or as intelligence gatherers at the Moghul court.

And it was not an isolated incident. Manuel da Nóbrega's 1556 treatise on conversion, the first meditation on such matters produced by a Jesuit in Brazil, insisted that winning Indian souls to Christ was really feasible only after some measure of subjugation had been indulged in. Just as Jesuits accompanied dragoons in Europe in the effort to re-Catholicize communities, so Jesuit chaplains accompanied punitive and pacifying expeditions across Asia and the Americas. In more fanciful moments, some members of the Society even suggested military invasions of Mecca, Angola, and the great Chinese empire itself. Jesuits knew the value of force, and tore down their share of temples, and they were not averse to exploiting European infrastructures to enforce their preferred brands of morality. At Goa, the official in charge of placing orphans in the hands of convert families, seizing them from their infidel relatives, was often a member of the Society.[20]

BUT RATHER MORE was going on. The relationship between the Society and the imperial authorities in Asia and the Americas was far from perfect, and the relationship between the Society and independent merchants and adventurers was worse yet. Jesuits were easily perceived as constituting an alternative source of power and influence in the New World, a perception that would make a major contribution to the fatal attack on the Society in the eighteenth century. More immediately, they had an awkward habit of criticizing colonial excess. Jesuits smashed idols, followed in the wake of European invasion, mocked and trampled on local customs and beliefs; but they could also, in the person of someone like António Vieira, denounce the sins of Maranhão.

Vieira asked his colonist congregation an awkward question in 1653: did they know what God wanted of them during this year's Lent? The answer, quite simply, was that God wanted them to break the chains of injustice and free those people they held in oppression and captivity. The congregation, he went on, was in a state of mortal sin, living in a state of condemnation, about to descend directly to hell. Pharaoh had held the Israelites captive and so the land was covered with frogs, the air was clouded with mosquitoes, the rivers flowed with blood, and thunder and lightning issued from the clouds. No surprise, then, that a land in which local populations were held in unjust captivity to serve the greedy ambitions of Portuguese settlers should suffer its own, God-given plagues: the plague of the Dutch, of smallpox, of famine and drought. Vieira predicted the colonists' response but gave it short shrift: "Who will fetch a pail of water for us or carry a load of wood? Who will grind our manioc? Will our wives have to do it? Will our sons?" Yes, the priest insisted, "and repeat again yes. You, your wives, your sons." It was better to live by your own sweat than by the blood of others. Take my advice, Vieira concluded, and you will go to heaven and not to hell.[21]

This all sounds very good and noble: "Any man who deprives others of their freedom, and being able to restore that freedom does not do so is condemned." But Vieira was no otherworldly saint. When not in Latin America he played the astute, wily politician back home in Portugal: this very sermon, fierce as it was, also took time to convince its audience that Vieira's recommendations made good economic sense. The fulcrum of his missionary career was the decidedly quirky notion that God wanted to establish a fifth universal monarchy under Portuguese control, and that this might be achieved in decidedly vicious ways: "the blood of heretics in Europe and the blood of Muslims in Africa, the blood of heathens in Asia and America" would all have to be spilled for the grand purpose of "conquering and subjugating all the regions of the earth under one sole empire."

Vieira had absolutely no objection to the colonial advance per se. Nor was he as enlightened as his inspired sermonizing might seem to suggest. He was entirely convinced of European cultural and moral superiority—God certainly wanted Indians to be freed, but "God is so favourable to the cause of liberty that he grants it even to those who do not deserve it." And his compassion was somewhat selective: what better way to remove the hideous burden from the backs of Native Americans than to increase the number of black African slaves coming into the colonies?

Vieira was no Peter Claver or Alfonso de Sandoval, winning a reputation at Cartagena, the terminus of the African slave trade, for distributing food, sympathy, and eternal salvation on board the ships lately arrived with their despicably treated human cargo. He was no Bartolomé de Las Casas, savaging, if exaggerating, Spain's treatment of indigenous populations and debating with Juan Ginés de Sepúlveda about the equality and rationality of the American people at Valladolid in 1550. But he *was* part of a robust, decent, clerical tradition that, in earlier guises, had forced European polities to enact the ameliorating Laws of Burgos in 1512 (which sought to codify the behavior of settlers in the Americas), and he had campaigned vigorously against as hateful an institution as the *encomienda,* whereby native inhabitants were blithely allocated for life to Spanish settlers: a system that did not, strictly, make for slaves, but did not make for autonomous, salaried employees either.

Jesuits, once more following Xavier's lead, would frequently criticize the morality of colonists. Complaints came in from Asia that "there are innumerable Portuguese who buy droves of girls and sleep with all of them and this is known publicly . . . there was one man in Malacca who had twenty four women of various races, all his slaves, and all of whom he enjoyed."[22] Back in Brazil, Manuel da Nóbrega thought it scandalous that some colonists had not been shriven for as long as seventeen years, not least because they surely had much to confess.[23] And Jesuits would sometimes go to extraordinary lengths to defend local populations. This could involve measured argument, as when Luis de Valdivia called for an end to personal service among the Araucanians of Chile,[24] or it could involve, in extremis, nothing less than a campaign to arm local populations with muskets.

Jesuits had maintained a missionary presence in Paraguay since the early years of the seventeenth century, most productively in the reductions established among the Guaraní between the Paraná and Paraguay Rivers. The trouble was that opportunists from São Paolo, much to the annoyance of the local authorities, would venture into this area in search of slaves. It has been calculated that as many as seventy thousand Guaraní were captured by these Paulistas, or *mamelucos,* many of them between 1629 and 1631. The Jesuit Antonio Ruiz de Montoya felt his only option was to march twelve thousand Indians to safety, four hundred miles downriver to lands between the Uruguay River and the coast.

It was an epic journey from which only a third of the migrants emerged with their lives, but it solved little: the slave raids continued. The Jesuits decided to seek permission to arm the Guaraní, and matters came to a head at the confluence of the river Mbororé. Here, in 1641, guided by Jesuit military advice, Guaraní troops repulsed five hundred Paulistas, and the seventeen hundred Indians they had in tow, in a series of land and sea skirmishes. This was not a battle between Jesuits and colonial authority: the unscrupulous slavers were lawless, independent adventurers. But it was, beyond a doubt, a famous battle between the Jesuits and the very worst kinds of European colonial behavior.[25]

THINKING THAT INDIGENOUS populations ought not to be mistreated or enslaved was not necessarily the same as thinking that they were the equals of the fine burghers of Spain, France, or Italy. The fabled Paraguayan reductions were ultimately an exercise (one that could never quite overcome the local population's annoying habit of thinking for itself) in paternalism. As for José de Acosta, he was much troubled by the brutal excesses of colonial life but he had no doubts about the overall legitimacy of the colonial enterprise and the cultural superiority of Christian Europe. He was adamant that the dross of paganism had to go, that any whiff of syncretism was to be avoided, and that Europe was the "better and more noble part of the world." Peru, by contrast, was like an ugly daughter, redeemed only by her mineral-rich dowry.[26] Acosta disapproved of slavery, but he also railed against the notion of mixed-blood, mestizo children growing up to be Catholic priests.

Jesuits would sometimes seek to protect their charges from unwholesome European habits. They enjoyed making less-than-flattering comparisons between the new Christians of Canada and the tired, corrupt Christians of France; they often refused to accept the value of Frenchifying or Hispanicizing entire communities. A few Jesuits in China became genuinely enchanted by the notions and nostrums of a sophisticated philosophy such as

Confucianism. Even more Jesuits regularly followed their colleague Francisco Suárez in insisting that an infidel was fundamentally different from a European heretic. The latter was stubborn, had had his chances to embrace the true faith, and had rejected them; the former was a rational creature who, until these latter days, had never been given the opportunity of seeking out salvation. This surely meant that, in ideal circumstances, he should be allowed to embrace Christ through free, unbullied choice.

Not that any of this prevented from Jesuits from being entirely typical early-modern Europeans; secure in their cultural status; eager, for the most part, to traduce and trample on rival beliefs; willing on occasion to exploit their association with empire. The fact that they thought indigenous populations *could* be converted was, by the standards of the time, generous enough. But they also thought that indigenous populations *should* be converted, which, to the peoples among whom the Society set up its evangelical stalls, was, at the very least, irksome.

At least the Society of Jesus thought its evangelizing mission through. It sometimes indulged in temple smashing but it also put great store in the concept of persuasion. Persuasion, of course, could mean many things: fierce sermons and horrifying woodcuts intended to reveal the tortures and indignities of hell, for instance. Fear was always a useful forerunner of faith, and Jesuits in New France were convinced of the "good effect" attainable from pictures of demons "tormenting [the] soul with different kinds of tortures—one applying to it the torch, another serpents, another pinching it with red hot tongs."[27] But there was also room for subtlety, caution, and gentleness—a duty, whether in Huronia or Peking, to decide how far, in the interests of securing conversions, it might be possible to adapt to local circumstances. The Society's enemies regarded this as an exercise in unholy compromise; the Society's supporters thought it a stroke of genius. It was absolutely not a Society-wide policy with which every Jesuit missionary agreed, but it is what made the Jesuit missions famous and what, as the decades piled up, got the Society into an awful lot of trouble.

Accommodation

When they have learned the languages and customs of the country, they put on the habit of the Indian penitents . . . comply with all their customs, though never so troublesome and disagreeable, and accordingly sit on the ground cross-legged; eat on the ground, never touching anything with their left hand, which, in the opinion of those people, would be contrary to all the rules of decency and politeness; keep a continual fast, eating but one meal a day, which is made up of fruit, herbs and some rice boiled in water . . . if the first missionaries of Madurai had refused to submit to that rigid life, their zeal would have proved ineffectual, and they could not have converted as they have actually done several Brahmins and above 150,000 idolaters.

The Travels of Several Learned Missionaries of the Society of Jesus into Divers Parts of the Archipelago, India, China and America, *1713*[28]

A foreign padre whose language, dress, tradition and customs were so ridiculous in our eyes that when we saw him in those first beginnings he served us no other purpose but to give us occasion to laugh at him, mock him, and ridicule him.

Sanga Hoki no Kami on the arrival of the first Jesuit missionary in Japan[29]

Members of the Society of Jesus knew rather too much about the perils of treating the attitudes and expectations of an alien culture with disdain. The Italian Jesuit John de Britto had already been in India for seven years when he moved into a house on the edge of the territories of Raghunatha Thevar, the ruler of Marava, late in 1686. The king's official stance, the result of legal action against de Britto and other Christians earlier in the year, was that Jesuits were forbidden to preach in his dominions, although he was probably willing to look the other way. But then a relative of the king, Tadiya Thevar, decided to convert to the strange new religion so despised by local Brahmins. Tadiya was a polygamist, and bolstered by his new faith, he gave up all but one of his wives.

This delighted his new spiritual counselors but devastated a woman named Kadalai, his youngest spouse and, rather more important, niece of the hitherto tolerant king of Marava. Convinced that his family's honor had been stained by these upstart missionaries and their curious moral standards, the king determined to hunt de Britto down. When sorcery failed to dispatch the missionary, the king sent him, Hamlet-style, with sealed instructions, to his brother Uriya Thevar. De Britto thought he was merely being exiled; Uriya knew that de Britto was to be killed. Having reached Urayur province in February, the Jesuit was beheaded with a scimitar (it took three swipes), his hands and feet were cut off and tied to his body, and the resulting spectacle hung, the most eloquent of warnings, on a tall wooden post.[30]

It would seem that preaching and promoting Western morality could carry an awful cost. Not that this ever hampered Jesuit missionaries in their effort to damn what they simply could not abide. The Society was known for its willingness to adapt to certain aspects of foreign cultures (de Britto himself was happy enough to wear local costume), but some things always seemed intolerable: it was all about drawing a line in the moral sand. Jacques Marquette, while missioning among the Illinois of North America, was once offered a peace pipe. Despite being painfully ill at ease with such a curious instrument, he saw no harm in participating up to a point: "You must not refuse it, unless you would pass for an enemy, or at least for being impolite. It is however enough to pretend to smoke."[31]

Measured cultural assimilation, which (once again) had its roots in Xavier's first apostolate, was to be found in virtually every Jesuit mission field, none more famous or more controversial than that of de Britto's predecessor, Roberto de Nobili. Arriving in Madurai in 1606, de Nobili was always a long way from going native, whatever his critics might have said, but he realized that to be taken seriously in Indian society he would do well to dress in the saffron robes of a sannyasi, since those in European dress were apt to be dismissed as *parangi*, detested foreigners. He also stopped eating meat, fish, and eggs, set about learning Tamil and Sanskrit, gave up speaking Portuguese, adopted a Tamil name, and while concentrating his own efforts on the illustri-ous Brahmin class, established a separate troop of priests for those at the lower reaches of the caste system.[32]

It was a very definite echo of the policy inaugurated in China by Matteo Ricci, when he had dressed as a Confucian scholar and observed the customs of the empire's intellectual elite, and of Alexander of Rhodes, the evangelist of Vietnam, who wore long braids and slippers. If Alessandro Valignano saw sense in pursuing a pastoral of the intellect in the ancient empires of the East, he also directed missionaries in Japan to acquire local "customs of good breeding," to decorate their houses after the Japanese style, even installing tea pavilions, and to eat rice and soup at Japanese-style low tables. It would also be an excellent idea, he suggested, if Jesuits took the time to wash themselves more frequently.

Even in New France, where the duty to denounce local moralities was taken especially seriously, cultural gaps were sometimes bridged. Paul Le Jeune seemed well aware of the shifting nature of cultural conventions. "Oh how weak are the judgements of men!" he declared. "Some place beauty where others see nothing but ugliness. The most beautiful teeth in France are the whitest; in the Maldive Islands whiteness of teeth is considered a defor-mity and they paint them red to be beautiful; and in China, if my memory serves me, they paint them black. Which is right?"[33] Condemning every last aspect of a culture was as intellectually flimsy as it was counterproductive, and perhaps, Le Jeune suggested, an apostolic man in New France would do well to cultivate affability, humility, patience, and a generous charity.[34]

Wise heads like Jean de Brébeuf urged their colleagues to bend to local mores and customs wherever possible, wherever a particular habit could be thought of as morally indifferent. When among the Huron, he counseled, never keep your hosts waiting, always carry a tinderbox to indulge their pas-sion for smoking, and do not ask too many questions since the Huron dislike the garrulous. Most especially, paddle in canoes only if you intended to keep it up for the entire journey—the Huron would not appreciate those who var-ied their work rate. It was a very good idea to respect the importance of gift giving in Huron culture, and during one encounter Brébeuf astutely "pre-sented to the assembly a collar of 120 beads of porcelain, telling them that it was given to smooth the difficulties of the road to paradise."[35] To dismiss this as an attempt at bribery would be to misconstrue it.

Jesuit attempts to discern what might please or disarm indigenous populations were often reductive, occasionally insulting, but some policies, such as the Canadian Jesuits' attempts to understand and mimic local rhetorical techniques, were extremely well thought out. What was more, as Jesuits were keen to stress, such strategies had a long and honorable pedigree within the Christian tradition. They had been good enough for Boniface and Cyril among the medieval tribes of northern Europe, and they had been good enough for the ur-apostle himself. Had Paul not advocated becoming all things to all men? Had he not criticized those within the early Christian community who had wanted to exclude gentiles from the faith because they had not been circumcised? Even God had been willing to adapt his message in order to render it accessible to the unworthy ears of mankind: "as God made himself man in order to make men God's . . . a missionary does not fear to make himself a savage, so to speak, with them in order to make them Christians . . . we must follow them to their homes and adapt ourselves to their ways, however ridiculous they may appear."[36]

But, the critics were quick to insist, if adapting to secular conventions— wearing the right sort of hat—was one thing, tinkering with the precious words of scripture or the sacramental and ritualistic norms of the Catholic Church was quite another. Was it really acceptable to extend the policy of adaptation and accommodation into more conspicuously religious arenas?

Behind much criticism of missionary accommodation was the persistent belief in an unsavory Jesuit tendency to tolerate, even admire, existing beliefs, to search for common spiritual ground, to rejoice when a Christian-looking image or idea—a flood myth, a serpent, a tree of life—was found in another culture's holy scripture. And if applauding something like Confucianism, claiming that beneath corrupt interpretations it had a worthy core, was bad enough, then the extremes of the "figurist" movement, the notion that Confucianism not only shared ground with Christianity but actually prefigured it, was the kind of audacious, intrusive analysis that was just the kind of thing to make enemies out of Chinese scholars happily operating within a *neo*-Confucian paradigm, and just the kind of thing to alarm those European critics of the Society who frowned on its efforts to enter into dialogue with infidel philosophies.[37]

Some maneuvers were much more superficial: livening up religious events in India with popular firework displays, juggling, and tightrope walkers; making altar decorations out of beads and porcupine quills in New France; blending local and Western architectural vernaculars in churches and religious art around the world. When Barthélemy Vimont found himself trying to say mass at Ville Marie in May 1642, where was the harm in using fireflies to light a phial displaying the Blessed Sacrament?[38] There was no better way to bolster the resolve of a converted samurai than to employ militaristic imagery in sermons and instruction: to abandon the faith in the face of persecution or social ostracism, it was regularly suggested, was to behave like the craven general who skulked away from battle when the odds began to stack up against him. If a culture had well-developed artistic tastes, what better way to engage potential converts than to indulge their fondness for music and spectacle?

But was it quite as innocent to exploit the Huron fascination with dreams (a grossly superstitious fascination by many accounts) to hasten conversion, or to replace pagan charms with new Christian amulets? Some critics claimed to observe sins of omission—a tendency to put off mentioning crucifixion in China (where it was a punishment reserved for common criminals) or to avoid talk of transubstantiation in New France (where missionaries worried that it might undermine their constant strictures against cannibalism).[39] Others objected to Jesuit missionaries allowing their converts to retain facets of the faiths and philosophies they had supposedly abandoned. Many eyebrows were raised when de Nobili did not insist that his Brahmin converts abandon their sacred threads, tufts of hair, and sandalwood paste marks on their foreheads. Surely, the critics alleged, such things had a religious significance antithetical to Christianity: they were not things indifferent.

What was Ricci's justification for allowing his new Christians to carry on with their ancestral rites and Confucius worship? Such a policy would surely lead to the vilest syncretism and a jumbled, polluted kind of Christianity. Ricci's insistence that such rites were, at heart, of civil rather than religious significance—acts of filial affection toward dead family members, conventions of a scholarly elite determined to offer homage to their philosophical master—was hotly disputed.

And then there was the problem of language. Ever since the first Pentecost the notion that all Christians should hear the word of God in their own tongue had been a reputable notion within the church. Jesuits (even if they tended to focus on elite languages, even if they often had to rely on translators, even if they were sometimes reduced to gesture) took this commitment very seriously indeed, and the missionary contribution to analyzing and codifying the world's languages was colossal.

Joseph Anchieta would produce Tupi and Guaraní grammars in Latin America; Enemond Massé and Jean de Brébeuf would produce a French-Huron dictionary in New France; de Nobili would become an accomplished scholar in Sanskrit, Tamil, and Telugu; Alexander of Rhodes would produce a Latin-Persian-Annamese dictionary, and his system of writing Vietnamese characters in Roman script still holds sway. The Jesuit effort to describe the various languages of Latin America still forms the basis of the linguistic categorization of the continent.[40] The scholarly effort to cope with clashing linguistic systems—the competing categories, inflections, parts of speech, ways of making verbs—was a mammoth achievement, even if many individual Jesuits tried and failed over long, frustrating years to master local languages.

But, the critics cautioned, while it was reputable enough to translate Aesop into Japanese or a Chinese classic like *The Art of War* into French, it was rather more hazardous to employ local tropes and images to explain intricate doctrines or to translate crucial religious concepts into local vernaculars. What if such languages lacked an appropriate vocabulary (the Huron simply didn't have a word for sin)? What if concepts of abstraction or the universal were inadequately developed? Although some Jesuits spent their careers trying to locate and codify universal grammars and the common roots of all the world's languages, speech and culture are never separate; each embodies the other, and the risk of shifting meanings or unintended connotation is always present.

Xavier had learned this in sixteenth-century Japan when, relying on imperfect advice, he had used the Japanese word *dainichi* to represent the Christian God; unfortunately the word really meant something like "a force of personal wisdom that illuminates the universe," and it made Christianity look like yet another Buddhist sect. When Ricci used the Chinese words *tian* (heaven) or *shangdi* (Lord on High) for God, some critics worried that the ideas provoked in Chinese minds were hardly consonant with what European Christians intended. But what was the alternative—the importation of clumsy transliterations like *De-us-e*, which was obviously much closer to the Latin *Deus* but which ran the risk of being an empty linguistic shell, devoid of any real meaning in Chinese minds?

Debate about such issues simmered away throughout the Jesuits' mission fields. Not everyone took the Ricci line: Claude Visdelou flatly rejected Ricci's policies; Jean Valat forbade his converts from indulging in ancestral rites; over in Ethiopia, some priests refused to make the slightest accommodation with long-standing, un-Roman, religious practice—enforcing Catholic calendars, trying to outlaw circumcision—and the Jesuits' mendicant and secular rivals steadily campaigned to have Ricci's and de Nobili's practices outlawed.[41]

The Jesuit response was often wise. Among the early Christians, de Nobili asked, was it not "always customary for the Holy Fathers to accommodate with the people in everything possible when it is a question of their conversion, by transferring even superstitious and idolatrous customs to Christian piety by giving them a new meaning"? "This was the case with holy water, foods, candles, branches at the doors of the churches, dances on the feasts of the saints, and many other things." It was as well to remember, others opined, that the story of early Christianity was one of taking on, adapting to the themes and philosophical concepts of Greek philosophy. And the response was sometimes witty.

De Nobili thought it impossible to outlaw everything in an alien culture that seemed to have a religious resonance. In a place like India, rituals and recitations seemed to accompany such humdrum tasks as brushing teeth, riding on horseback, and sweeping the floor. And besides, Europeans should be the last people to condemn the survivals of the superstitious past, or the common ground that pagan past and Christian present shared: "Which of them [in Europe] . . . ever abstained from marriage on the plea that the nuptial ceremony was regarded as presided over by the god of marriage? Or who ever scrupled to observe virginity on the ground that as heathens they considered that calling to be under the patronage of Diana?"[42]

Tracts were written, pleading emissaries were packed off to Europe, but ultimately Jesuits of the stamp of Ricci were fighting a losing, sometimes lonely, battle. The Malabar rites of de Nobili (the Brahminesque survivals) were smiled upon by Rome in 1623, but after a century of unholy wrangling, they were condemned by papal brief and constitution in 1734 and 1744. The Chinese rites were approved by Rome in 1615, condemned in 1645, and once more sanctioned in 1656. In 1704 and 1715 papal proclamations once more questioned the rectitude of Confucian and ancestral rites, the use of words like *tian* and *shangdi*, and a final proscription was issued by Benedict XIV in 1742. It was the kind of audacious Roman intrusion much resented by the Chinese emperor, a man much more at ease with the Ricci method. Having secured an edict of toleration in 1692, by 1717 the Christian community was facing an imperial edict that forbade the building of any new Christian churches and ordered the deportation of all but a few, scientifically useful, missionaries.[43]

A mess, frankly, contributed to by worthy men (of various evangelical complexions) who believed in what they said, by Frenchmen like Pascal who simply wanted to blight and blacken all things Jesuitical, and by the ever-vibrant, ever-baffling world of Vatican politics. And a mess that threatened to shatter Jesuit illusions. Fortunately, the Society had other ways of measuring success.

Head Counts and Martyrdoms: Missionary Success?

Prospects of missionary success sometimes seemed meager, as when Francis Xavier, genuinely frustrated, reported from India in 1549 that the local population did "not like to listen to anything that is not agreeable to its own manners and customs," covenants with Jesus Christ and all his saints included.[44] It is easy to assume that if Jesuit evangelical success was limited—and it was: the advertised aim was to Christianize entire empires and nations, and that simply never happened—then this must have been the fault of ill-advised Jesuit conversion techniques, or of untimely European squabbles like the Chinese rites controversy.

Jesuits did indeed alienate potential converts at times, and being informed by Rome that a century-old accommodationist missionary strategy was now illegal did not help the Society's cause. But these local populations were far from being passive recipients of the Jesuits' message. For the most part mission failed or stumbled because people in India, China, or New France did not want mission thrust upon them. They were happy enough with their familiar gods, their moralities, and their rites of passage.

Jesuits struggled to understand this. It seemed unfeasible that anyone would pass up the chance to worship the one, true faith, to cast off idolatry and superstition. And when the unfeasible happened, as it so often did, Jesuits routinely blamed it on local pride, local stupidity, or the urgings of the devil. But being certain of the righteousness, the inevitability, of their cause, Jesuits also lapsed into unwarranted optimism upon occasion, and this made them ideal targets for exploitation. It seems highly unlikely that the Chinese or Moghul emperors were ever going to embrace Christianity, but Jesuits thought they should and that, sooner or later, they probably would, and so Jesuits continued to beaver away at Peking and Fatehpur Sikri. Chinese and Moghul emperors were entirely happy with such a decision, since it got their calendars corrected, it allowed the tricks and techniques of Western art to be absorbed, it left behind a legacy of useful clocks, cannon, and mechanical toys.

There were, on the other hand, moments to be cherished, when, on the face of it, Jesuits turned things around. When Albuquerque was fighting for Malacca in 1511, his troops were confronted with massed ranks of war elephants, bizarre-looking creatures that could be repulsed only by stabbing them in the eyes and genitals. But only a few decades after Malacca fell it was not unknown for Indian neophytes to ride more obliging elephants to Sunday services at Christian churches.[45] Local populations sometimes seemed deliriously happy to welcome Jesuit priests into their communities. If we are to believe Jacques Marquette, missioning among the Illinois, he met with one such extraordinary greeting in 1672: "How beautiful is the sun, O Frenchman, when thou comest to visit us! All our towns await thee, and thou shalt enter all our cabins in peace . . . never has the earth been so beautiful, nor the sun so bright, as today; never has our river been so calm, nor so free from rocks . . . nor our corn appeared so beautiful as we behold it today."

When it was time for dinner, Marquette was apparently fed by hand, the bones were carefully removed from his fish, and someone even had the job of blowing on his food in case it was too hot.[46] As welcome a sign of favor, no doubt, as when the Ming emperor deigned to send missionaries delicacies from his own table.

The numbers can sometimes look impressive too. There was talk of 160 churches and three hundred thousand converts in China by 1675, of the same number of Japanese Christians as early as 1614. Among peoples like the Huron and the Guaraní large numbers undoubtedly came over to Christ. But what do such numbers really represent? What sort of Christians were produced? Xavier once boasted that "it often happens to me to be hardly able to use my hands from the fatigue of baptising: often in a single day I have baptised whole villages."[47]

Did such frantic efforts influence the quality of conversion? How much did the neophytes really know and understand about this puzzling new faith they were taking on? Omura Sumitada converted to Christianity in 1563 and within a decade there were twenty thousand Christians in his territories; but most of these converts were surely motivated by political pressure rather than heartfelt religious zeal. It was all rather reminiscent of the Holy Roman Empire after 1555, where, after the cozy compromise of the Peace of Augsburg, the religion of the prince automatically became the religion of his subjects. Spiritual autonomy had a tendency to abandon those on society's lower rungs during the sixteenth century.

On the whole, Jesuits were often very scrupulous about the depth of instruction that had to precede baptism. One of the first things they did in New France was criticize the mass-conversion policy of their predecessor, the secular priest Jesse Fleche, and although the dying could expect speedy entry into the church, those in better health would not usually experience any chrism-anointing moments until a decent amount of catechizing and edifying conversation had taken place. To ignore the possibility that genuine, devoted converts were secured is a huge mistake, and quite possibly demeaning and insulting to those new Christians who believed in what they were doing.

There were exceptions, of course, and when Eusebio Kino was criticized for doling out baptism rather too easily among the people of Lower California, he had to be summoned back to Mexico City in 1695 for consultation with his superiors. Spanish Dominicans spread rumors that Goan Jesuits were press-ganging local people, smearing their lips with beef (to defile them in Hindu eyes), and then baptizing them after three days' worth of instruction.[48] This was almost certainly unfounded propagandist exaggeration, but a clear enough signal that calculating an appropriate pace of conversion was a problem that never went away.

Neither did the fact that chances of evangelical success were often hopelessly at the mercy of political circumstances beyond the Society's control. Grateful converts were being won among the Huron during the 1630s and early 1640s, but then the Iroquois Confederacy began to wage war, and over the course of 1648 and 1649, the Huron were chased from their homeland and, effectively, wiped out as a distinct tribal presence in Canada. And when it wasn't the Iroquois it was the English, disrupting Jesuit missionary work by seizing Quebec in 1613 and again in 1629 and, after decades of dynastic conflict with France, ultimately removing the Jesuit missionary presence altogether, with the establishment of the Church of England as Canada's official faith in 1758. It was the Virginia English who, by invading Maryland in 1645, put an end to Andrew White's missioning among the Piscataway (White was sent back to England in chains); the Raj-making English who began to make their presence felt on the Indian subcontinent from the mid–seventeenth century; and the Dutch who, with their capture of Malacca in 1641, Ceylon in 1658, and Cochin in 1663, began to chip away at Portuguese and Catholic influence in Asia. Jesuits were well aware of what this meant for their missionary dreams: after the capture of Malacca and Cochin, those famously magical relics, two parts of Xavier's right arm, simply disappeared.

If a case study in the dire impact of political change is required, we need only turn to Japan. Centralized authority under an all-powerful emperor was much closer to myth than reality during the Jesuits' first evangelizing decades. With local warlords competing for land, tribute, and influence, the whole archipelago, in one commentator's phrase, seemed like "nothing else but a field of battle," and this was a boon for the missionary cause. By 1569 six daimyos on Kyushu, free to do whatever they chose in the absence of meaningful imperial authority, sometimes eager to make economic gains, sometimes keen to belittle the leaders of local Buddhist sects, came over to Rome.

But then a series of impressive soldier-politicians, beginning with Oda Nobunaga (who actually had few problems with Christian missioning) and culminating in the first giants of the Tokugawa shogunate, managed to restore a measure of political and social harmony to the empire. One corollary of such reform was a tendency to look askance at the liberties taken by European merchants and priests in less well governed times. In the corridors of power, Catholic influence began to be seen as a challenge to imperial discipline, and those with vested interests in seeing Catholics squirm did their best to harden this stance into orthodoxy. Dutch and English merchants, tired of Portuguese economic dominance in the East, ceaselessly counseled the court about how rebellious and rapacious southern European Catholics were, regaling it with stories of rabble-rousing and tyrannicide back home. Buddhist priests saw a wonderful opportunity to reassert their influence by stigmatizing Christianity as a deformed, foreign interloper of a religion, hazardous to Japanese purity and morality.

The first assaults on the mission were halfhearted. In 1587, Toyotomi Hideyoshi, Nobunaga's worthy successor, banished Jesuits from the empire, but after some 120 churches had been destroyed, the edict was not rigorously enforced. More damaging to Catholic interests was the shipwreck of the *San Felipe,* en route from Manila to Acapulco, off Shikoku in 1596, which led, as we have already seen, to the death of twenty-six Catholics at Nagasaki. Over the next two decades the tide of persecution rose and fell according to trading needs and the whims of political leaders, and perhaps seventy martyrs were burned or crucified.

The year 1614 marked a sea change. First came a nationwide ban on Jesuit activity, and although it did not prevent forty missionaries from continuing their ministry in secret, the next few years regularly witnessed fifty or sixty fatalities. Other grisly highlights were the deaths of fifty-one Christians at Nagasaki in 1622 and the burning of fifty more at Edo (present-day Tokyo) in 1624. The dreadful culmination was the Shimabara uprising of 1637. Partly inspired by Christian grievances, the rebels' cause was snuffed out by the final massacre at Hara Castle, during which upwards of thirty thousand people, hundreds of Catholics among them, lost their lives. In its aftermath only five priests were said to remain in Japan.

The exclusion edict of 1639 (temporarily indulgent to the Dutch) proclaimed that "for the future . . . let no-one, so long as the sun illuminates the world, presume to sail to Japan, not even in the quality of an ambassador, and this declaration is never to be revoked, on pain of death." Attempts to call the Japanese bluff proved to be misguided.

Over the coming decades hundreds of Christians were made to deny their faith by stamping on pictures of Jesus, and those who refused to comply were regularly exposed to the most horrific tortures (the *ana-tsurushi*, in which victims were hung over a pit of human excrement and a slit cut into their foreheads through which their blood could slowly drip away, probably being the worst). For the next three centuries Japan turned its back on the world. Any Japanese ship able to carry more than twenty-five hundred bushels of corn—substantial enough, in other words, to entertain the possibility of long-distance trade—was put to the torch.

A curious, covert kind of Christianity did manage to survive these years of isolation and neglect, but by the middle of the seventeenth century Jesuits had already learned a painful lesson: the shifting currents of high politics could blight the highest evangelical hopes. What they were unable to blunt was a very different kind of missionary success, one that could only be enriched by political downturns and adversity. Or so the propagandist story went.

AN EARLY-SEVENTEENTH-CENTURY history of the Japanese missions tells the story of Lucy, a native Japanese who was visited by a bizarre series of dreams. She had seen a beautiful young boy striding toward her, holding out his hands as though offering gifts. On the first night he would be carrying two precious jewels, on the second night two nosegays, and, finally, two lush red roses, but whenever Lucy reached out to claim her presents, the boy suddenly vanished. Tragic news that two of her fellow Christians had met their deaths made it all make sense. She had been warned in advance that God thought the souls of her two friends were so beautiful that he would one day bestow the priceless gift of martyrdom upon them.[49]

Centuries later, in November 1996, two thousand Japanese Christians gathered for a prayer vigil in Kyoto to commemorate the four hundredth anniversary of the Nagasaki martyrdoms, and a staggering 1.4 million people added their oblations over the Internet. Baptism by water was wondrous enough; baptism by blood—a sacrament by analogy, as the Catholic Church efficiently puts it—was more wondrous still.

Jesuits embraced persecution. In an era of reformation, when those claiming a monopoly on religious truth so often found themselves in jail or en route to the stake, it was of the first importance to put a positive spin on adversity. The trick was to insist that suffering was showered on the godly as often as the reprobate, as a means by which commitment to the truth might be assayed. It offered Christians the chance to share in the carrying of Christ's cross, the opportunity to partake of his passion, to join the long list of martyrs and good confessors who had learned that persecution was the inevitable lot of godly people living in an inimical, carnal world that did not understand them. Jesuits, desperate to prove that their faith was not built upon the sand but upon the immovable rock of Christ, signed up for the test with alacrity.

Such devotional empiricism—commitment verified by painful experience—was thought to work wonders in heretical lands, and it was every bit as potent in other corners of the world. Putting aside stories of apostasy—and many Christians, Jesuits among them, succumbed to their persecutors' pressures—books about heroic deaths in Nagasaki were reckoned to provide, "wrapped up in a few short sheets of ordinary paper," "a present of inestimable price, with a carcanet of the richest gems the Orient ever sent into Europe: jewels of Japonian pearl within the sea of persecution."[50] Jesuit novices would have martyrologies read to them at dinner; if they were in Rome they could visit the Church of Sant'Andrea al Quirinale, Jesuit-loving Bernini's masterpiece, and stand before the gruesome depictions of Jesuit martyrdom in Japan, India, and upon the Pacific Ocean.

So precious was the notion of dying for the faith that Jesuits in New France, unable to achieve the highest prize of actual bodily death, introduced any number of lesser martyrdoms into their missiological vocabulary. To observe the "the combats, battles, attacks and the general assaults against all nature which the gospel labourers suffer here every day," to have to sustain "patience, courage and their continual assiduity in pursuing their object" was surely, in its way, a petty martyrdom: "many persons could be found who would prefer to receive at once a hatchet blow upon the head than to spend their lives enduring the life that one must every day lead here." The choking smoke of native cabins, the fleas that "will keep you awake almost all night . . . not to speak of mosquitoes, sand flies and petty other like vermin" were likewise described as martyrdoms of a sort.[51]

Protestants felt obliged to undermine the Jesuit attempt to claim martyrs for the Catholic Church. It was the cause that counted, not the horrific circumstances of the death. As St. John Chrysostom had reminded his audience long ago, "the bodies of robbers, those who desecrate sepulchres and other evil-doers, are severely afflicted just as are the bodies of martyrs . . . but although their suffering is the same, the purpose differs."[52] Catholic "martyrs," it was suggested, were more often traitors than saints, inspired by pertinacity not constancy, by sin not virtue, by instigation of the devil rather than through the inspiration of God. They were more like suicidal zealots, like the Donatists of the fifth century, than men specially chosen by the Almighty. Jesuits would "force men to kill them," John Donne explained; they "boast of their hunting out of martyrdom in the new worlds and of their rage they will find it," but this was a pseudomartyrdom, inspired by pride and self-love.[53] And pride, it was important to note, had a tendency to evaporate when the flames began to lick: Jesuits about to die would speak in feeble voices, lose their strength, and begin to tremble: conclusive evidence of "what a graceless and comfortless religion popery is."[54]

Catholics, needless to say, were no less dismissive of Protestants who claimed to have died for their beliefs. As far as Richard Bristow was concerned, "no reasonable man will think those stinking martyrs of the heretics worthy in any respect to be compared with those most glorious martyrs of the Catholics . . . ours are God's martyrs and theirs the devil's . . . because ours died in the faith of St. Stephen, the first martyr, and of all his fellows, and theirs clean against the same."[55]

Of course, the majority of Jesuits would always be more interested in pursuing calm careers in pulpits and classrooms than dying horrible deaths.[56] But the battle for possession of true martyrdom was always hard fought, and it is a battle that throws up difficult questions for the historian. What to make, for instance, of those most celebrated Jesuit martyrs, the heroes of New France? The deaths were undoubtedly and unimaginably gruesome: the hagiographies tell us that Isaac Jogues had the skin stripped from his arms in 1646, that the eyes of Gabriel Lalemant were gouged from their sockets, to be replaced by burning coals, in 1649, the same year in which Jean de Brébeuf would be made to wear a necklace of red-hot hatchets. But defining such deaths as martyrdoms has troubled some later commentators. These men were killed during yet another outbreak of hostilities between the Huron and the Iroquois Confederacy: were they not, more accurately, casualties of war?[57]

Not that such questions have ever caused the faithful undue concern. Such men were prized as heroes, men for whom monuments would be built, men whose relics healed the sick and, in Brébeuf's case, were even capable of converting loudmouthed Calvinists.[58] They were, by any account, a crucially important part of a Jesuit missionary enterprise that tried, and felt the need, to bask in very different kinds of success. The success of martyrdom, but also of evangelism.

Sometimes conversion came slowly—during the early years in China, for instance. Sometimes it came with indecent haste, and sometimes, in places like Maryland or the Spice Islands, it hardly came at all. In other places—in India, in the Philippines, across Latin America—Christian communities, never as large as the Jesuits would have hoped, were established, and crucially, they endured, albeit in decidedly quirky ways. The emergence of distinct African, Asian, and American Christianities is something the Roman Catholic Church has, belatedly, come to see as dynamic and desirable, even if, for long decades and centuries, such uniqueness, marked (some said marred) by local adaptations and bothersome syncretisms, was often frowned upon. In the long term, though it took until the twentieth century, Jesuits of the Ricci school would even win the argument over Chinese rites in the end.

So the legacy of Jesuit mission is not simply one of ruins like the west front facade of St. Paul's in Macao, a facade packed with saints and angels jockeying for room, all that remains of a church erected in 1622, crushed by a nineteenth-century typhoon, the apses and altars long since crumbled. A symbol of Jesuit audacity, certainly, and a poignant reminder that what the Jesuits set out to achieve—the Christianization of continents—was a pipe dream. But it was a pipe dream with consequences. The historical legacy of mission (of which the Jesuits were only ever one, albeit a mighty, part) is enormous: Europe learned about the world and the world learned about Europe. Cultures met; they often sneered at and scarred one another; but sometimes they tried to understand, which did not always mean respect, the difference, the deposit of endless unseen, long-gone centuries.

But long before such legacies began to unravel, mission (as wrangling over the Chinese and Malabar rites made clear) had proven itself to be a much-frequented venue of the Society's critics. Jesuit strategy abroad could easily be likened to Jesuit strategy at home in Europe—give them what they want in China; give them what they want (they, the sinning herd) in France or Italy. A ludicrous claim, for the most part, but a very important aspect of the anti-Jesuit myth that had shown precious few signs of abating after close on two centuries of the Society's history.

5

"RHAPSODIES OF CALUMNY"[1]

The Creation of the Anti-Jesuit Myth

Slander is a monster, that is all mouth; it has no eyes to see the white and unspotted robe with which innocence is clad, no ears to be charmed with the sweet and melodious voice of truth, and no forehead to blush; and nothing but teeth and claws, and nothing but an evil spirit to set them at work.

The Most Humble Remonstrance
of the Jesuits of France, *1617*[2]

Had I been there when Charles [II] had changed his state
I'd decked the House of Death with bloody scenes
As strangling ravish'd maids not in their teens;
So great had been my spleen I should deflower
Virgins which lifeless lay besmirched with gore;
Laughed at young infants springing from the womb
To meet their mothers in a flaming tomb
Vomited flame upon the reeking stage
Without respect to greatness, sex or age.

St. Ignatius' Ghost, *1700*[3]

"Ecclesiastical Lechery": Sinning for Sinning's Sake

When early-modern Europeans wanted to describe or censure bad behavior, and it sometimes seems as if they wanted to do little else, they had a dazzling palette of metaphor at their disposal. "Sin is called poison, and sinners serpents," Thomas Goodwin explained in 1639. Sin was vomit and sinners were dogs; sin was the stench of graves, sinners were rotten sepulchres. Sows in a mire, blind men in darkness: these were the predicaments of the brazen and the ungodly. Sin was "shame, nakedness, folly, madness, death," just about anything, in fact, that might be thought "defective, infective and painful."[4]

And Goodwin had barely scratched the surface. Wastrels and heretics were weeds in a garden, rocks ready to inflict moral shipwreck, and a fantastical menagerie of beasts, real or imagined; what else were Jesuits but "bats [that] in the twilight of our security creep upon us" or the "ravening breed" of "that wolf-bred and wolf-breeding Romulus"?[5] But the best of all metaphors for sin was sordid sexuality.

People could either let themselves be "bewitched by that devilish harlot" of religious and moral transgression or drink the "nourishing milk of your loving mother's breasts" provided by the church.[6] To Protestant minds, in an era of reformation, the preeminent agent of sin was sure to be the whore of Rome, whose "filthiness, which being compared with the chastity of Christ's spouse set forth by holy writ, hath caused righteous men . . . to judge her children after the manner of harlots." Those who were tempted toward Rome's idolatry had, "like Dinah the daughter of Jacob . . . lost their virginity."[7]

And when it came to popish priests, describing their activities *in terms of* sexual deviance and promiscuity was all well and good—what else were Jesuits but men who indulged in "spiritual fornications," seducing youth and age alike with corrupting devotions and doctrines?—but not nearly so enjoyable as moving far beyond the figurative. Toward, for instance, the fictive, mischievous, seventeenth-century priest who seduced a Yorkshireman's wife by convincing her that adultery was only a venial sin—a priest who doubtless deserved everything he got, even if this included the aggrieved husband tying him "to a bed [to make] a capon of him, cutting out his stones to cool his courage." "Were all Romish priests so handled," the rural tale righteously concluded, "they would say [clerical] marriage were lawful and no more abuse other men's wives."[8]

And Jesuits, what were they, one critic asked, but men who "frequented the brothels themselves and kept mistresses for their pleasure and became epicures in sensuality"?[9] Men who, having finally managed to slake their own sexual thirsts, found time to pimp for their fellow Catholics: "No pander that ever Terence or Plautus mentioned in their comedies was so nimble at the trade of winning pretty wenches as are the Jesuits at this day."[10] This was mythmaking at its sordid, mendacious worst, but mythmaking with a habit of captivating audiences.

Priests, whether Jesuits or Friars
Are pious cheats, religious liars.
Who use their function as a gin
To catch unwary maids in.

Such was the doggerel served up, lavishly and ludicrously, by one Jeremy Jingle in 1732. "Priests, whether Jesuits or Friars"? But surely, for the most

part, members of Loyola's lascivious Society? Priests like Jean-Baptiste
Girard, for instance: "Pious Girard, Jesuit true / As ever pissed or trod in
shoe." This cartoon cleric might have had gargantuan sexual appetites:

> *Of wantons he had had half a dozen*
> *Whom he religiously did cozen.*
> *To him adultery, fornication*
> *Were nothing more than recreation.*

But

> *. . . half a dozen were too few*
> *And now he wanted something new.*
> *A virgin pullet, plump and white.*
> *To please his carnal appetite.*

Enter the ravishing Catherine Cadière, a deeply religious young woman
who had apparently managed to "set half the Gallic youth on fire." But how
could Girard possibly manage to scratch this particular sexual itch? How else
but through a stolen kiss in the confessional, and quite a kiss at that:

> *. . . straight the warm salival juice*
> *Did wonderful effects produce.*
> *Her pulse beats high, her bloods enflamed.*
> *Symptoms so plain her love proclaimed.*

Jingle's Girard wanted rather more than kisses, of course, and so he called
upon a tried and trusted Jesuit ally. Since

> *Cadières the object of his lust*
> *And none but she now suits his gust*
> *To maturate the growing evil*
> *He summons hell and plays the devil.*

Satan happily joins in the priest's designs and

> *Unseen before Cadière he dances*
> *And casts her into fits and trances*
> *Then like some conjuring politician*
> *Makes her believe she's seen a vision.*

But a very well-chosen vision: of heaven not of hell. Yield to me, Girard tells Cadière, and you will be showered in spiritual blessings; that part of you that craves to be a saint will be richly rewarded, even if it means "that you should now be naked stripped / And every part about you whipped," with even worse to follow.

> *Now with impetuous lust grown bolder*
> *He flings her clothes up to her shoulder.*
> *Three tender lashes then he gave*
> *Which she did willingly receive.*
> *This done he rubs her back, her bum*
> *He kissed, and eke her modicum . . .*

> *. . . He mounts the saddle, rides tantivee*
> *Tickling those parts that are most privy.*
> *He feeled, he looked, good folks, what then?*
> *Why then he looked and feeled again.*

Such fumblings carried quite a cost, an undesired pregnancy no less, and three months on, Cadière

> *. . . begins to loathe her meat*
> *Repents her folly, but too late.*
> *Her morning pukes and qualms of conscience*
> *To Girard tells, who calls it nonsense.*[11]

And he does rather more than that: he procures her an abortion and sends her off to a nunnery. But this was hardly surprising. As another account of the Girard story, *The Wanton Jesuit* of 1731, explains, the priest was apt to "kiss every woman in the parish" and "would quickly give them their bellies' full." Not that Girard suffered from the least remorse; quite the contrary, in fact:

I got to her garden by stealth,
A garden abounding with pleasure;
A rose I snatched from the bush,
More precious than Mexican treasure.[12]

THIS IS GROTTY, prurient stuff, bad poets doling out filth. But the only thing more astonishing than the abysmal rhymes is the fact that Jingle's poem and the *Wanton Jesuit* were based (so very, very loosely) on real-life events. There had indeed been a twenty-year-old Catherine Cadière, born in Toulon in 1709, and she had indeed employed a Jesuit called Jean-Baptiste Girard as her spiritual counselor. More important, there had been a court case before the Parlement of Aix-en-Provence early in 1731. Girard was accused of employing sorcery to bewitch Catherine for his sordid purposes; Girard offered counteraccusations that Cadière was guilty of perjury, that she was a disturbed young woman apparently addicted to the idea of becoming a saint, prone to hysterics and fits, but quite probably something of a charlatan. It was said that in order to fake a miracle, taking on the wounds of Christ, she had smeared herself with her own menstrual blood. While supposedly enduring religious fasts, she would sneak to the orchard at night to gorge on peaches.

The truth of the matter is impossible to pin down. Both sides ranted, and all comers seized upon the ranting. Perhaps Girard was fond of his spiritual charge, sending her doting letters and kissing her supposed stigmata (all a long way from whipping, of course). Perhaps Cadière was acting out of mischief, inspired to defame Girard by her Dominican brother. The Parlement of Aix-en-Provence certainly could not decide what was what. Twelve delegates voted for Girard to be burned alive (this was, in fact, the last formal witchcraft trial in French history), twelve other delegates voted for Cadière to be hanged. Faced with such an impasse, the president of the Parlement ordered that Catherine be sent home to her mother and Jean-Baptiste handed over to the ecclesiastical authorities. The priest died two years later, in 1733.

But the facts, for once, matter less than the fictions. It was at precisely the moment that Smollett's Peregrine Pickle embarked upon his curious odyssey that "the affair of Father Girard and Mademoiselle Cadière began to make a noise."[13] And it was the sort of noise not heard again until the Dreyfus affair at the end of the nineteenth century. Across Europe publishers rushed out—in French, German, Spanish, and Italian—dozens of accounts, many of which went through multiple editions, of the Jesuit's apparent moral turpitude. And the cruder and cheaper, the better. English audiences in the early 1730s could spend one shilling sixpence on *The Case of Mademoiselle Cadière*, and supplement it, for another shilling, with *The Defence of Father Girard*. Or, for a mere sixpence, lewd engravings included, they could invest in Jingle's jingles.

It was all too good an opportunity for the Society of Jesus's enemies to miss. As the author of *The Wanton Jesuit* explained, "for my own part I hate everything that comes from France except their wine and brandy," but he was not going to pass up the chance to convince London audiences that

> *A Jesuit is a clever man.*
> *When a maid comes to confession,*
> *He first does absolve, and next trepans*
> *And brings her to oppression.*
> *Then he kisses*
> *And does all he can,*
> *To multiply transgression.*[14]

And here was the crucial point: "a" Jesuit, *all* Jesuits, not this particular Jesuit, Girard—Girard, that is, as unflatteringly depicted in scurrilous verse. Sex and the confessional did have a shared history; sexually unscrupulous spiritual directors were a real, if fairly unusual, part of the early-modern Catholic landscape. To suppose that there has never been a Jesuit, Franciscan, or Dominican who did things that he should not have done, who lusted after boys or women, would be madness. Sometimes unwholesome things did (and doubtless ever will) go on and deserve ferocious criticism but uncritical generalizations about the entire personnel of the Society of Jesus remain unhelpful.[15]

Of course, for the Society's enemies (and by 1731 they were legion), the whole point of the Girard affair was to reveal that Jesuits "under a notion of infusing good principles . . . revel in forbidden pleasures without suspicion."[16] And if it happened in the confessional, then of course it must surely be happening in the schools.

In their dealings with the youth of Catholic Europe, Jesuits were sometimes merely charged with cruelty by their enemies. They would supposedly take municipal cash to look after destitute and orphaned young children, then proceed to kill them through neglect. Having been put out to debauched women, infected with the pox, babies would "suck poison instead of milk." And worse days were ahead. "Out of pure want of nourishment, the foreheads of these little wretches are full of dirt and earthiness . . . their eyes sink into their heads, where there should be cheeks there are only pits to be seen, their bones start out through the skin, so that at last the fatal morning comes that the nurse brings them home stone dead and dry as skeletons."

Very often, however, the mythmakers once more turned to sexual misconduct. There might have been much proud talk of Jesuit charitable and educational institutions, their glittering alumni, their innovative pedagogy, but one fantasy-wielding author, eager to "strip the long robe of hypocrisy" from the Society's shoulders, warned that such adulation obscured the fact that in these very institutions "the inhabitants of Gomorrah" were revived and "the highest parts of Sodomy acted over again." Witness "the effeminacy, the lascivious touches and embraces, the pollutions and the impurities which are so common among the younger students." Not to mention the older boys "that have made it no difficulty to persuade their scholars to unchaste gropings about the body, to raise in them the greatest inclinations to commit that abominable filthiness which nature trembles at." All of which was hardly surprising given the children's role models, like the master supposedly addicted to "ardently kissing and hugging between his knees and arms a young gentleman one of his scholars," or those who enjoyed committing "abominable sodomies," making students "walk around naked, untrussed . . . to contemplate their nakedness."[17]

And this, so the critics suggested, was hardly the worst of it. If Jesuits as individuals were capable of debauchery, the Society as a whole, with its devilishly well-thought-out strategies, was also corrupt and dangerous at an institutional level. A much more substantial threat. Pedophiles and pimps were one thing: an organized political campaign to take over the world was quite another.

Sinning as Strategy

In the shadowy, absurdist world of myth, Jesuits—stereotyped, stage-villain Jesuits—were peerless when it came to wooing political assassins. They would promise riches and salvation, of course—gold and diamonds in the here and now (doubtless from their secret mines in Mexico and Peru), eternal bliss sometime later. And when a suitable candidate had been identified, Jesuits apparently knew how to put on a show.

According to an especially outlandish account, published shortly after someone had killed Henry IV of France in 1610, Jesuits would "lay before [the future assassin] a knife folded up in a scarf and closed in a little casket of ivory, covered with an *agnus dei*, written round about with many sweet and perfumed characters." The bizarre ritual continued with Jesuits removing the knife from its box, sprinkling it with holy water, and attaching five or six beads of coral to the haft. These represented the five or six stabs to be made by the weapon, as well as the souls a successful assassination might be expected to release from purgatory.

In case the killer's nerve was failing, the Jesuits would offer encouragement by likening him to Samson, Jephthah, and Gideon, to David before he slew Goliath, or to Judith before she cut off the head of Holofernes. The assassin was reminded that he was being granted no less an honor than carrying the sword of the pope, "whereby he breaks the power of princes." "Be virtuous," he was told, "and God will strengthen thine arm." At this point "all the hellish company" would fall to their knees, with their leader declaring: "Come cherubim, come seraphim . . . come most blessed angels, angels of charity; come and fill this holy vessel of glory and eternity." They would tell their new recruit that "there is some deity dwelling in him, and they are so afraid of the splendour shining in him, as falling down, and kissing his hands and feet, they hold him no more for a mortal man." He could rest assured that he was now entitled to "go really and presently into paradise, without ever coming into purgatory." A passport any Catholic would presumably relish.[18]

And if subtler methods than stabbing were sometimes called for, the Society apparently had recourse to the expertise in chemistry and pharmacology it had been sure to cultivate for this purpose down the years. Some of the Society's milder critics merely accused Jesuit chemists of dupery. To Gui Patin, mid-seventeenth-century Hippocratically minded member of the medical faculty of the University of Paris, Jesuits, as well as being "hangmen," "fleas," and "bedbugs," were also the worst kind of quacks, conning gullible customers with their useless purgative confections and this hopeless new discovery called quinine.[19] Other voices spoke of rather more sinister goings-on. The chief duty of the Jesuit master poisoner, by one account, was to equip "assassins as shall be able to infect dishes, plates, salt cellars, basins, kettles and all sorts of utensils, though they be ten times washed and cleaned."[20]

Such, it was suggested, was the kind of influence behind Edward Squire, who, under the tutelage of the Jesuit Richard Walpole, had allegedly taken a job in the stables at Greenwich Palace in 1595 so that he might apply a lethal poison, blending opium and mercury, to the saddle of Elizabeth I, heretic queen par excellence: a task he attempted with pharmacological savvy—it was done "in the heat of the season, when the pores are most open to receive any malign vapour or tincture." Just one more instance, as a later commentator put it (these fictions died hard), of "the wily Jesuits, studying medicine and practising as physicians" in order to gain "a power over life, of which they made terrible use, for their knowledge of poisonous herbs and minerals often served them at a pinch when they desired secretly and safely to get rid of some active foe."[21]

SUCH EXTRAORDINARY TALES represent the marrow, the richest propagandist vein, of the Jesuit myth. If Jesuit education was such a fixture in the European cultural landscape, this, according to William Crashaw, was only because the Society had endeavored to pick "out the finest young wits of the world, and so trained them up that the pope shall never want instruments to kill kings."[22] The list of supposed Jesuit targets (some dispatched, others not) is dazzling: from William of Orange, Henry III, Henry IV, Louis XIV of France, Elizabeth I, James I, Charles I, and Charles II of England all the way through to that most favored institution of conspiracy theorists, the American presidency. Jesuits would be accused of trying to kill William Henry Harrison, Zachary Taylor, James A. Garfield, William McKinley, and inevitably enough, Abraham Lincoln. What was still more repugnant—the allegations were often quick to add—was the way the Society lauded as martyrs those who died in the throes of their treacherous designs: the "saint-traitorly crew," as the English Protestant Henry Gee described them.[23]

There was, so the theory went, always one overriding reason why such projects were hatched. Political influence, the pursuit of which sometimes demanded the removal of inconvenient politicians, was apparently the guiding principle of the entire Jesuit project. Whether the Society sought such power for itself or for the vicar of Christ was hotly debated, however. According to one Scottish Protestant writing in 1615, Jesuits believed that

the crowns of kings, their sceptres and subjects must all be at the pope's de-
votion. This is their special work, and the effect of their blind obedience,
that special vow, I mean, which they besides the three vows common to
other orders vow and swear at their receptions: to this point runs all their
service, to make the pope the lord of all the earth, emperors, kings and
princes his dependants, to be removed, altered, changed, deposed and
killed, when it pleaseth his holiness to give commission.[24]

Others suggested that the much-vaunted Jesuit obedience to Rome was more often than not a sham; that the superior general of the Society was ever apt to bully and sneer at the pope; and that when Jesuits killed monarchs it was only ever to further their own twisted political ends—or that, at the very least, Jesuit pride could never countenance unconditional submission to the supreme pontiff. As an English Protestant put it during his country's civil war, another political calamity often ascribed to the Society's machinations,[25] a Jesuit might seem like "the nimblest-pated fellow that the pope hath to send on his errand, and of most resolution and service," but he was also "least in awe." It was as well to remember that when Sixtus V annoyed the Society toward the end of the 1580s, "they gave him a dram to send him packing."[26]

It all rather depended on the mythmaker's agenda, on whether he was a Protestant with an animus against all things Roman, a Protestant intent on proving that some Catholics were worse than others (a perennial suggestion in Elizabethan and Jacobean England), or a Catholic unhappy with the role the Jesuits were playing in his or her church.

Of course, the critics sniped, assassination was only the most extreme tactic available. Jesuits sometimes had to settle for fomenting rebellion and bloodshed—the French Wars of Religion, for instance, blamed on the Society by Antoine Arnauld in 1594, or the bloody events of the St. Bartholomew's Day Massacre in 1572, the Gunpowder Plot of 1606, and even the Great Fire of London in 1666.[27] With such schemes always in the offing, Jesuits naturally saw the sense in being prepared. "Magazines of iron bullets, fire balls, ordinance, muskets, harquebuses, pikes [and] halberts" were apparently "concealed upon the tops, within the roofs, of their churches, both at Prague,

Cracow and other places" in case they had to "resist force by force should their secret intrigues meet with unexpected resistance."[28] Jesuits, some concluded, were Knights Templar for the new age.

Not that it always had to be about violence. What better way to manipulate Europe's laity than through the Jesuit network of schools and lay sodalities? And how better to influence European politics than to place Jesuits as confessors to as many Catholic monarchs as possible—"when they have insinuated themselves into the hearts of princes, they play with them like shuttlecocks"[29]—perhaps indulging in the black arts or striking Faustian bargains, or pushing for the promotion of their creatures to high office: Mazarin and Richelieu (and this was truly a bizarre leap of the imagination) would both be portrayed as Jesuit stooges. Jesuits would be accused of interfering in the internal politics of an Ethiopia ruled over by a much-divided royal house; the reductions of Paraguay would be criticized as an attempt to establish a Latin American Jesuit power base, a state within a state; and most bizarrely of all, the growth of the Quaker movement, with its "thous," "thees," and subversive, immodest hat wearing, would be seen as yet another Jesuit attempt to disrupt England's social and religious status quo.[30]

Sustaining this secretive, malignant policy naturally required a fiercely disciplined workforce, a membership that was, by some accounts, unthinkingly loyal to Rome, and by all accounts extraordinarily loyal to its superiors. The fact that Jesuits would disagree among themselves about everything from witchcraft to evangelical strategy—that, as one example of internal divisions, some sixteenth-century French Jesuits (such as Edmond Auger) would support the king, while others (such as Claude Matthieu) would side with the rival Catholic League—were easily passed over.[31] After all, did the Society's constitutions not demand that its members should resemble a cadaver—with no desire for self-determination—or the staff used by an old man, destined to serve him in whatever way he saw fit? The fact that these were stock images from the medieval monastic tradition, or that Loyola was not advocating brainwashed automatons but, rather, a commitment to honor and heed the inscrutable dictates of God's providence, was easily forgotten. So was the obvious realization that Jesuit employment of military metaphor and imagery (and the Society *did* employ it an awful lot) fitted very well into a long-standing, cross-confessional Christian tradition.

And if it was always tempting to liken the Society to a military machine, headed by generals, the brainchild of an ex-soldier, it followed that discipline meant everything to the Jesuits: and it could come in truly disturbing forms. If novices were foolish enough to become uppity, we are told, their superiors always had access to "a very strange library of cords, halters, racks, swords, axes, iron pincers, stocks, pillories, torches and several more instruments of torture, to tear those poor wretches joint from joint who have the misfortune to incur their displeasure." "Once they get a hint that any novice is wavering, or intends to desert them or is likely to betray the secrets of the Society, they clap him up in a pair of stocks and there keep him until he is almost starved to death with hunger and cold."[32]

But what use was obedience without financial solvency? Reason enough, the Society's opponents believed, to account for the Jesuits' establishing secret gold mines in Latin America, or their indulging in the smuggling of, among other things, holy relics, cattle, and chocolate. Rumors of vast, hidden Jesuit wealth were powerful enough to convince some Londoners to dig for buried Jesuit treasure at the Savoy Palace in 1679.[33] Jesuit schemes relied, by one account, on the "great estates engrossed out of the credulity of widows, who fall under their direction; and from the young gentlemen inveigled into their Society."[34]

The fabled *Monita Secreta*, which first appeared from the pen of Hieronymus Zahorowski, a dismissed Jesuit, in Cracow in 1613, would go through twenty-two editions in seven different languages by 1700, each of them detailing the secret rubrics by which Jesuits supposedly sought to undermine European civilization. When a wealthy man died, so the *Monita* revealed, Jesuits of "lively complexion and conversation" would begin to circle the now wealthy widow, counseling her that remarriage was a terrible idea, that she would be much better advised to take up a life of prayer and isolation and to allow the Society to disburden her of the distracting, demeaning consequences of a bountiful inheritance.[35]

But more important even than wealth was a genius for secrecy and mutability: an ability to have "as many shapes as Proteus had, and as many names as a Welshman."[36] One never knew who might be needed as an ally, so one had to be willing to be all things to all men (comparisons with the Society's accommodationist missionary policy cried out to be made at this point). Jesuits, according to one author, "scatter themselves like locusts over the whole world," able to "seduce the silly women," to "work themselves . . . into the courts, coaches and councils of princes," but also, at the opposite end of the social spectrum, to enter into "the conceits of the vulgar by a hypocritical austerity and dissembled devotion."[37] The author of *The Jesuit Discovered* observed that "the ways they have to ravish all sorts of affections . . . are well nigh infinite," and this was entirely predictable given the cunning, shifting nature of the Catholic Church as a whole.

> On the one side of a street you shall have a nunnery, or a cloister of virgins; on the other side a sty of courtesans. One day you shall have them all in masks, with all manner of obscenities and folly that can be imagined, or the corrupt nature of man desire: the day following they will be all in processions, whipping themselves until the blood cometh. On one door you shall have excommunications, throwing souls and bodies to hell: on another door, a jubilee, or full discharge of all villainies, murders, fornication, drunkenness, swearing, forswearing [and] poisoning.

Jesuits would pretend to be wise in the company of princes, voluptuous to the wanton, chaste to the pure. They would provide miracles for the credulous, and visions for the fanatical.[38]

And all such efforts, either because they were morally repugnant or because they were undertaken in hostile environments, demanded secrecy. "Jesuitism," a later commentator revealed, "is a region of secrecy and disguise, on which the sunlight falls not." To "tread softly, to whisper in the ear; to work mole-like underground; to glide to and fro, and in and out, like the serpent, through the windings of society; concealed behind whatever mask may best subserve their end": these were the hallmark talents of the Jesuit priest.[39] Why else, James Wadsworth asked, would Jesuit colleges always have their well-stocked costume departments, answering the needs of those who "sometimes being habited like soldiers very gallant . . . walk in the streets and highways, whoring and swaggering in the public stews," and those who "at other times, in the civil habits of citizens . . . pry up and down and listen in inns, in playhouses [and] in taverns"?[40]

It was natural to assume that such covert tactics were especially favored when Jesuit self-preservation was at stake, and nowhere was this more of a priority than in the hostile stews and byways of Protestant Britain. Accordingly, the figure of the cowardly, deceitful Jesuit became an especially useful weapon for the Elizabethan and Jacobean authorities, who, when they failed to hunt Jesuit priests down, could always attack their reputations. If the Jesuits' cause was so just, it was endlessly asked, why did they need to creep into England in disguise, under false names? And even if you did manage to catch a Jesuit, Protestant readerships were told, he was unlikely to answer your questions honestly and straightforwardly, but to hide himself behind half answers, barefaced lies, and equivocations; he would use words with double meanings, answer your questions with more questions.

Worst of all, according to Thomas Morton, was the Jesuitical practice of mental reservation, the notion that you could say half a sentence out loud and the other half in your head—God, after all, would hear it all. If someone asked a Jesuit if he was a Catholic priest, he might reply, "No! I am not a priest"—mentally adding, "Not of Apollo at Delphi." Such "equivocation by a mental reservation," Morton insisted, "is not a hidden truth but a gross lie," and it allowed priests "in a sort invisible unto Protestants to plot and practice against them what and when they will." It was "more subtle than any machiavellianism," and it would be better to "become speechless and handless than either in word or in writing to minister such a baneful conclusion unto the world."[41]

Stereotypes would endure, even when there was ample reason to question them. Given their special vow of obedience to the pope, there was always scope to portray the Jesuits as being in thrall to the whims and aspirations of the Roman court, utterly contemptuous of national churches. But from the earliest days of the Society, individual Jesuits had not balked from criticizing papal shortcomings. Giovanni Battista Viola, for instance, had offered this stinging advice to the briefly reigning Marcellus II in April 1555:

> *If the head of the church gave up the pomp, the splendour, and the worldly magnificence and reformed himself, and if, like predecessors such as Peter, he prayed frequently, preached God's word and set the example of a holy and blameless life, then all the prelates and church-leaders would be forced not to be so proud and arrogant and to lay their pomp and vanity aside. But if the pope does the opposite and carries on with the traditions of his predecessors then I think no fruit will be forthcoming, because all will look at the head and blame all their sins and bad lifestyles on his failures and abuses.*[42]

There would be many more tense moments of mistrust and antagonism between the Society and the Vatican. Jesuits have repeatedly defended what they perceived as the interests of their national churches against Rome-centeredness: François de la Chaise, who lends his name to the famous Parisian cemetery, was one of the most ardent Gallicans of the seventeenth century. As we have seen, in the Society's first century, various popes would challenge the very things about the order's organization that made the Jesuits stand out. More drastically, Innocent XI would intervene quite brazenly in the internal politics of the Society in 1687 when he engineered the election of Tirso González as superior general.

But none of this turbulent history managed to undermine the stubbornly resilient image—popular among both Catholics and Protestants—of Jesuits as papal lapdogs. In an imaginary popish cavalcade of 1714, the author describes Rome's greatest allies walking in military procession, and alongside "fanatical votaries," the cardinals, or "scarlet bullies," and the regiments of Dominicans and Carmelites, pride of place is given to the Jesuits—the pope's own cavalry, "the best light horsemen in the world."[43]

Gauging Myth

How to evaluate such stories and accusations? Was there ever a scoundrel who also happened to be a Jesuit? Or someone who took his Jesuit vows, not out of a deep-seated commitment to Ignatian spirituality, but because they represented an attractive career prospect? It is a simple matter of mathematics. There have been hundreds of thousands of Jesuits, and it is rather like asking if there has ever been a crooked judge, a negligent dentist, or an evil poet. Individual corruption tarnished, beyond a doubt, but it did not necessarily condemn the entire enterprise.

Moreover, behavior that might at first appear worryingly corrupt or disreputable was sometimes nothing of the sort. Jesuit missionaries, alert to the dangers of entering hostile Protestant lands, would make efforts to hide their heads, to avoid unnecessary dangers. The Jesuit Robert Abercrombie certainly wrote to his superiors in 1596 that, in Scotland, the name of papist was more "odious and abominable than that of Turk, Saracen or Jew. It is worse than calling a man a heathen or a member of the vilest sect on earth." In such a climate, he went on, "we are consequently obliged to travel by night" and "dare not enter an inn except after dark."[44] When his fellow Jesuit John Gerard had arrived in England a decade earlier, he had taken similar precautions, ordering "the ship to cast anchor off the point until night-fall. At the first watch of the night we were taken ashore . . . the night was dark and overcast. . . . Afraid we might wake the people . . . we decided to go off into a nearby wood and rest there until the morning. It was . . . raining and wet, and we passed a sleepless night. Nor did we dare talk, for the wood was close to a house."[45]

Theologically speaking, caution and prudence were usually regarded as entirely legitimate tactics under threat of persecution. Jesuits would adopt pseudonyms and wear decidedly unpriestly clothes: Michael Walpole posed as a Spanish servant when he arrived in England during Elizabeth's reign; Abraham de Georgiis went to Egypt dressed as an Armenian merchant in 1595; and Sebastián Vieira traveled from Manila to Japan in 1632 in the guise of a Chinese sailor. But this was simply what Edmund Campion described as disguising oneself to cheat the madness of the world.[46] Was it so obscene, as another Jesuit put it in 1583, if a harassed priest "frequently change his name, his dress, his horse and not come needlessly to places where search is being made for him"?[47] As Campion explained at his trial in 1581, there was a good deal of biblical precedent for such activities:

> *At what time the primitive Church was persecuted and that Paul laboured in the propagation and increase of the gospel, it is not unknown to what straits and pinches he and his fellows were diversely driven, wherein, though in purpose he were already resolved rather to yield himself to martyrdom than to shrink an inch from the truth he preached; yet, if any hopes or means appeared to escape, and if by living he might benefit the Church more than dying, we read of sundry shifts whereby he betook him to increase God's number and to shun persecution.*

He ended with the compelling point: "If these shifts were then approved, why are they now reproved in me?"[48]

Outright lying or denial of faith were never sanctioned by mainstream theology and there was always admiration for those who rushed undaunted and unprotected into the fray; they boosted morale if nothing else. But those who exercised caution and prudence were not committing a theological crime, and their Protestant critics knew it: in different circumstances they had adopted precisely the same tactics. There was fierce debate about where lines between cowardice and caution, between lying and acceptable reticence and equivocation ought to be drawn. Remaining silent under examination, offering ambiguous, doubtful answers—what Persons called "amphibology"—or employing words with double meanings was fairly easily defended, but the critics were wise to pounce on something like mental reservation, which some Jesuits certainly *did* advocate, and which was, undoubtedly, a controversial strategy. But all such efforts were far from being exclusively Jesuitical: they represented the knowledge that, as one Elizabethan casuistry manual put it, "not everyone can claim for himself the honour of being a martyr." Such men could "do anything they can—use equivocation, silence, reticence or any method he likes—to avoid matters of religion."[49]

On other occasions, Jesuit behavior might have been less than saintly, but members of the Society were not alone in their pursuit of power and influence. There had, after all, been Franciscans, Dominicans, Lutheran ministers, and Calvinist theologians who had schemed, manipulated, and sought prestige. It is unclear whether a Jesuit really did dress up as a ghost in order to scare the emperor Joseph I into dismissing his religious instructor Ferdinand von Rummel, but there was no shortage of less theatrical political maneuvering.[50] Louis XIII had to sack the Jesuit Nicolas Caussin as his confessor because he grew so critical of the king making treaties with Turks and Protestants and waging wars with his fellow Catholic monarchs; Richard Haller, confessor to Margaret of Austria, was pleased to offer his charge political advice and to serve as a champion of Austrian Habsburg interests at Philip III's Spanish court.[51]

Spanish politics also saw John Everard Nithard, confessor to Mariana, regent of Spain, accrue enormous influence as counselor and inquisitor general, and when Don John of Austria tried to secure the reins of power, Nithard was seen as a natural enemy—when Don John entered Saragossa in February 1669, Nithard was burned in effigy in front of the Society's buildings.[52] Jesuits at the eighteenth-century French court constantly campaigned to prevent their rivals from gaining too much sway with the king; Portuguese Jesuits were decidedly vocal about the benefits of freeing Portugal from Spanish control in 1640.[53]

It should be stressed, however, that some within the Society (Peter Canisius, for instance) voiced concerns about the distracting consequences of Jesuits becoming confessors to the rich and powerful, and when individuals such as Claude Matthieu and Edmond Auger became hopelessly embroiled in sixteenth-century French politics, their superior general, Claudio Acquaviva, ordered them to cease and desist.[54]

That some Jesuits may have schemed and known of plots—which was certainly true of some priests at the Spanish court of Philip II—is not the same as saying that Jesuits, over four centuries and more, sustained an institutionalized, Society-wide policy of poisoning kings and politicians who offended or obstructed them.[55] The wilier critics realized their vulnerability on this point and were eager to discredit any Jesuits who tried to suggest that, while an individual within the order might sometimes behave badly, that hardly justified tarring all of his companions with the same reputation. "Talk to a Jesuit about their bloody doctrines, intrigues and actions [and] he will join with you in their condemnation . . . and shudder at the relation of the direful effects of those counsels which have murdered kings." But this was simply a smoke screen: "Though singly the members of their Society may express their dislike, it is very certain that they are all rogues and murderers when they meet in consultation about ways and means to extend their power, to fill their coffers."[56] This was surely a less than convincing gambit on the part of the Jesuits' critics.

Jesuits have sustained a sense of purpose and a confidence in what they do. Jesuits have had their enemies and so Jesuits have campaigned, sometimes in underhanded ways, against those enemies. They spread rumors that their eighteenth-century adversary Jean le Rond d'Alembert was illegitimate, that Matteo Ripa, an artist in China associated with their rivals, had unhealthy sexual leanings; and when someone like Bishop Jerónimo Manrique of Cartagena, no friend of the Society, looked likely to be appointed visitor of their Spanish province in the sixteenth century, they were not slow to point out that, given his three bastard sons, he was perhaps not the ideal man for the job.[57] Jesuits, in fact, have been guilty of constructing precisely the kinds of insulting, reductive myths about their opponents of which they themselves have so often been victim.

All in all, the Jesuit response should be seen as entirely predictable, as something of a relief: as proof that human frailty permeates any multinational organization with a four-hundred-year-old pedigree. The obvious thought that the history of the Jesuits has been made up of a rich variety of people in a rich variety of times, places, and situations has always struggled for legitimacy. There have been Jesuit villains, Jesuits possessed of unseemly ambition, Jesuits who preferred politicking to preaching, but to corral all members of the Society into an ism—the devious, bloodthirsty, cruel, and cutthroat image of Jesuitism—was as intellectually mischievous as whitewashing the moments when this or that Jesuit sinned, stumbled, or satisfied his more worldly appetites.

THE SAFEST CONCLUSION is that much of the more extravagant Jesuit baiting is nonsense, but it is a very important kind of nonsense, and two questions demand answers: why did such a venomous anti-Jesuit campaign develop at all and, rather more interestingly, why did it develop in the specific ways it did?

Did the accusations fall from the sky to form a hodgepodge litany of Jesuit sins, or were they skillfully selected and cultivated? Robert Persons complained from England in 1581 that there was "tremendous talk here of the Jesuits and more fables perhaps are told about them than were told of old about monsters." He was adamant that such stories, from so many different sources, were often contradictory, self-defeating, bearing "a striking resemblance to dreams."[58]

But Jesuit baiters and haters were often more astute than that: careful, at least, to choose their myths according to their potency. Was it not sensible to attack precisely those cultural strongholds, such as its schools and its positions as spiritual advisers, from which the Society derived so much influence? In a curious way, the obsessions of the anti-Jesuit myth serve as an excellent indicator of where the Society had achieved its greatest successes. Jesuit science, to take another example, was one of the order's healthiest and most celebrated traditions, so it became an obvious target.

The corollary of Jesuit achievement in mechanics was apparently the ability to con the credulous by means of an ingenious representation of the Virgin. The seemingly miraculous moving eyes were, in reality, "performed by engine-work," and if the statue appeared to lactate "on the day of the nativity," this was only thanks to "small tin pipes at a great distance" through which offstage Jesuits conveyed the milk. It was just as tempting to claim that the Society's skills in medicine and pharmacology had really been developed only so that priests could pull off sham miracles. "A subtle Jesuit" would live in a community for "five or six years more or less," pretending to be blind by "dying the inner skin of the eye by a water distilled from a certain herb," or would pose as "lame, or leprosied," by an art of "raising an artificial leprosy, now used among some beggars, to move compassion in the charitable." When he was "well known, he shall come and implore the aid of such a saint" and "immediately he shall be as whole as a fish," his sight restored or his leprosy banished.[59]

And was there an overarching strategy to formulate myths that offered at least a hint of credibility? It made good sense to paint the Society as avaricious because, not being a mendicant order, it did seek to fund its evangelism through a phenomenal range of commercial activities—banking, mining, real estate, interest in the spice and silk trades. There was propagandist potential in the 38,435 vines under cultivation at the San Jerónimo hacienda in 1736, or the 245,820 pounds of sugar produced at the Villa hacienda in 1757, or the fact that as many as 10,000 lambs, 150,000 sheep, and 50,000 goats might be farmed in a single year at a single Mexican estate during the eighteenth century.[60]

Was it not wise to promote myths of Jesuit political scheming when, as we have seen, certain Jesuits did seek influence in the corridors of power? Or to talk endlessly about Jesuit equivocation and disguise because, undeniably, many a Jesuit missionary had entered England dressed in curious attire and, once in custody, had seen fit to talk his way out of trouble?

Of course, with such tactics, the fine print had to be smudged. Commercial profits (even if they sometimes came from an unsavory source like liquor production—a blight to local populations—or from the graft of an enslaved workforce) were almost always plowed back into the Society's ministries; politicking was not *quite* the same thing as regicide; disguise and equivocation were indulged in, but such behavior was usually grounded in sophisticated casuistical reasoning (when casuistry was a reputable theological science rather than just a dirty word). But myths had a far better chance of winning popular approval if, with a leap of the imagination, they could be understood as exaggeration rather than groundless fantasy.

The king killing is a case in point. No one could really deny the existence of controversial Jesuit political tracts, such as those of Robert Bellarmine, of Francisco Suárez, and above all, of Juan Mariana, whose *De rege et regis institutione,* published at Toledo in 1599, insisted that a monarch's power and position were, ultimately, conferred and sustained by the people. It is entirely fair to say that the Jesuit order itself worried about how some of these authors' works might be received, but ultimately, the kinds of arguments employed by someone like Mariana were so cautious and hedged around with qualifications that any threat that might have been latent within them was effectively neutralized.

Such works were also part of a long-standing, reputable scholarly debate about the nature of politics and civil society. Mariana's infamous work was commissioned by Philip II of Spain and, once published, faced no opposition in that country. But this was unlikely to stop the mythmakers from promulgating the idea that Jesuit authors were quite blatantly providing sophisticated justifications for hotheaded individuals to poison, stab, or strangle their enemies whenever the mood took them. It suited the Paris Parlement to condemn Mariana's work in 1610 and order it to be burned, and it suited James I to burn Suárez's *Defensio* on the steps of St. Paul's in 1613.

Propagandist myths and conspiracy theories often share techniques, vocabularies, and themes. They are lazy, in fact. But that does not prevent them from being suitable grist to the historical mill. The hallmark concepts of anti-Jesuit mythmaking often reflect what early-modern European society found most threatening: the things about which any right-thinking early-modern European was anxious. Harping on about Jesuit disguise in a culture, with its sumptuary laws and conventions of dress, where what a person wore was supposed to reveal so much about his private and professional life, was an intelligent tactic.

And a similar sort of intelligence resides in the three trends that characterized the anti-Jesuit tradition. There was the staggering consistency of accusations. The themes of the earliest critics of the Society, such as Antoine Arnauld and Etienne Pasquier in sixteenth-century France, would be faithfully regurgitated for several centuries; and when Bernardo Tanucci, the eminent Neapolitan politician, who hated the Jesuits as much as any *eighteenth-century* figure, required ammunition, he turned instinctively to the writings of Paolo Sarpi, who hated the Jesuits as much as anyone else in the *seventeenth* century.[61]

Jesuit haters have shared a sense of camaraderie: when the Society's Portuguese critics needed a hero in 1910, they turned directly to one of the Society's most determined eighteenth-century opponents, the marquis of Pombal, shouting at his statue on Lisbon's Avenida da Liberdade that his help was once again needed to vanquish the Jesuit enemy. Finally, there was the conviction that all members of the Society, whatever their time or place, shared in a common guilt, a continuum of crimes and misdemeanors, all related, all stemming from an ongoing commitment to mischief and cruelty.

A writer in the nineteenth century even blamed the Society for causing the American Civil War, and he was adamant that the hundreds of thousands of casualties should be added to precisely the same list that contained the victims of the St. Bartholomew's Day Massacre of 1572 and the bloodshed that followed the revocation of the Edict of Nantes in 1685: these were all the same kind of Jesuit offense, all evidence of the Society's dedication to earning Rome the "title, mother of harlots and abominations, drunk with blood."[62]

Say it often enough, they thought, and people will start to believe it. Which really leaves only one question: why did they say it at all?

THE "OLD MONKS," for all their shady scholasticism, were at least only ever interested in "hovering about their own cloister," not venturing "further than the contemplation of heaven, which was the bible, and of the stars, which were the devout interpreters thereof." The Jesuits, by troublesome contrast, "have found the use of the compass . . . and now they have not the patience to be fishers of men, but they are merchants of kingdoms and pirates both of spiritual and temporal treasure." They had become "corrupt and putrified carcasses as infect and envenom all places where they reside," they were "staves, as have swords sheathed in them, and such as wound and bruise even the in-wardest marrow of kingdoms." They infiltrated political life to such an extent that "the secrets of all states, and passages of all courts, had had no other register than the breasts of Jesuits."

What, John Donne continued, was "truly proper and peculiar" to this Society of Jesus? What else but "kindling and blowing, begetting and nour-ishing jealousies in princes, and contempt in subjects, dissension in families, wrangling in schools, and mutinies in armies, ruins of noble houses, corrup-tion of blood, confiscation of states, torturing of bodies, an anxious entan-gling and perplexing of consciences"? Jesuits might "pretend to forsake the world and to look all upward" but in truth they were "mixed and complex-ioned of all elements," hanging "between heaven and earth like meteors of an ominous and incendiary presaging," delighted when "an overture is given for the pope's advantage," but more than willing to dispatch turbulent, plotting missionary priests to a Protestant harbor like England, making pseudomartyrs out of them when righteous English justice ruined their designs.[63]

That Protestants disliked Jesuits is decidedly unremarkable, and a good portion of anti-Jesuit mythmaking is thus explained. But why would fellow Catholics launch into tirades every bit as merciless as those of John Donne? Why would, for instance, some Catholics want to portray the Jesuit experi-ment as an agricultural experiment gone awry? The Society was "as it were the vine, or plant that ought to have brought forth the antidote against the venom of heresy," but in place "of those two flourishing branches charity and poverty, which were almost dried up and withered," the devil himself had "engrafted one of self love and another of profit."[64]

As events in Paris back in 1594 had made clear, Jesuits were very easy to resent, not least by those they had displaced, challenged, or undermined, who saw the Society as a new, unwelcome power center within the already con-fused ecclesiastical politics of the Catholic Church. In Padua in 1591 gangs of university students smashed the windows of the Jesuit college, broke in, and started shouting obscenities at the priests. The college had been set up to teach Jesuit novices but had steadily expanded its educational reach, offering in-struction in philosophy to externs who might otherwise have taken up places at the university.[65] From Cracow to Prague, from Louvain to Bologna, rival Catholic educators likewise fumed against Jesuit intrusion, finding it more than a little irritating when, for instance, a Jesuit teacher like Juan de Maldonado proved so popular with his students at Clermont College in Paris that they queued for two or three hours to make sure of a seat.

Dominicans and Franciscans, meanwhile, were outraged when Jesuits set about replacing them as confessors to the high and mighty; they were ill at ease with the Jesuit response to the challenges posed by Galileo; and they were apt to see Jesuits as their all-too-successful rivals in missionary fields around the world. Oratorians would think of Jesuits as their main educational rivals in France; Capuchins would resent their evangelical efforts in Louisiana; Benedictines would complain that Jesuits were receiving far more than their share of the spoils recaptured from Protestant invaders during the Thirty Years' War.

As for members of the secular clergy, parish priests did not always appreciate snobbish Jesuit remarks about their moral and educational inadequacy, nor the overzealous progress of rural missionaries, nor the way in which communicants deserted local churches in order to receive the sacrament at Jesuit institutions. In a fledgling Catholic community like Mexico, Juan Palafox y Mendoza grew increasingly irate at Jesuits offering confession without obtaining the appropriate episcopal permits, at their providing sacraments outside of their settlements, and above all, at the Jesuit refusal to pay tithes and other ecclesiastical taxes. Bishops did not know quite how to react to a body of men who so often operated outside the rules and reach of ecclesiastical politics and justice.

In the troubled political atmosphere of Elizabethan England, secular priests who were trying extremely hard to sustain a cautious, nonprovocative ministry did not always relish the sight of Jesuit missionaries breezing into the country, full of bluster and political designs. An often vicious propaganda war would be waged between Jesuits such as Robert Persons and seculars such as Thomas Lister and William Watson.[66] Watson, as part of his "sparing discovery of our English Jesuits" in 1601, would complain of members of the order that "they stand so much upon the pumptoes in the overweened conceit of their puritanian perfection" that they saw "themselves [as] peerless, matchless and none to be compared with the meanest, puny father of their Society." Such fathers, with their penchant for stirring up political unrest and for adopting sneaky, equivocating tactics under examination, had "brought us poor secular priests, and other more honest and single-hearted Catholics," into "a gulf of danger and discredit." The Protestant authorities had begun "to give it forth that the Catholics are not to be trusted in anything they say."[67]

Others, committed to a particular ideal of independence for their national churches, rightly or wrongly perceived the Jesuits as intrusive agents of Roman hegemony. As we have already seen, the long, curious history of conflict between the Society and sections of the French establishment was well under way by the early seventeenth century. The heart of Louis XIII might have been buried in one of the Jesuits' Parisian churches, but in the same city the Society's enemies, who were rather more likely to recall that the regicidal Ravaillac had wanted his heart to be entombed at La Flèche, could look back with satisfaction on decades of blocking Jesuits' educational initiatives, accusing them of disloyal tendencies, and securing the banishment of the order between 1594 and 1603. It had been one thing to convince the bishop of Clermont and the cardinal of Lorraine to support the introduction of Jesuit education in France in the 1550s, but it had been rather more difficult, in the face of prolonged opposition from Parlement, university, and the bishop of Paris (all suspicious of this privileged, intrusive, novel order), to secure the letters of naturalization necessary to hold or inherit any property.[68]

It was a kind of suspicion and resentment replicated, to varying degrees, wherever the Jesuits—easily (if not always accurately) seen as a proudly supranational organization, explicitly loyal to Rome—made an appearance. Spanish kings, continually and actively suspicious of the Jesuits, eagerly provoked or prolonged internal struggles within the Society. When the pope placed Venice under interdict in 1606 for breaching ecclesiastical immunities, the Society obeyed his call to exclude members of the republic from the sacraments. It quickly became clear, once Jesuits were ordered to pack their bags, that the long tradition of polities exiling Jesuits in order to express their resentment at Roman interference had begun.

Such tensions can be overexaggerated. To describe the Jesuits as "mere Ishmaelites, whose arms are lifted up against all other orders, and theirs against them," was a little overdramatic.[69] A Dominican like Melchior Cano might have launched one of the most vicious early attacks on the Society of Jesus, but his superior would be quick to censure his actions. Dominicans and Franciscans, it ought to be remembered, were not averse to falling out among themselves, and mendicant-Jesuit rivalry—Spanish-backed Dominicans versus Portuguese-backed Jesuits in the Asian missions, for instance—was often more about long-standing national rivalries than anything else.[70] Jesuits might not have trained members of the secular clergy in precisely the ways Trent might have wanted, and outspoken missionaries such as Robert Persons certainly garnered any number of Catholic enemies, but faced with the challenges of reformation, the church was well aware of the massive potential represented by the Society of Jesus. This made for a tolerable, workable, if not altogether fairy-tale state of affairs.

Except there was one Catholic clique who insisted that the Society of Jesus posed a threat so fundamental, so disruptive, that any amount of Jesuit triumph and achievement became wholly irrelevant. It was amidst the rabble-rousing and rumor-mongering of the Jansenist party (if "party" is the word) that those two persistent strains of the anti-Jesuit myth—the personal immorality and the institutional self-love—would combine to devastating effect.

Jansenism was not, for the most part, about selling cheap and scurrilous copy, or about making up ludicrous allegations in order to titillate or trivialize. It grew out of a serious, rigorous theological quarrel, a quarrel that concerned not just "some useless nicety of the schools, but the main conduct of Christian life."[71]

It was about journeys toward salvation: important journeys, those. It was about the delicate, sometimes dissonant counterpoint between God's grace in all its puzzling, jargon-riddled variation and mankind's free will (or lack of the same). It was about how humanity's conspicuous addiction to sin ought to be accounted for and dealt with by the priest in the confessional, by the scholar in his study, by each lapsed, corroded prince and pauper in his lapsed, corroded life. It pitted worldviews against one another, breathed life into

Augustine's corpse; and as the Jesuit René Rapin observed, the animosity and importance of the contestants made it nothing less than the "most considerable matter" faced by Catholicism in the entire seventeenth century.[72]

Jansenism, like most isms, was a convenient, homogenizing fiction, but like most convenient fictions it was a shadow, a reflection, of a real, unruly squabble: a fault line running through the Roman Catholic Church. This was where the anti-Jesuit myth became serious, where cheap propaganda and earnest, wise theologizing met.

Unhappily it was a quarrel that regularly descended into gross exaggeration and political maneuvering, but it also gave the French language one of its undisputed gems: the *Provincial Letters* of Blaise Pascal. Through Pascal's hopelessly biased, subtly vicious satire, the notion of corrupt, corrupting Jesuitical casuistry was embedded in the popular imagination, and it has never really shifted since.

Jansenism

Religious fasting was an honorable tradition, an excellent spiritual discipline to boot, but did you really have to go without sustenance if you had a delicate stomach and ran the risk of sleepless nights if you missed out on your regular mealtimes? And what if you were already exhausted by extremes of profligacy the day before, more in need of nourishment than ever? And even if you had to pass up solid food, surely you were still allowed to drink wine, even in large quantities? As everyone knew, monks who took off their religious habits could be excommunicated, but were they not allowed to disrobe when they went out pickpocketing or headed to the brothel—think of the scandal that might be avoided. Servants stealing from their masters to make up for lousy wages, women dressing immodestly when haunting gambling dens, male parishioners frequenting mass so that they might ogle the fairer sex: the pillars, surely, of a thriving Christian commonwealth?

Not, Pascal insisted, that Jesuits—the men who apparently sanctioned such kinds of disreputable behavior—were trying to corrupt European morality; they simply did not feel obliged to reform it. Jesuits craved influence, and to that end they happily told their followers what they wanted to hear. On occasion a Christian yearned to be scolded, to be put through harrowing penances, and a Jesuit confessor would doubtless oblige. For the most part, though—for the vast majority of Europe's wayward population—laxist, easygoing advice was the order of the day. One more instance, Pascal was quick to point out, of Jesuit all-things-to-all-men mutability.

This was good news for the unreformable. Surely you were responsible for your sins only if you thought that what you were doing was wrong? Of course, Pascal's Jesuits would claim that whenever temptation faced a Christian, God, through an act of "actual grace" (divine assistance designed for specific needs), would sound a warning, prod the conscience—but wasn't this manifest nonsense? Was it not patently obvious that there were people who simply never thought of God and conscience, who boasted of their sins, who were happily immersed in avarice, impurity, blasphemy, dueling, revenge, robbery, and sacrilege? These people didn't seem to think they were doing wrong. One of Pascal's characters tells of those of his friends who spend all their days indulging in every kind of pleasure. He had always assumed that such behavior would lead to eternal perdition, but now, thanks to the Jesuits, it seems that these people will probably go straight to heaven. In such a world, he concludes, what point is there in sinning only in modest, half-hearted ways?[73]

Others were a little more scrupulous, of course, but there was no need to place intolerable burdens on their consciences. The confessional could be an embarrassing, daunting institution, so why not let Christians have one confessor for their commonplace venial sins and another for the more serious, mortal variety? No need to impose unduly harsh penances; no need, really, for the confessor to believe in a penitent's repentance. All very useful "lessons in finesse."

When tricky moral dilemmas cropped up, a vast array of conflicting advice was on offer, and most reasonable Christians might think that a person ought to follow the counsel that was most likely to keep a person out of sin. Not so, of course, the Jesuits. The baleful doctrine of "probabilism" was always available. It mattered not a jot if a hundred theologians agreed on the safest course of action: so long as one of their colleagues provided a more easygoing alternative, then a Christian could follow it in good conscience. Besides, sin was a tricky concept to pin down. What if you were doing a bad thing to achieve a worthwhile end? Imagine you were a servant holding the ladder so your adulterous master could climb to the bedroom of his latest conquest: if you were wise enough to think about—to "direct your intention" toward—the welcome reward you would receive, and put your master's liaison out of your mind, then where was the harm? A cash bonus was something worth having. So too was your honor, so although killing someone out of sport or unfounded vengeance was heinous, killing someone to preserve your reputation might also be an entirely legitimate act: as might bribing judges, disposing of false witnesses or corrupt jurors.

But what about tradition, all those church fathers, councils, popes, and verses of holy scripture that stood out against such strategies? Here it proved useful to be disconnected from, unbeholden to, the past. The Jesuits, so Pascal insisted, were happy to praise the old church fathers—Ambrose or Jerome or Augustine—for preaching morality that was appropriate to their times. But in the modern world, they had become irrelevant. And there was the magic name: Augustine. It was the battle over his reputation that lay behind the jaundiced genius of Pascal's creative, extraordinarily flimsy attack on the supposed cause and consequences of the Jesuit worldview. Unfortunately that brings us to none-too-easy theological terrain.

WHAT WAS THE relationship between a person's free will—her ability to have an impact on her salvation—and an omniscient, all-powerful God? Hardly anyone ever disputed the role and necessity of the Almighty in the equation; some species of his grace was always required. The difficult part was deciding what role people had in earning or rejecting it. To insist too much on a predestinarian universe, in which God dispensed unmerited grace on some people and flatly ignored the rest, seemed to rob people of any and all role in the divine economy, perhaps even to remove any responsibility from their shoulders—and that way lay license. On the other hand, to dwell too long on free will, on the role of mankind in its search for salvation, ran the risk of lapsing into Pelagianism, of undervaluing, underestimating the awesome power of God. Christianity had always struggled, and struggles still, with the dilemma.

Augustine had settled on a decidedly predestinarian outlook, and one that had been reputable, sometimes even normative, within the Christian tradition. The trouble for Catholics was that Augustine had become the champion of the predestinarian Protestants and his reputation had suffered a body blow as a result. But this, to some Catholics, seemed like too much of a sacrifice, a victory too easily given to Calvin and his unholy crew. Why should Catholicism abandon its Augustinian patrimony? Actually, a very good question.

What made matters even worse was the arrival on the theological scene of a novel account of grace and free will, as provided by the Jesuit Luis de Molina. There was, he insisted, absolutely no conflict between the necessity of God's grace and the human freedom to earn, accept, or reject it. God offered salvation—enough salvation for everyone who ever lived; this was called "sufficient grace." But not everyone was bound to respond to it. Only at the moment when God's grace was actually accepted did it begin to really mean anything in salvific terms; only then did it start to work: at this point it became "efficacious" grace. But while this seemed to empower the human will, did it not pose problems for the idea of God's omniscience, his divine foreknowledge about who would be saved and who would be damned? Not really, says Molina. Yes, God does know in advance (although talking about him in such temporal terms might be an error) who will and who won't accept his grace, but he did not dictate or arbitrarily determine who would do what. God, therefore, had all the knowledge a supreme being might reasonably expect, even if it was, as Molina termed it, a "middle knowledge," a *scientia media*.

Buried within this terminology was an optimism, a belief in mankind's potentiality, the notion that original sin was a terrible burden but not something that had corrupted human nature to such an extent that free will, an ability to choose between good and evil, had disappeared entirely. People were actually quite worthy—in theory, at least: worthy enough, many Jesuits suggested, to confess and then receive communion with a frequency that made their critics shudder.

The consequences for Jesuit moral advice were enormous. Because no one was irrevocably lost, because free will had a role in leading people toward or away from sin, there was perhaps room to be charitable and consolatory during an individual's moral off seasons—not in the absurd ways mentioned by Pascal, but in such a way as to sustain a person's sense of dignity and hope. People had the potential to do better, so moral advice did not always have to be about imposing Jean Delumeau's beloved sin and fear: rapping knuckles might be a wiser policy than pounding knuckles into reprobate, damned-and-there's-not-an-earthly-thing-you-can-do-about-it dust.

This was controversial—even a good many Jesuits were far from sanguine about Molina's position—and it was hopelessly at odds with the vision of those Catholics who wanted to rescue Augustine, who stressed the wounds of original sin, who sustained a far bleaker view of humanity's nature and potential. At the university of Louvain this battle had already been joined by the Jesuit Leonard Lessius and the Dominican Michael Baius; and when Molina's pivotal work, the *Concordia liberi arbitrii cum gratiae donis,* appeared in 1588, protests, not least from the Spanish Dominican Domingo Bañez, erupted; people called for the work to be examined at Rome, and the so-called *de auxiliis* ("of the helps") controversy raged from 1598 to 1607. No definitive judgment was reached, and Rome seemed to hope that granting Molinists, Thomists, and Augustinians the right to preach and teach whatever they chose would calm the theological waters. But the problem would not go away.

One of Baius's pupils, the Flemish theologian Cornelius Jansen, had died before the publication of his *Augustinus* in 1640—the title making the author's sympathies clear—in which man's concupiscence was portrayed as holding total sway over his free will in a universe wholly directed by God's gratuitous predestination. This was a subtle book, more often criticized out of hand than actually read, but a book that Rome, under no little Jesuit pressure, nonetheless felt obliged to condemn as too Calvinistic. But by this point it had already gained a following in France, not least in the person of the Abbé de Saint-Cyran, spiritual director of the Cistercian convent at Port-Royal and, fatefully, an opponent of the absolutist governance of Cardinal Richelieu.

With followers such as Antoine Arnauld, the "Jansenists" set about attacking the lax moral theology of the Jesuits—a consequence, they claimed, of the Society's rosy view of human nature. Mankind needed rigorous moral counseling to check its vile and corrupt nature; it needed to distance itself from the creaturely, to embrace asceticism. Jesuits might think that people deserved to take communion quite often; Jansenists insisted that most people were rarely morally clean enough to deserve such an honor. It was not enough to confess sins because you feared the fires of hell: you had to be truly and painfully sorry.

Needless to say, none of this pleased the Jesuits; it did not please Richelieu and his successor Mazarin, who saw Port-Royal as a challenge to royal authority; and it did not please Rome, which saw Jansenism as subversive of the centralizing mission of the Tridentine church. Such combined pressure led, in 1653, to papal condemnation of five propositions on grace and human nature supposedly contained in Jansen's book. And then the chaos set in. Antoine Arnauld suggested that the propositions were genuinely disreputable but were simply not to be found within the covers of the *Augustinus;* more papal condemnation followed in 1656; Arnauld once more disputed the facts; and in that same year Pascal's *Provincial Letters* and their vicious attack on Jesuit moral theology began appearing. The arguments rumbled on. Members of the French clergy would be obliged to sign anti-Jansenist formularies, Port-Royal would be disbanded, Arnauld would head into exile in Holland, and at the start of the eighteenth century an overly Augustinian book by Pasquier Quesnel reopened the controversy all over again. Finally, in 1713, the papal bull *Unigenitus Dei Filius*—which denounced many of Quesnel's propositions—*seemed* to toll the death knell of French Jansenism.

There had been exaggeration and misrepresentation on all sides. Pascal sometimes indulged in levelheaded controversy with Jesuits—disputing with

Antoine de Lalouvère about cycloids, with Etienne Noël about the existence of vacuums—but his account of Jesuit moral advice was grossly unfair. It quoted selectively, often out of context, from a very limited pool of Jesuit theologians—most notably Antonio Escobar y Mendoza. As Pascal himself admitted, it was not unknown for Jesuits to be among the most rigorous moral counselors of the period, sometimes criticizing the very casuistry manuals produced by their colleagues as little more than "fodder for the vulgar to feed on."[74] The serial adulterer Louis XIV, for one, had had to endure his share of Jesuit disapproval. Something like probabilism was real enough, but not quite as ludicrous as Pascal made out and not, for the record, a Jesuit invention: it had first been systematically introduced by the Dominican Bartolemé de Medina in 1577.

There *were* excesses within the Jesuit casuistical tradition, and popes would oppose them as eagerly as they stood out against Jansenism, but Pascal's reductive analysis of mysterious-sounding theological terms and opinions left him vulnerable to the criticism enshrined in one of his own pithy aphorisms: "The world is content with words; few think of searching into the essence of things."

On the other hand, it was every bit as easy to stereotype Jansenism as it was to stereotype Jesuitism. The concept itself—insofar as it represented a unified, organized sect—is not uncontroversial, and to a degree, it was an invention of Jesuit opponents hoping to create a political-theological bogeyman. The precise theological content of Jansenism is likewise difficult to identify: it was manifestly not a Catholic kind of Calvinism—Arnauld, one of its most celebrated champions, hated Calvinists with unseemly passion. At root it was a Catholic attempt to reclaim Augustine, and this did not strike some people as an especially disreputable cause. It seemed unfair to Pascal that the machinery of Molinism had been allowed to turn Catholic verities upside down. Why was it that Jesuits could get away with preaching ideas that had been damned in the Semi-Pelagians? Why was Arnauld blamed for saying things that Augustine had said? Was the Catholic Church not supposed to stand for tradition, to be wary of innovation?[75]

This was simplistic and inflammatory, but that (for our purposes especially) is what made the Jansenist controversy important. What may have looked like an erudite, obscure theological quarrel could actually inspire its share of popular passion: Catholics in Toulouse would take to the streets in 1645, bearing Jansenist placards and showering Jesuits with personal insults.[76] And it was a quarrel with consequences. Jesuits would never learn to forgive Jansenism. When Theophilus Darrington visited the Jesuit college at Liège in 1698, he noticed that the chained-up, prohibited shelves in the library contained the works of the hated Martin Luther and Cornelius Jansen side by side.[77] No amount of papal pronouncements could really undo the damage done to the Jesuits' reputation by the *Provincial Letters* of Blaise Pascal. The notion that the Society of Jesus had furnished sinful, sinning Christians with a moral theology ideally suited to their depravity would have a long and healthy future ahead of it. Jesuits had, as one nineteenth-century commentator would put it, managed to "make law, religion and the general conventional honesty of mankind a burlesque."[78]

Jesuits, so the anti-myth continued to insist, indulged in immorality themselves, forgave the moral inadequacies of others, told people in France and China whatever they wanted to hear. Devotions were made easy, religious services were turned into carnival, "bewitching men's senses with pomp and show."[79] Thin, austere Jansenists were behaving as good Christians ought to behave; fleshy, sensual Jesuits, Tartuffes to a man, were seeking influence, wealth, and carnal gratification at every opportunity. "All the world knows," sniped one author, "that they live in fair sumptuous cells . . . repose upon soft beds of down, and surfeit (as it were) upon all the pleasures that the world can afford."[80] Jesuits catered to the baser instincts of the sinning herd: Jesuits, in fact, *were* the sinning herd.

An awful lot of enemies, then. So many, in fact, that at the beginning of the eighteenth century the Society of Jesus had managed to become every bit as controversial as it was popular, as hated as it was loved. But this, in a perverse kind of way, was a sign of health and vitality. Chinese rites controversies, brilliant French satire, unceasing Protestant vilification were troublesome, beyond a doubt, but the critics would not have felt compelled to criticize unless they saw the Jesuits as a threat: and if you posed a threat you must have made your mark. In 1700 there were more Jesuits than there had ever been, doing more things, and doing them in colleges, princely courts, and communities around the world. And yet, in a little more than seventy years, the Jesuits would be destroyed, suppressed by papal fiat, obliged to seek out new careers.

6

"THE JESUIT IS NO MORE"[1]

Enlightenment and Suppression

In the middle of the eighteenth century, Voltaire ruled unchallenged over France and over civilised Europe. They had finally discovered and proclaimed liberty over the ruins of fanaticism. They sang, especially after drinking, about tolerance and brotherhood; they kissed passionately and even the most restrained wept tears of joy for humanity; it was truly wonderful to see. . . . Men had finally become so perfectly happy that they could move beyond God and replace him, to their great advantage, with philosophy and reason.

A highly sarcastic sketch of the Enlightenment by the Jesuit Auguste Carayon, 1865[2]

Legacies

On July 16, 1724, the Blessed Sacrament was carried in procession around a church in the Polish city of Torun. The Jesuit account of what happened next tells of a "mean Lutheran burgher" who, with exceptional audacity, refused to bare his head. Appalled at such blasphemy, one of the Society's local students pulled the offending hat off the head of the offensive Protestant, for which troubles he was promptly assaulted by other Lutherans (probably students at the rival grammar school) and locked up. More Jesuit students, apparently unknown to their teachers, then kidnapped and incarcerated a Lutheran, with the intention of making an exchange of prisoners. This, in turn, prompted a mob to attack the Jesuits' college, where, having beaten up some priests and torn down some altars, they "hewed down the sacred statues, and tore and hacked to pieces the images, and especially that of the Holy Virgin." They then "dragged to the public square before the schools the statue of the Blessed Virgin, of St. [Francis Xavier], Casimir and others, where they burned them openly, impiously exulting and leaping all the while over the fire."

The alternative, Lutheran account could hardly deny the attack on the Jesuits' college, but it offered an entirely different version of events. First of all, the church around which the sacramental procession took place had been unjustly taken from the Lutherans. Next, the Jesuit student was attacked only because he had forced people to kneel down before the sacrament, which was an awful assault on Protestant consciences. Yes, the student had been locked up, but his release was promised for the next day. Not that this calmed his classmates, who, without any real provocation, took to the streets with sabers and, so it was alleged, even threw one poor Lutheran, dressed in his night-gown, into the river.

What was truly outrageous, however, was the punishment inflicted on the Lutheran perpetrators—and this part, at least, is clear in the historical record. Despite protests from several governments, and even despite calls for leniency from a papal envoy, a special committee—and the Protestant account insisted that it was acting directly under Jesuit influence—ordered the execution of nine ringleaders, including the mayor, Jan Roesneck. The only remaining Lutheran church in Torun was handed over to the Franciscans.

To the author of an English account of the atrocity, the message was clear. He called "on the Protestants of all denominations to lay aside their private, trifling disputes, and cordially to unite and exert themselves against an enemy who aims at no less than the utter extirpation of Protestantism."[3]

Here was compelling proof that the eighteenth century would witness no lessening of hostilities between the Society of Jesus and its habitual rivals. The real cause for concern would be the emergence of newer, perhaps subtler, but no less determined adversaries.

Sharp in Rome, 1765

Give what scope you please to your fancy, you will never imagine half the disagreeableness that Italian beds, Italian cooks, Italian post-horses, Italian postillions and Italian nastiness offer to an Englishman in an autumnal journey." Thus Samuel Sharp in 1765, a lazy inheritor of a proud English tra-dition: an urge to visit Italy (one could hardly deny the cultural and artistic draw of the place) coupled with a duty to launch into barbed criticism as soon as one arrived, to complain (as Sharp surely did) of the dirty sheets, of the complete lack of curtains, and of tablecloths and napkins more suitable for the sausage-eating mob. Sausages that were apparently only one of the many Italian insults to the palate: Sharp claimed that he was lucky if he managed to dine on "a couple of fowls . . . boiled to rags without any the least kind of sauce," while the bread "all the way is exceedingly bad, and the butter so rancid, it cannot be touched." Butter so rancid, in fact, that Sharp and his companions were reduced to buying some cream and making their own.[4]

This was age-old English snobbery, much on a par with the comment made two centuries earlier that all an English tourist was likely to get out of a trip to Italy was an empty purse and an upset stomach.[5] "Suffer not thy sons to pass the Alps," William Cecil had advised English parents way back in the reign of Elizabeth I, "for they shall learn nothing there but pride, blasphemy and atheism."[6] But talk of blasphemy and atheism points to the other thing that Protestant Englishmen believed to be so terribly wrong with Italy. "What," Roger Ascham had asked in 1552, "is an Englishman Italianated? He that by living and travelling in Italy bringeth home into England . . . the religion, the learning, the policy, the experience, the manners of Italy." And that meant "papistry or worse."[7]

Sharp was heir to these particularly English kinds of sentiment, but the letters he sent home from Italy over the course of 1765 and 1766 show that he was also infected with typically eighteenth-century qualms about all things Roman Catholic. "I do not know a more melancholy place than modern Rome," Sharp confessed. There was the world-class religious art to be appreciated, of course, but was it not all a little over the top? "The excellent pictures to be seen in their churches and palaces are ambrosia to some palates, but I confess that after having paid my respects to fifty thousand of them, I am satiated and grow indifferent in my visits to the second fifty thousand." What was more, "the association of ideas spoils my relish for these goodly and sumptuous objects, as I cannot look on their golden altars, and their fat priests, without reflecting on their deserted *campania* and starving laity." This "pride of modern Rome" was one "of the causes of her wretchedness. She boasts of her gold and silver lying dead in her churches," but made not the slightest effort to put such precious booty to more constructive, socially responsible use.

Not that everything glimmered like the shining altars. "A man, on his first arrival at Rome, is not much fired with its appearance; the narrowness of the streets, the thinness of the inhabitants, the prodigious quantity of monks and beggars give but a gloomy aspect to this renowned city," and this only made the curious activities of the Roman Catholic Church seem all the more absurd to an upstanding Protestant Englishman. A visit to a ceremony in the pope's chapel revealed levels of "mummery, farce and pageantry" that "one would have thought impossible to be introduced into any religion." Sharp was plainly irritated. "I am now in a country where the sovereign is a priest, at a time of the year too, when the priesthood displays all its pomp, not to call it arrogance, and I assure you it is a trial for the patience of reason."[8]

"Reason," that favorite eighteenth-century word, uttered by a man who, admittedly, is more usefully thought of as a tetchy English traveler than any kind of *philosophe*. But uttered, nonetheless, in a city which seemed to be under siege, where a century's worth of architectural and cultural endeavor, from the Trevi Fountain and the Spanish Steps to the Capitoline Museum, seemed no longer able to sustain Rome's glamour and prestige. And in a Europe that was supposedly captivated by the charms of enlightenment: the nostrums of which, according to one's taste, have supplied either the beauty or the blight of modern Western civilization. The same Europe, in fact, which, over the past seven years had seen the Jesuits (Rome's favorite sons, it was convenient to think) banished from Portugal and France, which in the coming decade would witness their expulsion from Spain, Naples, and Parma, and by August 1773, the worldwide suppression of the entire Society.

It had not been the happiest of centuries for the Jesuits. Mission had faltered in China, Canada, and India—Catholic European empires were not what they used to be—theological squabbles had continued to simmer, the anti-Jesuit mythmaking machine was showing no sign of fatigue. Nonetheless, the decades of suppression still represented an extraordinary collapse from a midcentury position of apparent strength, when some 22,589 Jesuits around the world helped to staff 1,180 schools, professed houses, novitiates, and residences. A result, it is tempting to conclude, of the Society of Jesus being hopelessly out of step, just like the mummery, the fat priests, and the gloomy monks; a trial for the patience of reason, to borrow Sharp's phrase; the quintessence of all things Roman—like the gleaming altars, glamorous but decayed. Tempting, but not necessarily so.

Light

Enlightenment was all well and good, but your response to it rather depended upon what sort of light you were interested in. The frontispiece to the *Encyclopédie,* that thirteen-volume literary monument to the eighteenth century's anticlerical vogue, offers one alternative.[9] Reason, depicted as a classically dressed woman, pulls away the veil of error and superstition from Truth. Above and behind, the heavens part and a pure white light breaks through. Huddled beneath, grouped on clouds, more toga-wearing women are seen consulting geometrical diagrams and cradling scientific instruments.

But there were other lights available: in the Church of Sant'Ignazio in Rome, for instance. Here, on a ceiling painted by the Jesuit brother Andrea Pozzo in the middle of the seventeenth century, God sends a ray of light to the Sacred Heart of Jesus. From here it passes on to Ignatius Loyola, splits into four beams, and travels out to four far-flung continents. This is the light of faith, of the Jesuit missionary spirit; the light of Isaiah, perhaps—"I will make you a light for the gentiles that you may bring my salvation to the ends of the earth"; or the light of Thomas à Kempis, a privileged author within Jesuit ranks—"Enlighten me, good Jesus, with the brightness of internal light, and take away all darkness from the habitation of my heart"; doubtless the sort of light Jesuits on rural missions claimed to have seen in the skies above Bavaria in 1721, taking it as a sure sign that "the new light of truth would enlighten the dull minds of men."[10]

It is a very different kind of light indeed. Or so, at least, it might seem.[11]

This chapter follows the Jesuit order through the most troubled century it had yet negotiated, culminating in 1773 with the papal brief of suppression,

Dominus ac Redemptor. As one quietly delighted author would later put it, "Maternal Rome stretched out her withered hands over her child and her champion, grieving, while she herself united in one common sacrifice to peace—and the Jesuits were immolated."[12] Rome, to borrow another writer's phrase, had performed a cesarean on itself, but the child had not survived. It was all, as John Henry Newman would later calculate, "one of the most mysterious matters in the history of the Church."[13]

Suppressions Great and Small

It had begun in Portugal: the country, ironically enough, from which the great Jesuit missions had first embarked more than two centuries earlier. The horrendous Lisbon earthquake of 1755 struck at nine-forty on the morning of All Saints' Day, leaving only a tiny proportion of the capital's houses intact and killing thirty thousand people, many of them crammed, helplessly and hopelessly, into the city's churches. When certain Jesuits were impolitic enough to describe the tragedy as a timely punishment for Portugal's sins—talk of divine intervention that had always been unpopular with ruling elites and which, by 1755, was regarded by self-styled forward thinkers as superstitious claptrap—one politician in particular was deeply unimpressed.

Sebastião José de Carvalho e Mello, the future marquis of Pombal, was a man much risen in influence since the accession of Joseph I in 1750 (a "feeble, timid and voluptuous" monarch, easily manipulated, by one hostile account)[14], a man who would emerge as Portugal's chief minister in 1756. By the time of the Lisbon earthquake he was already fuming at what he regarded as Jesuit attempts to flout royal authority in Paraguay. With the Treaty of Madrid in 1750, Portugal had exchanged Sacramento colony for Spanish lands east of the Uruguay River that happened to take in seven of the Jesuits' Paraguayan reductions. Some twenty-nine thousand Guaraní now came under Portuguese governance. Led to their newly alloted home on the other side of the Uruguay

Francis Xavier

The Gesù

PHOTOS COURTESY
OF PAUL KILDEA

Vnus non sufficit orbis. { Een alleen
                           VVas my te kleen.

G Hy die hier siet dit kleyne kindt,
  Siet oock den aerdt van een die mint,
Van een die boogh en pijlen draeght,
En die gheduerigh sielen iaeght.
Al schijnt hy kleyn en sonder maght,
Sijn handen hebben groote kracht:
VVant krijght hy iemant in't ghesicht,
En dat hy waeght maer eenen schicht,

Daer

The Jesuit missions: "One world is not enough"
AF-BEELDINGHE VAN D'EERSTE EEUWE DER SOCIETEYT JESU (ANTWERP, 1640), P. 204,
COURTESY OF THE TRUSTEES OF THE NATIONAL LIBRARY OF SCOTLAND
AND THE SCOTTISH CATHOLIC ARCHIVES

The Society at 100

AF-BEELDINGHE VAN D'EERSTE EEUWE DER SOCIETEYT JESU (ANTWERP, 1640),
FRONTISPIECE, COURTESY OF THE TRUSTEES OF THE NATIONAL LIBRARY OF
SCOTLAND AND THE SCOTTISH CATHOLIC ARCHIVES

Bernini's Fontana dei Fiumi

PHOTOS COURTESY OF
PAUL KILDEA AND THE AUTHOR

Kircher's world

Robert Bellarmine
PHOTO COURTESY OF
PAUL KILDEA

Trampling on
heresy, the Gesù
PHOTO COURTESY OF
THE AUTHOR

Pozzo's ceiling, Sant'Ignazio

FRANCISCI AGVILONII

E SOCIETATE IESV

OPTICORVM
LIBER QVINTVS
DE
LVMINOSO ET OPACO.

ARGVMENTVM.

 IBRO *primo propofitione* 30. *& fequentibus explicata eſt quadamtenus natura luminis, quoad ſcilicet ad obiectum viſus primò attinebat,eiuſque cognitio ad intelligentiam viſibilium ſpecierum conducibilis erat. Quo etiam loco de coloribus vtcumque eſt actum, quatenus nimirum ab ipſis alij quidam tenuioris eſſentiæ colores exoluti ac luminis ope ad aſpectum delati,illos qui in rebus ſunt, velut propriæ imagines repræſentät. Nunc de luminis profuſione ac propagatione, de luminü concurſu & occurſu,de luminis illapſu in varias corporum formas,de vmbrarum productione, deȷ̃ varia figuratione luminis per foramen traiecti non pauca proponenda occurrunt,*
quæ

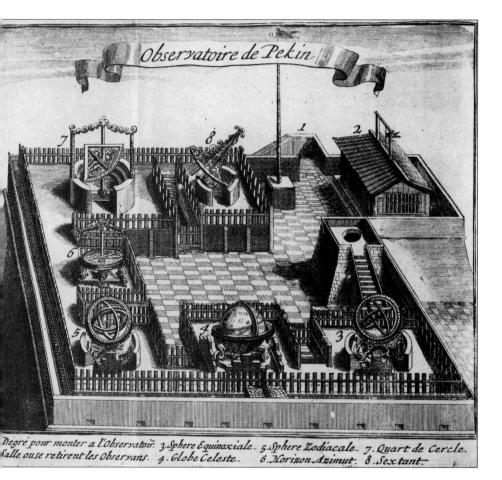

Observatoire de Pekin

Degré pour monter a l'Observatoir. 3.Sphere Equinoxiale. 5.Sphere Zodiacale. 7.Quart de Cercle.
Salle ouse retirent les Observans. 4.Globe Celeste. 6.Horizon Azimut. 8.Sextant.

The Peking Observatory

A Chinese woman

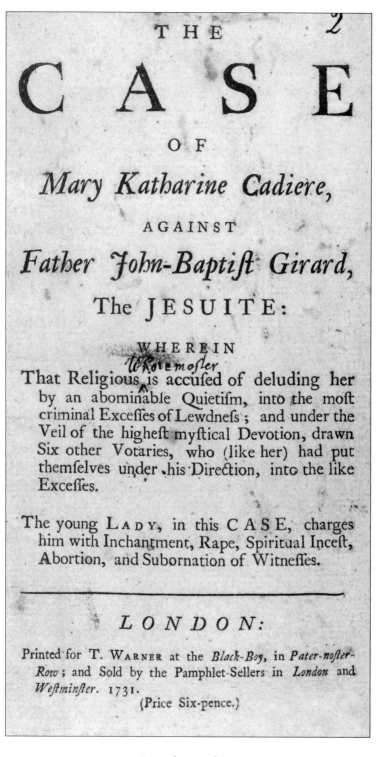

THE
C A S E

OF

Mary Katharine Cadiere,

AGAINST

Father John-Baptist Girard,

The JESUITE:

WHEREIN

Whoremofter

That Religious is accufed of deluding her by an abominable Quietifm, into the moft criminal Excefles of Lewdnefs ; and under the Veil of the higheft myftical Devotion, drawn Six other Votaries, who (like her) had put themfelves under his Direction, into the like Excefles.

The young LADY, in this CASE, charges him with Inchantment, Rape, Spiritual Inceft, Abortion, and Subornation of Witnefles.

L O N D O N:

Printed for T. WARNER at the *Black-Boy*, in *Pater-nofter-Row* ; and Sold by the Pamphlet-Sellers in *London* and *Weftminfter.* 1731.
(Price Six-pence.)

Girard v. Cadière

Father De Smet

by Jesuit missionaries, many among the Guaraní, who had been happy enough being loyal to Spain, rose up in resistance, even kidnapping some of the Europeans entrusted with laying out the new borders.

Long energized by bizarre (groundless) rumors of hidden Jesuit wealth and a Jesuit effort to establish a state within a state (Pombal was especially aggravated by rivalry between the Society and his Brazilian trading company), enemies of the order were outraged when some Jesuits in Lisbon seemed to preach in the Indians' defense, claiming that asking them to leave behind their homes and possessions was despicably cruel. Unfounded rumors circulated that the Society was behind the Indians' rebellion (in fact, local Jesuits were certainly angry but under orders from their general not to intervene).[15] Portuguese and Spanish troops succeeded in crushing Guaraní resistance and the Indians were obliged to choose between submission and resettlement. But the anti-Jesuit bandwagon was only just beginning to gather steam.

Over the next months and years Pombal engineered the expulsion of several Jesuit preachers and confessors from court, and an increasingly outlandish anti-Jesuit propaganda campaign was waged in the press: Jesuits were even accused of being behind riots against the governmental wine monopoly at Oporto in 1757, during which they had supposedly quipped that the company's wine did not even taste good enough to be used in the Eucharist. By the middle of 1758, Cardinal Saldanha, the papally appointed investigator of Jesuit affairs in Portugal, had concluded that scandalous commercial activity was rife inside the Society's Portuguese houses.

And then, on the night of September 3, 1758, someone shot the king in the right shoulder and arm. At first, the crime was kept quiet and reports were circulated that the king had simply suffered a fall in his garden. When it finally emerged that his illicit affair with Teresa de Távora, and the wounded pride of her relations, was probably to blame for the full-fledged assassination attempt, the suspected culprits, including the duke of Aveiro, were arrested. This was a welcome opportunity for Pombal to attack what he perceived as the willful independence of the Portuguese nobility, but he did not forget his other, more priestly enemies, and almost inevitably, the Jesuits began to attract suspicion. By one typically outlandish account, the would-be assassin had been encouraged by Jesuits at their local professed house, and told that killing the king would count only as a venial sin.

By early January, Jesuits were being arrested. One of them, the aged Gabriel Malagrida, endured a particularly vile imprisonment, showed signs of going mad (if holding conversations with God, the Virgin, Ignatius Loyola, and Charles Borromeo can be so construed), and was finally strangled, his remains burned, on September 21, 1761: denounced, as one contemporary reported, as "puffed up with pride and insolence which made him in his own conceit superior in merit to the rest of mankind."[16] Even Voltaire thought the treatment of the old priest was unnecessarily cruel.

In February all of the capital's Jesuits were restricted to three of their houses and the selling off of surplus food and kitchen equipment began. In April the entire Society was formally banished from Portugal, and by September the first ships began leaving Lisbon, heading for refuge in the Papal States, where the first boatload of priests, men denounced as being in rebellion with the Portuguese crown, would arrive on October 24. In all some eleven hundred Jesuits would be banished, another 250 being consigned to Pombal's prisons. In the ensuing months and years the shock wave moved around the world, and Jesuit priests were thrown out of Portugal's overseas possessions.[17]

As these events unfolded Pombal endeavored to bad-mouth the Society to any foreign diplomat who would listen—a self-justifying propaganda campaign that culminated in the viciously anti-Jesuit *Dedução cronológica e analística* of 1767. It was a project that continues to smart among Portuguese Jesuits, who, in one of their magazines published in 1982, described Pombal's methods as anticipating those of Goebbels and Stalin.[18]

One contemporary resident of Lisbon was no doubt delighted by all that had transpired. English audiences, in the very year of banishment, read his fanciful complaints that, for decades, Jesuits had been trying to isolate Portugal from the rest of Catholic Europe, had been trampling on the rights of the king in Paraguay, and had subtly gained influence in every sphere of society—"into the esteem of the literati . . . into the confidence and commerce of the merchants." They had apparently sought to dispose of all and any rivals and acted in such a way that even the fearsome Inquisition dreaded them.

Banishment, he reported, would surely answer "the prayer of every unje-suited Catholic here."[19]

ACROSS IN FRANCE, which had witnessed its own attempt at regicide as recently as 1757, at least one un-Jesuited Catholic was avidly suggesting that Portugal's lead should be immediately followed by Louis XV. What big-ger hint was needed, he wondered, than the recent appearance of a comet—"a demonstrative proof," as he called it, that "the horrors of this Society" should be expunged? He realized that some people scoffed at the notion that comets were portentous (not to mention earthquakes!), but then again, some people actually believed that the Jesuits could care less about the interests of France.[20] Those who shared his sentiments were offered a chance to strike when a scandal broke concerning the shady business practices of Father Antoine Lavalette.

Lavalette had been in Martinique since 1746, where promising beginnings and useful administrative reforms had given way to less and less edifying busi-ness transactions. As a priest he was quite entitled, in the eyes of canon and civil law, to increase productivity, to sell produce at a reasonable price, and to plow the profits back into the mission. Less legitimate were his purchasing of lands on Dominica and the production of cash crops such as coffee, indigo, and especially sugar, and his decision to act as an agent for Martinique resi-dents wanting to transfer monies to France. Despite chastisements from his superiors, and despite being summoned back to France in 1754–55, Lavalette continued his wayward commercial ventures, building up considerable debts and commitments with a number of French financial houses in the process. Amidst the chaos of the Seven Years War, ships carrying the Jesuit's produce were lost.

These losses contributed to the bankruptcy of some of Lavalette's credi-tors (notably the Lioncy and Gouffre brothers in Marseilles), who decided to seek redress from his superiors. Eventually, in 1760, they gained a judgment from the consular court of Paris that the Society of Jesus as a whole was culpable for Lavalette's debts.[21] The Society decided to appeal the decision and, foolishly, turned not to the Grand Conseil but to the Parlement of Paris, one of the Jesuits' oldest and fiercest rivals.

Even in distant Peking there was a growing sense that the Society was in trouble. As the Lavalette affair unraveled, the Jesuit Antoine Gaubil wrote to his brother that "the Jesuits, especially in Paris, have very powerful enemies, and these Jesuits presently have great need of protection." At such a time, Gaubil counseled, it was crucial to "know how to distinguish those clerics who were good Catholics from those were not." "Above all," he suggested, "one must not trust the Jansenists," those hypocrites who "deceive the world under their fine appearances" but who never missed an opportunity to "animate others against the Jesuits."[22] These were prescient words, and very much in keeping with recent scholarly emphasis on the role Jansenism played in the Society's downfall in France.[23]

Jansenism had moved on since the days of Pascal and Arnauld. Despite the apparent defeat embodied in Clement XI's *Unigenitus* of 1713, the spirit of Jansenism, and its enduring critique of all things Jesuitical, had managed to survive: more than that, it had transformed itself from a theological pressure group into an influential political party, concerned with asserting the rights of the French church and resisting papal power and pretensions. Along with disgruntled Sorbonnistes, opportunist *encyclopédistes,* and figures as redoubtable as the duc de Choiseul and Madame de Pompadour (who was still smarting from the refusal of her Jesuit confessor to forgive her adulterous liaisons), members of the Jansenist party scattered throughout France's political and ecclesiastical establishments would lead the charge against the Society by astutely linking their aim of crushing the Jesuits with the causes of parliamentary authority and Gallican ecclesiastical liberty.

In May 1761, the Paris Parlement dutifully upheld the decision of the lower court regarding the Jesuits' financial responsibilities, but quickly seized the opportunity to launch a much broader attack on the Society: a body, it would soon declare, that was obnoxious to civic order.[24] Over the next two years the Society's constitutions would be examined and denounced, most fiercely in the *extraits des assertions* of March 1762; it would be claimed that the Society had never enjoyed genuine legal status in France, the works of twenty-three Jesuits would be ordered to be burned, and plans to close all of the Society's schools and to sequester all its property would be put in place. The full gamut of hackneyed anti-Jesuit accusations—that they were king killers, sorcerers, and dispensers of shameful moral advice—was dutifully trotted out.

There were efforts to reach a compromise—the idea of establishing a French branch of the Society independent of Rome was floated, and French Jesuits, much to the dismay of the Society's leadership, would show themselves amenable to reaching such a settlement. Considerable support came in from some quarters, most notably from the higher echelons of the French clergy.[25] The bishop of Carpentras, for instance, tired of allegations of Jesuit immorality and disloyalty, pointed out that "I have been acquainted with the Jesuits from my earliest youth . . . [and have] often been with them in Italy, at Rome, at Malta, in Switzerland and Paris." He was happy to report that "I owe every maxim of morality, Christianity and submission to the powers commissioned by God to govern his people, to their care and institution." "Far from observing in their conducts any grounds for those odious aspersions thrown at present against them, I have always found them steady in the pursuit of the opposite principles."[26]

But all would be in vain, and by November 1764 the Society was dissolved, not just within the jurisdiction of the Paris Parlement, but across the whole realm, by edict of a reluctant king. Unlike in Portugal, former members of the Society were allowed to remain in France, but this was small comfort to those who believed they were witnessing the culmination of two and a half centuries of French anti-Jesuit sentiment, of the "complex of intrigues, calumnies and persecutions to which the Society of Jesus has been exposed from the moment of its birth until the time of its destruction, during which the hatred and wickedness of its enemies has not slowed down for an instant."[27] It was just like Aristides being banished from Athens, another commentator complained: no one could say exactly what crime the Society had committed but it was found guilty anyway. The Society was like Philomela, he suggested: it had been ravished, only then to have its tongue ripped out to deny it any right of reply.[28]

But at least there was still Spain. Until, that is, the sombreros intervened.

IN MARCH 1766 the population of Madrid rioted. Prices were high, harvests had been bad, and the finance minister (an Italian to boot) had become wildly unpopular. Into this mix a royal decree was issued that forbade Spaniards in provincial capitals and royal and university towns from wearing flowing cloaks and sombreros: such clothes were far too useful to criminals in need of a disguise. The sombrero was to be replaced by the French three-cornered hat. Amidst the violence, property was damaged, ministers fled hither and thither, and petitions were submitted.

Once the count of Aranda (very much in the mold of the marquis of Pombal in Portugal or the duc de Choiseul in France) had calmed the situation, typically ridiculous rumors began to circulate that the Jesuits (who else?) had been behind the disturbances, prophesying the king's death and using their secret presses to satirize the political situation. If Louis XV of France had been reluctant to countenance the destruction of the Jesuits—he had used delaying tactics on several occasions—his Bourbon cousin, whose ears had been filled for several years by the anti-Jesuit ravings of the Neapolitan politician Bernardo Tanucci, had no such qualms. Long-standing resentment of the Jesuits—from a new class of politicians unhappy with the Jesuits' dominance in education; from a monarchy angry with the Jesuits' fierce opposition to the proposed canonization of Bourbon-backed saints—seemed to be approaching a critical moment.

The Extraordinary Council of Castille was charged with investigating complaints against the Society, finding against it by January 29, 1767. Copies of the edict of banishment (produced by printers watched over by armed guards) were circulated, and on the night of March 21, without the slightest warning, the Jesuits' six Madrid houses were entered by troops. The residents were allowed to take with them the clothes they wore, their breviaries, and any snuff, chocolate, and small change they happened to have. Every spare coach and carriage in the capital was requisitioned and the next morning the arrested priests and brothers began their journey into exile, headed for the port of Cartagena.[29] Colleges across Spain were then visited and orders were dispatched to the colonies, reaching Buenos Aires at the beginning of June; 2,267 Jesuits would ultimately be dispatched to Europe. The memory of such arbitrary Bourbon power would later play a role in the anticolonial movements of nineteenth-century South America.[30]

When news reached the Papal States that a new consignment of exiles was on the way, the very merchants who had made a healthy profit from transporting their Portuguese brethren again offered their services, only to be disappointed when Rome refused to take in any more Jesuits: there was neither the room nor the money to support them.[31] The Spanish Jesuits were sent off to Corsica, and within a year, the satellite states of Spain—Naples, Parma, and Sicily—had all followed Madrid's lead and banished the Society.

IN THE FACE of such dismal, disheartening events, there were still signs of life. As late as 1769 the Jesuits of Freiburg would embark on a major renovation of their grammar school.[32] But the question that was on almost everybody's lips was whether the Society as a whole would now be suppressed. In Rome, John Thorpe lamented in 1767 that "more stories are now told and printed of the Jesuits than all the pagan poets recount of their fabulous monsters." A sign, perhaps, that "if destruction continues to rage much longer (and it seems every day to gather new force) we will scarce be able to find a safe corner in any part of the world."[33] The Catholic powers who had carried through their national banishments eagerly pushed for total suppression—it was the perfect way to justify their unilateral actions—and for the next six years they would apply enormous pressure on Rome. When the pope reacted harshly to Parma's newly enacted anticlerical legislation, Naples responded by seizing the papal towns of Benevento and Pontecorvo, and France (employing a tactic often used before when Rome needed threatening) took Avignon and Venaissin. Useful bargaining counters all.

With the death of Clement XIII, the conclave set up to elect his successor was dominated by the issue of suppression. *Zelanti* cardinals pushed for a pope who would defend the Jesuits, while *politicanti* cardinals and ambassadors of the great powers campaigned for a pope who would do their bidding: it was the most blatant example of secular governments using a papal conclave as a political playground since the epic election process of 1740, the longest since the Western Schism, which delayed the election of Benedict XIV for six months.

In Rome, Thorpe grimly reported in May 1769 that "the unanimous election of Cardinal Ganganelli was no sooner divulged about the city than everyone looked upon the Jesuits . . . to be inevitably ruined."[34] In fact, despite his anti-Jesuit credentials, the new pope, Clement XIV, would play an astute political game over the next four years, postponing any direct promise to suppress the Society, gaining time by attacking the Jesuits in limited ways—stopping their pensions, removing the Roman and Irish Colleges from their control, not letting them use papal musicians and the Swiss Guard on ceremonial occasions—to appease their critics and to avoid destroying them outright.[35]

With hindsight, it is easy to talk of the inevitability of suppression during these years, and a strain of fatalism (couched in terms of providentialism) can certainly be discerned within the Society. But even as late as January 1773, when the Jesuit John Carroll reported that everyone was saying that "our catastrophe is here at hand," he was also careful to note that although "we have been alarmed so often during the present pontificate with like reports and the date of our destruction has been fixed so often," as yet, nothing had come of it.[36] The key issue was the reaction of Catholic Austria—would Maria Theresa (who had until now balanced a suspicion of Jesuit influence—attacking the Society's dominance in Austrian education, for instance—with a willingness to employ the talents of individual members of the Society) support the

Jesuits, support the Bourbon powers, or simply remain silent? Thorpe was aware that the Viennese court was "constrained by its many connections with the Bourbon compact" and as a result "does not make any public declaration either for or against the Jesuits," but "nevertheless it is said every now and then to give words of consolation." In the end, however, the lure of marriage alliances with France convinced Maria Theresa to overlook any objections she might have had.[37]

The final obstacle was removed, and the suppression document—prepared under the firm influence of the Spanish ambassador, José Moñino y Redondo—was dusted off. With the papal brief *Dominus ac Redemptor,* a curious document that does not make any specific accusations against the Jesuits, but claims their removal is necessary for the sake of Christian peace, the Society of Jesus was destroyed.

On August 16, 1773, the brief was read to the general of the Society, Lorenzo Ricci, who by late September would be languishing in the papal prison of the Castel Sant'Angelo. On the same day, the sixteenth, John Thorpe wrote from the English College that "we had passed the day in the usual occupations and were sat down to supper in peace. The news of the day had not furnished anything that could either augment our hopes or fears." But then word of the papal decision arrived and Thorpe and his fellow Jesuits had found themselves in "something like the swimming of drunkenness." Thorpe noticed that "the multitude of sparrows that for many years beyond the measure of any man had every night taken shelter in the great orange and lime trees in the garden entirely disappeared on the night of the execution."[38] More mundanely, he observed that, what with so many ex-Jesuits in need of new careers and the clothes that went with them, at least the tailors of Rome would be happy.

"SUCH," CROWED D'ALEMBERT, was "the fate of all human grandeur and power." It was "in their very nature to grow worse and become extinct when they have arrived at a certain degree of greatness and lustre."[39] It had happened to the Persians, to the Assyrians, and even to ancient Rome, he explained, and now it had happened to the Jesuits. But was that really fair? Had the Society of Jesus really grown worse, or did a few Europeans simply think it had? And more than that, was it really within the gift of those few Europeans to destroy a centuries-old, worldwide religious order that had long since grown inured to criticism? Column inches, as men like d'Alembert knew, were easy to rack up during the eighteenth century; political influence, an ability to actually convince Bourbon monarchs and popes to suppress the Jesuits, was rather more difficult to come by. Contributing to a climate in which destroying the Jesuits became easier was one thing: actually causing such destruction was something else entirely. Perhaps the suppression might be best understood as a naked act of eighteenth-century statecraft: something that did not have to happen and something, after the accrued bruises and wisdom of thirty years, that popes and Catholic monarchs would come to regret.

Enlightenment

An early-nineteenth-century literary concoction offered its readers a glimpse of an imaginary "catalogue of the most eminently venerable relics of the Roman Catholic Church" which had supposedly been "disposed of by auction at the Church of St. Peter's at Rome . . . for the benefit of a young gentleman of great rank" back in 1752. Sought-after items apparently included

> The ark of the covenant [and] the cross of the good thief: both somewhat worm-eaten
> St. Joseph's axe, saw and hammer, and a few nails he had not driven: a little rust eaten

The water pots of the marriage at Canaan, in Galilee. NB These are
   not the pots shown at Pisa, Cluny and Andegavi, but the true,
   original ones
Crumbs of the bread that fed the five thousand
The towel with which [Jesus] washed his disciples' feet: very rotten
The holy linen cloth upon which St. John the Baptist was beheaded:
   wants new hemming and darning[40]

Vicious and brilliant satire that made it seem as if all those so-called miraculous relics had lost their power as objects of veneration and become something to poke fun at. Jesuits, relic hoarders without equal, always keen,
according to our author, to employ falsification and chicanery "to make their
collection more glorious and raise the larger sum," had, it was suggested, finally been exposed for the charlatans they were.

As heirs to the Enlightenment, in an era when it was still respectable to ad-
here to the notion of a unified, easily defined thing called the Enlightenment,
many a nineteenth-century European saw the suppression of the Jesuits as but
one more step in the proud march toward the triumph of reason, the banishment of superstition, and (as an inevitable, doubtless pleasurable consequence) the humbling of Rome. In 1826, thinking of the Voltaires, the
Diderots, and the d'Alemberts, a speaker at the Cheltenham Auxiliary Reformation Society, no less, portrayed a time when "a crowd of men of talent,
disgusted with the form in which religion met their eyes . . . revolted against
the legends, the miracles, the tyranny and the ignorance, which they pro-
nounced to be the bulwark of the priesthood."[41] A priesthood, it was endlessly
averred, that had been addicted to moribund forms of scholarship, pining for
a time when Aristotle had ruled the scientific roost and mired in the absurdi-
ties of medieval scholasticism: the "boundless labyrinth of unintelligible opinions," as one disgruntled ex-Jesuit had put it in 1717, where words were
valued instead of things, "quibbles instead of answers, quotations instead of
reasons, passion instead of sense."[42]

The familiar, and still voiced, explanation of what the eighteenth century was all about has Europe refusing to believe in relics and miracles, insisting that if religion has to exist it must be a natural kind of religion, whose tenets, much like the laws that governed gravity or the expansion of gases, could be deduced by anyone through the exercise of reason alone, and not by means of revelation or the parochial dogmas of any particular church. God, at least by extreme Deist accounts, was *Deus absconditus,* a blind watchmaker who set the universe in motion but did not intervene in human affairs by blithely inflicting plague, famine, and war. The Bible could be usefully mined for moral content, but to ask people to believe in things which patently defied the laws of nature and stood outside their reasoning or experience was wholly untenable. This might have been acceptable to a Jesuit—a person, as Henry Isaac Roper later explained, who had been "reduced from a being of volition to a mere piece of animal clockwork, a instrument to be put in motion by another"—but that was precisely why the Jesuits, men who were still poisoning youth in their schools, had become irrelevant and had to go.[43]

That the Enlightenment killed the Jesuits is a seductive enough idea, not least because it was peddled both by a *philosophe* like d'Alembert—which annoyed the Jansenists, who wanted their role in destroying the Society to be fully acknowledged—and by Jesuits such as Augustin Barruel, who did much to harden this view of enlightenment and suppression into historical orthodoxy. In his *Memoirs Illustrated by the History of Jacobinism,* a book that had a profound influence on Edmund Burke among others, a conspiracy is detailed in which the plotting of the *philosophes* led from the *Encyclopédie* to suppression of the Jesuits to revolution itself. Voltaire, he explained, would have gladly seen all the Jesuits at the bottom of the sea, each with a Jansenist hung to his neck, and Voltaire had seemingly had his way.[44]

But there are real problems with this view. For one thing, the notion of a unified priest-hating "enlightenment" movement, *à la française,* does a huge disservice to the rich variety of national "enlightenments," many of which cannot sensibly be thought of as anticlerical. For another, the vast majority of Europe's population remained unimpressed by, even unaware of, the fashionable ideas circulating in Parisian and Viennese salons, and remained firmly attached to notions of a providentialist, interventionist God. Even the sophisticated advocates of untrammeled reason, it should be remembered, were, on the one hand, fairly easily duped by mesmerism, and on the other, rather keen to let superstition maintain its hold over the lower echelons of society—organized Christianity was no bad thing for the servants.

More fundamentally, whatever the Enlightenment was, seeing it as representing an eighteenth century defined by a neat schism between forward-looking rationalism and moribund religious faith is invalid. Recent scholarship has profitably reminded us that all those cleric-hating *philosophes* (some of whom also happened to be sacrament-partaking *philosophes*) shared a worldview, a font of imagery and rhetoric, and an intellectual method much influenced by the Christian past (of what, after all, is that frontispiece of the *Encyclopédie* reminiscent if not depictions of the seven liberal arts—that product of the medieval, clerical university and the scholasticism from which so many eighteenth-century bright young men were keen to fly?). Many a cleric, meanwhile (Jesuits sometimes included), was a keen advocate of the fashionable theories of Newton, Wolff, or Leibniz, and happy to employ the scientific and philosophical obsessions of his age in order to defend and revitalize Christianity.

Jesuits, of course, set a premium on the enlightenment of faith (it was ultimately, as Juan Polanco had long ago said, "a better light than human reason") and balked at an overreliance on man's rational faculties,[45] but they were part of a Christian tradition that reviled fideism and insisted on the role of reason in the spiritual life: not using reason to create belief, perhaps, but seeing it as a tool with which belief could be explored and expanded. It was the Jesuits' enemies, the Jansenists, whose religious sensibilities were far more suspicious of reason. The chasm between what Jesuits and the Enlightenment supposedly stood for can all too easily be overstated, which brings us back at last to those two kinds of light: the light of reason and the light of faith, the age of Enlightenment standing for one, the Jesuits standing for the other, implacable enemies. A neat dichotomy, certainly, but somewhat wrongheaded.

Voltaire, eager to undermine the claims of conventional religion by contrasting the infighting of the Catholic Church with the sedate purity, unity, and rationality of the students of Euclid, boasted that there were no sects among geometers. This, with the arrival of non-Euclidean geometry in the next century, would prove to be overly optimistic, but more important, invoking geometry as some kind of antithesis of revealed religion was a rhetorical mistake. After all, some of the best geometers of the past two centuries (including Christopher Clavius, the author of the preeminent early-modern version of Euclid's *Elements;* including Francois d'Aguilon; including Giovanni Girolamo Saccheri, author of books which, after a period of long neglect, would help lay the basis for non-Euclidean geometry) were Jesuits.

This success, replicated in most other areas of scientific endeavor, in just the sort of pursuits deified on that frontispiece of the *Encyclopédie* does much damage to the division, so crucial to the familiar postmortem account of the suppression, between Jesuit priests and an interest in so-called rational pursuits.

And this is only one facet of the deep irony of the Jesuits' suppression. The culture that destroyed the Society of Jesus owed many of its hobbies and fashions to the reportage of Jesuit missionaries—this was, after all, the century of chinoiserie. Fashionable talk of noble savages, of the universal roots of language, of the origins of the world's religious diversity were influenced by, had been anticipated by, members of the Society. Dispensing with a religious order was very different from discarding the vast store of Chinese knowledge and observation contained within the Jesuits' long-running *Lettres édifiantes* (they would be reprinted in their entirety in the years after 1773), or the studies of national histories, sciences, flora, and fauna that had been provided by Jesuits from Manchuria to Latin America.[46] And the irony runs deeper yet. For all the differences between the Society's outlook and the anticlerical bent of some Enlightenment figures, their worldviews could sometimes be strikingly similar. An optimistic view of mankind's capacities, a forceful emphasis on mankind's free will, an unshakable faith in the transformative power of education: such things are often posited as summing the Enlightenment project up, but they also very much remind one of the Jesuits.[47]

The Jesuits were, in fact, part of the culture that destroyed them. More important, they had helped to create the culture that destroyed them. Their suppression, in this scheme, looks rather like a patricide, however wayward and occasionally out of touch the father might have become. But then, if you believe in such things, ungrateful sons turning against their enfeebled fathers, imagining, with the brash confidence of youth, that they are making things new and better, is not the most ridiculous image of historical development.

And perhaps most curious of all is the fact, already hinted at, that the darling endeavor of the eighteenth century, the pure, clean world of science, had been a proud and profitable Jesuit domain from the earliest days of the order. Jesuit science had its emphases, and these, because they did not always mesh with the obsessions and assumptions of certain eighteenth-century scientists, had undoubtedly rendered the Society less reputable and influential on the European academic scene. Jesuit science had its favored disciplines, its reluctance in some quarters to abandon one paradigm, that of Aristotle, for another, but could anyone really deny that when the Jesuits were suppressed in 1773 they could look back on two and a half centuries of worthwhile, influential, and—let us stress the point—supremely rational scientific endeavor?

Jesuit Science

Tables of the satellites of Jupiter, telescopes, books about botany and anatomy, sea charts, two quadrants, three great pendulums, an equinoctial dial, burning glasses of twelve and twenty inches, lodestones, microscopes, thermometers, barometers, and "all the tubes and machines that serve in making experiments of vacuity": an appropriate enough cargo for the seven men, bearing the title of the king's mathematicians in the Indies and China, sent to Asia by Louis XIV in 1685, granted special membership of the Royal Academy of Sciences, one of their chief duties to continue the effort to "correct the geographical maps, facilitate navigation and raise astronomy to its perfection," to "observe in their travels by sea and land the longitudes of the chief places, the declinations and variations of the needle and all that can serve to certify and improve our charts and navigation."

These were men who also happened to be Jesuits, and who, during their long voyage, found time to mount daily religious services, catechize sailors, and, wisely enough, offer nine masses to the Virgin before the perilous Cape of Good Hope was tackled. But they were also men of ample curiosity, who observed the night sky and corrected their star charts at every opportunity, who dissected sharks, marveled at enormous turtles and typhoons, and, when given the chance to examine a porpoise, confirmed that it was a warm-blooded creature by plunging their hands into its entrails. When their ship arrived at the Cape, it was suggested that the presence of Jesuits would probably "offend the nicety of a Dutch commander in a pretty new colony and make him suspect something else than what we pretended," so the priests were advised to meet their Protestant host in disguise. They refused, but all worries evaporated when the Jesuits set about instructing their host in Giovanni Cassini's new method of calculating longitude by means of the satellites of Jupiter. They were sent on their way up the east coast of Africa with presents of wine and tea, given by the grateful Dutch in exchange for a microscope and a burning glass.[48]

Here, amidst unusual cross-confessional calm, was a typical Jesuit example of science blending in with, serving as the handmaiden of, evangelism. These and other French missionaries would continue the pastoral of technology established in China a century earlier by Matteo Ricci.

NOT THAT OVERTLY evangelical causes always lay behind the researches of Jesuit scientists, and this brings us to Maximilian Hell, director of the observatory at Vienna University since 1756, who found himself above the Arctic Circle in 1769, at the end of a decade in which his fellow Jesuits had been banished from most of Catholic Europe. He was on the desolate island of Vardø, off the Norwegian northeast coast: not as an exile but, thanks to the sponsorship of Christian VII of Denmark, in order to observe the transit of the planet Venus across the surface of the sun.

Such transits were frustratingly rare—they came in pairs, eight years apart, every twelve decades—but they were vital for anyone interested in calculating how far the earth was from the sun. At the start of the eighteenth century, estimates for this crucial distance—what we today call an astronomical unit—ranged between 8 million and 111 million miles. A sorry state of affairs, as Sir Edmund Halley pointed out, but rectifiable if, as he suggested, astronomers would cooperate in observing the next two Venusian transits, in 1761 and 1769. The idea was that if they were observed from as wide a variety of locations as possible around the world—locations for which the longitude and latitude would have to be calculated to perfection—and if the times it took Venus to cross the sun (in the region of seven minutes) were precisely recorded, then an accurate number for the solar parallax could be arrived at, and from this a reliable measure of the sun's distance would emerge.

To this end, in 1761, English and French astronomers had risked crossing enemy lines at the height of the Seven Years War; John Winthrop had traveled to Newfoundland; others had headed to St. Helena, Siberia, and Madagascar; and Charles Mason and Jeremiah Dixon (soon to be famous, after surveying the disputed Pennsylvania-Maryland border, for their Mason-Dixon line) made for South Africa. Eight years later, in consort with Hell in Vardø, observations were made, among other places, at Hudson Bay, in California, Mauritius, and, courtesy of Captain James Cook, on the island of Tahiti. Collation completed, the mean distance to the sun was calculated to within 1 percent of its currently accepted value—just shy of 93 million miles.

What some people could not ignore, however, was that Hell was a Jesuit, the sort of person who, upon arriving at Vardø on October 11, had launched into a *Te Deum*. Enemies of the Society, hardly in short supply at the end of the 1760s, suggested that he had falsified his calculations—although the Danish astronomical society seemed happy to publish his results—and the accusation was still reverberating when, in 1835, Carl Ludwig Littrow found Hell's astronomical diary in Vienna and claimed to be able to make out blatant erasures and alterations. Jesuit deception, it was suggested, extended even to the hallowed world of science. It took almost fifty years for Hell to be vindicated, thanks to the intervention of the astronomer Simon Newcomb, who pointed out that, while there were most certainly rubbings out and corrections in the diary, these had been made, in good faith, at the time. Hell had, in fact, been striving for accuracy; Littrow had been theorizing from prejudice.[49]

ANOTHER INDIVIDUAL PRONE to anti-Jesuit sentiment was Samuel Johnson, who, as he once revealed, could recognize the "many helps to get to heaven" that Roman Catholicism seemed to offer, but could not make use of them since "an obstinate rationality prevents me."[50] In an early, unfinished translation of Paolo Sarpi's history of the Council of Trent, Johnson had readily allied himself with the Venetian's virulently antipapal posturing. The notions that "the pope is invested with all the authority of heaven and earth . . . that all princes are his vassals, and that he may annul their laws at pleasure" were "maxims equally shocking, weak, pernicious and absurd." It was with apparent sympathy that Johnson quoted Sarpi's opinion that, in order to chasten Rome, "there is nothing more essential than to ruin the reputation of the Jesuits."[51]

But in 1760, when Johnson dined with the Dubrovnik-born Jesuit Roger Boscovich, who had arrived in England looking every inch the gentleman in powdered wig, white stockings, and knee breeches, Johnson decided to discuss the theories of Sir Isaac Newton. It was a wise choice of table talk, since Boscovich was one of the most accomplished and celebrated scientists of his time.

The priest endured uncomfortable moments during his time in England—being asked, for instance, to celebrate Guy Fawkes Night at Cambridge (not the most pleasurable evening's entertainment for a Roman Catholic)—but on the whole, his visit was a success. The highlight came on January 15, 1761, when, on the same occasion as Sir Joshua Reynolds, he was elected to the Royal Society of London. As his nominators soberly put it, he was "well qualified by his knowledge on astronomy and other parts of natural philosophy to be a useful member."[52]

In fact, there were few areas of science that Boscovich had left untouched. As an astronomer he had calculated the sun's diameter, had observed the 1736 transit of Mercury, and in 1748 had supervised an observation of the solar eclipse at the Jesuits' Roman College in the presence of three cardinals, fifty prelates, and a handful of princes. He had made contributions to hydraulics, geometry, and the mathematics of probability, had helped convince Benedict XIV to remove Copernicus from the Index, and would go on to supervise the draining of the Pontine marshes. His architectural expertise was sought when problems emerged with the dome of St. Peter's and the belfry of Milan cathedral, and by the empress Maria Theresa when the structural integrity of the imperial library was in question. His influence on such scientific luminaries as Faraday, Kelvin, and Clerk Maxwell has been well established, and his advanced atomic theory has been seen as a precursor of modern field theory and quantum mechanics. Such conspicuous success has meant that Croats, Serbs, and Dalmatians have competed to claim him as a son, and far beyond such Balkan squabbles he even has a crater, forty-six kilometers in diameter, named for him on the surface of the moon.

BOSCOVICH WAS IN many ways exceptional. Regarding some fellow Jesuits as insufficiently progressive, Boscovich was himself mistrusted by others in his order as perilously avant-garde. But he was, like Hell and the French Jesuits of 1685, part of an enduring Jesuit contribution to science. If Boscovich is honored with a crater on the moon, so are Hell, Athanasius Kircher, and Matteo Ricci, and thirty-one other Jesuits. Indeed, one of the first detailed selenographs of the lunar surface—one that gave us names as familiar as the Sea of Tranquility and which is still proudly displayed at the Smithsonian in Washington—had been produced by the Jesuit Giovanni Battista Riccioli, based upon the crucial astronomical observations of his fellow Jesuit Francesco Maria Grimaldi.[53]

However often they might have been made during the eighteenth century, suggestions that Jesuits had offered nothing to the store of human knowledge were palpably false. They had contributed to the development of pendulum clocks, pantographs, barometers, reflecting telescopes, and microscopes, to scientific fields as various as magnetism, optics, and electricity. They observed, in some cases before anyone else, the colored bands on Jupiter's surface, the Andromeda nebula and Saturn's rings. They theorized about the circulation of the blood (independently of Harvey), the theoretical possibility of flight, the way the moon affected the tides, and the wavelike nature of light. Star maps of the Southern Hemisphere, symbolic logic, food control measures on the Po and Adige Rivers, introducing plus and minus signs into Italian mathematics—all were typical Jesuit achievements, and scientists as influential as Fermat, Huygens, Leibniz, and Newton were not alone in counting Jesuits among their most prized correspondents.

Jesuit science had not always been popular. When Christopher Clavius supervised the changeover to the Gregorian calendar in 1582, Jesuit houses across Europe were stoned by crowds blaming the Society for the theft of the ten days stolen from them in the name of astronomical accuracy. Sometimes Jesuit scientific ambition ran ahead of Jesuit scientific expertise—Bartolomeu de Gusmão made something of a fool of himself when he tried to demonstrate hot air ballooning to the Portuguese court in 1709 (he descended from a tower with panache but proved less skilled at reascending and even managed to set part of the king's palace on fire)—but the dozens of Jesuit-run observatories, pharmacies, and weather stations, in Europe and beyond, were welcome additions to the eighteenth-century scientific landscape.

Why, then, was it so easy for eighteenth-century polemicists to attack Jesuits as pathologically and institutionally opposed to worthwhile, rigorous scholarship? Part of the answer lies in the challenges thrown up by the previous two centuries of scientific endeavor and how Jesuits had reacted to them—or more accurately, how they were perceived as having reacted to them.

And challenges there had been. Aristotelian certainty, with its neat system building, its conviction that the physical world could be perfectly categorized and the essence of things truly understood, had been undermined by a science of doubt, of measured skepticism, by the replacement of certainty with probability. Mathematical formulae—allowing things like pressure and motion to be described numerically—would strive to replace verbal analysis; Galenic medicine, with its humoral theory and vital spirits, would come under siege; experiments with falling bodies and pendulums, ballistic science's talk of objects moving in parabolas, would threaten Aristotelian physics; advocates of a mechanistic universe would pour scorn on notions of providentialism, of God's hand being involved in every cause and effect.

And of course, there was also the challenge posed by Copernican and Galilean cosmology: a development that intruded upon existing scientific power struggles within the church; that hinted at a different model of the role, scope, and autonomy of scientific study; and that, more worryingly still, tried to turn the universe upside down—or better, inside out.

But if we ask how the Society of Jesus responded to all this, a picture of greater complexity than the hackneyed view of Jesuits as the stubborn, unyielding champions of the medieval Aristotle, the irrational persecutors of the likes of Galileo, the sworn enemies of Descartes, begins to emerge. Eighteenth-century polemicists had, let us say, half a point. There were, patently, moments when the Roman Catholic Church had been stubbornly, unreasonably reactionary in the face of scientific advance. Many Jesuits *did* defend Aristotle (though not, in all cases, out of laziness or spite); some Jesuits were certainly involved in the campaign against Galileo (though, as we will see, this was not necessarily part of some epochal, dastardly struggle between religion and science). And if some Jesuits attacked Descartes, they did so most often when Descartes, dismissing the Aristotelian division between matter and form, undermined one of the linchpins of Catholic teaching on transubstantiation.

It is worth suggesting, however, that, from the perspective of their times, Jesuits were sometimes perfectly entitled to do all of these things without being tarred as scientific cheats and dullards—liking Aristotle was not necessarily some species of disreputable scientific heresy, much as it looks that way to us. Talk of forward marches, of the elusive *P*-word, "progress," is rarely, if ever, sensible in historical discourse—progress is in the eye of the beholder, and the beholder is always the person living in the seemingly inevitable, but actually contingent, present. Second, although broad Jesuit scientific trends can be made out (this was, after all, a religious order with active censors and rigidly defined curricula), many members of the Society bucked them by losing faith in Aristotle, by admiring Galileo, and by being seduced by Cartesianism. That did not make them somehow better or brighter Jesuits, but it did make them different, and it is in the difference, in the diversity, that the most efficient answer to the eighteenth-century model of monolithic, idle, habit-ridden Jesuit science can be located.

Man's mutable, imperfect understanding of the physical universe changed over the course of the Jesuits' first two centuries. Jesuits, like everyone else, struggled to come to terms with this transformation, but, on occasion, they struggled in measured, subtle, and reasonable ways.

Crystal Spheres and Vacuums

That the Church is the implacable foe of "Science" is a charge so constantly repeated as to have acquired in the popular mind the character of a primary truth—one that requires no proof beyond its own self-evidence.

John Gerard, S.J.[54]

On earth, in the sublunary world, things grow, decay, and die; it is a place of change and corruption. The four elements engage in intermingling and transmutation in their quest to reach their natural homes: the concentric shells below the moon in the case of fire, air, and water. As for the element of earth, one need only throw a stone in the air to see it falling toward its inevitable destination, the very center of the universe, the habitat of mankind.

In the heavens, by absolute contrast, all is perfect and unchanging. A system of spherical shells of ether, stretching from the moon to Mercury, Venus, the sun, Mars, Jupiter, and Saturn, as far as the firmament of fixed stars, is tightly fitted together (no vacuums here), each with its own perfectly circular rotation. All at once a universe where mankind might feel important, at the center of things, and yet a universe endlessly dependent for its motion upon the unmoved Prime Mover beyond the starry firmament.

Thus Aristotle's universe, the blueprint for its successor, a medieval universe that shunned unpalatable Aristotelian features—an eternal cosmos, for instance, without beginning or end—but that also introduced its strange accretions, like a Christian God beyond the starry firmament and angels delicately turning the crystalline spheres, making perfect music in the process. And yet, as the great Egyptian astronomer Ptolemy was aware, things were not quite so simple. As any observer could see, the planets did not seem to move in perfect circles, their speed appeared to be variable, on occasion they even seemed to stop and reverse course across the sky. Venus, Mars, and Jupiter patently looked more or less bright at different times of the year.

The solution lay in the geometrical models and mathematical constructs of eccentrics, epicycles, and equants. These damaged Aristotelian notions but, in the final analysis, could be treated as hypotheses, ways to save the observed phenomena, not necessarily corresponding to any physical reality. The fundamental notion of an earth-centered cosmos, divided absolutely between realms of immutable perfection and volatile corruption, was the only notion any right-thinking medieval European ought to entertain.

What, then, to make of the new star that appeared in the constellation of Cassiopeia in 1572 and then vanished two years later, or the comet of 1577 that seemed to exist above the moon? How, exactly, could comets *move through* or stars *appear in* heavens that were supposed to be unchanging? And worse yet, once Galileo and his telescope arrived on the scene, how to account for the mountains on the moon or the spots on the sun—bodies that were supposed to be unblemished, as smooth as mirrors? And what about the rings of Saturn—a planet that, like any other, was supposed to be perfectly spherical?

What about the phases of Venus, or the satellites of Jupiter, which rather dented another Aristotelian axiom: that there was only one center of motion in the universe, the earth?

Ingenious efforts were made to explain such things away. Might not sunspots, as the Jesuit Christoph Scheiner held for a while, be the shadows of nearby satellites? Perhaps, since the moon was a perfect mirror, its so-called mountains might be reflections of the earth? Ultimately, however, although some astronomers, including the Jesuit Adam Tanner, proved unwilling to alter their opinions, most people felt able to abandon the Aristotelian notion of unchanging heavens, even if, like the Jesuit Christopher Clavius, some of them continued to insist that the heavens were still *less* corrupt than the sublunary world.[55]

Far more threatening was the idea, posited by Copernicus and supported by Galileo, that the sun, rather than the earth, was at the center of the cosmos, that the earth moved and the sun stayed still. This seemed to contradict a number of biblical passages—passages in Joshua, for instance, that talked quite clearly about the sun moving across the sky. This raised troublesome questions of scriptural exegesis—was it going to be necessary to analyze such passages in nonliteral ways? Christoph Scheiner was eventually willing to concede that sunspots might be on or near the sun's surface but he never accepted the Copernican model of the universe. Jesuits such as Jacques Grandami and Charles Malapert would produce detailed rebuttals of the Copernican paradigm.

Indeed, in the trials and tribulations of Galileo we can almost certainly detect the roots of the popular perception that the Catholic Church, Jesuits included, was irrationally addicted to an obsolete cosmology and determined to crush the epochal scientific breakthrough of a plucky Paduan genius. The trouble is that, as recent scholarship has amply demonstrated, things were not so straightforward. Before Galileo, few within the church were especially troubled by the theories of Copernicus: they seemed to account far more efficiently than any other system for the observed phenomena of the universe. So long as Copernican ideas were treated as a *mathematical hypothesis,* useful for calculating the apparent motions of the heavens, rather than being touted as an accurate account of the physical *reality* of the cosmos, there was really no problem.

But this was the line that Galileo crossed: he insisted that the Copernican model was a precise description of how the universe actually was. Unfortunately, he did not have any clinching proof for this assertion. His insistence that churchmen ought to start interpreting passages of scripture in new, less literal ways was bound to smart. No one questioned—indeed the Jesuit Robert Bellarmine explicitly said this to Galileo—that the book of nature and the Bible had to agree: this was a matter of logic, since both had God as their author. If there was an apparent contradiction, then this was simply a failure of interpretation, and if an irrefutable proof of the heliocentric theory could be provided, then words such as those in Joshua would have to be looked at afresh. But as Bellarmine insisted, unless you had an irrefutable proof, was it not reasonable to stay with the traditional interpretation?

In the meantime the theory could certainly be used as a useful, perhaps even a preeminent hypothesis, but for a scientist to stray into comments about the role and competence of biblical exegesis—quoting Baronius's famous "The bible tells us how to get to heaven, not how the heavens go" and suchlike—was inevitably going to cause irritation. Not least in a Tridentine church that was fiercely committed to making biblical interpretation a matter for theologians alone (none of that Lutheran exegetical free-for-all) and which, after a century of change and novelty, was suspicious of any kind of innovation.

Galileo annoyed the Jesuits, but not because they were unusually resistant to everything he had to say. Before the famous drama, from gagging orders in 1616 through to trial in 1633, got under way, Jesuits at the Roman College (from whom, it has been argued, Galileo actually derived some of his physical theories) had absolutely no problem with looking through telescopes and confirming Galileo's observations.[56] Galileo was a friendly correspondent of a Jesuit like Christopher Clavius; a Jesuit like Christopher Grienberger would defend Galileo in the face of early criticism; Galileo would be received at the Roman College in 1611 as an honored guest, worthy of elaborate celebrations; and Jesuits would use the subject of Jupiter's satellites in their sermons.

There would be rows between individual Jesuits and Galileo—with

Scheiner over sunspots; with Horatio Grassi about comets—but on the whole, the genius of Galileo's observations was fully recognized by the Society of Jesus. Adam Schall von Bell, although stopping short of discussing heliocentrism, would even take news of them to China, happily including talk of moon mountains and the phases of Venus in his astronomical treatise of 1626.[57] An undoubted affinity between Galileo and the Society's scientists had caused, or rather deepened, institutional rivalries between Jesuits and members of the Dominican order—who routinely refused any dialogue with the new theories. This was a consequence that some within the Society could accept: theological and philosophical threats could perhaps be contained, allowing the practical benefits to be fully exploited. But when Galileo insisted, without sufficient proof, that the Copernican system was literally true, he pushed the Jesuits too far.[58]

We know, and applaud, that Galileo was right. And of course, it was hardly impossible for people at the time to think that Galileo was *probably* right. But the response of the church, of someone like Robert Bellarmine, for instance, really ought not to be demonized. The Galileo affair did not represent a battle between religion and science but between competing scientific paradigms; and the desire to hang on to a well-established Aristotelian model of science when there was no overwhelming reason to abandon it was an intellectually viable policy in the 1610s and 1620s.

Just as important, talk of a unified Catholic or Jesuit response to Galileo makes little sense. Some Jesuits attacked Galileo with no little vitriol, some reluctantly and cravenly abandoned him, others sought compromise in the cosmology of Tycho Brahe, still others would push very forcefully for the use of the Copernican system as an ideal hypothetical model. Honoratus Fabri would spend fifty days in prison in 1671 for doing this with such gusto. Some Jesuits, such as Wenceslaus Kirwitzer and a number of astronomers in Spain and Portugal, even seem to have accepted that the Copernican theory was an accurate depiction of physical reality.

Indeed, such diversity is entirely emblematic of a Jesuit science that, throughout the seventeenth and eighteenth centuries, was anything but monolithic. In eighteenth-century Portugal the Jesuit José Veloso would roundly condemn the ideas of Newton and Gassendi, while Inácio Monteiro would emerge as an arch anti-Aristotelian. Yes (as Monteiro discovered), the Society's leadership was entirely willing to criticize and silence individual scientists who overstepped the mark. Giuseppe Biancani would find it extremely difficult to get his theories about the liquid nature of the heavens (through which, as he poetically put it, extraterrestrial bodies moved "as a fish through water") past the Society's censors.[59] Yes, many Jesuits would emerge as dyed-in-the-wool Aristotelians, refusing, like Niccolo Zucchi, to accept the possibility that vacuums could exist, refusing, as Leibniz discovered to his cost, to abandon the Aristotelian notion of the immutability of species. Aristotle would remain a Jesuit champion—a massive commentary on his works would be produced by the Jesuits of Coimbra from 1592 onward; the 1730 general congregation would reaffirm loyalty to fundamental Aristotelian principles.

Not that loyalty was ever the same thing as blind obedience. Galileo had made great sport of distinguishing between the historical Aristotle—an innovative, open-minded scientific theorist—and the massed generations of subsequent, unimaginative Aristotelians. "If Aristotle had been such a man as they imagine," he suggested, "he would have been of intractable mind, obstinate spirit, and barbarous soul—a man of tyrannical will who, regarding all others as silly sheep, wished to have his own decrees preferred over the senses, experience and Nature itself. But it is the followers of Aristotle who have crowned him with authority, not he who usurped it or apportioned it to himself."[60]

This sentiment is strikingly similar to the Jesuit Niccolo Cabeo's assertion that "if you never question Aristotle's doctrines your commentary will not be that of a philosopher [i.e., a natural philosopher] but that of a grammarian."[61] José de Acosta knew full well that Aristotle had ruled out the possibility of people living in the equatorial zones—they were far too hot—but Acosta also knew from firsthand experience in Latin America that people manifestly *were* living in the equatorial zones, not least because the weather was not as uniformly oppressive as Aristotle had supposed. "I went into the sun to get warm," Acosta reported, "and what else could I do but laugh at Aristotle . . . and his science, seeing that in that place and at that season, when all should be scorched with heat . . . I and all my companions were cold." Aristotle was the master—he was most certainly Acosta's master—but he was not to be followed slavishly at every turn.[62]

Some Jesuits did hold on to what were perceived as moribund ideas and scientific concepts out of laziness and convenience, and the Society's reputation suffered as a result. But some of their colleagues also emerged as prominent supporters of newer scientific trends and not always simply because they wanted to avoid being dismissed from their academic posts. A Cartesian Jesuit was not an unknown figure on the European intellectual scene, while Jesuits like Kaspar Sagner and Josef Stepling would be instrumental in promulgating the ideas of Newton across Europe and beyond. Jacopo Belgrado would make a major contribution to the emerging science of electricity.

And besides, whatever scientific paradigm a particular Jesuit subscribed to did not necessarily influence the quality of his research. You could make important astronomical observations whether or not you believed that the earth orbited the sun; you could advance the technology of microscopy regardless of whether you believed in modern botanical theories. Filippo Buonanni worked entirely within an Aristotelian interpretative framework but no one could question the importance of his studies of seashells. Ignace Gaston Pardies criticized Newton's color theory but his criticisms actually served to improve and refine Newton's ideas.

I T   W O U L D   B E absurd to position the Society of Jesus as one of the more go-ahead, adventurous, or innovative scholarly and scientific institutions of the eighteenth century: it simply was no such thing. At the moment of suppression Jesuit science did not count for nearly as much as it once had. National academies had managed to dilute the earlier importance of institutionalized Catholic science, the educational emphases of official Jesuit curricula were often anything but adventurous, and many Jesuit scientists proved unwilling to move beyond traditional disciplines such as geometry and optics.

But although some contemporaries were apt to plead to the contrary, neither was it some disconnected, disenfranchised relic. As was cheekily pointed out, many of the articles contained within the much-vaunted *Encyclopédie* were derived, sometimes even plagiarized wholesale, from the scholarship of Jesuit priests such as Claude Buffier. A publication such as the French Jesuits' *Journal de Trévoux* was not to everyone's taste but its role in eighteenth-century academic discourse, not unlike the thirty astronomical observatories controlled by the Society in 1773, not unlike the twenty-six chairs of mathematics occupied by Jesuits in Europe in 1762, could not be seriously questioned any more than the manifest contribution of the previous two centuries' worth of Jesuit scientific endeavor.[63]

For all that, it can hardly be denied that when people in the eighteenth century wanted to advertise themselves as especially "enlightened" they often felt obliged to voice their profound dislike for the Society of Jesus: when the Bavarian Academy of Science was established in 1759 it excluded Jesuits on principle.[64] In spite of the unsung contributions of priests like Claude Buffier, Jesuits could readily be portrayed as sworn enemies of a project like the *Encyclopédie,* not least when a Jesuit like Guillaume-François Berthier undertook a sustained attack on the project from the publication of the prospectus onward. His main objection, that the great work was riddled with plagiarism, contradictions, and bizarre choices of subject matter—was it not odd to exclude St. Augustine entirely but make room for a recipe for apricot jam?—could be easily overlooked. As could the fact that his main aim had been to convince the editors to include quotation marks when they were citing material, and to properly acknowledge their sources.[65]

A key protagonist of the century, Voltaire certainly had his Jesuit adversaries (even if he also found time to be extremely complimentary to some of those Jesuits who had educated him), although it is difficult to avoid the conclusion that this sometimes came down to nothing more noble than personal animosity. Louis Bertrand Castel, for instance (a man of quirky theories, it must be admitted), was, in Voltaire's opinion, an "ingenious philosopher" and "Euclid Castel." Until, that is, Castel allowed unpleasant comments to be written about Voltaire in the *Journal de Trévoux,* upon which transgression

Castel suddenly became the "Don Quixote of mathematics," an "enraged dog," and a mathematical jester.[66]

It was a custom that survived into the next century. Henry Isaac Roper insisted that the Jesuits were "a barrier against all that is progressive in the onward reach of human society. When you speak of Jesuitism you call up the spirit of the past, the dull dark past. . . . Its mission is not to take the world onward, but to drag the world backward, to get it again amidst that rickety infancy of intellect, and those dim shadows which are Rome's best hope."[67]

Such a statement is questionable on several levels. The teleology of it all, the forward march, gives pause, and it neglects to mention that a sturdy—if sometimes overstated—case can be made that it was in the dull, dark past of the medieval universities, where so many crucial translations of scientific texts where undertaken and where a spirit of free, rational inquiry was often at least aimed at, that much of the groundwork of the scientific revolution was laid: through the experimentalism (albeit an experimentalism drowned in metaphysics) of Robert Grosseteste and Roger Bacon, through the emergence of Thomist realism, which, rejecting the abstractions of Platonic forms, talked of an ordered universe of concrete, particular things, understandable according to physical laws. And if it was *God's* universe, then that was all the more reason to observe and understand it accurately and precisely, to marvel at the creation rather than make the pagan error of fearing it.

Medieval Aristotelian science, it can be claimed, not only provided modern science with much of its terminology—"form," "genus," "species," "quantity," and so forth—but, up to a point, afforded scientists the right, independent of issues of faith, to acquire knowledge through the senses and the use of reason. St. Ambrose might have insisted that nothing "shows such darkness as to discuss subjects concerned with geometry and astronomy . . . to measure the depths of space, to shut up heaven and earth within the limits of fixed numbers," but medieval Christianity was having none of it.[68] And if all that is true, then it was precisely an organization such as the Society of Jesus that was perfectly placed to serve as a bridge between these achievements and the scientific advances of the seventeenth and eighteenth centuries.[69]

But just because the Society of Jesus was not hopelessly out of kilter with the intellectual fashions and achievements of the eighteenth century, that hardly stood in the way of the high priests of enlightenment saying that it was, that it was a bulwark against progress, a cabal of irrational, superstitious obscurantists. Which leaves us in a quandary. Just because criticism of Jesuit intellectual horizons was laced with exaggeration and moments of outright falsification does not mean that such criticism was discounted by the European public. Perhaps everyone believed the biased propaganda. Perhaps enlightenment—a very specific version of enlightenment—did kill the Jesuits after all?

Except it didn't. First, because the French Enlightenment, at the risk of repetition, did not represent the totality of eighteenth-century thought and culture. Philosophers could spill untold amounts of ink, they could have crowned heads as their correspondents, but none of that amounted to the wherewithal to destroy one of the pillars of the Roman Catholic Church. Second, because suppression, however much it delighted *encyclopédistes,* however much their intellectual whispering campaign made it more palatable, was largely about politics.

Politics and Consequences

The national suppressions of the Society of Jesus, those extraordinary, quasi-comical events detailed at the start of this chapter, were discrete phenomena, not facets of some united pan-Bourbon conspiracy. The personalities of individual politicians, hideously bad luck (think of the wayward fiscal choices of Father Lavalette), and long-standing grievances (of the Jansenists in France, most notably) all played their very specific parts in the Society's downfall. But that does not mean that the suppression was an isolated, freakish accident.

It would be tempting, for instance, to place the suppression in the context of burgeoning anti-Roman political thought that seemed to enrapture

Catholic courts from Vienna to Versailles over the course of the eighteenth century. An occasional pope (Benedict XIV, for instance) would maintain good relations with the rulers of Catholic Europe, but for the most part the encounter was a story of mistrust and antagonism.

It was easy for monarchs and their minions to believe that the Roman Church represented a rival hub of power and influence in their dominions. After all, priests who ultimately derived their power from Rome were educating populations, directing their consciences, imposing social and moral regulation, all the while enjoying substantial economic and legal privileges. In country after country the church had managed to accrue a mighty portion of the national wealth, while a sizable fraction of those nations' manpower was devoted to filling the clergy's ranks. The radical, leading edge of such sentiment was contained within the writings of Johann Nikolaus von Hontheim (usually referred to as Febronius) and the future reforms of Emperor Joseph II of Austria. Europe, so the theory and the limited practice went, ought to be made up of state-controlled national churches. The pope's role should be limited to maintaining church unity.

Such thought was undoubtedly radical, but it also had an impressive pedigree. National governments' resenting the claims and influence of the bishop of Rome was no new departure. The sight of money leaving local coffers and heading to Italy, the attempted interventions of the papacy in national politics, the more radical interpretations of the papal primacy, had been irritating secular politicians for centuries. This was felt not least in France, a country that well remembered its squabbles with ambitious medieval popes such as Boniface VIII, that had always endeavored to secure concordats that protected the interests of the national, Gallican church. Recent history was replete with episodes in this proud tradition—the Estates General declaring in 1614 that the French king derives his power from God, not the pope; a prolonged dispute over the rights of the king to make ecclesiastical appointments and collect revenue from vacant bishoprics; the enshrining of Gallican liberties in the articles of 1682. Popes, these articles insisted, clearly had authority, but it was subject to the superiority of a general council of the church; the ancient rights and traditions of the French church ought to be respected.

The consequences of the declaration of 1682 were troubling—bishoprics would remain empty, secret excommunications would be issued from Rome. Although there was soon a return to more polite relations, the nostrums of 1682 continued to be taught and resentment was apt to resurface whenever the papacy became overly assertive. And who were suspected as the most likely agents of such papal self-aggrandizement? Well, the issuing of the papal document *Unigenitus* in 1713 was aimed at outlawing the neo-Jansenist teachings of Pasquier Quesnel, but it was construed by many as yet another instance of unwelcome papal intervention in French religious affairs. And who were the document's main beneficiaries if not the Jesuits, the Jansenists' fiercest and loudest enemies? The fact that individual Jesuits of the past—such as Fathers Coton and la Chaise—had actually been decidedly Gallican in their sympathies were unlikely to erase the image of Jesuits as disruptive, devious lieutenants of the papacy. They were denounced as an instrument of papal pestering and pretension. They summed up everything that secular leaders had against papal meddling.

Whenever a national government grew tired of Roman behavior—and Spain and Portugal were more than capable of sharing that kind of weariness—it was likely to voice its dislike of the Society of Jesus, a body of men with (notionally at least) a supranational identity who even went so far as to swear a special fourth vow of obedience to the pope. It was significant that in France the destruction of the Jesuits was orchestrated by the Paris Parlement, the longtime spiritual home of Gallican ideals. It was orchestrated, in large degree, by supporters of Jansenism, a movement that had long since, and wisely, allied itself with the cause of protecting the Gallican liberties of the French church.

Jesuits as Rome's henchmen, Jesuits as a challenge, a rival, to the authority of secular power: the image was flawed—many a French, Spanish, or Portuguese Jesuit was far more concerned with promoting his nation's interests than in doing Rome's bidding—but to men like the marquis of Pombal, heavily addicted to squashing all and any political competition, it was an image that convinced. Just as Pombal sought to humble and enfeeble the Portuguese nobility, so he was more than prepared to rid his country of the Jesuits: men, so he believed, who had been undermining royal authority at home and in Paraguay for far too long.

✳

CLEMENT XIV, BY one account, was "a person of universal learning, indefatigable in his enquiries . . . regular and devout in the exercises of religion." "In his person" he was "of the middle size, rather inclining to be fat."[70] It fell to this pope to destroy the Society of Jesus. He did so because the secular powers of Catholic Europe left him with little choice. He delayed, so they bullied. Securing the worldwide suppression of the order became an urgent, self-justifying political priority. Something like a logic of suppression took over, and it could be suggested that many within the Society simply gave up the fight, adopting the fatalistic view that providence had ordained their annihilation.

When news of the dissolution of the Jesuits reached Lisbon, the marquis of Pombal, with a flourish of costly extravagance, ordered that the city's lights should burn all night in celebration.[71] And if we wanted to blame the Jesuits' demise on the philosophical Enlightenment, that would doubtless be a perfect symbol; but Pombal was largely unmoved by the theorizing of the likes of Voltaire.

On one level the suppression was about traditional dynastic politics, about the wrangling that had been going on between Rome and Catholic Europe for centuries, the wrangling that had produced any number of victims over the years, the wrangling that allowed French and Spanish ambassadors to turn papal elections into grotesque diplomatic farces. On another, it was about that sequence of events, specific to France, Portugal, and Spain, which were recounted earlier: the earthquakes, the riots, the ships lost at sea, the bankruptcies, the assassination attempts.

But it was also part of a transformation of the role and reputation of the Catholic Church. In the years after 1773, in a variety of countries, papal nuncios would be expelled more than they had ever been expelled before, monasteries (rich sources of wealth and manpower) would be dissolved, the state would seek greater control over education, civil marriages would be introduced, and contacts between local priests and Rome would be ever more strictly controlled.

Even popes themselves seemed to be losing something of their former grandeur. Back in the eleventh century a German emperor, trapped by political necessity, had been willing to travel to Canossa to see the pope, to stand outside castle gates for three days in the clothes of a penitent, weeping. In 1782 it was down to the pope to make the journey, to Vienna, in the hope of tempering the radical ecclesiastical reforms of Joseph II. His counsel was not heeded in the slightest; he was treated with outrageous disrespect by the minister, Wenzel Kaunitz; and the emperor cheekily suppressed a monastery within an hour of the pontiff's departure back to Rome. It was all a long distance from 1077, a long distance from the castle at Canossa. And the suppression of the Jesuits, a reluctant action of a bullied pope, had been a stop along the way.

JESUITS WOULD BE affected in a hundred different ways by the suppression. Some of those who found themselves far distant from European surveillance simply stayed where they were, blithely ignoring calls to return home. The geographer Joseph Tieffentaller would be buried at the missionary cemetery in Agra; Jean-Jacques Casot would continue his residence at Quebec until 1800; Louis de Poirot would live out his life in China, dying at Peking in 1815.

Suppression did not inevitably signal disaster or destitution; not everyone ended up languishing in Pombal's prisons. Ex-Jesuits could quite legitimately continue their clerical careers as either secular priests or members of other religious orders. Something like fifty-five former members of the Society would enter the episcopate. Others carved out quite glamorous careers: Franz Paula von Schrank would emerge as a successful director of the Munich botanical gardens; Benedict Stattler would continue his eminent academic career at Ingolstadt, launching broadsides against the novel philosophy of Immanuel Kant (a philosophy with a turbulent but curiously enriching future in the history of Catholic theology); at the court of Maria Theresa (who had dealt with Jesuits in her own inimitable way for years), Martin Dobrizhoffer would enchant the empress with tales of his adventuring in South America, Georg Pray would serve as her imperial historiographer, and Joseph Eckhel would hold the posts of custodian of the imperial cabinet of medals and director of the imperial treasury.

Even the forced return of Jesuits from around the world could pay unexpected dividends. Lorenzo Hervas y Panduro, suddenly exposed to the experiences and recollections of so many of his brethren, made great strides in his comparative linguistic studies. In the scholarship of Jesuits such as Francisco Xavier Clavijero, the uniqueness and importance of Latin America's history and natural environment would do much to develop a cultural climate which would eventually lead to campaigns for independence.[72] As for Roger Boscovich, the erstwhile dinner companion of Samuel Johnson, a position as director of optics in the French navy and a pension of eight thousand francs per annum awaited him.

Some Jesuits took the time to enjoy the more unlooked-for benefits of suppression. Persistent myths had been dented, after all, and one Roman priest noted with obvious satisfaction that troops, addicted to stories of hidden Jesuit wealth, had been disappointed when they found no "immense treasures . . . ingots of gold, caskets of diamonds, quantities of bank notes."[73]

This was small comfort, however, when one considered the 728 educational establishments that were disbanded, a quarter of a million students forced to make other arrangements. Or the six hundred abolished libraries in Europe with their half a million books, three quarters of which were sold off for their scrap paper value. Or the Brueghels and Van Dycks the Belgian province was forced to sell off at bargain rates. The poignant physical evidence of change was everywhere: the professed house in Vienna was transformed into a war office; buildings in Quebec and Augsburg were reborn as military stores and barracks.

Others enjoyed windfalls from the suppression. Seized wealth helped to support education funds in Austria; Catholic art collections acquired new treasures; secular priests in Palermo, Lazarists in Heidelberg, Piarists in Bohemia all gratefully took up the teaching positions recently vacated by Jesuits. But the odd thing about the disappearance of the Society of Jesus is that it never disappeared entirely. The partition of Poland in 1772 had placed 201 Jesuits within the territories of Catherine the Great. Not being inclined to do whatever the pope told her, Catherine refused to allow the bull of suppression to take effect in her realm. Russian Jesuits would sustain the Society's corporate existence all the way down to 1814, and for a while, until 1786, Jesuits in Prussia were allowed to do much the same thing. Over the coming years small Jesuit communities would reemerge across Europe: in Parma, in England, in Naples.

Even when former Jesuits were not granted official permission to regroup they were able to found new associations which sought to sustain the Jesuit ethos: thus the Fathers of Faith, the Fathers of the Sacred Heart, and the Select Body of the Clergy in the United States, established by former Jesuits in 1784.

This survival, the link between the old and new Societies, helped to define the man who would emerge as one of the most influential Jesuits of the nineteenth century, the Dutchman Johann Philipp Roothaan, twenty-first general of the order. He was born in Amsterdam in 1785, and part of his early education was supervised by an ex–Jesuit priest, Adam Beckers. Through him, Roothaan also learned of the survival of the Society in White Russia, and having sailed to Riga in 1804, Roothaan set out to pursue the time-honored route of Jesuit formation, taking his first vows in 1806, being ordained in 1812.

By the time he returned to Europe, forced out of Russia with his Jesuit brethren by Tsar Alexander I in 1820, the re-formed Society was already six years old. The challenges it faced—the legacy not just of the troubled pre-suppression years but of the ensuing decades of revolution and reaction—were colossal.

"The Catholic world demands with unanimous voice the reestablishment of the Society of Jesus." So claimed the papal bull for the Society's reestablishment. For one thing, this was not quite true—even in the wake of revolutionary excess there was still no shortage of un-Jesuited Catholics. For another, the Catholic world was simply not the privileged, secure place it used to be, or at least had claimed and aspired to be.[74]

7

"STILL ON A MILLION TONGUES"[1]

Jesuits Since 1814

. . . these new enemies of the Jesuits, to whom their former enemies have bequeathed their hatred, their fury, their ignorance and their perfidy; that is to say, they are even more hateful, more furious, more perfidious and, above all, more ignorant.

A Frenchman defends the Jesuits in 1827[2]

There is no doubt the Jesuits are the real men in Rome—i.e., we fall in with none others. I don't mean to say how great they are, but only they are the prominent men.

John Henry Newman, 1846[3]

They are attacked because of their pre-eminence. In this consists their guilt.

T. W. Allies, 1872[4]

Revival

In 1816, John Adams wrote to Thomas Jefferson about the return of the Society of Jesus. "I do not like the late resurrection of the Jesuits," he confessed; "shall we not have swarms of them here, in as many shapes and disguises as ever a king of gypsies . . . himself assumed?" Adams had been rereading his Pascal, along with a four-volume history of the Society, and had reached the conclusion that if "any congregation of men could merit eternal perdition on earth and in hell . . . it is this company of Loyola." Adams had to allow that, given "our system . . . of religious liberty," the United States might be obliged to "afford them an asylum," but he remained adamant that, given their history, "if they do not put the purity of our elections to a severe trial, it will be a wonder." Jefferson was apparently of a like mind—"I dislike with you their restoration, because it makes a retrograde step from light towards darkness"—and nor was it a uniquely American sentiment.[5] A letter had appeared in *The Times* of London on January 27, 1815, in which a correspondent registered "considerable surprise at the apathy and indifference which are manifested on the subject by the states of Europe in general, and by this country in particular."[6]

The mood was very different in Rome. "Amidst these dangers of the Christian republic," as the bull of Jesuit reestablishment put it, "we should deem ourselves guilty of a great crime towards God if . . . we neglected the aids which the special providence of God has put at our disposal." The bark of Peter was seemingly "tossed and assaulted" by continuous storms, so why not turn to the Jesuits, those "vigorous and experienced rowers who volunteer their services"?[7]

Revolution

There had never been a shortage of people eager to mock the telltale pomp and ritual of Catholicism, and religious processions had often struck such people as preeminently mockable. Take the "Protestant Gentlemen" of late-seventeenth-century London, for instance, whose "popish cavalcade" had moved out from Whitechapel, through Aldgate, along Leadenhall Street and Fleet Street, all the way to Temple Gate in November 1680. A series of floats carried men dressed as Franciscans, Minims, Benedictines, Dominicans, and, of course, some forty Jesuits, "a sore burden to the whole world, corrupters of all morality, Christianity and government." Then came bishops and cardinals, nuns dressed as whores, and "the man of sin himself," the pope, on a throne, being offered counsel by the devil. All intended to remind Londoners of the unfathomable depths of Catholic treachery, of popish plots, great fires, and the like, "to raise a just abhorrency of such popish practice."

Apparently, such reminders could draw an impressive crowd. "Never were the streets, windows and balconies more thronged with spectators." As fitting culmination, an "abundance of fuses like falling stars" were set off, a "great store of wine and other liquors were profusely poured out to the multitude," and, inevitably enough, the pope was burned in effigy. The prints memorializing these events, available from Nathaniel Porter at the Peacock near the Stock Market, John Wilkins at the Star in Cheapside, or Samuel Lee at the Feathers in Lombard Street, doubtless sold rather well.[8]

That Protestant Englishmen enjoyed lampooning Catholicism would have struck any European Catholic as unsavory but eminently par for the course. A century later, by contrast, it must have been much more alarming to hear that

Frenchmen, in the grip of revolution but also heirs to centuries of Catholic practice and devotion, were mounting mock processions of their own, complete with donkeys decked out in priestly vestments and bishops' miters. The anticlerical mood of revolution had found its outlet in the performance of antiritual.

At much the same time, sansculottes in the provinces were sending relics, or "disgusting bones" as they termed them, to Paris, plate and bells were being melted down, churches were being dedicated to a cult of Reason. When revolutionary troops reached Liège in 1794, the body of the Jesuit martyr Peter Wright, which had been lovingly cared for by local Jesuits for more than a century, suffered the indignity of being hurriedly stashed in a lead coffin and buried in the Jesuit college's garden.[9]

Here was a culture that, for a while, abandoned the Christian calendar, declared monastic vows illegal, and strove to replace religious martyrs with secular martyrs of liberty. In 1793, an urn containing the heart of the recently murdered Jean Paul Marat was greeted with applause as though, much like Voltaire recently entombed in the Pantheon, he were some new and better kind of saint: a saint, indeed, who would even be portrayed in paintings and busts with a halo around his head.

Such anticlerical excess was but a temporary stage in the lengthy, meandering course of revolution. Not everyone in France (perhaps not even *many* people in France) approved of such behavior, but such events did take place and they, quite reasonably, made Catholic Europe shudder. Nor could it have been any easier to hear about French priests, former Jesuits among them, who, refusing to swear an oath to the new Civil Constitution of the Clergy (seen by some as an effort to turn servants of Rome into salaried servants of the state), were being forced into exile or murdered. One traveler, arriving at Southampton in 1792, was so astonished at the number of Frenchmen he encountered there that he wondered whether his coach "had made a mistake and had carried us to a French town instead of an English one."[10]

Back in Paris in September 1792, some 220 priests (along with three bishops and no few aristocrats and prostitutes) would be massacred by crowds who were panicked by the arrival of a Prussian army at Verdun (a worryingly close 150 miles away) and who were eager to eradicate any potential traitors to the revolutionary cause. In 1768 it must have seemed to the Jesuit Alexander Lanfant that things had got as bad as they were ever likely to get. His religious order had been expunged from the French religious landscape, he had been granted sixty livres to buy some "secular clothes," and he had seen his possessions hastily sold off: couches, cupboards, a checked cotton mattress, a pine desk with four drawers (fifty livres), a copper candlestick (eighty sous).[11]

In fact, matters did start to improve over the next two decades. Lanfant would have his critics, but his clerical career did not wither away: he would preach to Maria Theresa in Vienna and to Louis XVI at Versailles. But his refusal to accept the Civil Constitution—"monstrous principles that are the scourge of religion"—led to his murder by a mob on September 5, 1792, by which date twenty-two of his fellow ex-Jesuits had shared a similar fate. September days that, by Thomas Carlyle's account, were on a par with the horrors of the St. Bartholomew's Day Massacre and the Sicilian Vespers, and which offered a glimpse into the "dim phantasmagory of the pit."

Mercifully, the radically anticlerical stage of revolution would not last, but it must still have been unsettling for a certain kind of Roman Catholic to be present at the Champ-de-Mars, in front of the Ecole Militaire, in July 1798, when booty from French military success in Italy arrived in Paris: bronze horses from St. Mark's, the wooden Virgin of Loreto, artworks and manuscripts from the Vatican and Capitoline Museums.[12] It would have been extraordinary if the papacy had not been affected by having one of its number, Pius VI, die in French captivity in 1799. As for Pius VII, while he was still only bishop of Imola he had suggested that seeking some accommodation with the ideals of revolution was not out of the question. Being abducted and carried to France in 1812, being held in captivity and virtual isolation, was always likely to radicalize his position.[13]

BY 1814, THE year in which the Jesuits fully reemerged, the Catholic Church was scandalized and stunned by the events of the previous two and a half decades. It was worried about the future security of thrones and altars, unsure of how to respond to the political and philosophical legacy of the revolutionary era and the previous century of novel, unsettling theorizing.[14] Over the coming decades there would be a troubling duty to engage with fashionable concepts like liberalism, capitalism, rationalism, free presses, democracy, pluralism, and religious toleration.

The nineteenth century did not represent some monolithic campaign to banish organized religion any more than the nineteenth century was descended exclusively from events in one country, France, over a couple of decades. The cultural and philosophical trends that emerged had a much lengthier, more impressive, and at times entirely separate pedigree. But as the decades advanced, the Catholic Church, not least its popes, did feel compelled to respond, to react, to what it found unpalatable in the postrevolutionary world. The material seemed to be stealing a march on the supernatural, and those eighteenth-century pundits who had merely denounced Catholicism as ludicrous were giving way to nineteenth-century pundits, be they Marx or Feuerbach or Nietzsche, who denounced it as something rather worse, as a blight, as a man-made illusion, as a positive evil. Philosophies emerged that rejected metaphysics and theology as pointless, impossible pursuits, beyond the scope of human experience, investigation, or observation.

It would seem as if the very things that defined the Catholic Church's place in society—a special, legally established place in former times—were in jeopardy. Many of the old clerical duties—from education to dispensing moral advice, to marrying and burying people—would continue to come under threat. Long-cherished links between church and state, the neat, mutually legitimizing contract between the spiritual and the secular (troubled as it had often been), would be seriously weakened. In America, an idealized, infectious model for the complete separation of church and state would be forged, and certain founding fathers would suggest that people's consciences and religious beliefs were entirely beyond the power and competence of government. Catholicism would be criticized for being out of step, for being too hierarchical, too centrist, too eager to claim a monopoly in helping human beings to salvation, too keen to squash protest in the pope's own territories.

Places where a person couldn't even waltz without censure, where, it was averred, fear of progress even prevented the arrival of gas lighting or steam trains.

Familiar internal squabbles between center and periphery (between Rome and national churches, between clergy and laity) would continue throughout the nineteenth century, and they became that much more confused when the very nature, the political identity, of the center was transformed. After the defeat of Austria at the battle of Solforino in 1859, region after region fell under the spell of Piedmontese-driven unification. By 1861 the pope lost control of most of his possessions, and with the withdrawal of a French protectionary army in 1870 the city of Rome itself was absorbed into the new Italian state. So-called Italian patriots had, so far as a papal pronouncement was concerned, outdone the shamelessness of the prodigal son by robbing the pope of his political independence, threatening his spiritual autonomy in the process. Reluctance to accept the concessions offered for the loss of the papal temporal power—a pension and continued control over the Vatican and Lateran Palaces—would distract the Catholic world and sour relations between the pope and the Italian government for decades to come.

Catholicism found itself in a quandary. How to deal with a Europe of towns and industry, with that curious new addition to Catholic flocks, the capitalist worker? What to make of a new addiction to democratic institutions, to the cult of the individual? How involved should Catholics become in the political life of the new Europe? How should they respond to a dazzling array of new and urgent social problems? And what of new departures in scholarship and science? Were innovative, disruptive ways of analyzing scripture and the Christian tradition legitimate?

Historical burdens, the pull of tradition and the deposit of faith, had to be placed in the balance with the need to accommodate, to engage, to do that thing which Catholicism has always taken its time in doing: change.

NOT, AS JESUITS well knew, that it was always just about intricate philosophical and theological debate. If Catholics had to formulate a response to the challenges of the nineteenth century, they also had to consider an enduring history of insult, dispersion, and violence of which revolutionary terror was really only the embarkation point.

Born in Switzerland in 1815, John Bapst arrived in New York in 1848 with barely a word of English. After missioning among the Penobscot, and a spell at the town of Eastport, Bapst moved to Ellsworth in 1853: a town with a population of four thousand, including some six to eight hundred Irish Catholic immigrants. Bapst made good headway, offering pastoral care to the Catholic community (until now without a priest), attracting Protestants to his Sunday afternoon lectures, and even winning over a number of converts—including the daughter of the Hancock County sheriff. But then he had the audacity to lend his support—organizing petitions, attempting to direct legal action—to the family of a Catholic girl who refused to read the Protestant King James Bible at school.

Such efforts won Bapst harsh criticism from the Protestant pulpits in the town. Articles and cartoons directed against the priest began to appear in the press, and in June 1854, the Protestant mob stoned the priest's house (he happened to be away) and the nearby Catholic church. Bapst was advised to stay clear of Ellsworth for his own safety, returning only in October. Then, on the night of the fourteenth, Bapst was dragged from a friend's house, his watch was smashed, and his wallet stolen. The crowd next undressed the priest, tarred and feathered him, and rode him on a rail to a shipyard a half mile away. Bapst, perhaps lucky to escape with his life, went on to a successful priestly career in Bangor and Boston, but the memory of these bizarre humiliations was said to have stayed with him until his death in 1885.[15]

Horrible enough indignities, yet not the worst the Society of Jesus would have to endure during the nineteenth century.

Jesuits and Their Enemies

Dear Philotheus, you have, I know, a strong, and to me, unaccountable partiality for the Jesuits; will you listen to me patiently if I ask you a few questions about them? . . . . There must be something very bad about the Jesuits when we see them driven with one accord from almost every country in Europe.

Philotheus and Eugenia, *1850*[16]

Unlike Samuel Sharp, Michael Hobart Seymour seemed rather taken with all that Rome had to offer when he visited the city during the 1840s. There was an opportunity to "gratify and indulge my taste for the arts among the most exquisite sculptures, and the most beautiful pictures, the greatest miracles of art in the world," or else "to wander among those scenes where lived and walked the heroes of the past." Time also to spend "mornings among the Jesuits," to learn a little more about the Roman Catholic faith, to discuss any number of burning theological issues. Seymour realized that many of the priests he encountered were trying to convert him—he was perceived as a conspicuously high church Anglican, after all—but he seemed to take this in good sort, and whatever his reservations about some aspects of "Romanism," he certainly did not balk at admiring the sensuality and spectacle of Catholic ritual in full flow.

Invited to a service at the Gesù, the Jesuits' mother church, he marveled at the pope singing the *Te Deum* surrounded by cardinals, at priests "in robes of white silk, damasked with the richest foliage of gold," all surrounded by "antique marbles and costly decorations" and the "sweetest and most beauteous music." From his privileged vantage point—a private gallery which he shared with an Italian princess and her companion—he confessed that "nothing could surpass the picturesque beauty of the spectacle, especially at the moment of the elevation of the host." An illuminated altar, boys from the Propaganda Fide dressed in scarlet, great wax candles, five feet tall, all in the spiritual center of the Society of Jesus: what tourist in search of a show could have asked for anything more?[17]

A decade or so later, it was the turn of Francis Amherst, future bishop of Northampton and a great friend of the Society of Jesus, to visit Rome and enjoy moments every bit as calm and leisurely. There was ample time to enjoy the pope's hospitality—he was "very kind, and has sent me presents of cakes and oranges"—and an opportunity to indulge in a little gossip: "The poor old king of Prussia," Amherst revealed to a correspondent, "goes about with his mouth open, looking quite idiotic. He washed his hands in the soup the other day, dining with the grand duke of Tuscany." A few years on, life in Rome appeared to be continuing on this gentle, untroubled keel and Amherst wondered if just about everyone in Europe was trying to get there. On his way to the city he had been on board a ship which also carried three cardinals and thirty-three bishops. When he reached Rome in early June 1862, preparations for a mass canonization were at such a pitch and "the carriages are in such requisition that some bishops are paying five pounds to go to the Vatican and back."

And if the hierarchy of the Catholic Church was inordinately busy, its laity seemed as passionate as it had ever been about their leader. When the pope had appeared one day in May, Amherst reported, "Swiss Guards were drawn up across the staircase to prevent people from passing, but a troop of French ladies made a violent charge and some succeeded in breaking the line of soldiers." Papal admirers, Amherst decided, were a sure sign that "the enthusiasm for the pope seems to be increasing, and one would think that Victor Emmanuel has no chance here." Here was a remark that would very quickly prove to be wildly overoptimistic.[18]

THE SON OF a cabinet maker from Reggio nell' Emilia, Angelo Secchi entered the Jesuit novitiate in Rome in 1833, aged fifteen. It had been some time since John Carroll, ex-Jesuit and the first bishop of Baltimore, had sensibly declared that "many years will be necessary to reproduce such men as formerly adorned the Society by their virtues and talents."[19] Secchi would undoubtedly play his part in refurbishing Jesuit reputations, but, crucially, contained within his story were both the potential for new and enviable Jesuit achievements and the threats and challenges that the Society of Jesus would be obliged to face during the nineteenth century and beyond.

Secchi's fame rests on his contributions to astronomy—an enduring Jesuit field of study, as we have already witnessed in the careers of priests like Ferdinand Verbiest and Maximilian Hell, and one that still thrives today thanks to the Society's guardianship of the Vatican Observatory and the thousand-pound mirror of the Mount Graham telescope near Tucson, Arizona. Over the course of his career Secchi would study the physical composition of comets, the rings of Saturn, solar radiation, storms in the atmosphere of Jupiter, and nebulae. He would be the first to refer to the "canals" on Mars, and the system he devised for categorizing stars according to their spectra—red giants, white dwarfs, and all—still bears his name.

Less happily, along with other Jesuits in the city (including theological luminaries such as Giovanni Perrone and Johann Baptist Franzelin), he would be compelled to leave Rome when the short-lived republic was established in 1848—not long after Seymour basked in ritual at the Gesù. He would find temporary shelter at the Jesuits' Stonyhurst College in England—where his forced arrival prompted one Jesuit to conclude that "irreligion and misrule seem to be the order of the day"—and at Georgetown University in Washington, D.C. Secchi returned to Rome in 1850 and was still there two decades later when the troops of a united Italy arrived in the city and stripped the Jesuits of their colleges and libraries. Most of his brethren headed into temporary exile at Florence and then Fiesole; Secchi, lauded scientist that he was, was granted permission to continue his work at the observatory. For all Francis Amherst's recent confidence, it turned out that Victor Emmanuel had rather a good chance in Rome after all.[20]

This was, in miniature, the story of the Jesuits in nineteenth-century Europe: efforts to rekindle the influence of an earlier era running in tandem with an endless stream of setbacks. And the story was hardly limited to the confines of Rome. Witness the journey of a fictional wandering Jew.

※

T H E M Y T H O F the wandering Jew had impacted on Europe's culture—literary, artistic, and oral, high and low—for several centuries. Ahasuerus, so the odd, uncomfortable story went, had made the foolish mistake of not showing pity to Christ as he carried his cross through the streets of Jerusalem en route to Calvary. He had refused to let Jesus rest at his door, urging him instead to "go on, go on." As punishment, Ahasuerus would be condemned to wander the earth for centuries, millennia perhaps, until the Second Coming: the time, it was suggested, when, among much other business, the Jews would voluntarily convert to Christianity.

Easily the most famous wandering Jew of the nineteenth century was the creation of Eugène Sue, ship's doctor–turned–serializing feuilletonist, who used his variation on the myth to launch a pitiless, far-fetched—though, for 1840s France, hardly exceptional—assault on the Jesuits, those so-called avaricious scoundrels and corrupters of French society. Men, apparently, of hideous appearance—with "almost invisible lips . . . little reptile eyes, half concealed by their flabby lids"; men with a penchant for beating the individuality out of people—exercising "that frightful species of influence which, acting only by despotism, suppression, and intimidation, breaks down all the living forces of the soul, and leaves it inert, trembling, and terrified."[21]

And needless to say, men with a dastardly plan to take over the world. Looking at his globe, one such Jesuit was sure to contemplate "in profound silence, the innumerable little red crosses, which appeared to cover, as with an immense net, all the countries of the earth. Reflecting doubtless on the invisible action of his power, which seemed to extend over the whole world, the features of this man became animated, his large grey eyes sparkled, his nostrils swelled, and his manly countenance assumed an indescribable expression of pride, energy, and daring."

Sue's *Le Juif errant* was a spectacular hit: during its serialization in *Le Constitutionnel* in 1844–45, the circulation of the newspaper leapt from thirty-six hundred to twenty thousand. However, it is another fictional wandering Jew, the creation of an author who looked rather more kindly on the Jesuits than Eugène Sue, who demands rather more of our attention. He has certainly heard of Sue—"a French novelist of no mean celebrity"—but as he tells a midcentury British audience, the Frenchman's decision to become his biographer, to use "me as the representative of a set of principles, which, in his judgement, would secure the happiness of mankind," was something of a disaster. "For 1800 years," he explains, "I have kept silence under every kind of ignominy." "Though I watched the rise and progress of the art of printing, from the wooden types at Haarlem, to the steam press of the Times newspaper, I have never before obtruded myself on the notice of the public." And this despite being "painted in red and yellow, with long beard and tattered garments, a grotesque caricature"; despite being made into a "bugbear to frighten children, a scapegoat for the crimes and follies of the multitude." "Every scandal," he complains, "and every indignity have been heaped in turn upon my head."

Now, however, it is time to break his silence. Having his own reputation ruined is one thing, but "I cannot agree to have history falsified and good men slandered." The good men are the Jesuits, pilloried in the wandering Jew's name by Eugène Sue, and not by Sue alone. Old enemies of the Society will be chastised over the course of this alternative wandering Jew's narrative: the Pombals and the Pascals, whose *Provincial Letters* are denounced as the armory from "which the enemies of the Jesuits have drawn their weapons" for two hundred years. But it is modern-day hatred of the Society that seems to alarm him most of all. He tells the reader of a journey through contemporary Europe, the most notable feature of which is that wherever he goes he seems destined to meet people who utterly loathe the Society of Jesus. He serves, in fact, as a reliable guide to many of the key sites and sources of anti-Jesuit sentiment, and his trail is worth following: the fictional characters he encounters and external, historical realities worth juxtaposing.[22]

IN SWITZERLAND, HE meets a man armed with sword and musket on his way to help "drive the Jesuits beyond the Alps." "They are wretches," he explains, "and not one of them shall be allowed to pollute the free soil of Switzerland."[23] As things turned out, in the real world of Swiss politics, he would soon get his way. Long worried about the preservation of their sovereignty and religious freedoms, the seven Catholic cantons of the Swiss Confederation formed a protective alliance, the Sonderbund, in 1845. An unimpressed, anticlerical-leaning diet declared this union illegal and called for the expulsion of the Jesuits (seen, quite unfairly, as the influence behind Catholic agitation). The Catholic cantons protested, a particularly nasty civil war broke out, the Catholic cantons were soundly defeated, and in 1847 the Jesuits were banished from Switzerland. They were not granted official permission to return until 1973.

Such events would doubtless have pleased another person encountered by the wandering Jew: a German student "basking in the sun." Striking a grand attitude with a telltale beard and pipe, the student talks "much of Greek plays and Roman antiquities, of Goethe and the German Fatherland," and recounts his dream of an entirely rational religion: "It is coming," he insists, "the day of the emancipation of the human mind—the triumph of reason over superstition, of liberty over priestcraft." His "worst enemies" in this struggle are, of course, the Jesuits: "We must drive them out of Germany, cost what it may"; we must paint "their black gowns blacker with the ink of twice ten thousand pens."[24]

By the time the German Empire was established in 1871 there was no shortage of real-life Germans—anticlerical liberals, Prussian Protestants concerned about union with the Catholic states of southern Germany, a chancellor troubled by the influence of Catholic parties in German politics—eager to contribute to such a task, even if not all of their motivations were quite so idealistic. A great deal happened over the course of Bismarck's Kulturkampf (culture war) of the 1870s: the freedom of Catholic pulpits was seriously curtailed, the Catholic contribution to German education was undermined, a bishop's right to freely make ecclesiastical appointments was attacked, candidates for the priesthood were even obliged to train only at those seminaries or universities recognized by the state.

In such a climate it was always unlikely that the Society of Jesus would emerge unscathed. Denouncing them as emissaries of Rome, the Reichstag enacted laws on July 4, 1872, that brought the Jesuits under the supervision of the police authorities. It was soon decided that they had no right to exercise any ministry in the German Empire—either in education or spiritual matters—and hundreds of Jesuits had little choice but to leave the country. Signs of dissent—such as the demonstration in Essen in which the mob attacked the home of a freemason (traditionally thought to be a fierce enemy of the Jesuits)—were only sporadic.[25]

It was a familiar story across Europe, and as politics twisted and turned, with regime supplanting regime, with antithetical ideological currents constantly in flux, there was always a good chance that, with the arrival of a new or newly energized government or political elite, the status of the Jesuit order would be one of the first items of business. Jesuit fortunes were apt to rise, fall, and rise again with almost comical frequency. It was like the 1760s all over again.

Take Spain, for instance. Welcomed back to the country in 1815, the Jesuits would be suppressed in 1820 when the insurrection of Major Rafael del Riego forced Ferdinand VII to swear to an unpalatable modernizing constitution. They would be back by 1823, after French armies had helped restore Ferdinand to his full authority, but when the dynastic struggle between his daughter Isabella and brother Carlos erupted in the 1830s, Jesuit fortunes would again plummet. When a cholera epidemic hit Madrid in July 1834, some of the citizenry accused the Jesuits (easily perceived as arch-Carlists) of poisoning the city's water supply. On July 17, crowds gathered at three of the city's main squares, where they chanted "Death to the Jesuits" and "Death to the friars." They converged on the Jesuits' San Isodoro Church and their Colegio Imperial, and fourteen members of the Society were killed. They were soon joined in the grave by dozens of Franciscans and Dominican fathers, and the next year the Society was once more banished from Spain. And so it went on. When Isabella came of age in 1851 Jesuits were welcomed back, the revolution of 1868 once more saw their dispersal, but they returned yet again with the Bourbon restoration of 1875.

Such dizzying stories were common across Europe: Jesuits were back in Portugal in 1829, exiled during the 1834 revolution, gained gradual reentry until official readmittance in 1858, and were suppressed again with the revolution of 1910. Which hardly leaves time to mention banishments from, among other places, Belgium in 1816, Russia in 1820, Galicia in 1848, and, further afield, Mexico in 1821, Guatemala in 1872, and Nicaragua in 1881.

It was in France, however, that the wandering Jew claimed to have witnessed the "anti-Jesuit fever at its height." People "would behold a Jesuit at every corner, lying in wait for their wives and children. I do not know what they feared the most—the Jesuits or the English." France's bizarre political chronology over the course of the nineteenth century would certainly have a hugely disruptive impact on the Society. Jesuit bashing emerged from a curious blend of political opportunism and deep-seated, long-standing prejudice.[26]

Already by 1823, François Dominique, comte de Montlosier, was complaining that the Jesuits (as it happened, present in the realm only in small numbers by this stage) were one of the "fleas" that all good Frenchmen ought to try to eradicate.[27] In 1828 the eight Jesuit educational establishments in France were closed down, and then, in 1830, came the decidedly anticlerical July revolution. A militantly resurgent Catholicism and a king, Charles X, who was seen by some as a reactionary Jesuit stooge were presumably in the minds of those crowds who attacked the archbishop of Paris, tore down missionary crosses, and on July 29 attacked and pillaged the Jesuits' Parisian house at Montrouge, taking time to drink a sarcastic toast to the health of Ignatius Loyola.[28]

In the wake of such events, the first years of the July Monarchy (1830–48) were much happier for the Society, but success was apt to breed resentment. Once representatives of a newly confident Catholicism began to criticize the secular hold over education, academics like Jules Michelet and Edgar Quinet at the Collège de France and writers such as Eugène Sue launched a bitter critique of the Jesuit presence in the country. One disgruntled Scottish Catholic mumbled that, in imitation of such men, it had become a rule on the European literary circuit that "every unfledged scribe must flourish his quill, and every self-important declaimer enounce his twaddle against the papacy and the Jesuits."[29] The government, in pursuit of calm as much as anything else, petitioned Rome to suppress the French branch of the Society, and although this remained out of the question, the closing of Jesuit establishments in Paris, Lyons, and Avignon was secured in 1845.

After the revolutionary days of 1848, the first two decades of the Second Empire were profitable times for the Society: the Falloux Laws of 1850 even enshrined the Jesuits' right to teach in the country. But then came the Paris Commune of 1871: a city under siege, freed from the control of a government languishing at Versailles, and containing radicals with undisguised anticlerical sympathies. At midnight on April 3, the college of St. Genevieve was surrounded by an armed battalion. After spells in the Conciergerie and the Mazas prison, during which supporters managed to smuggle the Blessed Sacrament in to the captives, the Jesuits Léo Ducoudray and Alexis Clerc were shot at La Roquette on May 24; for a while their bodies were abandoned, coffinless, in a pit at the Père Lachaise cemetery. Two days later in Belleville, Pierre Olivaint (rector of the house in the rue de Sèvres), Jean Caubert, and Anatole de Bengy met similar fates.[30]

After such harrowing events, the first few years of the Third Republic once more witnessed encouraging Jesuit growth in France—twelve new colleges were established after 1871—but then increasingly hostile ministries began to wield power, Catholic efforts to rally to the republic remained half-hearted, and Jesuits inevitably came under fire. In March 1880 the Council of Deputies carried a motion to dissolve the Society within three months, and by the end of June police were evicting Jesuits from the thirty-seven houses around France and sending them on their way across the border. A steady flow of these exiles began to return, but supposed involvement in the Dreyfus affair (a Jesuit conspiracy, by some accounts)[31] and the determinedly anticlerical ministries of Pierre Waldeck-Rousseau and Emile Combes brought the

Society into increasing disrepute. By 1905 Jesuit education had vanished from France and the Catholic Church had been wholly disestablished.

※

OF COURSE, SOME of the national representatives encountered by the wandering Jew never had the opportunity to bask in moments of outright Jesuit banishment, but there was still much satisfaction to be gained from hurling insults and rumor-mongering.

In 1851 Jean Claude Pitrat urged Americans to be wary of the "Jesuits, who fill the Roman Catholic Churches, invade your colleges, and educate your children, who are scattered everywhere in the richest cities of the United States, who are in Oregon, in California, wherever money is made, who you meet aboard of the steamboats and the railroads with a studied smile, eyes cast down, very modestly dressed, and with the most reserved posture."[32] Very much the kind of warning that the fictional American encountered by the wandering Jew seems to have taken to heart. They meet near Mont Blanc: "a very fine sight," the American has to admit, but hardly "finer than the falls of Niagara! After all, I have seen nothing superior to what may be found on the great American continent." He has in mind "our boundless plains, our trackless forests, our magnificent lakes, our mighty rivers, our cultivated fields, our thriving cities and our happy, happy people," not to mention "the just laws and free institutions under which we live and flourish."

But all this peaceful grandeur is apparently threatened by growing public suspicion of the Roman Catholic Church. The Jesuits, it seems, "have lately increased amongst us, and their doctrines are not compatible with the free spirit of the American people." Public order has grown fragile, and at present, Americans "have no mercy on rats, Jesuits and abolitionists." Jesuits might not have lit the fires that burned Catholic churches and Irish homes in Philadelphia in 1844, he admits, but they were surely responsible for aggravating those who did.[33]

Anti-Catholic sentiment was rife in the nineteenth-century United

States—a country that, despite the proud boasts of the religion clauses of the First Amendment, was very much a de facto Protestant society. Eminent, otherwise sensible people (Samuel Morse, as in the code, for instance) could talk of papal invasion forces; Ursuline convents could be burned in Boston in 1834; riots could erupt in Philadelphia in 1844 when local Catholics demanded the removal of Protestant Bibles from public schools. Charles Chiniquy claimed that the Society was behind the outbreak of the Civil War and Lincoln's assassination, and the Connecticut minister and revivalist Lyman Beecher warned of the dangers of letting Jesuits—men who were already "in full organisation, silent, systematised, unwatched, and unrestricted action amongst us"—travel around the new lands of the West as missionaries.[34]

It was in the West, Beecher suggested, that the "religious and political destiny of our nation is to be decided," and Thomas Jefferson Morgan, commissioner of Indian Affairs, was far from happy that Jesuits and nuns, "educated in foreign lands, who speak the English language indifferently, who know nothing by experience or training of public school work, who are not imbued with American ideas," were given free rein on the frontier.[35]

Most worrying of all, a national political party—the Know-Nothings—could stand on a xenophobic, antiimmigration, anti-Catholic platform and secure dozens of seats in the 1854 Congress. The same year, in fact, that John Bapst suffered those unfeasible indignities at Ellsworth, Maine.

Jesuits, one critic averred, were wily enough to realize that times had changed. They recognized the fact that, in the new age, "the scavenger had as much political power as the millionaire, and the ignorant labourer who was not fit for better work than the opening of a sewer, counted the same by his vote as the most cultured citizen." But this only made the Jesuits more dangerous. Beneath a veneer of democratic respectability they were apparently mobilizing Irish and German political influence from New York and Baltimore to Chicago and Cincinnati, to New Orleans and San Francisco.[36]

Popular resentment against the Jesuits often clothed itself in noble-sounding talk of the liberal, democratic spirit of the new republic, to which the Society of Jesus was allegedly antithetical: a throwback to medieval, theocratic political designs. Catholicism, by one account, was little more than "a system of darkness and slavery, mental, bodily and spiritual," and "nothing more directly at the antipodes to all our republican civic theories in legislation, and political economy can possibly be imagined." More often than not, however, Protestant Americans disliked all things Catholic because all things Catholic were associated with all things immigrant.[37]

THE UNITED KINGDOM may have lacked frontiers and American-style party machines, but it was certainly not short of equally fierce, equally outlandish—if rather differently motivated—anti-Jesuit feeling. Such, at least, is the impression given by the next group encountered by the wandering Jew. "I knew they were Englishmen at a glance," he explains, "by their keeping aloof from the rest, and looking as if the whole universe belonged to them by right of birth." Chief among their concerns are the unchecked rise of Catholic education in Britain and the Jesuits' sponsoring of Irish political activism: "Were it not for them, the Irish would starve upon potatoes and yet be contented and happy."[38]

And this, so the Reverend William Patterson told an Edinburgh audience in 1893, was only one aspect of the "great Jesuit plot of the nineteenth century." He hoped his audience would "watch with an intelligent eye the further development of the intrigue for the subjection of the nation to Rome." "In the recent work of the [Jesuit] order," he warned, "the popish world is reconstructed," and a "new fresh project for the conquest of the globe and for the reconstruction of human society" was being devised, the ultimate aim being to "plant the foot of the pope on the neck of a prostrate mankind."[39] Some Protestant Britons believed they had much to fear from events of the nineteenth century—Anglicans like Newman and Manning were going over to Rome; Catholic educational establishments were being founded and financially supported across the country (which, a Cheltenham audience heard in 1826, represented the "christening and endowing [of] the bitter tribes of Jesuitism with a property in the British soil");[40] there had been the revival of a

Catholic hierarchy of bishops in England and Wales in 1850 (the famous act of "papal aggression"); and who could ignore the loud campaigns by Catholics and Irishmen to assert their rights?

If one required an explanation for such troubling developments, it was regularly suggested that one need look no further than the Jesuits. The religious sympathies of Albert Close are not immediately discernible by looking at the titles of some of his books—*The Dover Patrol Naval Operations* or *The Truth about Jutland,* for instance—although others, such as *The Great Harlot on the Seven Hills* or *Babylon the Scarlet Woman,* offer heavier hints. By the time he composed his *Jesuit Plots from Elizabeth to George V* in 1936, he was adamant that he could look back on a century of steady Romanist infiltration and damage. There were the Catholic historians turning out falsified accounts of the past, Catholics winning unseemly influence in the media and the Foreign Office, the unwholesome spectacle of kings of England, princes of Wales, and prime ministers visiting the pope, of the Royal Navy saluting the pope as though he were some sovereign head of state.

Close had been accustomed to launching such rants on a speaker's platform near the Tower of London and he had apparently received an excellent response. "Tower Hill crowds," he was happy to report, "contrary to the popular conception are, with the exception of say about ten percent of a rough element, the best educated, most intelligent and influential open air crowds in Britain."[41] He had doubtless been preaching to the choir, and to assume that large swaths of the British public were amenable to such rampant anti-Catholicism would be a mistake. But sentiments such as Close's had been able to find a receptive audience over the past century, and the Englishmen the wandering Jew encountered on his travels were not simply a figment of his creator's imagination.

Jesuits, some had claimed, where just about everywhere. Not just infiltrating the press or Parliament, but on every street corner. A story was said to have circulated in a Cambridge senior common room about an Englishman who, returning home after years abroad, was shocked to see a Jesuit he had once met now disguised in the humble blue apron of a butcher. It was a foolish person who, "relying upon the assumed irresistible advances of the human intellect," now chose to "contemplate the doctrines of popery with any less disgust."[42]

※

IT IS IMPORTANT to realize that when a nineteenth-century politician or propagandist shouted "Jesuit" or "Jesuitism" he was not necessarily referring specifically to members of the Society of Jesus. Such words had long since emerged as general anti-Catholic terms of abuse. But even when actual Jesuits were being attacked, it would also be wrong to assume that all their enemies hated them for the same reason. It was not always a simple matter of self-styled forward thinkers, people imbued with fashionable nineteenth-century notions of democracy and liberalism, railing against the so-called backwardness of the Society of Jesus—a body, it was suggested, that was patently undemocratic, that was ruled over by a hierarchy that suppressed individualism, and that dreamed of a return to a disreputable kind of political culture.

Sometimes it was about nationalism, about resentment of a body of men with a supranational loyalty to Rome; sometimes it was about age-old Protestant prejudice or anti-immigrant bigotry; sometimes it was about not much more than the backbiting and intriguing of parliamentary politics. Thinking about rebellion and agitation in Ireland and Poland, John Elliot, rather than seeing them as agents of reaction, criticized the Jesuits for stirring up unhealthily modern, liberal attitudes. Jesuits were apparently behind those observers who never stopped invoking "popular platitudes about liberty and tyranny," those who complained about nasty, authoritarian regimes like "hysterical young lasses." Jesuits failed to see that subduing Polish nationalism, rescuing Poles from their "natural temperament" and "bigoted religion," was rather a good thing: no more heinous, Elliot suggested, than ridding the Welsh of their ugly, impenetrable language. It represented nothing more sinister than "the policeman seizing with resolution an unmanageable street ruffian" or "the executioner inflicting due pain upon a scoundrel."[43]

It is also worth noticing that, for much of the time, the charges leveled at the Jesuits would bear a striking, unimaginative resemblance to those rolled out in earlier centuries. Familiar accusations of peddling corrupt moral advice would certainly endure, and a Glasgow audience in 1831 would hear jaded tales of Jesuits—"the pope's bodyguard"—counseling that "smutty conversation is a thing indifferent in itself" and that "it is lawful for persons of all qualities, conditions and sexes to go into places of common prostitution."[44] Politicking was also still reckoned to be a peculiarly Jesuit addiction and members of the Society were still portrayed as "designing political agents, creeping up backstairs into the cabinets of princes, familiar with trapdoors and sliding panels." Events as wildly disparate as the meeting of the socialist First International in 1864, the Franco-Prussian conflict of 1870–71, and the Boer War would all be linked to the Society. Even William Gladstone was thought by some to be a Jesuit agent.[45]

In spite of such subtleties and continuums, it remained very easy for nineteenth-century Roman Catholics (many Jesuits among them) to attribute their woes first and foremost to novel, disruptive, peculiarly nineteenth-century cultural and intellectual trends. Of course, this process of blame, analysis, and reaction was not all that nineteenth-century Catholicism was about. Not every Catholic, and certainly not every Jesuit, would agree that fashionable political and philosophical trends were the devil's work. Some would avidly seek to baptize revolution, to see potential and protection in free churches in free states. But the balancing of conflicting urges to react and to refashion, to augment tradition and reassert the Church's relevance and uniqueness, certainly devoured a disproportionate amount of Catholic energies.

Beyond the Mountains: Rome's Response

In times of crisis and upheaval, the Catholic Church, eager to foster unity and courage, has always turned to its symbols. And as the nineteenth century came to a close, the pope decided to talk about the Sacred Heart of Jesus—"a symbol and a sensible image of the infinite love of Jesus Christ." It was needed "in these latter times especially" because there was "a wall being raised between the church and civil society" aimed at securing the "exclusion of religion from having any constant part in life." The ultimate goal was nothing less than "the banishment of God himself from the earth."[46]

Of all objects, as a Jesuit put it in the eighteenth century, the Sacred Heart was "the noblest, the holiest, the greatest, the most divine and altogether the most sweet and most amiable that can possibly be conceived." Not merely "an inanimate piece of flesh" but something burning with the love of God, filled with news of the salvation of mankind, the place from which the church and its sacraments had flowed. But also something fragile, a heart "that is offended, insulted and despised by unthinking man, by sinners void of all sense of gratitude and unaffected by [Christ's] love," people besmirched by trepidity and pride.[47]

And this, some Catholics had been heard to say more and more during the nineteenth century, was the real risk, the real and urgent problem. The role of the Sacred Heart was not merely to "raise us to most ardent love" or to offer consolation, but also to inspire the "greatest sorrow." There was room for "reparation for [the] wrongs and outrages" the Sacred Heart suffered daily, room to "make amends."[48] St. Gertrude had been told, centuries earlier in medieval Saxony, that knowledge of the Sacred Heart had been reserved until a later, colder age. As a decade of revolution seemed to give way to a nineteenth century in thrall to secularism, liberalism, and anticlerical posturing, those Catholics, many Jesuits included, who believed their church to be under siege turned to the Sacred Heart of Jesus as an act of contrition, to apologize for their modern times, but also as an act of defiance and solidarity.

The bleeding, burning heart of an incarnate, miraculous God was something easily ridiculed. A certain breed of intellectual could see nothing but farce in something that claimed to represent the mystical, twofold nature of Jesus Christ: the incarnate Word, possessed of divinity, but also of fleshy, frail humanity—woundable and killable. But the louder the scoffing grew, the more important it was to offer devotions to a symbol of Catholicism so easily understood: the "fountain of all graces," the "furnace of love," an "ocean of bounty," the "terror of the devils" and "delight of all the saints."[49] Care had to be taken to prevent devotion descending into mawkish sentimentality, but devotion there had to be. There was no better way to survive the challenges of the nineteenth century than to dwell on something that made Catholicism special.

As the nineteenth century progressed, devotion to the Sacred Heart, a regional, if always reputable, phenomenon in earlier periods, expanded at a fantastical rate. The feast of the Sacred Heart, authorized since 1765, was extended to the whole church in 1856, becoming a grandiloquent-sounding "double rite of the first class" in 1889. Jesuits, who had adored the heart for centuries, counseling its visionaries, putting its image on the walls of their churches, as a frontispiece in their books, were eager to sustain the tradition. They established apostleships of prayer to secure its devotion; a Jesuit such as Joseph Mary Rubio would mold a five-thousand-strong honor guard of the Sacred Heart in Madrid, and the Society would dedicate all of its provinces to the Sacred Heart in 1872. Individual cities and countries (Ecuador in 1873, for instance) steadily followed suit: in 1875 the pope would dedicate all Catholics to the Sacred Heart and, in 1899, the entire human race. When proof had been required that the Catholic world would welcome such momentous developments, Jesuits like Henri Ramière had avidly helped the cause, collecting signatures of approval from bishops in their hundreds and the laity in their millions.

The Sacred Heart was always about traditional kinds of devotion—medals, prayers, and meditations—and its intercession was doubtless always welcome. It could apparently save houses from flooding, heal the sick from Amiens to Bohemia, help the pious when fighting righteous lawsuits, and get suitably Catholic-minded mayors elected. It was even suggested that it could speed up postal services so that a much-needed telescope might reach a Catholic-run observatory in time for a transit of Venus. But sometimes there was something overtly political about the heart's place in Catholic affections.[50]

It had been a symbol for the peasants of the Vendée as they faced revolutionary troops in 1795, for the four cantons of the Austrian Tyrol as they faced a French revolutionary army a year later.[51] And after the war of 1870–71, in the wake of German invasions and the anticlerical excesses of the Paris Commune, what better rallying call could there be for French Catholic revival than the Sacred Heart, what better object to name votive churches for? Paris would erect its impudent symbol of modernism, the Eiffel Tower, but the city's skyline could also offer the beginnings of an ovoid-domed alternative in the Sacré Coeur baptistry on Montmartre: not very far, as it happened, from the place where the Jesuit experiment had begun three centuries earlier.[52] The Sacred Heart would be adopted by extremists on the Catholic right, it would become a refuge for Catholics who basked in an exaggerated (and officially frowned upon) brand of fideism, but it would also sustain a special place, a special power, in the affections and strategies (devotional and political) of the Catholic mainstream.[53]

AND IF REMINDING the world of a uniquely Catholic devotion was one way of confronting the nineteenth century, turning to the detail of Catholic ecclesiology was another.

Papal infallibility does not mean that whatever the pope says is infallibly true. If he were to announce over dinner one evening that parmesan is the best cheese in the world, every Catholic would not have to agree. Advocates of camembert or cheddar could conclude that the Holy Father has a poor palate, and their eternal souls would be unlikely to suffer as a result.

But as the First Vatican Council (1869–70) declared, things are very different when, ex cathedra, "as the pastor and teacher of all Christians in virtue of his highest apostolic authority," he defines "a doctrine of faith and morals that must be held by the Universal Church." At such a juncture, the papal teacher is held to be empowered, "through the divine assistance promised him in blessed Peter," with the infallibility that Christ "willed to endow his Church." Ultimately, only God is infallible, and once more, the pope is merely imbued with the infallibility that Christ gave to the church. It is about a *charism*, a gift: it concerns the pope as the pastor of all Christians, not the pope as one more brilliant or mediocre theologian. At such moments, when the magisterial authority is exercised in the highest degree, the church—and this can sometimes mean not only the pope alone but, on occasion, the pope in consort with others—cannot, by definition, fall into error. Whatever doctrinal pronouncement emerges must be consented to by Roman Catholics from Glasgow to Mexico City to Seoul.

The First Vatican Council—only the twentieth general, or ecumenical, council in the history of the church, the first since the Council of Trent—was a momentous, endlessly discussed event. Francis Amherst, one of the seven hundred bishops to participate, admitted that it was "rather difficult sometimes to be quite guarded as to our obligation of secrecy," what with all the rumors circulating about divisions among the delegates. The press doesn't "know what to write and are obliged to invent" tales of discord, he complained, whereas, in fact, "nothing can be more quiet, orderly and cordial than the relations of the bishops at all the meetings; and the liberty of speech is perfect."[54]

Perhaps, but what Amherst would have struggled to deny was that formulating a definition of papal infallibility was creating serious rifts within the Catholic world. Some feared that a *"magna carta* of ecclesiastical absolutism" was in the offing. Others suggested that much more careful theological thought was needed before making such a momentous pronouncement—just what did "a doctrine of faith and morals that must be held by the Universal Church" really mean? And what of ecumenical relations with other Christian churches? How would an Anglican or a Lutheran react to talk of infallible popes?

Some delegates left Rome to avoid participation in the voting on infallibility; two bishops—of Cajazzo, southern Italy, and of Little Rock, Arkansas—went so far as to oppose the measure at the final solemn session; all the rest assented to (which was not the same as approved of) the declaration that emerged. It was instantly rebelled against by small sections of the faithful in Austria, Germany, and Holland, who fell into schism with Rome and emerged as the so-called Old Catholics.

As a matter of history, papal infallibility has, by most calculations, only ever been exercised on one occasion—with the declaration in 1950 that Mary, Mother of God, had been taken up in body as well as soul into heaven. As a matter of theology, papal infallibility as defined at Vatican I could be construed as something of a fudge. It was certainly less than extreme ultramontanes had hoped for, and it would lead to ongoing debates about just what had been defined—it has nicely been referred to as "a kind of Pickwickian infallibility."[55] Discussing it in controversial ways would still be able to blight a brilliant theological career such as that of Hans Küng as late as 1979.

Nonetheless, perception and point making mattered at least as much as substance, and enshrining the notion of the "infallible magisterium of the Roman pontiff" can reasonably be seen as the high-water mark of papal efforts to bring order, authority, and energy to the church in face of a world with which it had serious, enduring problems. This lengthy campaign was hopeful that persistent critiques of papal absolutism could be blunted (although the risk was that they might be aggravated) by sending out loyal nuncios around the Catholic world, by striving for control over the church's hierarchy and ever more assertive laity, by encouraging the delation of turbulent priests to the Holy Office, by promoting characteristically Roman devotions and papally approved pilgrimage sites, by devising a Code of Canon Law (1917) and compelling bishops to make regular trips to Rome to meet the pope face-to-face. If a pope enjoyed a reign as long as Pius IX (1846–78), the potential for stamping his authority on the church was considerable: by the time Vatican I met, those bishops who had been consecrated under earlier popes were in a tiny minority.

THE CHURCH HAD settled on two broad strategies, then: emphasizing the sources of Catholic pride and originality (witness the Sacred Heart) and dwelling on the nature of papal power. And if such tactics could have been combined, then the mid-nineteenth-century Vatican would naturally have been delighted. Such an opportunity had arisen in December 1854, with the promulgation of the dogma of the immaculate conception.

Despite a common misunderstanding, the immaculate conception is not about Jesus Christ being born "immaculately" from the virginal body of Mary. It refers to the perhaps equally controversial assertion that Mary, unlike the rest of humanity, was herself born as an immaculate being: a person, "all fair and perfect," without the stain of original sin. This is an explosive idea. Theologians down the centuries have worried (though sophisticated rebuttals are available) that it chips away at the significance of Christ's sacrifice on Calvary. If Mary was without original sin, then why did she need Christ to save her? And if she did not need Christ to save her, then does that not demolish the notion of the absolute universality of Christ's salvific work?

By the nineteenth century the idea of an immaculate Mary was broadly acceptable within the Roman Catholic tradition: she was making appearances in the Savoyard countryside, she was being chosen by American bishops when they needed a figure to which the United States could be consecrated, and an Immaculate Heart of Mary was emerging as a privileged object of devotion alongside the Sacred Heart of her son. The idea continued to appall a good many Protestants and philosophical opponents of Catholicism, but that only meant that talking about it served to announce what made Catholicism unique: an announcement rendered all the louder by visions of the Virgin at La Salette in 1846, at Lourdes in 1858, and at Fatima in 1917—at the height, significantly enough, of a Portuguese anticlerical storm.

But the real opportunity was to assert the dogma of the immaculate conception without calling or consulting anything as democratic as a general council. Consultation with the worlds' bishops there certainly was, but the papal bull *Ineffabilis Deus,* promulgated on December 8, 1854, was precisely that—a *papal* bull. Catholic uniqueness and papal power combined in a single gesture. "Hence, if anyone shall dare—which God forbid!—to think otherwise than as has been defined by us, let him know and understand that he is condemned by his own judgement; that he has suffered shipwreck in the faith; that he has separated from the unity of the Church."[56]

The Society of Jesus was reckoned to be delighted with such developments, with this molding of a resurgent, ultramontane church. Jesuits were not represented at Vatican I in huge numbers, but their influence, not least through the contributions of Johann Franzelin and Superior General Pieter Beckx, was considerable. To be sure, many Jesuits had been supporting the idea of papal infallibility for centuries—ever since Diego Laínez at the

Council of Trent—so it was probably fitting that Giovanni Perrone, professor at the Roman College, should have helped prepare the first draft of the infallibility pronouncement. The fiercer critics of infallibility such as the English historian John Acton and his former teacher, the Munich-based theologian Johann Ignaz von Döllinger, suspected that the Society of Jesus was the main impetus behind the declaration.

As for the immaculate conception, the Jesuit Carlo Passaglia, although he grew rebellious later in his career, contributed to the first draft of the papal declaration, which, again, placed him firmly in a long-standing Jesuit tradition. Sixteenth-century pictures representing an immaculate Mary had been provided for the Society's Florentine church by Bartolomeo Carducci; Jesuits had imposed vows in eighteenth-century Sicily to shed blood if necessary in defense of the immaculate conception. If it looked as if popes were determined to create a revitalized Catholic civilization, then the Jesuits' influential journal *Civiltà Cattolica* would steadily lend its support to the pope's initiatives.

Not that Catholic revanchism was limited to bold, positive assertions of what made the church special. Just as much energy needed to be expended on criticizing those trends, within the ranks of the faithful as well as in the wider world, which needed to be resisted. This was never a common Catholic cause. It did not appear obvious to every member of the church that democracy, or disestablished churches, or modern trends in scholarship and philosophy were anathema. As we will see, even successive bearers of the papal tiara managed to reach different conclusions about such issues. But for a good many Catholics, the modern world was riddled with errors that needed to be exposed and placed in sharp contradistinction to more righteous alternatives. Once again, the Society of Jesus would play a starring role.

THE FAMOUS SYLLABUS of Errors, an eighty-item-strong list of despicable propositions, had been in the offing for many years before it was attached to the papal encyclical *Quanta cura* in 1864: it was actually built upon papal announcements and allocutions from the previous decade and more. For all that, its timing was exquisite. Döllinger and the supporters of Catholic academic freedom, and advocates of liberal Catholicism, a Catholicism that sought accommodation with contemporary society, had met, respectively, at Munich and Malines in the previous year. It seemed to some that the mighty rebuttal of the idea that the Roman "pontiff can and ought to reconcile himself with progress, liberalism, and modern civilization" was urgently needed.

Efforts were made, by Bishop Dupanloup and others, to put a conciliatory gloss on the Syllabus—the pope, so the theory went, despaired only of what was noxious in modern civilization, not every last aspect of it—but Pius IX's uncompromising anatomization of his culture's sins and mistakes struck many onlookers as part of an attempt to rivet medievalism on the neck of the church. Along with his securing of papal infallibility, the Syllabus was pivotal in the creation of Pius IX's image as reactionary, dictatorial pope par excellence, a man who wanted nothing whatever to do with the nineteenth century—an image that still provoked misgivings in some Catholic circles when Pio Nono was up for beatification during the 1990s.

Papal criticism of modern civilization was a many-headed creature. The special role of Catholicism was avidly defended. Suggestions that the church did not enjoy eternal rights, that it was up to the civil power to determine the church's status, or the idea that politics and society could be conducted without reference to God or religion were bitterly pilloried. There was thought to be a terrible and growing risk of Europe collapsing into the chaos of indifferentism: was it not absurd to suggest that every man should be allowed to profess whatever faith the light of reason led him to, or that salvation was possible outside of the Catholic tradition, or that liberty of conscience and worship and freedom of speech were inalienable rights?

Extreme rationalism—the idea that reason alone should dictate mankind's religious, or any other, beliefs—was no less dangerous than immanentism or pantheism, the idea that God could be wholly identified with his creation. And both were just as horrific as materialism and naturalism, heresies that outlawed the supernatural, the providential actions of God, and suggested that the physical world was the be-all and end-all of the cosmos. There was much talk of liberalism, but did that not really mean license? True liberalism surely meant being granted the opportunity to live one's life in conformity with the divine law. There was much talk of the individual, but did such talk not damage precious notions of the communal and the social?

And if there was no shortage of big ideas, it was as well to realize that they often turned out to be godless ideas. Laissez-faire capitalism and the command economics of socialism seemed to be at opposite extremes of the political spectrum, but both of them produced class antagonism, and both lacked the slightest moral content, replacing God with empty laws of the market or dialectical materialism. Prophets of an inevitable progress, so the papal line went, were surely damned by the products of their own theorizing.

And worse yet, such ideas had infiltrated the church itself. Frenchmen like Joseph de Maistre (diplomat and fervent royalist) and François René de Chateaubriand (rationalist critic of Christianity–turned–devoted Catholic) had done much in the early nineteenth century to enunciate a conservative reaction to revolution and its aftermath. Thrones and altars were to be seen as safeguards, as buffers against a return to the tragedies of the Terror. Christianity was to be privileged above philosophy, powerful popes were preferable to overconfident national churches, kings and established churches were better than elected assemblies and liberal constitutions, tradition was a safer bet than innovation. As had been manifestly proven, national churches could not always rely on the protection of national governments: far better to shelter in the ultramontane glow of a powerful pope.

The French priest Félicité Robert de Lamennais did not disagree with all of this: he was as committed a supporter of ultramontanism as any of his contemporaries. What he did not accept was the idea that religion and civil authority ought to be united: such union, he suggested, had always carried more risk than advantage. In the modern world, in which Catholicism was undoubtedly threatened, was it not better to separate church and state, to permit religious liberty, to allow Catholicism to become a free church in a free state, one more option in the marketplace of ideas? This was the finest guarantor of Catholic rights. For the church to be free, all must be free: special privileges should give way to the rule of law, to free presses, free consciences, to expanded suffrage. Advertising such ideas, calling for the reconciliation of Catholicism and democratic liberalism—a cause shared by liberal Catholics such as the historian Charles René de Montalembert and the Dominican preacher Henri Lacordaire—infuriated Rome. Magazines such as *L'Avenir* were quashed, and the liberal Catholic agenda was denounced in the encyclicals *Mirari vos* (1832) and *Singulari nos* (1834).

The perils of adapting to the times could even trouble a relatively progressive pope like Leo XIII. When, later in the century, it began to look as if certain American, especially Irish-American, theologians and church leaders were arguing for a new kind of church designed to suit contemporary tastes, Rome once more felt obliged to act. There was no place for a version of apologetics aimed at winning over non-Catholics, nor for an integrated Catholicism at ease with a separated church and state and the religious freedoms of the First Amendment. The apostolic letter *Ad testem benevolentiae* of 1899 insisted that Catholic teaching was the same in all times and all places— not something to be conveniently adapted, not a pick-and-mix theology, the more difficult aspects of which could be downplayed in order to put modern audiences at their ease.

Worse yet was the creeping tide of modernization and adaptation within the Catholic academy. What was this talk of utilizing Kant, Fichte, or Hegel in Catholic theology, or of allowing Catholic theologians total freedom of inquiry? Applying the rubrics and techniques of secular historians to the study of scripture and church tradition, writing lives of Christ as though he were just one more historical figure, doubting the literalness or historical veracity of the Bible: these were surely lamentable developments. Could it sensibly be asserted that what the church teaches had been determined by local, time-specific factors just like every other historical process? Was church teaching to be regarded not as a matter of cast-iron dogmas, but as an organic, evolutionary process to which the whole Catholic community ought to contribute?

When such trends seemed to culminate in the so-called Modernist crisis of the early twentieth century, with the radical theorizing of Catholic priests like Alfred Loisy and George Tyrrell, the decree *Lamentabili* and the encyclical *Pascendi dominici gregis* (both 1907) sought to outlaw them from Catholic discourse. By 1910 all teachers at seminaries and Catholic universities, all priests and candidates for the priesthood were obliged to swear an anti-Modernist oath.

The trouble with the attacks on liberal Catholicism, Americanism, and especially Modernism was that Rome was more interested in creating bogeymen than responding to complex, diverse intellectual movements. Many of those ruined by accusations of Modernism—and a veritable witch-hunt took place—were simply not part of a systematized, synthesized movement. But attacking conveniently stereotyped schools of thought was a useful way for the Catholic Church to impose an idealized response to the modern world, and it was an attack to which members of the Society of Jesus often contributed.

It was perhaps no coincidence that the doyen of ultramontanes, Joseph de Maistre, had a father with the decidedly Jesuitesque name of François Xavier de Maistre, nor that his family went into private mourning when the Society was suppressed in France, nor that some of the research for de Maistre's pope-adoring classics was undertaken, in exile, at the Jesuits' St. Petersburg Library.[57] The Jesuits' journal *Civiltà Cattolica* would lead the calls for a syllabus of modern errors, and when such a syllabus emerged in 1864 professors at the Jesuits' Roman College played a major role in its drafting. Its content was disseminated by Jesuit journals such as *Stimmen der Zeit* and *Stimmen aus Maria-Laach* in Germany, *Etudes* in France, and *The Month* in England; it was translated into German by the Jesuit Klemens Schrader.

Civiltà Cattolica also called for a denunciation of Americanism, and the papal letter which answered that call was prepared by the Jesuit Camillo Mazzella. Jesuit approval of the papal line would sour relations between the Society and sections of the American parish clergy well into the twentieth century. In the early part of the nineteenth century, the German philosopher and theologian George Hermes had begun suggesting that the thought of Immanuel Kant might make a useful contribution to Catholic theology: he would later be roundly condemned by the influential Jesuit theologian Giovanni Perrone. And when modern biblical exegesis needed to be undermined, the German Jesuit and renowned biblical scholar Karl Josef Rudolf Cornely helped produce the encyclical *Providentissimus Deus* in 1893.

A major strategy in the papal reaction to such modernizing academic trends was to turn to the systematized scholastic thought of Thomas Aquinas. As the encyclical *Aeterni Patris* put it in 1879, because "false conclusions concerning divine and human things . . . have now crept into all orders of the state," the wisdom of Aquinas was much needed: "like the sun he heated the world with the warmth of his virtues and filled it with the splendour of his teaching." Aquinas was the model that right-thinking theologians ought to follow, and this was what Italian Jesuits such as Matteo Liberatore, sometime editor of *Civiltà Cattolica,* had been saying for years. When the Pontifical Biblical Institute was established in 1909 to enshrine this theological orthodoxy, it was placed in Jesuit hands.

GEORGE TYRRELL WAS the Jesuit rebel par excellence, an eloquent champion of the Modernist agenda so despised by Rome. Having been expelled from the Society of Jesus, having been excommunicated from the church, he would be denied the right of Catholic burial when he died in 1909. Four years earlier he had written to Superior General Luis Martin that "the Society has become an avowedly reactionary institution; I am, and always will be, impenitently progressive. As such, my position in her ranks is dishonest, unfair to her and to myself."[58]

Was this fair comment? Given Jesuit support for the main pillars of papal resurgence—infallibility, the immaculate conception, the Syllabus, the return to Aquinas—it might seem as if it was. It should be noted, however, that Tyrrell was not the first Jesuit to take up unpopular positions. Franz Quarella had argued *against* the declaration of infallibility, suggesting that the consent of the world's bishops was required for a doctrinal statement to be reckoned infallible. Luigi Taparelli d'Azeglio was an advocate of a unified Italy and of a liberalism stripped of its anticlerical leanings. Carlo Curci made the mistake of suggesting that the loss of papal temporal power was no bad thing since it would allow the pope to concentrate more fully on matters of the spirit.

Others had subscribed to the view that broad religious freedom was the most likely way to protect Catholic interests in the modern world. So many Jesuits had been suspected of holding pro-Lamennais sympathies in the 1830s that public denunciations of liberal Catholicism and a swath of expulsions from the Society were thought necessary. A similar crisis rocked the Society in the years of the Modernist crisis.

Nineteenth-century Jesuits were not simply papal lapdogs. Relations between the Society and the Vatican were often as strained as they had ever been, and although *Civiltà Cattolica* was, as we have seen, a reliable supporter of papal positions, it is as well to remember that the Jesuits' superior general had resisted the journal's foundation precisely because he feared it would bring the Society into unnecessary controversy.

For all that, if a normative nineteenth-century Jesuit mentality existed at all, it was surely dominated by a desire to react cautiously and conservatively to the political, social, and intellectual maelstrom of the post-revolutionary world. This did not mean that everything the Society, or the church as a whole, did was blinkered and negative. There was, as one example, imagination and courage involved in the response to capitalism's seemingly unstoppable ascent. But the fact that many within the Catholic Church, not least the Jesuits, felt more alienated from Western civilization than at any time in the previous millennium, the fact that they lived in perpetual fear of the spread of socialist and communist ideas, and that they were tempted toward (or backward to) philosophies and theologies that others (rightly or wrongly) saw as moribund, would make the coming century interesting, to say the least. It would also make the transformation of the Society into what it is today—a very distant cousin of its nineteenth-century self—all the more extraordinary.

8

The Fifth Jesuit Century

Today we bring this counter-cultural gift of Christ to a world beguiled by self-centred human fulfillment, extravagance, and soft living, a world that prizes prestige, power, and self-sufficiency. In such a world, to preach Christ poor and humble with fidelity and courage is to expect humiliation, persecution, and even death.

Decree 26, thirty-fourth general congregation, 1995

The Legacy

As reward for his evangelizing efforts among the Ruthenians of southeast Poland, Andrew Bobola had endured horrible tortures in the early summer of 1657. A group of Cossacks had dragged him with a rope, whipped him, plucked one of his eyes from its socket, slit his lips and nostrils, cut out his tongue, stretched him on a butcher's table, torn the skin from his head and hands, stabbed him with an awl, hung him by his feet, and finally dispatched him with a saber.

Miracles associated with him after his death (a necessity for any prospective saint) included giving sight to a blind baby, curing dropsy, raising a nine-year-old girl from the dead, and (less spectacularly but doubtless just as welcome) letting "three noble ladies escape from manifest peril of being destroyed in a precipice." In later years, as partition followed upon partition, Bobola would emerge as a symbol of Polish independence: it was reported that he was apt to appear to statesmen, promising that when, through God's mercy, a true Polish kingdom finally emerged, he would serve as the country's patron.

Finally, after the Soviets moved his remains from Polotsk in White Russia to a medical museum in Moscow in 1922, Rome was sufficiently alarmed to send two Jesuits to get him back. After strained negotiations (Jesuits and Bolsheviks never having shared the fondest of relationships) and the securing of customs permits, Bobola would travel by train from Moscow to Odessa, by sea to Constantinople, and on board an Italian steamer back to Rome. Finally, in 1938, the year of his canonization, his remains would be transferred, via Budapest and Cracow, to Warsaw.[1]

Here was one more example of Jesuits caring for their past, remembering earlier adventures to better withstand the present. It was a policy that the modern Society of Jesus had long since learned to cultivate.

For all the adversity, for all the awful muddle, the nineteenth century had not been an altogether bitter cup for the Society of Jesus. The glory days of mission had, with an ounce or two less verve, been revisited, even if Protestant rivals were now more numerous and influential than ever before, even if some local people (as if they hadn't been thinking this all along) wondered ever more loudly why the Western Christ assumed he had a special place in their cultural landscapes. Many of the old evangelical theaters (not to mention old arguments about missionary methods) had once more opened up—in Mexico from 1816, Canada and China from 1842, Malabar in 1837, Bombay in 1856, Goa in 1890, to name only a few. In Africa (along the Zambezi, in Matabeleland, in French Algeria) and in the United States (from the Rockies to the Pacific, from the Mexican border to Alaska), new outlets for the irrepressible Jesuit evangelical impulse would continue to emerge.

All those unwelcome setbacks, in Europe and across the world, even had a habit of triggering off exciting new initiatives elsewhere. Jesuits were thrown out of Spain in 1835, so many of them headed to Argentina; when they were evicted from Argentina in 1842, they moved on to Paraguay and Uruguay. Exiled from Germany during Bismarck's Kulturkampf, Heinrich Pesch would travel to England, where he embarked upon his scathing indictment of working-class conditions in Liverpool, London, and Manchester.

Such forced itineraries could have the most delicious, unexpected consequences. Fathers Kranewitter and Klinkowstroem fled Austria in 1848, but by 1851 they were helping to establish the Sevenhill community in Australia's Clare Valley, where, as an imaginative complement to boarding schools and horseback missions, the vines planted by brothers John Schreiner and George Sadler would continue to yield substantial harvests down to the present day. In addition to the wine produced for use at the altar (something like 25 percent of Catholic Australia's communion wine at last count), oenophiles the world over can today treat themselves to St. Ignatius Red (a blend of Cabernet Sauvignon, Merlot, Malbec, and Cabernet Franc), St. Aloysius White (mixing Chardonnay, Chenin Blanc, and Verdelho), or even Jesuit Fine Old Tawny Port at $175 per case. One more striking example of Jesuit versatility.

Mission would continue to carry its familiar risks—as Jesuits who perished during the Maronite massacres in Lebanon (1860) or the Boxer Rebellion in China (1900) were to discover—but there were happier reminders of the past as well: hints, for instance, that the stalled evangelism of earlier times had not been entirely in vain.

Japan had effectively been closed to European influence for two centuries and more by the time a bullish, treaty-demanding American fleet arrived at Tokyo harbor in 1853. But over the coming years, Western visitors would discover sixty thousand hidden Christians, *kakure kirishtan*, descendants of the people converted by Jesuits and their mendicant counterparts in the sixteenth and seventeenth centuries. Crucifixes had been passed down over long decades, the rituals of Buddhism and Shinto had been adapted so that Christian devotions might be furtively indulged in, and most imaginatively of all, the ubiquitous Japanese tea ceremony had been harnessed as a coded way of celebrating holy communion. Centuries of isolation had, admittedly, bequeathed some strange transformations. The puzzling Latin of the liturgy had disintegrated into a meaningless jumble of vowels and consonants, and the gospel of the hidden Christians had acquired some bizarre accretions: Noah was now remembered for surviving the flood in a canoe rather than an ark. Nonetheless, the fact that, despite years of official prohibition, a curious but recognizable version of the Christian faith had been sustained was a huge boon to Catholics back in Europe.[2]

And a world away, in the United States, there was another reminder of past adventures when Rocky Mountain Indians arrived at St. Louis in 1839, asking for a Jesuit missionary to visit their lands. A cultural memory of the Society had been passed down from their Iroquois descendants, and their invitation launched careers as spectacular as that of the Belgian Jesuit Peter De

Smet. As well as establishing permanent missions among the Flatheads, Kalispels, and Coeur d'Alenes, traveling as many as sixty-five hundred miles a year by foot, horse, canoe, and steamboat, De Smet served as a diplomat in negotiations between various tribes and the U.S. government. Whatever his role in such a strained and sometimes sordid process—whether he should be seen as a well-intentioned peacemaker or a pawn (unwitting or otherwise) in the republic's effort to dispossess indigenous populations of their lands—it was hardly every Jesuit who could claim to have met and talked with Sitting Bull, even giving him a crucifix, which the great Sioux chief promised to wear for the rest of his days.[3]

Such links to the past were, and still are, cherished by the postsuppression Society. They were deliberately enhanced by the publication of source materials from the early years of the order, by new editions of Loyola's *Spiritual Exercises,* and by exhaustive accounts of the Society's various national histories: works of rigorous and objective scholarship (such as Bernhard Duhr's history of the German Jesuits, or Antonio Astráin's account of the Spanish branch of the Society) which remain indispensable to any historian of the order.

In many ways, Jesuit business went on as usual. Educational ministries were augmented by the network of high schools and colleges in the United States, Jesuit spirituality would flourish, and Jesuit science would continue to thrive, not least in the spheres of astronomy, seismology, and meteorology. When Benito Viñes published a hurricane warning in Havana newspapers on September 11, 1875, a prediction that was part of a lifetime's study of the formation and circulation of Caribbean hurricanes and cyclones, he was only being the most useful out of those Jesuit colleagues at meteorological stations around the globe, from Manila to Calcutta to Shanghai.[4] When Foucault and his earth-rotation-proving pendulum hit scientific headlines in 1851, Angelo Secchi made sure to offer a demonstration of the experiment at the Jesuits' Sant'Ignazio Church.

Such apostolates and vocations represented a continuation of a centuries-old tradition, and those of the twentieth century would certainly not aspire to any fundamental break with the past. Jesuits have rarely neglected to position themselves as the direct heirs of Ignatius Loyola, and the official documents of the thirty-fourth general congregation, held at Rome in 1995, are crammed with references to the aims and ethos of the Society's founder, obsessed with the challenge of how the Loyolan vision ought to be applied and interpreted in the modern world. Symbolically enough, at the culmination of the congregation, Urbano Valero would place flowers, ten roses, at the feet of Loyola's statue.

Tradition, of course, is a difficult thing to curate. By the time of the 1995 congregation, after a curious, disruptive hundred years, members of the Society of Jesus, a religious order transformed, knew this as well as anyone. The legacy of the nineteenth century, the stances and the directions taken up by the Catholic Church, had combined with the baffling, often baleful events of the twentieth.

ALTHOUGH MANY JESUITS remained unimpressed by the dramatic conclusions of Charles Darwin, the French paleontologist Pierre Teilhard de Chardin would put them to extraordinary theological use. While digging for fossils in Africa and China, he would borrow the concepts and vernacular of evolutionary theory in order to suggest that Christianity itself was an evolutionary process, a story of ever-increasing complexity, of ever-rising levels of consciousness. Eventually, he believed, mankind would live in the highest level of human society, with the risen Christ at its center, with charity as its propelling force. Whatever was made of Teilhard's theories, and the Vatican would not permit their publication during the Jesuit's lifetime, the optimism at their core was undeniable. And yet, the one thing it was inordinately difficult to be in Teilhard's century was optimistic.[5]

It was to be the century of Auschwitz and Dachau, places where, amidst far deeper, wider death and suffering, some Jesuits would also perish. It was to be the century of Hiroshima's destruction, the American-conjured nightmare witnessed firsthand by the Jesuit Pedro Arrupe. A century during which the European colonial enterprise was finally dismantled; and if Jesuits had been there at the start, they would be there at the end, and in the afterlife of consequence, adjustment, and blame. There had been times when the rise of a certain brand of global capitalism would seem inevitable, an inevitability about which Roman Catholicism, Jesuits included, would not always remain sanguine. During the Jesuits' fifth century the bastardized communism of Lenin, Stalin, and Mao would paint half the world red, a global transformation which terrified the Roman Catholic Church. Technology, communications, mass popular culture would thrive; Jesuit theologians like Karl Rahner—a giant, let it be said—would feel the need to write about the Beatles. Debates would rage, on race, on gender, and Jesuits would feel obliged to have their say.

Catholicism, however changed, however challenged, is still a fascinating, at times infuriating, at other times exhilarating, thing to behold. It has become a Catholicism of the causes, of radical social conscience but of unyielding moral postures too. It has become a Catholicism of the apology, where popes say sorry for persecuting medieval heretics like the Bohemian rebel Jan Hus, where popes almost say sorry for the Vatican's stance during the Nazi era, where Filipino bishops express their regret for siding with the colonial powers during the country's struggle for independence. It has become a Catholicism of technology, where Irish Jesuits set up Web sites so that the online faithful can come and pray, where Catholics in León, Spain, can pay their tithes by credit card at an automated terminal. It has become a Catholicism easily mocked, a place where Catholics feel obliged to moan about the church's depiction on American television shows; a Catholicism rocked, in recent years, by scandal, by newspaper headlines, court cases, and financial settlements thrown up by tales, too often true, of sexual abuse. But also, let us not forget, still a Catholicism of the day-to-day, of the weekly round of sacrament and spectacle, of rites of passage, of spiritual identity, of a thousand parishes not jolted by infamy or argument.

In reaching this point, competing Catholic urges to react and to refashion had continued to jostle for influence, the campaign to cling to tradition had been frustrated by spasms of novelty and dissent, and the modern Jesuit identity had warily emerged.

Right and Left

There was an ideal view of what the world should look like—its morals, its structures, its aspirations—but there was also the reality of how the world actually turned out to be. Obviously, it would be preferable if the ideal could be attained—and philosopher-theologians would often refer to this as the *thesis*. But this did not mean that everything below the ideal was necessarily evil, something to be shunned—and philosopher-theologians, Jesuit ones not least, often referred to this pragmatic dispensation as the *hypothesis*. To put it in more concrete terms: nineteenth-century Europe, sad to say, was no longer ruled over by kings, by good Catholic kings, and the church's importance seemed to be waning by the decade, but Catholics still had to live in and interact with the world in which they found themselves. It was about accepting reality—accepting the imperfect *hypothesis*—in such a way that the fundamentals of the faith, the dogmas and the duties, remained inviolate. The thesis, so the joke went, was to call a constitutional liberal as many horrid names as came to mind; the hypothesis was to have dinner with him.

As we saw in the last chapter, Rome went to extraordinary lengths to denounce all that was seemingly rotten in modern civilization. Nonetheless, a pope such as Leo XIII still managed to emerge: a pope who urged French Catholics to make their peace with, to rally to, the republic, who brought the crisis of the German Kulturkampf to an end, and who never so much as thought of doing anything as provocative as exercising the newly enshrined powers of papal infallibility. Leo was, in many ways, as conservative as either his successor or his predecessor—the much more obviously reactionary Pius IX and Pius X—but his quarter-century reign between 1878 and 1903 did encapsulate a much-needed papal quality: realism.

There had to be some sort of recognition that Catholics could not live entirely separate lives, that if the church's hierarchy insisted that they *did*, then a hemorrhage of disenchanted Catholic laymen would be the inevitable, lamentable result. They might even be seduced by the siren call of socialism. It was necessary to accept that unpalatable regimes were here to stay and that they had to be bargained with: modern popes would grow adept at securing satisfactory concordats, making sure, at the very least, that Catholics in a particular country could enjoy freedom of worship, that the papacy could control ecclesiastical appointments, that those appointees could maintain free communication with Rome.

But if it became increasingly apparent that an encounter with the modern world was unavoidable, there was still much work to be done in defining its scope and parameters. If Christianity was vanishing, if the Christian foundations of society were crumbling, then what was the best way to slow the decline? Given the dynamism of the post-1945 Christian democratic movement, it is striking to recall how very long it took Rome to countenance direct Catholic involvement in the modern political process. Such involvement was an established fact in Germany and Belgium, but no Italian Catholic party even came close to gaining papal approval until Luigi Sturzo's Popular Party in 1918: Italian Catholics were simply forbidden from voting until the removal of the papal *non placet* in the following year. And even this was something of an aberration. General papal approval of the democratic process—of its potential for protecting Catholic rights—would not truly emerge until after the Second World War.

This was largely because an alternative model of Catholic mobilization was instinctively given preference: the so-called Catholic Action movement. The direct involvement of the laity in politics might have been beyond the papal pale, but that did not exclude the possibility of a lay apostolate, of organizations of Catholic men, Catholic women, Catholic youth, workers, and students dedicated to confronting social and economic issues. Such groups, so the theory went, should certainly be controlled and guided by the clergy. They should sustain a proud confessional identity, making devotions and worship part of their mission. But Jesuits like Henri Leroy, who sought to alleviate working-class suffering through the Action Populaire initiative, like Gustave Desbuquois, who established centers of social action and research, like Stanislaus du Lac, who set up the Syndicat de l'Aiguille to provide loans, benefits, and special restaurants for Parisian seamstresses and dressmakers, all contributed to the emergence of a socially engaged Catholicism that would come to dominate the church's history over the course of the twentieth century. It was all a long way from today's more radical branches of social Catholicism. It was a process dominated by a constricting paternalism, by an adherence to cumbersome medieval concepts of natural law and of social classes neatly ranged in mutually respectful guilds. But it was also a long way from the isolation and indignation of the Syllabus of Errors.

The trouble was, Catholics of the early twentieth century did not only have to contemplate engagement with the social ills of Western Europe. They were also confronted with the flourishing, atheistic menace of communism. "For the first time in history," Pope Pius XI warned in 1937, owing to the "false messianic idea" of Bolshevism, "we are witnessing a struggle, cold-blooded in purpose and mapped out to the last detail," between man and God. If Catholic Action represented a step forward, fear of the red peril would convince a good many Catholics to take several steps backward.

A MECHANIC, a chauffeur, a beggar, a street sweeper: these were just a few of the disguises employed by the Jesuit Miguel Agustín Pro in 1920s Mexico. This was the place where the sacraments stopped, where the anti-clerical presidency of Plutarco Elias Calles saw Catholic property seized, Catholic schools and churches closed, foreign priests deported, the debilitating clauses of the 1917 constitution fully enacted. And where, on November 23, 1927, Miguel Pro was executed by firing squad, falsely accused of trying to assassinate ex-president General Alvaro Obregón.

Born in Guadalupe in 1891, the son of a mining engineer, Pro had been among those Mexican Jesuits forced into exile in 1914, only three years after he entered the Jesuit novitiate at El Llano. After a year at Las Gatos, California—where a handkerchief soaked in the martyr's blood is still displayed—he moved to Spain, to Belgium in 1924, and in 1926 back home to Mexico, easily one of the most dangerous places on earth for a Roman

Catholic priest to find himself. Over the coming months Pro would secretly celebrate mass and dispense sacraments, narrowly escaping arrest on several occasions. Then, when a car previously owned by Pro's brother was involved in the bomb attack on Obregón, the government seized the opportunity to rid itself of the turbulent, charismatic priest. Just before he was shot, without a blindfold, crucifix in one hand, rosary in the other, Pro shouted, *"Viva Cristo Rey!"*—long live Christ the King—the slogan of the Cristeros, Mexico's forty thousand Catholic rebels.[6]

Such was the fate of a Jesuit living under a left-leaning, Marxist-inspired regime. The Roman Catholic Church was philosophically opposed to, and profoundly frightened of, communism, or anything that even slightly resembled it. Popes, most notably in the 1937 encyclical *Divini Redemptoris,* would denounce it, Jesuits would point to the dangers and distractions it had brought to their worldwide ministry: to the forty-eight Jesuits who died during the anticlerical violence of the Spanish Civil War in 1936, to the fact that it was now necessary to send a Jesuit like Michel d'Herbigny on secret missions to the Soviet Union to carry out covert ordinations. As the century progressed, the experiences of Eastern Europe—harassment by the Stasi in East Germany, show trials and long spells in prison and monastery camps in Czechoslovakia, persecution in Hoxha's Albania—would do little to endear institutionalized Marxism to the Society of Jesus.

Jan Korec, sent as a secret bishop to Czechoslovakia in 1951, would work as a night watchman and an elevator repairman in order to keep his true identity a secret; having finally been exposed in 1960, he would be sentenced to sixteen years in prison. Walter Ciszek, under the pseudonym Vladimir Lypinski, would enter the Soviet Union in 1940, be arrested a few months later, and after a spell of torture, endure a fifteen-year term in Siberia. Here, he would continue his priestly duties, offering masses, confession, and retreats, making communion wine out of raisins stolen by Polish prisoners, using a shot glass as a chalice. Given such harrowing experiences, it was easy to think that the Society of Jesus would do anything within its power to attack the communist menace. It was even suggested that Jesuits at Georgetown University were behind the witch-hunts of the Jesuit-educated Senator Joe McCarthy—Jesuits like Edmund Walsh, who, as well as lecturing to rooms full of soldiers and FBI agents about the evils of Leninism and Stalinism, had led the protests against Franklin Roosevelt's official recognition of the Soviet Union in 1933.

※

IT IS OFTEN suggested that the fear and loathing of communism contributed to a political lurch to the right in twentieth-century Catholicism. To be sure, many Catholics had sustained faith in thrones and altars during the previous hundred years, supporting the Carlist cause in Spain or the Orleanist cause in France. Popes had tended to respect established authority rather than support popular rebellion, even when, as in Belgium and Poland, the rebels happened to be Catholics. An extreme, integrist party certainly existed within the church, a party that flatly refused to accept any of the consequences of the Enlightenment, that preached the virtues of hierarchy, order, and tradition, that dreamed of medieval guilds and a corporatist social structure, that sometimes spiked its theorizing with anti-Masonic, anti-Jewish outbursts.

When authoritarian governments took power in Portugal under Antonio de Oliveira Salazar (1932), in Spain under Francisco Franco (1939), or in Austria under Engelbert Dollfuss, some Catholics—including Jesuit professors at the Gregorian University—seemed decidedly pleased. When an influential right-wing political movement such as Charles Maurras's Action Française incurred the wrath and censure of the Vatican in 1926, some Catholics, including the Jesuit cardinal Louis Billot, registered their displeasure. As payment for offering sympathy to the vanquished movement, Billot would be forced to resign his cardinal's hat: the only cardinal to suffer such an indignity in the entire twentieth century.[7]

But—not least because of what came next, the atrocities of the Nazi era—enormous care has to be taken before concluding that Catholicism was somehow predisposed toward the goals and beliefs of the extreme far right, of fascism. In the case of Mussolini's Italy, for instance, appearances had a habit of being deceptive. After decades of anticlerical bullying, the church was undoubtedly heartened by promises to restore state support for churches and church schools, by the relative courtesy with which Fascist officials treated clerics, by the return of Catholic religious education to public schools, and of crucifixes to hospitals and courtrooms. Jesuits rejoiced at having their mother church, the Gesù, restored to them. Even the decades-old "Roman Question," the relationship between Rome and the Italian government that had grown ever more uneasy since 1870, looked as though it might be resolved. After lengthy negotiations—in which Jesuits were deeply involved—the Lateran Treaties of 1929 saw the pope finally recognizing the existence and legitimacy of an Italian kingdom; in return, he was to be regarded as the head of a sovereign Vatican State and granted sizable financial compensation for the loss of his territories.

But things were never quite as cozy as they seemed. Mussolini soon made it clear that he regarded religion as subservient to the state; the anticlerical violence that had always marked Italian Fascism would continue; and energetic church organizations such as the Catholic youth groups would attract the regime's suspicion. Dubious actions, such as the alliance with Hitler and the invasion of Abyssinia, would divide Catholic opinion. At the heart of such tensions was the fact that Catholicism and Fascism were incompatible doctrines. Fascist corporatism and Catholic corporatism were simply not the same thing—a point made very forcibly by the pope in 1931—and more fundamentally, the Fascist conception of society could not be squared with Catholicism's understanding of how the religious and the secular ought to interact. Fascism was a philosophy of totality: the whole of life was to be controlled by the state, the state was all there was, the state could not countenance any rival sources of morality or belief. It was far from clear how an institution such as the Catholic Church could fit into such an ideology.

As for the fascist ascendancy in Germany, it is true that the country's bishops withdrew their overt opposition to the Nazi Party in 1933 (though this was hardly the same as replacing it with overt approval), it is true that Rome negotiated a concordat with Hitler in the same year (although Rome was in the habit of negotiating concordats with almost any legally established regime), and it is true that the papal critique contained within the encyclical *Mit brennender Sorge* of 1937 was more concerned with breaches of that concordat than with the government's racist, anti-Semitic policies (although a more forthright, though still inadequate encyclical had been prepared, by Jesuits, just before Pius XI died).[8]

Beyond a doubt, anti-Semitism had been an institutionalized canker within the Roman Catholic tradition, within the broader Western cultural tradition, for as long as anyone could remember: during the nineteenth century a Jesuit journal such as *Civiltà Cattolica* would continue to publish noxiously anti-Jewish material, and it is important to recall that the Jesuit prohibition of those with Jewish ancestry entering the Society would remain in force until as late as 1946. It is also entirely possible to criticize the wartime papacy for not speaking out more clearly against the assault on the Jews than it did, for not acting with more dynamism when explicitly asked to do so by the bishop of Berlin in 1943—although sensationalist denunciations of "Hitler's pope" surely go a little too far.

But Nazism and Catholicism were hardly allies. After all, the German invasion of Poland would result in the death of 2,650 priests, eighty Jesuits among them. Yes, there were Catholic Nazis; yes, there were Catholic supporters of Vichy; but—if we bring our focus back to the Society of Jesus—there were also special Gestapo files devoted to Jesuit priests; Jesuits who would be prohibited from acting as chaplains in the armies of the Reich (even if a handful did manage to make it as far as Stalingrad); Jesuits who the Bavarian police would denounce for "reactionary activities," for trying to "undermine the Third Reich and bring contempt even on the Führer himself" in 1935.[9] Hitler played a wily game with Catholicism—happily exploiting its appeal for a time—but ultimately he was determined to expunge its influence, to remove the threat posed by the network of Vatican spies (Jesuits included) he believed to exist.

The Second World War was hardly the proudest era in Roman Catholic history, but at least there were occasional edifying moments. The Jesuit Jacob Raile helped to protect the Jews of Budapest, the Jesuit Alfred Delp would be assassinated for his involvement in the anti-Hitler Kreisau circle, Robert Regout would be sent to Dachau for criticizing the Nazi regime, Rupert Mayer would spend time at Sachsenhausen for the same offense. In France, the Jesuit Gaston Fessard was almost the only Catholic voice to speak out against the anti-Jewish laws of 1940, and his magazine, *Témoignage Chrétien*, would continue, along with the Jesuit journal *Etudes*, to prod Catholic consciences.[10] Jesuits would be involved in the resistance movements in France, Luxembourg, Holland, and Yugoslavia: Yves de Montcheuil would be a chaplain to the maquis. When a group of German generals, having concocted a plan to overthrow Hitler, sought a secret diplomatic channel to the allied forces, it was the Jesuit Robert Leiber who served as intermediary. Faced with the atrocities of Nazism, a great many Catholics, a great many Jesuits, chose to sit on their hands. A few, Jesuits among them, did not.

What the Third Reich's abominations helped to bring into terrible clarity was the fact that the Catholic Church, however ill at ease with modern civilization, however much it pined for former times, could no longer stand apart, insulted and insulting. Connections had to be made, misgivings overcome.

Flirting with Modernity

The bilious hatred of communism and the tendency of some Catholics to conclude that right-wing, authoritarian regimes were perhaps not the most serious threat to Christian civilization were, in part, the legacy of nineteenth-century Catholic reaction. Jesuits of the old guard would certainly remain influential within the Society. A superior general such as Wladmir Ledochowski (1915–42) would despair that the modern world resembled nothing so much as the poor paralytic of Bethesda, lacking the strength to arise from its sickbed. But it is wrong to assume that this conservative trend within the church, this refusal to have anything to do with the modern world, was all that Catholicism or the Society of Jesus was about. Ledochowski would give way to superiors general as innovative and provocative as Jean-Baptiste Janssens and Pedro Arrupe.

For the Catholic Church, as an institution and a fellowship of the faithful, it was, above all, the twentieth century that led up to Vatican II, the Second Vatican Council of 1962–65: technically speaking the continuation of Vatican I, disrupted in 1870 by the outbreak of the Franco-Prussian War, but in terms of what was sought and what was done, a striking discontinuity, an attempt, as Pope John XXIII had hoped, at aggiornamento, at bringing up to date.

Vatican II can best be understood as a culmination of a desire to reform the church, in its ritual and liturgy, and to enshrine a new and fuller role for the Catholic laity. And also as a theological culmination. However savagely the Modernist movement had been squashed in the century's first decade, many of its preoccupations—the effort to understand the church and its dogma in historical terms, to apply modern scholarly standards to the Catholic academy—refused to disappear. French Jesuits like Henri de Lubac and Jean Daniélou, the so-called New Theologians, would be denounced by the papal encyclical *Humani generis* in 1950, accused of undermining traditional teaching on original sin, grace, and liturgy. The American Jesuit John Courtney Murray would incur the hierarchy's displeasure as a result of his meditations on religious pluralism and the desirability of separating church and state. Karl Rahner, with his talk of an instinctive knowledge of God possessed by every person, Catholic or otherwise, would raise eyebrows by advocating a heightened commitment to ecumenism and interreligious dialogue. But it was to be precisely such men as de Lubac, Murray, and Rahner who dominated proceedings at Vatican II, a council that declared a new openness to the modern world, to those of other Christian faiths or wholly non-Christian religions, to any men of goodwill.

But perhaps most important of all, Vatican II was the place where the Catholic Church's dynamic engagement with modern social questions came of age. It had fallen, tellingly, to Pope Leo XIII to issue the groundbreaking encyclical *Rerum novarum* in 1891—a document to which the Jesuit Luigi Taparelli d'Azeglio contributed greatly. It was the first of the momentous social encyclicals, the attempt to respond to the revolutionary impact of capitalism and industrialization. Socialism was, of course, denounced, but so was the tendency of unregulated capitalism to alienate workers, to create unwelcome class antagonism. Employees should have the right to unionize, they should receive a living wage, and they should enjoy decent working conditions.

As radical as such claims were, it is important to stress that papal teaching was as distant from socialism as could be imagined. It was rooted in medieval notions of natural law and the just wage. But *Rerum novarum* did instigate a century of papal cautioning of the possible drawbacks of capitalism—a voice that, at times, would stand virtually alone in the West. *Quadragesimo anno* ("Forty Years After," again the work, in part, of Jesuits, Austrian and German) would follow in 1931 with its call for states to further protect the worker, its criticism of both communism *and* capitalism, its search for a middle way between laissez-faire and command economies. *Octogesima adveniens* and *Centesimus annus* ("The Eightieth Anniversary" and "The Hundredth Year") would arrive in due course, and by stages, a fully evolved social Catholicism would emerge.

Already by the era of Vatican II papal teaching would be suggesting that the laws of the market, left to themselves, were no guarantor of justice, that the globalization of the international economic system was riddled with pitfalls. People had rights: to shelter, education, health care, and unemployment benefits. Vatican II itself, especially in its Pastoral Constitution on the Church in the Modern World, would accept that, as always, the church was a mystery, a sacrament, but also that the pursuit of justice and peace, not least through the lay apostolate, ought to be normative to the Catholic experience.

The Catholic social teaching that has emerged in the wake of Vatican II, the church would doubtless insist, is very much a unity. It is not really something from which eminent rock stars can pick and choose, praising it when it denounces Third World debt, land mines, or the death penalty, turning against it when it outlaws abortion and contraception. All of these things, so it is suggested, are interlinked. Providing people with a decent wage is a good in itself, but it also reduces the chances of pregnancies being terminated because they cannot be afforded. Of course, the modern Catholic laity, not to mention the modern Society of Jesus, has grown quite adept at simply ignoring those aspects of the church's official social vision with which it does not agree—the American church is a spectacular example of this—and that is no doubt to the good. But whatever one's distaste for particular papal positions, the overall architecture of Catholic social teaching is a decidedly impressive thing.

It starts from an insistence on individual human dignity—a dignity that derives from man being made in God's image—but one that can be fully protected only within the context of the wider community. It stresses the crucial role of the state in solving social problems, but also demands an underlying principle of subsidiarity—problems should be solved at the most local level possible. It has also moved away from its natural law origins toward a philosophy based fundamentally on the notion of justice, of a blend of rights and duties; it has insisted upon a preferential option, amidst all the world's dilemmas, for the poor. However it is to be judged, it can at least be credited with offering an alternative, a radical alternative, and an alternative that the Society of Jesus has tended, in ways too outlandish for some tastes, to embrace.

VATICAN II—WITH its attempt to encounter the world, to assess the church's liturgical identity and the role of the laity, its suggestion that the Catholic Church is not the only means of salvation, its pronouncements on social teaching—was controversial. It was not enough for some, far too much for others. And even when the deeds were done, when the elegant papal documents were issued, it was far from clear whether it had all been about a starting point or a stopping point, a signal toward the road ahead or a marker of this-far-and-no-further. Little wonder that the post–Vatican II Roman Catholic Church, not least the post–Vatican II Society of Jesus, would turn out to be a confused, conflicted place to be.

It would be a church full of dissent, with Catholics arguing about birth control, gay rights, celibate priests, and vernacular liturgies; full of diversity, with African and Asian Catholicisms, inculturated Catholicisms, throwing off the yoke of Latinized, Western tradition. It would be energized by talk of justice, of preferential options for the poor, of the gospel's role in liberating people from the structures of oppression. And it would be populated by Jesuits, the radical Jesuits, the gay Jesuits, the archneoconservative Jesuits, the Jesuits (it ought to be remembered) trying to ignore all the squabbling and get on with their ministries, not to mention the thousands of ex-Jesuits who had chosen to abandon their order.

As of January 2003, there were 20,408 members of the Society of Jesus, a Society that has witnessed and responded to the busiest century in human history, and which has played no small part in the church's journey to Vatican II and its aftermath. A Society, also, whose role and raison d'être is as contentious as it has ever been.

TODAY, JESUITS, AS their tradition insists, can be found in almost every country, in almost every workplace imaginable. If a war zone or trouble spot is named—Sudan, Angola, Rwanda, East Timor, the Moluccas, the Balkans—the likelihood of a Jesuit presence is high. There are Jesuit biochemists, Jesuit bosses of retreat houses, Jesuit musicians, Jesuit professors at business schools, the Jesuit who took up a place on the board of the Disney corporation, the Jesuit who turned to an academic career after giving up his seat in the United States Congress. Jesuits continue to speak out: on the rights and wrongs of animal vivisection and clone technology; declaring, in recent years, that cremation is an acceptable way to dispose of Catholic corpses, that hell is not quite the place many people think it is, that there ought to be senior nuns in the College of Cardinals, that sex education in Latin America ought to take on a far more realistic, relevant aspect.

The twentieth-century Society of Jesus would be as diverse as any of its predecessors, producing some three hundred martyrs, teachers for the twenty-eight American colleges affiliated to the order, the man (Daniel Berrigan) who was sentenced to three years in prison in 1970 for destroying Vietnam draft cards, and another (John McLaughlin) who served Richard Nixon and emerged as one of his key apologists. Jesuits are sometimes to be found at the heart of the Roman establishment, promoting the canonization of Pius XII in the case of

Peter Gumpel, defending his reputation in the case of Pierre Blet. Sometimes they are found annoying the Roman establishment more than members of any other religious order. The astonishing incident in 1981, when John Paul II imposed his own personal representative, Paolo Dezza, on the Society, rather than allowing the ailing superior general's vicar general, Vincent O'Keefe, to wield full authority, was only the most spectacular moment of antagonism between the Jesuits and the supreme pontiff. When Jesuits sought to remove the traditional hierarchy within the Society, the pope felt obliged to intervene. When Jesuit theologians such as Anthony de Mello, Roger Haight, and Jacques Dupuis talked controversially about religious pluralism, about bridging the gaps between Eastern and Western spirituality, about Jesus not being the only route to God, Rome and its censorship machine were quick to act.

But when the thirty-fourth general congregation tried to assess the true nature of the modern Jesuit mission, it did manage, faced with a diverse, conflicted membership, to fasten upon themes that revealed the Society to be a direct heir of the aspirations of the Second Vatican Council. Relations with those of other Christian faiths, those of non-Christian faiths, and those of no faith at all; a commitment to a regionalized, inculturated Catholicism that was responsive to local circumstances and traditions; an acceptance that the Society was part of an ecclesiastical system that had historically been unfair to women—these, it was declared, were some of the things Jesuits should think about and act upon.

But, again very much in consort with the ethos of Vatican II, it seemed that quite the most important word in a Jesuit's vocabulary ought to be "justice": like "tradition," an easy word to say but an endlessly difficult concept either to define or to pursue.

On November 16, 1989, six Jesuits at the University of Central America, their housekeeper, and her daughter were murdered by soldiers of El Salvador's army. The brains of some of the corpses had been scooped out:

a warning, so one imagines, not to think too hard about, or denounce too loudly, the human rights abuses of the government. This was the price to be paid for commitment to a particular interpretation of Vatican II's message.[11]

Justice has become a Jesuit rallying cry. Christian liberty, so the sages of liberation theology insist, is about freedom not only from sin, but from poverty and injustice. The world is full of dictators and economic inequality, full of international structures of oppression and iniquity. The job of the gospel is to set such wrongs right. And in that work, some, though hardly all, suggest that it might even be reputable to recruit the most unexpected allies. Marxism, as a way of life, is untenable, so the logic goes; but the structural analysis offered by Marxist philosophy has something to commend it. Just as modish literary theorists do not become Marxists by utilizing *The Eighteenth Brumaire* in their close readings of texts, so Jesuits do not become Marxists when they use Marx to understand and denounce iniquity.

There are, of course, a host of ways to combat injustice, but as advocates of preferential options for the poor and the marginalized usually suggest, if the fight can be fought at the local level, then all to the good. In Honduras, the Jesuit Jack Warner would establish the Teatro La Fragua to help young people rediscover their unique cultural identity in the face of economic and cultural globalism. In Nicaragua, Fernando Cardenal would take up a position as education minister in the Sandinista government; Xavier Gorostiaga would become its director of planning. When the pope declared that priests ought not to cross the line into politics so blatantly, Cardenal would choose to leave the Society of Jesus. In the Philippines, Godofredo Alingal would fight for farmers' rights and be murdered for his trouble. Jan Sobrino would write speeches for Archbishop Oscar Romero, another priest killed in El Salvador for his opinions. In Europe, almost as an echo of the pioneering worker priests of the 1940s, Jesuits would be drawn to depressed inner cities, to the dilemmas faced by immigrant populations. And when a barbecue to celebrate the opening of the Channel Tunnel was in need of outside catering, the thirty-five hundred covers were supplied by the Table de Cana, a firm established by the Jesuit Franck Chaigneau to provide employment for the dispossessed youth of Paris.

Many within the Society of Jesus would undoubtedly like to be defined by, perhaps remembered for, such initiatives as the Table de Cana, for organizations as dynamic as the African Aids Network or the Jesuit Refugee Service, or the Society's work in the slums of Manila or the prisons of Italy, among the Dalits of India. Returning to Goa, where we began this book, it is possible to see tradition and modernity overlapping. There is the Francis Xavier Institute for Historical Research and the Thomas Stephens Center for Konknni, named for the sixteenth-century English missionary who inaugurated European interest in the Konknni language. But there are also the initiatives to alleviate local poverty, to promote adult literacy, to serve the interests, through the Janajagaran organization, of local employees as diverse as shepherds and power-loom workers.

But the Society's commitment to justice, as important to contemporary Jesuits as combating the Reformation or evangelizing the far reaches of the globe was to their forbears, is not entirely uncontroversial. For all the adaptations and syncretisms of local churches around the globe, for all the explosions of indigenous priesthoods, there are still, on occasion, resentful outbursts against representatives of a Western belief system taking it upon themselves to solve the ills of Indian or African society. There is sometimes talk of a breadbasket Christianity, mumbling over the number of converts who are dependent on the church for what little health and wealth they possess. There is always, always will be, the memory of colonialism.

Within the ranks of the faithful, not least among the higher echelons, there is concern that the Jesuit pursuit of justice sometimes goes too far, that it embroils Jesuits in radical politics, that it turns Jesuits into social workers, men who seem to have forgotten that they are, first and foremost, priests, dispensers of sacraments.

And this is only one problem among the many that the Society of Jesus faces. There is the sometimes uneasy relationship with the papacy, the fact that numbers have fallen by sixteen thousand in the past thirty-five years, the need to reflect seriously about the nature of the Jesuit educational ministry, the grumbling from some Jesuits that countercultural trends and tendencies have swamped the Society's traditional mission, the parade, in recent years, of unpalatable stories detailing Jesuit sexual abuse.

There is energy too, of course: in Asia, where the number of novices entering the Society has even been known to rise year on year; in the ministries of the thousands of well-intentioned, scandal-free priests who, faced with a world that often dismisses them as irrelevant, endeavor to sustain the Loyolan vision. As ever, Jesuit history is marked by both crisis and accomplishment.

What the Jesuits will do next is simply not the pressing issue it was in 1540 or 1814, the moments when the Society of Jesus was born and then reborn, but it is still an issue that bears watching. The Society of Jesus has always been a cultural weather vane, a way to understand the intellectual trends and fashions of a certain time and place. But it has also always been curiously unique and disjointed from whatever time or place it happened to find itself in, maintaining a defiantly idiosyncratic way of looking at the world. It is in this collision, a collision between contingency and enduring tradition, that the fascination of Jesuit history has always resided, and doubtless always will.

Acknowledgments

DURING THE FINAL stages of preparing this book for publication, news came of the death of Giles Gordon, my agent and friend. I will always be grateful for the faith Giles showed in me, and I will miss him terribly.

I first thought of writing a book on the Jesuits during a year at the University of Pennsylvania, so first thanks go to the organizers and officers of the Thouron Awards. I did much of the early research while enjoying a fellowship in Germany, so thanks to those at the Institut für europäische Geschichte in Mainz.

I am grateful to the staffs of the British Library, Lambeth Palace Library, and the Archives of the English Province of the Society of Jesus (all in London), the Bodleian Library in Oxford, Durham University Library, the Martinus-Bibliothek in Mainz, and the National Library of Scotland, Edinburgh.

Thanks also to Paul Kildea (for some of the photos of Rome), Christopher Haigh, Anthony Upton, Kate Johnson (for her judicious editing), Gordon Wright and Peter Taylor, to Michael Fishwick and Kate Hyde at HarperCollins, and to Andrew Corbin at Doubleday.

I am grateful to the Trustees of the National Library of Scotland for permission to reproduce the following items: D. Bouhours, *The Life of St. Francis Xavier* (1688), frontispiece (for which acknowledgment is also made to the Library of St. Andrew's College, Drygrange); *Af-beeldinghe van d'eerste eeuwe der Societeyt Jesu* (Antwerp, 1640), frontispiece and p. 204 (for which acknowledgment is also made to the Scottish Catholic Archives); A. Kircher, *Mundus subterraneus* (Amsterdam, 1678), frontispiece; F. Aguilonius, *Opticorum libri sex* (Antwerp, 1613), p. 356; L. Le Comte, *Nouveaux memoires sur l'état présent de la Chine* (Amsterdam, 1697), p. 99 and p. 192 (for which acknowledgment is also made to the Library of St. Andrew's College, Drygrange); *The Case of Mary Katherine Cadière* (1731), title page; P.-J. de Smet, *Voyages aux Montagnes Rocheuses* (Brussels, 1873), frontispiece.

Notes

Introduction: The Afterlife of Francis Xavier

1. J. Balmes, *Protestantism and Catholicity Compared in Their Effects on the Civilization of Europe,* trans. C. J. Hanford and R. Kershaw (1849), 220.
2. J. Brodrick, *The Economic Morals of the Jesuits: An Answer to Dr. H. M. Robertson* (Oxford, 1934), 8.
3. G. Schurhammer, *Varia* (2 vols., Rome, 1965), I:346.
4. S. Neill, *A History of Christianity in India: The Beginnings to AD 1707* (Cambridge, 1984), 146; G. Elison, *Deus Destroyed: The Image of Christianity in Early Modern Japan* (Cambridge, Mass., 1973), 35. The definitive biography of Xavier is G. Schurhammer, *Francis Xavier: His Life, His Times* (4 vols., Rome, 1973–82).
5. M. Foss, *The Founding of the Jesuits, 1540* (1969), 185–86; B. W. Diffie and G. D. Winius, *Foundations of the Portuguese Empire, 1415–1580* (St. Paul, Minn., 1977), 253; M. N. Pearson, *The New Cambridge History of India,* 1.1: *The Portuguese in India* (Cambridge, 1987), 88–115; David M. Kowal, "Innovation and Assimilation: The Jesuit Contribution to Architectural Development in Portuguese India," in J. W. O'Malley et al., eds., *The Jesuits: Cultures, Sciences and the Arts, 1540–1773* (Toronto, 1999), 480–504.
6. G. Schurhammer and J. Wicki, eds., *Epistolae S. Francisci Xaverii aliaque eius scripta* (2 vols., Rome, 1944–45), I:121–22.
7. J. A. de Polanco, *Vita Ignatii Loiolae et rerum Societatis Jesu historia* (6 vols., Madrid, 1894–98), VI: 781.
8. C. R. Boxer, *From Lisbon to Goa, 1500–1750: Studies in Portuguese Maritime Enterprise* (1984 ed.), 111.
9. *Monumenta Xaveriana ex autographis vel ex antiquioribus exemplis collecta* (2 vols., Madrid, 1899; 1912–14), II:911.
10. P. Rayanna, *St. Francis Xavier and His Shrine* (Goa, 1998), 141–216; T. Johnson, "Blood, Tears and Xavier-Water: Jesuit Missionaries and Popular Religion in the Eighteenth-Century Upper Palatinate," in R. Scribner and T. Johnson, eds., *Popular Religion in Germany and Central Europe, 1400–1800* (1996), 183–202.
11. L. Châtellier, *The Religion of the Poor: Rural Missions in Europe and the Foundations of Modern Catholicism, c. 1500–c. 1800* (Cambridge, 1997), 149–50.

12. R. G. Thwaites, ed., *The Jesuit Relations and Allied Documents: Travels and Explorations of the Jesuit Missionaries in New France, 1610–1791* (73 vols., Cleveland, Ohio, 1853–1913), 53:73–75.

13. J. Pilkington, *Works,* ed. J. Scholefield (Cambridge, 1842), 147.

14. J. Calvin, *Traité des reliques,* in F. Higman, ed., *Three French Treatises* (1970), 84, 90–91.

15. J. Waterworth, ed., *The Canons and Decrees of the Sacred and Oecumenical Council of Trent* (1848), 235–36.

16. L. Richeome, *Defence des pèlerinages . . . avec un discours des sainctes reliques* (Paris, 1605), sig. A2r, fols. 39, 44v, 45r.

17. *Monumenta Xaveriana,* II:777.

18. *News from Heaven: or A Dialogue Between S. Peter and the Five Jesuits Last Hang'd* (1679), 1–4.

19. H. Linde, *Via Tuta: The Safe Way* (1630), 324.

20. Jesuit English Province Archives, Mount Street, London, MS M2/3C, "Father John Thorpe's Notes on Passing Events in Rome, etc., Before, at the Period of, and After the Dissolution of the Society," fol. 52.

21. W. J. Callahan, *Church, Politics and Society in Spain, 1750–1874* (Cambridge, Mass., 1984), 153–54.

22. J. Lockman, *Travels of the Jesuits into Various Parts of the World* (1743), xii–xiii.

1. "New Athletes to Combat God's Enemies": Jesuits and Reformations

1. P. Matthieu, *Histoire de France* (2 vols., Paris, 1631), I: 253, cited in M. Yardeni, *"L'entrée des jésuites dans l'historiographie française,"* in G. Demerson, B. Dompnier, and A. Regond, eds., *Les jésuites parmi les hommes aux XVIe et XVIIe siècles* (Clermont-Ferrand, 1987), 225.

2. M. Chemnitz, *Examination of the Council of Trent,* part I, trans. F. Kramer (St. Louis, 1971), 25.

3. A. Bower, *The History of the Popes,* vol. VII (1766), 457.

4. J. W. O'Malley, S.J., *The First Jesuits* (Cambridge, Mass., 1993), 17.

5. H. Rahner, "Der Tod des Ignatius," *Stimmen der Zeit* 158 (1955–56): 248.

6. Thwaites, *Jesuit Relations,* 27:49; 29:169.

7. P. Caraman, *Ignatius Loyola* (1990), 199.

8. H. Rahner, "Der kranke Ignatius," *Stimmen der Zeit* 158 (1955–56): 81–90.

9. M. O'Rourke Boyle, *Loyola's Acts: The Rhetoric of the Self* (Berkeley, Calif., 1997).

10. J. Le Rond d'Alembert, *An Account of the Destruction of the Jesuits in France* (1766), 4–5.

11. *Alumbrado* was the term applied to those mystical individuals in sixteenth-century Spain who claimed direct divine illumination and regarded much of the apparatus of mainstream Catholicism as superfluous.

12. *St. Ignatius of Loyola: Personal Writings,* ed. and trans. J. A. Munitz and P. Endean (1996), 48.

13. R. Knecht, *Francis I* (Cambridge, 1982), 248–52.

14. T. Becon, *Prayers and Other Pieces,* ed. J. Ayre (Cambridge: Parker Society, 1844), 270, 261.

15. J. Foxe, *Acts and Monuments,* ed. J. Pratt (8 vols., 1870), 6:278; J. Fines, *A Biographical Register of Early English Protestants, 1522–1558* (2 vols., Abingdon, 1981), I: alphabetical entry.

16. P. J. Winstone, *A History of the Church in Clapham,* North Yorkshire Record Office Publications 29 (1982), 26; T. Rogers, *The Catholic Doctrine of the Church of England,* ed. J. J. S. Perowne (Cambridge: Parker Society, 1854), 284.

17. W. V. Bangert, *A History of the Society of Jesus* (2nd ed., St. Louis, 1976), 97.

18. R. P. McBrien, *Lives of the Popes: The Pontiffs from St. Peter to John Paul II* (New York, 1997), 281.

19. On the Parisian scene in which these events took place, see L. Taylor, *Heresy and Orthodoxy in Sixteenth Century Paris: François Le Picart and the Beginnings of the Catholic Reformation* (Leiden, 1999), 113–25; A. Sutcliffe, *Paris: An Architectural History* (New Haven, Conn., 1993), chaps. 1 and 2.

20. O'Malley, *First Jesuits,* 29.

21. T. J. Campbell, *The Jesuits 1534–1921* (1921), 31.

22. T. Griesinger, *The Jesuits: A Complete History of Their Open and Secret Proceedings from the Foundation of the Order to the Present Time* (1903), 2.

23. J. H. Pollen, ed., "The Memoirs of Father Robert Persons," CRS Miscellanea 2, Catholic Record Society (1906), 187–88.

24. C. de Beaumont du Repaire, *Instruction pastorale . . . sur les atteintes données à l'autorité de l'église, par les jugements des tribunaux séculiers dans l'affaire des jésuites* (Paris, 1829), iii–iv.

25. O'Malley, *First Jesuits,* 16.

26. P. Van Dyke, *Ignatius Loyola: The Founder of the Jesuits* (Port Washington, N.Y., 1986), 296–97.

27. P. Van Marnix von Sant Aldegande, *The Bee-Hive of the Romishe Church,* trans. G. Gilpin (1580), fols. 4v, 353.

28. L. Hicks, *Letters and Memorials of Father Robert Persons,* CRS Miscellanea 39, Catholic Record Society (1942), 120.

29. *All Is Not Gold That Glisters* (1648), 13.

30. D. Owen, *The Puritan Turn'd Jesuit* (1652), sig. A3.

31. J. Brooks, *A Sermon Very Notable* (1553), sig. B2v.

32. J. N. Tylenda, *Jesuit Saints and Martyrs* (Chicago, 1998), 155–56.

33. H. Foley, *Records of the English Province of the Society of Jesus* (7 vols., 1877–84), I:339–46.

34. A. Walsham, *Church Papists: Catholicism, Conformity, and Confessional Polemic in Early Modern England* (1996).

35. K. Noreen, "Ecclesiae Militantis Triumphi: Jesuit Iconography and the Counter-Reformation," *Sixteenth Century Journal* 29 (1998): 695.

36. J. H. Pollen, ed., "The Memoirs of Father Persons Continued," CRS Miscellanea 4, Catholic Record Society (1907), 45.

37. E. Towers, "The Opening Years of the Venerable English College, Rome," *Ushaw Magazine* 20 (1910): 29–30.

38. L. Taylor, *Soldiers of Christ: Preaching in Late Medieval and Reformation France* (Oxford, 1992), 218.

39. F. J. McGinness, *Right Thinking and Sacred Oratory in Counter-Reformation Rome* (Princeton, N.J., 1995), 38–39.

40. C. F. Black, *Italian Confraternities in the Sixteenth Century* (Cambridge, 1999), 272; H. Kamen, *Spain in the Later Seventeenth Century, 1665–1700* (1980), 180.

41. O'Malley, *First Jesuits*, 268.

42. L. Châtellier, "Les jésuites et l'ordre social," in L. Giard and L. de Vaucelles, eds., *Les jésuites à l'âge baroque* (Grenoble, 1996), 144.

43. Black, *Italian Confraternities in the Sixteenth Century*, 94. Jesuits also served as editors of the massive *Acta sanctorum* project begun in Belgium in 1623, which would do much to outlaw legend and apocrypha from Catholic hagiography,

44. A. Lynn Martin, *Plague? Jesuit Accounts of Epidemic Disease in the Sixteenth Century* (Kirksville, Mo., 1996), 110.

45. R. Brendt, *Petrus Canisius: Humanist and Europäer* (Berlin, 2000).

46. M-L. Rodén, "Queen Christina of Sweden, Spain and the Politics of the Seventeenth-Century Papal Court," in E. M. Ruiz and M. de Pazzis Pi Corrales, eds., *Spain and Sweden in the Baroque Era, 1600–1660* (Puertollano, 2000), 783–800.

47. G. Huppert, *Public Schools in Renaissance France* (Urbana, Ill., 1984), 107.

48. B. Duhr, *Geschichte der Jesuiten in den Ländern deutscher Zunge* (4 vols., Freiburg, 1907–28), I:337–38.

49. E. I. Hogan, *Distinguished Irishmen of the Sixteenth Century* (1894), 789–94.

50. G. Parker, *The Thirty Years War* (1987), 67–68, 128; R. Bireley, *Religion and Politics in the Age of the Counterreformation: Emperor Ferdinand II, William Lamormaini, S.J., and the Formation of Imperial Policy* (Chapel Hill, N.C., 1981).

51. See, for instance, J. W. O'Malley, *Trent and All That: Renaming Catholicism in the Early Modern Era* (Cambridge, Mass., 2000).

52. W. Crashaw, *The Bespotted Iesuite* (1641), sig. A3.

53. W. Crashaw, *Loyola's Disloyalty* (1643), introduction.

54. R. Mousnier, *The Assassination of Henry IV: The Tyrannicide Problem and the Consolidation of the French Absolute Monarchy in the Early Seventeenth Century*, trans. J. Spencer (1973), 217–24.

55. A shift observed in Claude Sutto, "Le père Louis Richeome et le nouvel esprit politique des jésuites français (XVIe–XVIIe s.), in *Parmi les hommes*, 175–84.

56. M. Fumaroli, *L'âge de l'éloquence: Rhétorique et "res literaria" de la Renaissance au seuil de l'époque classique* (Paris, 1994), 237.

57. J. Lough, *France Observed in the Seventeenth Century by British Travellers* (Stocksfield, 1984), 188. In fact, members of the Society had been officially exempt from participation in processions since 1576.

58. E. Coffin, *A True Relation of the Last Sickness and Death of Cardinall Bellarmine* (St. Omer, 1623), 389–406. J. Brodrick, *Robert Bellarmine, Saint and Scholar* (1961), remains the best English study of the cardinal.

59. W. Whitaker, *A Disputation on Holy Scripture Against the Papists, Especially Bellarmine and Stapleton*, trans. and ed., W. Fitzgerald (Cambridge, 1849), 3–6.

60. Owen, *The Puritan Turn'd Jesuite*, 33.

61. Bellarmine's suggestion was that the pope's temporal power, his right to intervene in temporal matters, was only indirect: an ability to become involved only when a ruler's actions threatened the spiritual interests of his or her subjects. Frustratingly, Bellarmine's theories were perceived by some critics as granting too much power to the pope, by others as providing too little.

2. "One World Is Not Enough": The First Jesuit Century

1. Cited in A. G. Dickens and J. Tonkin, *The Reformation in Historical Thought* (Cambridge, Mass., 1985), 97.

2. *The Jesuit Libel Case: Father Bernard Vaughan, SJ, v. "The Rock"* (1902), 6.

3. A. Olearius, *The Voyages & Travels of the Ambassadors Sent by Frederick Duke of Holstein, to the Great Duke of Muscovy, and the King of Persia . . . Whereto Are Added the Travels of John A. de Mandelslo . . . from Persia, into the East-Indies* (1662), passim.

4. L. Giard, "La devoir d'intelligence ou l'insertion des jésuites dans le monde du savoir," in L. Giard, ed., *Les jésuites à la Renaissance* (Paris, 1995), xix.

5. G. E. Ganss, trans., *The Constitutions of the Society of Jesus* (St. Louis, 1970), 292–93.

6. Ganss, *Constitutions*, 176.

7. F. Edwards, ed. and trans., *The Elizabethan Jesuits of Henry More* (1981), 31.

8. M. R. O'Connell, *Thomas Stapleton and the Counter-Reformation* (New Haven, Conn., 1964), 41.

9. Ganss, *Constitutions*, 86, 88, 135, 127, 129.

10. Whitaker, *Disputation on Holy Scripture*, 4.

11. See G. Switek, "Der Eigenart der Gesellschaft Jesu im Vergleich zu den anderen Orden in der Sicht des Ignatius und seiner ersten Gefährten," in M. Sievernich and G. Switek, eds., *Ignatianisch: Eigenart und Methode der Gesellschaft Jesu* (Freiburg, Basel, and Vienna, 1990), 204–32.

12. J. Donne, *Pseudo-Martyr: Wherein Out of Certaine Propositions and Gradations, This Conclusion Is Evicted, That Those Which Are of the Romane Religion in This Kingdome, May and Ought to Take the Oath of Allegiance*, ed. A. Raspa (Montreal, 1993), 106.

13. O'Malley, *First Jesuits*, 68.

14. H. Phillips, *Church and Culture in Seventeenth-Century France* (Cambridge, 1997).

15. On the growing worry that the interior spirituality of the Society was becoming neglected, see M. de Certeau, "La réforme de l'intérieur au temps d'Acquaviva," in *Les jésuites: Spiritualité et activités* (Paris, 1974), 61–65.

16. B. Dompnier, "La Compagnie de Jésus et la mission de l'intérieur," in Giard and de Vaucelles, *Les jésuites à l'âge baroque*, 177.

17. C. M. Burgaleta, S.J., *José de Acosta, S.J. (1540–1600): His Life and Thought* (Chicago, 1999), 6–8.

18. L. Châtellier, *The Europe of the Devout: The Catholic Reformation and the Formation of a New Society* (Cambridge, 1989), 52–53.

19. A. Ziggelaar, *François de Aguilon SJ (1567–1617), Scientist and Architect* (Rome, 1983).

20. R. Pörtner, *The Counter-Reformation in Europe: Styria 1580–1630* (Oxford, 2001), 103.

21. M. R. Forster, *The Counter-Reformation in the Villages: Religion and Reform in the Bishopric of Speyer, 1560–1720* (Ithaca, N.Y., 1992), 66–69.

22. V. Duminuco, *The Jesuit Ratio Studiorum: 400th Anniversary Perspectives* (New York, 2000).

23. The nature of Jesuit education, how much it was allied to humanistic ideals, how much it represented a throwback to classical formalism (drumming in information rather than cultivating formation), is a much-debated issue. See A. Scaglione, *The Liberal Arts and the Jesuit College System* (Amsterdam, 1986); J. C. Olin, "Erasmus and Ignatius Loyola," in *Six Essays on*

Erasmus (New York, 1979); A. P. Farrell, *The Jesuit Code of Liberal Education* (Milwaukee, 1938).

24. W. H. McCabe, *An Introduction to the Jesuit Theater* (St. Louis, 1983), 20.

25. J. Donne, *Ignatius His Conclave: An Edition of the Latin and English Texts*, ed. T. S. Healy (Oxford, 1969), xxxii; R. Bireley, "Les jésuites et la conduite de l'état baroque," in Giard and de Vaucelles, *Les jésuites à l'âge baroque*, 229, 232.

26. L. Lazar, "The First Jesuit Confraternities and Marginalised Groups in Sixteenth Century Rome," in N. Terpstra, ed., *The Politics of Ritual Kinship: Confraternities and Social Order in Early Modern Italy* (Cambridge, 2000), 132–49. A good overview of the Marian congregations is found in Châtellier, *Europe of the Devout*.

27. J. D. Selwyn, " 'Schools of Mortification': Theatricality and the Role of Penitential Practice in the Jesuits' Popular Missions," in K. J. Lualdi and A. T. Thayer, eds., *Penitence in the Age of Reformation* (Aldershot, 2000), 201–21.

28. B. Dompnier, "Les jésuites et la dévotion populaire: Autour des origines du culte de Saint Jean-François Régis (1646–1676)," in *Parmi les hommes*, 295–308.

29. Thwaites, *Jesuit Relations*, 68:37, 94; 65:14; 67:321.

30. A. Poncelet, *Histoire de la Compagnie de Jésus dans les anciens Pays-Bas* (Brussels, 1927), 546.

31. Not that Jesuits were slow to defend their title: see A. T. Wilson, ed., *History of the Missions of the Fathers of the Society of Jesus Established in Persia* (Hertford, 1925), 5.

32. T. Worcester, *Seventeenth Century Cultural Discourse: France and the Preaching of Bishop Camus* (Berlin and New York, 1999), 51. Coton (hardly a saint) was thought to have great influence over Henry IV, which was much resented in some quarters—the painful joke was that the king had too much cotton in his ears. See J.-C. Dhôtel, *Histoire des jésuites en France* (Paris, 1991), 26.

33. See O. Hufton, "Altruism and Reciprocity: The Early Jesuits and Their Female Patrons," *Renaissance Studies* 15 (2001): 328–53.

34. A. L. Fisher, "A Study in Early Jesuit Government: The Nature and Origins of the Dissent of Nicolas Bobadilla," *Viator: Medieval and Renaissance Studies* 10 (1979): 397–431; G. Lewy, "The Struggle for Constitutional Government in the Early Years of the Society of Jesus," *Church History* 29 (1960): 141–60.

35. Scaglione, *Liberal Arts*, 62.

36. G. R. Dimler, "The *Imago Primo Saeculi:* Jesuit Emblems and the Secular Tradition," *Thought: A Review of Culture and Ideas*, 56 (1981); 435, 438.

37. Thwaites, *Jesuit Relations*, 18:63–77.

3. "Over Many Vast Worlds of Water": The Jesuit Missionary Enterprise

1. *The Palme of Christian Fortitude: Or the Glorious Combats of Christians in Japonia* (St. Omer, 1630), preface.

2. D. Bouhours, *The Life of St. Francis Xavier*, trans. J. Dryden (1688), 1–2.

3. L. Thorndike, *A History of Magic and Experimental Science* (8 vols., 1923–58), VII:568.

4. P. Conor Reilly, *Athanasius Kircher, SJ: Master of a Hundred Arts, 1602–1680,* Studia Kircheriana 1 (Wiesbaden and Rome, 1974), 179.

5. S. J. Gould, *Rocks of Ages: Science and Religion in the Fullness of Life* (2001), frontispiece comment.

6. J. G. Keysler, *Travels Through Germany, Bohemia, Hungary, Switzerland, Italy, and Lorrain: Giving a True and Just Description of the Present State of Those Countries* (4 vols., 1760), II: 174–76.

7. S. J. Harris, "Mapping Jesuit Science: The Role of Travel in the Geography of Knowledge," in O'Malley et al., eds., *The Jesuits,* 220–21.

8. G. J. Bender, *Angola Under the Portuguese* (1978), 62.

9. J. Correia-Afonso, *Letters from the Mughal Court: The First Jesuit Mission to Akbar (1580–1583)* (Anand, 1980), 38–43.

10. See, for instance, D. E. Mungello, *The Forgotten Christians of Hangzhou* (Honolulu, 1994).

11. N. P. Cushner, *Lords of the Land: Sugar, Wine, and Jesuit Estates of Coastal Peru, 1600–1767* (Albany, N.Y., 1980), 30.

12. Reilly, *Kircher,* 147–48.

13. D. Block, *Mission Culture on the Upper Amazon* (Lincoln, Neb., 1994).

14. For instance, G. Schurhammer, S.J., "Xaveriuslegenden und Wunder: Kritisch Untersucht," *Archivum Historicum Societatis Iesu* 32 (1963): 179–92. Loyola, when the Society was campaigning for his canonization, posed an even greater problem: just what had he done that could be classed as miraculous? On this, see F. R. Guettée, *Histoire des jésuites, composée sur documents authentiques en partie inédits* (3 vols., Paris, 1858–59), I:99.

15. Thwaites, *Jesuit Relations,* 8:195; 42:127.

16. Tylenda, *Jesuit Saints and Martyrs,* 142–44, 99–101, 72. Kino has also recently been commemorated with three identical statues—one in Tucson, Arizona (the center of his missionary activities), another in Magdalena, Mexico (where he died), and another in Segno, Italy (his birthplace).

17. G. Edmundson, ed. and trans., *Journal of the Travels and Labours of Father Samuel Fritz in the River of the Amazons Between 1686 and 1723,* Hakluyt Society, 2nd. series 51 (1922), 60, 66.

18. J. Brodrick, *St. Francis Xavier, 1506–1552* (1952), 286.

19. C. W. Polzer, "Kino on People and Places," in C. Chapple, ed., *The Jesuit Tradition in Education and Missions: A 450-year Perspective* (1993), 234.

20. Ganss, *Constitutions,* 79–80.

21. O'Malley, *First Jesuits,* 55. See T. V. Cohen, "Sociologie de la croyance: Jésuites au Portugal et en Espagne (1540–1562)," in *Parmi les hommes,* 24–25, for a statistical breakdown of the desired careers of those who joined the Society: something like 40 percent in the period under discussion expressed an interest in a missionary life in the "Indies," 25 percent of these with extreme enthusiasm; 10 percent ruled missionary work out altogether, usually pleading ill health or lack of appropriate learning. Also see his "Why the Jesuits Joined, 1540–1600," *Historical Papers* (Canadian Historical Association, 1974), 237–58; A. Lynn Martin, *The Jesuit Mind: The Mentality of an Elite in Early-Modern France* (Ithaca, N.Y., 1988).

22. J. P. Donnelly, S.J., *Jacques Marquette, S.J., 1637–1675* (Chicago, 1985), 17.

23. J. Brodrick, S.J., *The Progress of the Jesuits (1556–79)* (1946), 207–8.

24. See T. McCoog, review essay, *Sixteenth Century Journal* 18 (1987): 462–63.

25. Thwaites, *Jesuit Relations,* 8:167.

26. J. T. Axtell, *The Invasion Within: The Contest of Cultures in Colonial North America* (New York, 1985), 78.

27. *Palme of Christian Fortitude,* preface.

28. J. P. Donnelly, "Antonio Possevino's Plan for World Evangelisation," in J. S. Cummins, ed., *Christianity and Missions, 1450–1850* (Aldershot, 1997), 55–56.

29. Tylenda, *Jesuit Saints and Martyrs,* 70–72, 387–91; J. P. Ronda, "We Are Well as We Are: An Indian Critique of Seventeenth Century Christian Missions," *William and Mary Quarterly* 34 (1977): 66–82; Thwaites, *Jesuit Relations,* 14:51; 8:56.

30. B. Prasad, *History of Jahangir* (Allahabad, 1930).

31. P. A. Cohen, "The Anti-Christian Tradition in China," *Journal of Asian Studies* 20 (1960): 171; H. W. Bowden, *American Indians and Christian Missions: Studies in Cultural Conflict* (Chicago, 1981), 82.

32. Elison, *Deus Destroyed,* 321.

33. C. R. Boxer, *The Christian Century in Japan 1549–1650* (Manchester, 1993), 58–64.

34. M. Conte-Helm, *The Japanese and Europe: Economic and Cultural Encounters* (1996), 3.

35. Thwaites, *Jesuit Relations,* 36:111; 30:151; 47:293, 48:223, 32:65; 30:149; 45:125; 49:155; 34:37; 47:221; 43:27; 35:29.

36. B. Hinsch, *Passions of the Cut Sleeve: The Male Homosexual Tradition in China* (Berkeley, Calif., 1990), 2.

37. L. Le Comte, *Memoirs and Observations Topographical, Physical, Mathematical, Mechanical, Natural, Civil, and Ecclesiastical: Made in a Late Journey Through the Empire of China, and Published in Several Letters* (1697), 95–100, 59, 64, 128, 126, preface, 123. On Le Comte see M. Lazard, "Les tribulations d'un jésuite en Chine: Le père Le Comte et la conversion," in *Parmi les hommes,* 351–61.

38. W. Wright, *A Briefe Relation of the Persecution Lately Made Against the Catholike Christians in the Kingdome of Japonia* (St. Omer, 1619), 21–23.

39. Elison, *Deus Destroyed,* 16.

40. J. F. Moran, *The Japanese and the Jesuits: Alessandro Valignano in Sixteenth-Century Japan* (1993).

41. D. E. Mungello, *Curious Land: Jesuit Accommodation and the Origins of Sinology* (Stuttgart, 1985).

42. C. E. Ronan, ed., *East Meets West: The Jesuits in China 1582–1773* (Chicago, 1988).

43. C. Pagani, " 'One Continuous Symphony': Automata and the Jesuit Mission in Qing China," in B. H. K. Luk, ed., *Contacts Between Cultures: Eastern Asia: History and Social Sciences* (Lampeter, 1992), 279–84.

44. A. Rowbotham, *Missionary and Mandarin: The Jesuits at the Court of China* (Berkeley, Calif., 1942), 79–101. Other Jesuit directors of the astronomy bureau were Kilian Stumpf (1711–20), Ignatius Koegler (1720–46), and Augustin von Hallerstein (1746–74).

45. J. Waley-Cohen, "God and Guns in Eighteenth-Century China: Jesuit Missionaries and the Military Campaigns of the Qianlong Emperor (1736–1795)," in Luk, ed., *Contacts Between Cultures,* 94–99; J. Spence, *The China Helpers: Western Advisers in China, 1620–1960* (1969).

46. J. S. Cummins, "Two Missionary Methods in China: Mendicants and Jesuits," in V. Sánchez, ed., *España en Extremo Oriente* (Madrid, 1979), 103–4.

47. P. M. D'Elia, *Galileo in China* (Cambridge, Mass., 1960), 21.

48. Alden, *Making of an Enterprise,* 56.

49. Le Comte, *Memoirs,* 124.

50. Thwaites, *Jesuit Relations,* 19:39.

51. M. Pomeldi, "Beyond Unbelief: Early Jesuit Interpretations of Native Religion," *Studies in Religion* 16 (1987): 275–87.

52. B. Keen, ed., *Latin American Civilisation, History and Society, 1492 to the Present*, 5th ed. (1991), 204.

53. Thwaites, *Jesuit Relations*, 1:173.

54. Thwaites, *Jesuit Relations*, 8:173.

55. J. P Ronda, "The European Indian: Jesuit Civilisation Planning in New France," *Church History* 41 (1972): 385–95. For accounts of such debate see A. Pagden, *The Fall of Natural Man: The American Indian and the Origins of Comparative Ethnology* (Cambridge, 1982).

56. Thwaites, *Jesuit Relations*, 16:63, 77–83.

57. Thwaites, *Jesuit Relations*, 26:282.

58. H. Hosten, "Father Nicholas Pimenta," *Journal and Proceedings of the Asiatic Society of Bengal*, new series 23 (1927): 68.

4. "Sometimes Sweetly, Sometimes with the Sword": Missionary Methods

1. T. Middleton, *A Game at Chess*, ed. T. H. Howard-Hill (Manchester, 1993), 11.

2. The image—from D. Bartoli's *Dell'istoria della Compagnia di Giesu l'Asia* (1657–63)—is reproduced in D. Alden, *The Making of an Enterprise: The Society of Jesus in Portugal, Its Empire, and Beyond, 1540–1750* (Stanford, Calif., 1996), facing 38.

3. Lockman, *Travels*, xii.

4. S. Purchas, *Purchas His Pilgrimage, or Relations of the World and the Religions Observed in All Ages and Places Discovered, from the Creation unto This Present* (1617), 5, 14, 19.

5. A. Kircher, *China Illustrata*, ed. and trans. Charles D. Van Tuyl (Muskogee, Okla., 1987), 98.

6. Purchas, *Purchas His Pilgrimage*, 14–16.

7. M. Geddes, *The History of the Church of Malabar, from the Time of Its Being First Discover'd by the Portuguezes in the Year 1501* (1694), 74.

8. L. de Camões, *The Lusiad: Or, the Discovery of India*, tr. W. J. Mickle (1798), 1.

9. D. Lach, *Asia in the Making of Europe*, vol. 1 (Chicago, 1965).

10. M. Trudel. *The Beginnings of New France, 1524–1663* (Toronto, 1973), 9–10.

11. P. Seed, *Ceremonies of Possession in Europe's Conquest of the New World, 1492–1640* (Cambridge, 1995), 69.

12. Thwaites, *Jesuit Relations*, 1:55.

13. Purchas, *Purchas His Pilgrimage*, 61.

14. J. Metzler, "Foundation of the Congregation de Propaganda Fide by Gregory XV," in Metzler, ed., *Sacrae Congregationis de Propaganda Fide memoria rerum*, vol. 1.1, *1622–1700* (Rome, 1971), 79–111.

15. Neill, *History of Christianity in India*, 156–57.

16. On Priber see K. Mellon Jr., "Christian Priber's Cherokee Kingdom of Paradise," *Georgia Historical Quarterly* 57 (1973): 319–33.

17. Elison, *Deus Destroyed*, 87.

18. E. Sanceau, *Knight of the Renaissance: D. João de Castro, Soldier, Sailor, Scientist, and Vice-Roy of India 1500–1548* (1949), 108.

19. See F. Goldie, *The First Christian Mission to the Great Mogul; or, The Story of Blessed Rudolf Acquaviva, and of His Four Companions in Martyrdom* (Dublin, 1887); T. R. de Souza, "Why Cuncolim Martyrs? An Historical Reassessment," in T. R. de Sousa and C. J. Borges, eds., *Jesuits in India in Historical Perspective* (Macao, 1992), 35–47.

20. C. R. Boxer, "A Note on Portuguese Missionary Methods in the East," *Ceylon Historical Journal* 10 (1965): 77–90.

21. C. R. Boxer, *A Great Luso-Brazilian Figure* (1957); E. B. Burns, ed., *A Documentary History of Brazil* (1966), 82–89.

22. Neill, *India*, 97.

23. T. Cohen, "Who Is My Neighbour? The Missionary Ideals of Manuel de Nobrega," in J. Gagliano and C. E. Ronan, eds., *Jesuit Encounters in the New World: Jesuit Chroniclers, Geographers, Educators and Missionaries in the Americas, 1549–1767* (Rome, 1997), 216.

24. B. Blum, "Luis de Valdivia: Defender of the Araucanians," *Mid-America* 24 (1942): 109–37.

25. P. Caraman, *The Lost Paradise: An Account of the Jesuits in Paraguay, 1607–1768* (1975).

26. S. MacCormack, *Religion in the Andes: Vision and Imagination in Early Colonial Peru* (Princeton, N.J., 1991), 263–64.

27. P. Goddard, "Converting the Savage: Jesuits and Montagnais in Seventeenth-Century New France," *Catholic Historical Review* 84 (1998): 119–39.

28. *The Travels of Several Learned Missionaries of the Society of Jesus into Divers Parts of the Archipelago, India, China and America* (1713), sig. A3.

29. Elison, *Deus Destroyed*, 31.

30. Neill, *History of Christianity in India*, 305–7.

31. J. G. Shea, *Discovery and Exploration of the Mississippi Valley* (New York, 1852), 22.

32. V. Cronin, *A Pearl to India: The Life of Roberto de Nobili* (1959).

33. Thwaites, *Jesuit Relations*, 5:105.

34. Thwaites, *Jesuit Relations*, 8:177.

35. Thwaites, *Jesuit Relations*, 10:1. On the importance of gift giving in Huron culture, see H. W. Bowden, *American Indians and Christian Missions: Studies in Cultural Conflict* (Chicago, 1981), 66–67.

36. Axtell, *The Invasion Within*, 80; G. H. Dunne, *Generation of Giants* (1962), 4–14.

37. P. A. Rule, "The Confucian Interpretation of the Jesuits," *Papers on Far Eastern History* 6 (1972): 1–61.

38. Thwaites, *Jesuit Relations*, 22:169.

39. Bowden, *American Indians*, 86–87.

40. A. Métraux, "Jesuit Missions in South America," in J. H. Steward, ed., *Handbook of South American Indians*, vol. 5 (New York, 1963), 645–54.

41. Witek, "Controversial Ideas in China," 110–15.; J. S. Cummins, *The Travels and Controversies of Friar Domingo Navarrette, 1618–1686* (Hakluyt Society, 1960), xliii.

42. X. Rajamanickam, "The Newly Discovered 'Informatio' of Robert de Nobili," *Archivum Historicum Societatis Iesu* 39 (1970): 229–30, 237.

43. D. E. Mungello, *The Chinese Rites Controversy: Its History and Meaning* (Nettetal, 1994).

44. H. J. Coleridge, ed., *The Life and Letters of Saint Francis Xavier* (2 vols., 1890), II:67.

45. Diffie and Winius, *Foundations of the Portuguese Empire*, 258.

46. Shea, *Discovery*, 22–23.

47. Coleridge, *Life and Letters*, I:152.

48. C. R. Boxer, *The Church Militant and Iberian Expansion 1440–1770* (Baltimore, 1978), 100.

49. Wright, *Briefe Relation*, 78.

50. *Palme of Christian Fortitude*, preface.

51. Thwaites, *Jesuit Relations*, 17:16; 7:39; 10:89.

52. J. E. Sherman, *The Nature of Martyrdom: A Dogmatic and Moral Analysis According to the Teachings of St Thomas Aquinas* (Paterson, N.J., 1942), 61.

53. J. Donne, *Biathanatos*, ed. E. W. Sullivan (Newark, 1984), 61.

54. *True Relation . . . Ogilvie*, 33.

55. R. Bristow, *A Briefe Treatise of Divers Plain and Sure Wayes* (Antwerp, 1599), fols. 73–73v.

56. T. Reef, "In the Shadow of the Saints: Jesuit Missionaries and Their New World Narratives," *Romance Philology* 53 (1999): 165–81.

57. G. Laflèche, "Les jésuites de la Nouvelle France et le mythe de leurs martyrs," in *Parmi les hommes*, 35–43.

58. Thwaites, *Jesuit Relations*, 33:89.

5. "Rhapsodies of Calumny": The Creation of the Anti-Jesuit Myth

1. Thorpe, "Notes," M21a, 10.

2. *Occasional Letters on the Present Affairs of the Jesuits in France* (1763), 95.

3. *St. Ignatius' Ghost, Appearing to the Jesuits, upon the King's Signing the Act Against the Growth of Popery: A Satyr* (1700), 9–10.

4. T. Goodwin, *Aggravation of Sinne, and Sinning Against Knowledge and Mercie* (1643), 4.

5. J. Gee, *The Foot Out of the Snare: With a Detection of Sundry Late Practices and Impostures of the Priests and Iesuits in England* (1624), 2.

6. St. Vincent, *The Waie Home to Christ*, trans. J. Proctor (1556), sig. C5v.

7. H. Ainsworth, *Counterpoyson: Considerations Touching the Points in Difference Between the Godly . . . and the Seduced Brethren* (1642), 3v; Gee, *The Foot Out of the Snare*, 2.

8. *Trust a Papist and Trust the Devil* (1642), 4.

9. *Jesuitical Policy and Iniquity Exposed: A View of the Constitution and Character of the Society of Jesus* (Glasgow, 1831), 14.

10. J. Wadsworth, *The Memoires of Mr. James Wadswort, a Jesuit That Recanted* (1679), 51.

11. J. Jingle [pseud.], *Spiritual Fornication: A Burlesque Poem* (1732), 5–23.

12. *The Wanton Jesuit; or, Innocence Seduced* (1731), II.i.

13. T. Smollett, *The Adventures of Peregrine Pickle* (Oxford, 1936), 699.

14. *Wanton Jesuit*, I.i.

15. See S. Haliczer, *Sexuality in the Confessional: A Sacrament Profaned* (Oxford, 1996).

16. *Wanton Jesuit*, I.i.

17. *A Further Discovery of the Mystery of Jesuitism* (1658), 23, 22, preface, 28.

18. *A Discoverie of the Most Secret and Subtile Practises of the Jesuites* (1610), sigs. A1–B1.

19. Thorndike, *A History of Magic and Experimental Science*, 532.

20. *The Doctrines and Practices of the Jesuits* (1759), 41.

21. *Authentic Memoirs of the Exquisitely Villainous Jesuit, Father Richard Walpole* (London, 1733),

13. See also F. Edwards, "Sir Robert Cecil, Edward Squier and the Poisoned Pommel," *Recusant History* 25 (2001): 377–414; M. Murphy, *St. George's College, Seville, 1592–1767,* Catholic Record Society 73 (1992), 11.

22. Crashaw, *Bespotted Jesuit*, 43.

23. Gee, *Foot Out of the Snare*, 44.

24. *A True Relation of the Proceedings Against Iohn Ogilvie* (Edinburgh, 1615), 5–6.

25. A. Hopper, " 'The Popish Army of the North': Anti-Catholicism and Parliamentary Allegiance in Civil War Yorkshire, 1642–46," *Recusant History* 25 (2000): 15.

26. *The Jesuits Character; or, A Description of the Wonderfull Birth, Wicked Life, and Wretched Death, of a Jesuit* (1642), sig. A2r.

27. M. de Waele, "Pour la sauvegarde du roi et du royaume: L'expulsion des jésuites de France à la fin des guerres de religion," *Canadian Journal of History* 29 (1994): 267; *Pyrotechnica Loyolana: Ignatian Fire-Works, or The Fiery Jesuit's Temper and Behaviour* (1667), 122–23.

28. *The Doctrines and Practices*, 39.

29. *The Doctrines and Practices*, 20.

30. See, for instance, *A Brief Account of the Rebellions and Bloodshed Occasioned by the Anti-Christian Practises of the Jesuits and Other Popish Emissaries in the Empire of Ethiopia* (London, 1679).

31. A. L. Martin, "The Jesuit Mystique," *Sixteenth Century Journal* 4 (1973): 31–40.

32. Wadsworth, *Memoirs*, 54.

33. T. McCoog, S.J., " 'Laid up Treasure': The Finances of the English Jesuits in the Seventeenth Century," in W. J. Sheils and D. Wood, eds., *The Church and Wealth, Studies in Church History* 24 (Oxford, 1987), 258.

34. *The Doctrines and Practices*, 18.

35. J. Gerard, *The Secret Instructions, Monita Secreta, of the Jesuits* (1901).

36. *Jesuits Character*, sig. A2v.

37. Crashaw, *Bespotted Jesuit*, sig. A4.

38. *The Jesuit Discovered, or, A Brief Discourse of the Policies of the Church of Rome* (London, 1659), 1, 3.

39. H. I. Roper, *The Jesuits* (1848), 13.

40. J. Wadsworth, *Memoirs*, 50.

41. T. Morton, *A Full Satisfaction Concerning a Double Romish Iniquitie: Hainous Rebellion, and More Than Heathenish Aequivocation* (1606), dedicatory epistle, sigs. A3v, A4r; part III, 49, 55; A. Jonsen and S. Toulmin, *The Abuse of Casuistry: A History of Moral Reasoning* (Berkeley, Calif., 1988), 205.

42. Cited in H. J. Sieben, "Option für den Papst: Die Jesuiten auf dem Konzil von Trent, dritte Sitzungsperiode 1562/1563," in *Ignatianisch*, 239.

43. *The Popish Courant* (1714), 1.

44. W. F. Leith, *Narratives of the Scottish Catholics* (Edinburgh, 1885), 227.

45. P. Caraman, ed., *John Gerard: The Autobiography of an Elizabethan* (London, 1951), 9.

46. B. Basset, *The English Jesuits from Campion to Martindale* (London, 1967), 41–43.

47. Hicks, ed., *Letters and Memorials of Father Robert Persons*, 331.

48. *Cobbet's Complete State Trials* (1809), I: 1059.

49. P. J. Holmes, ed., *Elizabethan Casuistry*, Catholic Record Society 67 (1981), 72.

50. C. Ingrao, *The Habsburg Monarchy 1618–1815* (Cambridge, 1994), 113.

51. A. Lloyd Moote, *Louis XIII, the Just* (Berkeley, Calif., 1989), 243; M. Sánchez, *The Empress, the Queen and the Nun: Women and Power at the Court of Philip III of Spain* (Baltimore, 1998), 21–22.

52. J. Lynch, *The Hispanic World in Crisis and Change* (Oxford, 1992), 360–65; R. Trevor Davies, *Spain in Decline, 1621–1700* (1957), 118.

53. T. E. Kaiser, "Madame de Pompadour and the Theatres of Power," *French History* 19 (1996): 1025.

54. M. Heimbucher, *Die Orden und Kongregationen der katholische Kirche* (Paderborn, 1965), II:179.

55. See A. Douarche, *L'Université de Paris et les jésuites* (Paris, 1888).

56. *The Doctrines and Practices*, 58.

57. D. E. Mungello, *The Great Encounter of China and the West, 1500–1800* (Lanham, Md., 1999), 48; Bangert, *History*, 99.

58. *Letters and Memorials*, 83.

59. *Jesuit Discovered*, 3–4.

60. Cushner, *Lords of the Land*, 69; H. W. Konrad, *A Jesuit Hacienda in Colonial Mexico: Santa Lucía, 1576–1767* (Stanford, Calif., 1980), 176–86.

61. L. Pastor, *The History of the Popes from the Close of the Middle Ages* (40 vols., London, 1891–1953), 37:33.

62. W. Paterson, *The Great Jesuit Plot of the Nineteenth Century* (Edinburgh, 1894), 20.

63. Donne, *Pseudo-Martyr*, 106–8.

64. *The Policy of the Jesuits* (1658), sigs. B1v–B2r.

65. J. P. Donnelly, S.J., "The Jesuit College at Padua: Growth, Suppression, Attempts at Restoration: 1552–1606," *Archivum Historicum Societatis Iesu* 51 (1982): 45–79.

66. A useful survey of these writings is in P. Milward, *Religious Controversies of the Elizabethan Age* (1977), 116–26.

67. W. Watson, *A Sparing Discoverie of Our English Iesuits* (1601), preface, 11–12. Divisions that such authorities were delighted to exploit: see P. E. McCullough, *Sermons at Court: Politics and Religion in Elizabethan and Jacobean Preaching* (Cambridge, 1998), 123.

68. H. O. Evennett, *The Cardinal of Lorraine and the Council of Trent* (Cambridge, 1930), 57–62.

69. Squire, *Authentic Memoirs*, 23.

70. H. M. Goodpasture, ed., *Cross and Sword: An Eyewitness History of Christianity in Latin America* (Maryknoll, N.Y., 1989), 30–32.

71. *A Journal of All the Proceedings Between the Jansenists and the Jesuits* (1659), sig. A2.

72. *Mémoires du père René Rapin*, ed. Léon Aubinau (3 vols., Lyon, 1865), I:i.

73. The edition of the letters consulted was H. F. Stewart, ed., *Les lettres provinciales de Blaise Pascal* (Manchester, 1920).

74. See, for instance, J. Viner, "Secularizing Tendencies in Catholic Social Thought from the Renaissance to the Jansenist-Jesuit Controversy," *History of Political Economy* 10, no. 1 (1978): 142.

75. L. Ceyssens, "Que penser finalement de l'histoire du jansénisme et de l'antijansénisme," *Revue d'Histoire Ecclésiastique* 88 (1993): 108–30; "L'antijansénisme à la cour de Madrid au tournant des 17e–18e siècles," *Revue d'Histoire Ecclésiastique* 94 (1999): 15–29.

76. A. Auguste, *Les origines du jansénisme dans le diocèse de Toulouse* (Paris, 1922), 40–41.

77. F. Courtney, "English Jesuit Colleges in the Low Countries 1593–1794," *Heythrop Journal* 4 (1963): 257.

78. *Exposure*, 18.

79. *The Missionaries Arts Discovered* (1688), sig. A3.

80. L. Owen, *Speculum Jesuiticum* (1632), 15.

Notes

6. "The Jesuit Is No More": Enlightenment and Suppression

1. M. P. Harney, *The Jesuits in History: The Society of Jesus Through Four Centuries* (New York, 1941), 345.
2. A. Carayon, *Les prisons du marquis de Pombal, ministre de S.M. le roi de Portugal, 1759–1777* (Paris, 1865), vii.
3. *A Faithful and Exact Narrative of the Horrid Tragedy . . . Lately Acted at Thorn, in Polish Prussia, by the Contrivances and Instigation of the Jesuits* (London, 1725), 1–13; *The Speech of the Reverend Father, the Advocate for the Jesuits of Thorn* (Dublin, 1725); J. Kloczowski, *A History of Polish Christianity* (Cambridge, 2000), 134.
4. S. Sharp, *Letters from Italy, Describing the Customs and Manners of That Country, in the Years 1765 and 1766: To Which Is Annexed an Admonition to Gentlemen Who Pass the Alps in Their Tour Through Italy* (London, 1767), 43–46.
5. H. Turlerus, *The Traveiler of Jerome Turler* (1575), 66.
6. C. Howard, *English Travellers of the Renaissance* (London, 1923), 73.
7. R. Ascham, *The Schoolmaster*, ed. L. V. Ryan (Charlottesville, Va., 1974), 67.
8. Sharp, *Letters from Italy*, 69–70, 61, 50, 191, 194.
9. J. E. Barker, *Diderot's Treatment of the Christian Religion in the Encyclopedia* (New York, 1941). The article on the Jesuits, which rehearsed the usual litany of disreputable behavior (tyrannicide, political scheming, affection for the dark arts, etc.), appeared in vol. 8 in 1766.
10. Isaiah 49:6; Johnson, "Blood, Tears and Xavier Water," 198.
11. On the emergence of the term "enlightenment"—a relative newcomer compared with *Aufklärung*—see J. Lough, "Reflections on Enlightenment and Lumières," *British Journal for Eighteenth Century Studies* 8 (1985): 1–15.
12. I. Disraeli, *Despotism, or The Fall of the Jesuits: A Political Romance* (1811), vii.
13. C. S. Dessain, ed., *The Letters and Diaries of John Henry Newman*, vol. 12 (1961), 117.
14. J. N. Loriquet, *Pombal, Choiseul et D'Aranda, ou L'intrigue des trois cabinets* (Paris, 1830), 1.
15. D. Francis, *Portugal 1715–1808: Joanine, Pombaline and Rococo Portugal as Seen by British Diplomats and Traders* (1985).
16. *The Proceedings and Sentence of the Spiritual Court of Inquisition of Portugal, Against G. Malagrida, Jesuit, for Heresy, Hypocrisy, False Prophecies, Impostures, and Various Other Heinous Crimes; Together with the Sentence of the Lay Court of Justice* (1762), 5; M. Cheke, *Dictator of Portugal* (1938), 152–57.
17. A. Weld, *The Suppression of the Society of Jesus in the Portuguese Dominions* (1877).
18. K. Maxwell, *Pombal: Paradox of the Enlightenment* (Cambridge, 1995), 20.
19. *The Doctrines and Practices of the Jesuits* (1759), 3, 4, 6, 68.
20. *L'apparition de la comète: Preuve astronomique contre les jésuites* (Paris, 1759), 19, 7, 14.
21. A good summary of the Lavalette affair, and one which confronts the tricky issue of just what Lavalette's superiors did and did not know about his activities, is D. G. Thompson, "The Lavalette Affair and the Jesuit Superiors," *French History* 10 (1996): 206–39.
22. A. Gaubil, *Correspondance de Pékin 1722–59*, ed. Renné Simon (Geneva, 1970), 858.
23. See especially D. Van Kley, *The Jansenists and the Expulsion of the Jesuits from France, 1757–1765* (New Haven, Conn., 1975); D. Van Kley, *The Religious Origins of the French Revolution: From Calvin to the Civil Constitution, 1560–1791* (New Haven, Conn., 1996).

24. Julia Swann, *Politics in the Parlement of Paris Under Louis XV, 1754–1774* (Cambridge, 1995).
25. D. G. Thompson, "General Ricci and the Suppression of the Jesuit Order in France, 1760–64," *Journal of Ecclesiastical History* 37 (1986): 426–41.
26. *Occasional Letters on the Present Affairs of the Jesuits in France* (1763), 125–26.
27. Beaumont du Repaire, *Instruction pastorale*, preface.
28. *Occasional Letters*, 4, 7.
29. J. Lynch, *Bourbon Spain 1700–1808* (Oxford, 1989).
30. M. Mörner, ed., *The Expulsion of the Jesuits from Latin America* (New York, 1965).
31. Thorpe, "Notes," M21a, 2.
32. M. R. Forster, *Catholic Revival in the Age of the Baroque: Religious Identity in Southwest Germany, 1550–1750* (Cambridge, 2001), 223.
33. Thorpe, "Notes," M21a, 1, 3.
34. Thorpe, "Notes," M24, 3
35. J. A. M. Crétineau-Joly, *Clément XIV et les jésuites* (Paris, 1847).
36. T. O'Brien Hanley, ed., *The John Carroll Papers* (Notre Dame, 1976), I:27.
37. Thorpe, "Notes," M23c, 1.
38. Thorpe, "Notes," M23c, 49.
39. D'Alembert, *Account of the Destruction*, 8.
40. *A Catalogue of the Most Eminently Venerable Relics of the Roman Catholic Church . . . Which Are to Be Disposed of by Auction, at the Church of Saint Peter's at Rome, the 1st of June, 1753, by Order of the Pope, for the Benefit of a Young Gentleman of Great Rank . . .* (1818), 8.
41. *An Exposure of the Jesuits* (Cheltenham, 1828), 15–16.
42. F. de La Pillonière, *An Answer to the Reverend Dr. Snape's Accusation, by F. de La Pillonnière, Formerly a Jesuit, Now Living with the Bishop of Bangor: Containing an Account of His Behaviour . . . Amongst the Jesuits, of His Leaving Their Society, and Afterwards Turning Protestant* (1717), 8.
43. H. I. Roper, *The Jesuits: A Lecture* (London, 1848), 10.
44. B. N. Schilling, *Conservative England and the Case Against Voltaire* (New York, 1950), chap. 13.
45. See, for instance, F. A. Kafker, *The Encyclopedists as a Group*, Studies in Voltaire and the Eighteenth Century 345 (Oxford, 1996), 163.
46. J. Hardy Jr., "French Jesuit Missions and the Enlightenment," *Bucknell Review* 12 (1964): 94–108.
47. M. Góngara, *Studies in the Colonial History of Spanish America* (Cambridge, 1975), 228–29.
48. G. Tachard, *A Relation of the Voyage to Siam, Performed by Six Jesuits, Sent by the French King, to the Indies and China, in the Year, 1685: With Their Astrological Observations, and Their Remarks of Natural Philosophy, Geography, Hydrography, and History* (1688), 1–27.
49. H. Woolf, *The Transits of Venus: A Study of Eighteenth Century Science* (Princeton, N.J., 1959), 2–4, 126–33.
50. J. Cannon, *Samuel Johnson and the Politics of Hanoverian England* (Oxford, 1994), 22.
51. D. J. Greene, *The Politics of Samuel Johnson* (New Haven, Conn., 1960), 109. Johnson was also critical of the Society's activities in Ethiopia, on which see J. L. Gold, "Johnson's Translation of Lobo," *Proceedings of the Modern Language Society of America* 80 (1965): 51–61.
52. J. Torbarina, "The Meeting of Boskovic with Dr. Johnson," *Studia Romanica et Anglica Zagrabiensia* 13–14 (1967): 6; L. L. Whyte, ed., *Roger John Boscovich S.J., F.R.S., 1711–1787: Studies of His Life and Work* (1961).
53. T. L. MacDonald, "Riccioli and Lunar Nomenclature," *Journal of the British Astronomical Society* 27 (1967): 112–17.
54. J. Gerard, *The Church Versus Science* (1905), 5.

55. W. G. L. Randles, *The Unmaking of the Medieval Christian Cosmos* (Aldershot, 1999), 92–94.

56. W. Wallace, *Galileo and His Sources: The Heritage of the Collegio Romano in Galileo's Science* (Princeton, N.J., 1984).

57. P. M. D'Elia, *Galileo in China: Relations Through the Roman College Between Galileo and the Jesuit Scientist-Missionaries* (Cambridge, Mass., 1960); B. Szcześniak, "Notes on the Penetration of Copernican Thought in China," *Journal of the Royal Asiatic Society* (1945): 30–38.

58. R. Feldhay, *Galileo and the Church: Political Inquisition or Critical Dialogue?* (Cambridge, 1995), 10; I. Kelter, "The Refusal to Accommodate: Jesuit Exegetes and the Copernican System," *Sixteenth Century Journal* 26 (1995): 273–83, on early anti-Copernican Jesuits.

59. Randles, *Cosmos*, 94.

60. G. Galilei, *Dialogue Concerning the Two World Systems,* tr. S. Drake (Berkeley, Calif., 1953), 110.

61. J. L. Heilbron, *Electricity in the Seventeenth and Eighteenth Centuries: A Study of Early Modern Physics* (Berkeley, Calif., 1979), 110.

62. T. R. Ford, "Stranger in a Foreign Land: José de Acosta's Scientific Realizations in Sixteenth-Century Peru," *Sixteenth Century Journal* 29 (1998): 32.

63. R. R. Palmer, "The French Jesuits in the Age of Enlightenment: A Statistical Study of the *Journal de Trévoux,*" *American Historical Review* 45 (1939–40): 44–58. On the emergence of mathematics as a Jesuit discipline, see A. Meskens, "The Jesuit Maths School in Antwerp in the Early Seventeenth Century," *Seventeenth Century* 12 (1997): 11–22.

64. D. Sorkin, "Reform Catholicism and Religious Enlightenment," *Austrian History Yearbook* 30 (1999): 201.

65. A. Cazes, "Un adversaire de Diderot et des philosophes," in *Mélanges offerts par ses amis et ses élèves à M. Gustave Lanson* (1922), 235–49.

66. R. Trousson, "Deux lettres du P. Castel à propos du 'Discours sur les Sciences et les Arts,' " in J. Pappas, ed., *Essays on Diderot and the Enlightenment in Honor of Otis Fellows* (Geneva, 1974), 293.

67. Roper, *The Jesuits*, 10.

68. St. Ambrose, *'On the Duties of the Clergy'*, in *A Select Library of Nicene and Post-Nicene Fathers,* series II, vol. 10 (1896), 122.

69. S. Jaki, *The Road of Science and the Ways to God* (Edinburgh, 1978); A. Funkenstein, *Theology and the Scientific Imagination* (Princeton, N.J., 1986); D. Noble, *A World Without Women: The Christian Clerical Culture of Western Science* (New York, 1992); M. Biagioli, "Jesuit Science Between Texts and Contexts," *Studies in the History and Philosophy of Science* 25 (1994): 637–46.

70. *A Translation of the Bull for Effectual Suppression of the Order of Jesuits* (1774), 35.

71. Pastor, *History of the Popes*, 38: 295.

72. Mariano Picón-Salas, *A Cultural History of Spanish America from Conquest to Independence* (Berkeley, Calif., 1962), 137–38.

73. Thorpe, "Notes," M21a, 6

74. *The Bulls of Popes Clement XIV and Pius VII for the Suppression and Re-Establishment of the Order of Jesuits* (1815), 7.

7. "Still on a Million Tongues":
Jesuits Since 1814

1. *Der Ex-Jesuit* (1774), 22.

2. *Relation de ce qui s'est passé entre l'un des éditeurs des documents . . . concernant la Compagnie de Jésus, et MM les rédacteurs du Journal des Débats* (Paris, 1827), 3.

3. *Letters and Papers*, XI: 275.

4. T. W. Allies, *Germany, Italy and the Jesuits* (1872), 18.

5. C. F. Adams, ed., *The Works of John Adams*, vol. 10 (Boston, 1856), 216–32.

6. *The Times*, January 27, 1815.

7. *Bulls of Clement*, 8.

8. *The Solemn Mock-Procession: or, The Tryal & Execution of the Pope and His Ministers* (1680).

9. F. Courtney, "English Jesuit Colleges in the Low Countries 1593–1794," *Heythrop Journal* 4 (1963): 263.

10. D. A. Bellenger, *The French Exiled Clergy in the British Isles After 1765: A Historical Introduction and Working List* (Bath, 1986), 3.

11. H. Fouqueray, "Une victime des journées de septembre: Le père Lanfant," *Etudes* 105 (1905): 50–75.

12. D. M Quynn, "The Art Confiscations of the Napoleonic Wars," *American Historical Review* 50 (1944–45): 437–60.

13. F. J. Coppa, *The Modern Papacy Since 1789* (1998), 34.

14. A. J. Reinerman, "Metternich Versus Chateubriand: Austria, France and the Conclave of 1829," *Austrian History Yearbook* 12 (1976): 155–80.

15. *New Catholic Encyclopedia*, alphabetical entry.

16. E. Bellasis, *Philotheus and Eugenia* (1874), 3.

17. M. H. Seymour, *Mornings Among the Jesuits at Rome* (1850), 155–56.

18. Letters of F. K. Amherst, Jesuit English Province Archives, BU/7 (January 21, 1860); BU/8 (June 7, 1862; May 26, 1862).

19. T. O'Brien Hanley, ed., *The John Carroll Papers*, (3 vol., Notre Dame, 1976), III:351.

20. F. O'Reilly, "Stonyhurst and Angelo Secchi," *Stonyhurst Magazine* (2000): 28–34.

21. E. Sue, *The Wandering Jew* (1990 edition), 73, 80, 387.

22. *Notes on the Wandering Jew, or the Jesuits and their Opponents* (Dublin, 1873), ix–x, 100.

23. *Notes on the Wandering Jew*, 13–14.

24. *Notes on the Wandering Jew*, 17–18.

25. R. J. Ross, "The Kulturkampf and the Limitations of Power in Bismarck's Germany," *Journal of Ecclesiastical History* 46 (1995): 614. For a German compendium of anti-Jesuit stories see B. Duhr, *Jesuiten-fabeln* (Freiburg im Breisgau, 1899).

26. *Notes on the Wandering Jew*, 20–21; G. Cubitt, *The Jesuit Myth: Conspiracy, Theory and Politics in Nineteenth Century France* (Oxford, 1993).

27. G. de Bertier de Sauvigny, *The Bourbon Restoration* (Philadelphia, 1967), 382.

28. D. H. Pinkney, *The French Revolution of 1830* (Princeton, N.J., 1972), 268–69.

29. J. S. MacCorry, *The Jesuit* (Edinburgh, 1853), 4.

30. A. Frogier de Ponlevoy, *Acts of the Captivity and Death of the Fathers P. Olivaint, L. Ducoudray . . . and A. de Bengy* (1871).

31. M. Larkin, *Church and State After the Dreyfus Affair* (1974), 84–85; Louis Caperan, *L'anti-clericalisme et l'affaire Dreyfus, 1897–1899* (Toulouse, 1948), 267.

32. J. C. Pitrat, *Americans Warned of Jesuitism* (New York, 1851), 13.

33. *Notes on the Wandering Jew*, 14–16.

34. L. Beecher, *A Plea for the West* (New York, 1835), 148, 11. See J. George Jr, "The Lincoln Writings of Charles P.T. Chiniquy," *Journal of the Illinois State Historical Society* 69 (1976): 17–25.

35. B. M. Smith, "Anti-Catholicism, Indian Education and Thomas Jefferson Morgan, Commissioner of Indian Affairs," *Canadian Journal of History* 23 (1988): 227.

36. Paterson, *Plot*, 12.

37. R. Baxter, *Jesuit Juggling: Forty Popish Frauds Detected and Disclosed* (New York, 1835), xii.

38. *Wandering Jew*, 19.

39. W. Paterson, *The Great Jesuit Plot of the Nineteenth Century* (Edinburgh, 1900), 2, 3, 11.

40. *Exposure of the Jesuits*, 3.

41. A. Close, *Jesuit Plots from Elizabeth to George V* (1936), 15.

42. *The Confessor: A Jesuit Tale of the Times* (1854), xi.

43. J. H. Elliot, *Russia, Poland, and the Jesuits* (1863), 3–9.

44. *Jesuitical Policy and Iniquity*, 34.

45. W. H. Anderson, *The Jesuits* (1880), 4.

46. *Annum sacrum* (1899).

47. *The Devotion to the Sacred Heart of Jesus* (Bruges, 1767), 6–10.

48. *Devotion*, 10, 16.

49. *Devotion*, 42–43.

50. J. A. Keller, *The Sacred Heart* (1898), 108 ff. Earlier in the Society's history, Jesuits such as Loyola, Borgia, and Canisius had all been devotees of the Sacred Heart, as had Jean Eudes (educated by the Society) and the seventeenth-century visionary Margaret Mary Alacoque (spiritually advised and publicized by Jesuits). Significantly, Jansenists had disapproved of such devotion, as had enlightened eighteenth-century Tuscan dukes, who claimed that it represented superstitious "cardiolatry." During the years of suppression, when the ex-Jesuit Peter John de Clorivière wanted to form a congregation that might sustain the ethos and purpose of his old order, he would name it the Society of the Heart of Jesus.

51. R. Jonas, "Anxiety, Identity and the Displacement of Violence During the Année Terrible: The Sacred Heart and the Diocese of Nantes, 1870–1871," *French Historical Studies* 9 (1975): 57; T. C. W. Blanning, "The Role of Religion in European Counter-Revolution," in D. Beales and G. Best, eds., *History, Society and the Churches: Essays in Honour of Owen Chadwick* (Cambridge, 1985), 209–10.

52. R. Jonas, "Sacred Mysteries and Holy Memories: Counter-Revolutionary France and the Sacre Coeur," *Canadian Journal of History* 32 (1997): 347–59.

53. W. A. Christian Jr., *Moving Crucifixes in Modern Spain* (Princeton, N.J., 1992).

54. Amherst Letters, BU/12 (December 20, 1869; January 21, 1870).

55. B. Tierney, *Origins of Papal Infallibility 1150–1350*, Studies in the History of Christian Thought 6 (Leiden, 1972), 1; Klaus Schutz, S.J., *Papal Primacy, from Its Origins to the Present* (Collegeville, Minn., 1996).

56. *Ineffabilis Deus*, December 8, 1854.

57. J. Godechot, *The Counter Revolution: Doctrine and Action 1789–1804* (1972), 84–102.

58. E. Leonard, *George Tyrrell and Catholic Tradition* (New York, 1982), 22; J. D. Root, "English Catholic Modernism and Science: The Case of George Tyrrell," *Heythrop Journal* 18 (1977): 271–88; M. Ranchetti, *The Catholic Modernists* (Oxford, 1969).

8. The Fifth Jesuit Century

1. P. Monaci, *The Life and Martyrdom of the Blessed Andrew Bobola* (London, 1855); L. J. Gallagher, "How We Rescued the Relics of the Blessed Andrew Bobola," *The Month* 143 (1924): 116–29; J. Murray, "St. Andrew Bobola and Poland," *The Month*, 172 (1938): 22–29. On Bobola as a symbol of nationalism, see B. Grabinski, *Das Übersinnliche im Weltkriege* (Hildesheim, 1917), 169–81.

2. A. Harrington, *Japan's Hidden Christians* (Chicago, 1993).

3. R. C. Carriker, *Father Peter John de Smet: Jesuit in the West* (Norman, Okla., 1995); G. E. Tinker, *Missionary Conquest: The Gospel and Native American Cultural Genocide* (Minneapolis, 1993).

4. A. Udia, "Jesuits' Contribution to Meteorology," *Bulletin of the American Meteorological Society* (1996): 2307–15.

5. H. J. Birx, *Interpreting Evolution: Darwin and Teilhard de Chardin* (1991).

6. F. Royer, *Father Miguel Pro* (Dublin, 1955).

7. D. Gwynn, *The Action Française Condemnation* (1928).

8. G. Passelecq, *The Hidden Encyclical of Pius XI* (New York, 1997).

9. J. S. Conway, *The Nazi Persecution of the Churches* (1968), 258; V. A. Lapomarda, "The Jesuits and the Holocaust," *Journal of Church and State* 23 (1981): 241–58.

10. W. D. Hallis, *Politics, Society and Christianity in Vichy France* (Oxford, 1995), 97.

11. T. Whitfield, *Paying the Price: Ignacio Ellacuría and the Murdered Jesuits of El Salvador* (Philadelphia, 1994).

Bibliography

WHAT FOLLOWS IS merely a list of items cited in the book's endnotes along with other books and essays that were particularly useful. Where more than one essay from a collected volume has been cited in the endnotes, only the collection is listed. For reasons of economy, the many volumes of source material contained within the *Monumenta Historica Societatis Iesu* are not listed; specific volumes from this series are referred to in the endnotes.

Those readers wanting more are directed to the mammoth bibliographical achievements contained within Carlos Sommervogel et al., *Bibliothèque de la Compagnie de Jésus* (12 vols., Brussels, Paris, Toulouse, 1890–1932), and László Polgár, *Bibliographie sur l'histoire de la Compagnie de Jésus, 1901–1980* (3 vols., Rome, 1981–90), and the continuing reviews and surveys of Jesuitica contained in successive volumes of the *Archivum Historicum Societatis Iesu* (abbreviated as *AHSI* below). Another major contribution to Jesuit scholarship is the *Diccionario histórico de la Compañía de Jesús* (4 vols., Rome and Madrid, 2001).

Those readers wanting less are directed to those items marked with an asterisk. These books are all in English, all relatively recent, and all serve as particularly useful launching pads for closer study of various aspects of Jesuit history.

Place of publication is London unless otherwise indicated.

Bibliography

Achilli, G., *Dealings with the Inquisition, or, Papal Rome, Her Priests and Her Jesuits* (1851).

Ainsworth, H., *Counterpoyson: Considerations Touching the Points in Difference Between the Godly . . . and the Seduced Brethren* (1642).

*Alden, D., *The Making of an Enterprise: The Society of Jesus in Portugal, Its Empire, and Beyond, 1540–1750* (Stanford, Calif., 1996).

Aldrich, R., *Greater France: A History of French Overseas Expansions* (New York, 1996).

All Is Not Gold That Glisters (1648).

Allies, T. W., *Germany, Italy and the Jesuits* (1872).

Amherst, F. K., Letters, Jesuit English Province Archives.

Anderson, W., *The Jesuits: A Sermon Preached . . . in Advent, 1880* (1880).

L'apparition de la comète: Preuve astronomique contre les jésuites (Paris, 1759).

Appleton, W., *A Cycle of Cathay* (New York, 1951).

Arnal, O., *Ambivalent Alliance: The Catholic Church and the Action Française* (Pittsburgh, 1985).

Ascham, R., *The Schoolmaster*, ed. L. V. Ryan (Charlottesville, VA., 1974).

Astráin, A., *Historia de la Compañía de Jésus en la asistencia de España* (7 vols., Madrid, 1902–25).

Auguste, A., *Les origines du jansénisme dans le diocèse de Toulouse* (Paris, 1922).

Aveling, H., *The Jesuits* (1981).

*Axtell, J., *The Invasion Within: The Contest of Cultures in Colonial North America* (Oxford, 1985).

————, "White Legend: The Jesuit Missions in Maryland," *Maryland Historical Magazine* 81 (1986): 1–7.

*Bailey, G. A., *Art on the Jesuit Missions in Asia and Latin America, 1542–1773* (Toronto, 1999).

Bakewell, P., *A History of Latin America: Empires and Sequels 1450–1930* (Oxford, 1997).

Balmes, J., *Protestantism and Catholicity Compared in their Effects on the Civilization of Europe*, trans. C. J. Hanford and R. Kershaw (1849).

*Bangert, W., *A History of the Society of Jesus* (St. Louis, 1976).

Barker, J. E., *Diderot's Treatment of the Christian Religion in the Encyclopédie* (New York, 1941).

Basset, B., *The English Jesuits from Campion to Martindale* (London, 1967).

Baxter, R., *Jesuit Juggling: Forty Popish Frauds Detected and Disclosed* (New York, 1835).

Beaumont du Repaire, C. de, *Instruction pastorale* (Paris, 1829).

Becker, C., *The Heavenly City of the Eighteenth-Century Philosophers* (New Haven, Conn., 1932).

Becon, T., *Prayers and Other Pieces*, ed. J. Ayre (Cambridge, 1844).

Beecher, L., *A Plea for the West* (New York, 1835).

Bellasis, E., *Philotheus and Eugenia* (1874).

Bellenger, D. A., *The French Exiled Clergy in the British Isles After 1765: An Historical Introduction and Working List* (Bath, 1986).

Bender, G. J., *Angola Under the Portuguese* (1978).

Berger, P., *The Sacred Canopy* (1969).

Bernard, P., *Jesuits and Jacobins: Enlightenment and Enlightened Despotism in Austria* (Urbana, Ill., 1971).

Berndt, R., *Petrus Canisius SJ (1521–1597)* (Berlin, 2000).

Bertier de Sauvigny, G., *The Bourbon Restoration* (1966).

Biagioli, M., "Jesuit Science Between Texts and Contexts," *Studies in the History and Philosophy of Science* 25 (1994): 637–46.

Binchy, D., *Church and State in Fascist Italy* (1970).

*Bireley, R., *Religion and Politics in the Age of the Counterreformation: Emperor Ferdinand II, William Lamormaini, S.J., and the Formation of Imperial Policy* (Chapel Hill, N.C., 1981).

Birx, H. J., *Interpreting Evolution: Darwin and Teilhard de Chardin* (1991).

Bitterli, U., *Cultures in Conflict* (Cambridge, 1989).

Bibliography

Black, C. F., *Italian Confraternities in the Sixteenth Century* (Cambridge, 1999).

Blanning, T. C. W., "The Role of Religion in European Counter-Revolution," in D. Beales and G. Best, eds., *History, Society and the Churches: Essays in Honour of Owen Chadwick* (Cambridge, 1985).

*Block, D., *Mission Culture on the Upper Amazon* (Lincoln, Neb., 1994).

Blum, B., "Luis de Valdivia: Defender of the Araucanians," *Mid-America* 24 (1942): 109–37.

Borges, C., *The Economics of the Goa Jesuits 1542–1759* (Delhi, 1994).

Bouhours, D., *The Life of St. Francis Xavier*, trans. J. Dryden (1688).

Bowden, H. W., *American Indians and Christian Missions: Studies in Cultural Conflict* (Chicago, 1981).

Bower, A., *The History of the Popes, vol. VII* (1766).

Boxer, C., *From Lisbon to Goa, 1500–1750: Studies in Portuguese Maritime Enterprise* (1984).

*———, *The Christian Century in Japan 1549–1650* (Manchester, 1993).

———, *The Church Militant and Iberian Expansion 1440–1770* (Baltimore, 1978).

Brading, D. A., *Church and State in Bourbon Mexico: The Diocese of Michoacán, 1749–1810* (Cambridge, 1994).

A Brief Account of the Rebellions and Bloodshed Occasioned by the Anti-Christian Practices of the Jesuits and Other Popish Emissaries in the Empire of Ethiopia (1679).

Bristow, R., *A Briefe Treatise of Divers Plain and Sure Wayes* (Antwerp, 1599).

Brodrick, J., *Saint Francis Xavier* (1952).

———, *The Life and Works of Blessed Robert Francis Cardinal Bellarmine* (1928).

———, *The Economic Morals of the Jesuits* (Oxford, 1934).

———, *The Progress of the Jesuits (1556–79)* (1946).

Brooke, J., *Reconstructing Nature* (Edinburgh, 1998).

Brooks, J., *A Sermon Very Notable, Fruictefull and Godlie Made at Paules Crosse* (1553).

The Bulls of Popes Clement XIV and Pius VII for the Suppression and Re-Establishment of the Order of Jesuits (1815).

Burgaleta, C. M., *José de Acosta, S.J. (1540–1600): His Life and Thought* (Chicago, 1999).

Burrus, E., *Ducrue's Account of the Expulsion of the Jesuits from Lower California* (Rome, 1967).

Callahan, W., *Church, Politics and Society in Spain, 1750–1874* (Cambridge, Mass., 1984).

Camões, L. de, *The Lusiad: Or, the Discovery of India*, trans. W. J. Mickle (1798).

Campbell, T. J., *The Jesuits 1534–1921* (1921).

Camps, A., and J.-C. Muller, eds., *The Sanskrit Grammar and Manuscripts of Father Heinrich Roth* (Leiden, 1988).

Cannon, J., *Samuel Johnson and the Politics of Hanoverian England* (Oxford, 1994).

Caperan, L., *L'anticlericalisme et l'affaire Dreyfus, 1897–1899* (Toulouse, 1948).

Caraman, P., *The Lost Paradise: An Account of the Jesuits in Paraguay* (1975).

———, *The Lost Empire: The Story of the Jesuits in Ethiopia* (1985).

———, *Ignatius Loyola* (1990).

———, *John Gerard: The Autobiography of an Elizabethan* (1951).

Carayon, A., *Les prisons du marquis de Pombal, ministre de S.M. le roi de Portugal, 1759–1777* (Paris, 1865).

Carlen, M. C., ed., *The Papal Encyclicals* (5 vols., Wilmington, N.C., 1981).

Carriker, R. C., *Father Peter John de Smet: Jesuit in the West* (Norman, Okla., 1995).

The Case of Mrs. Catherine Cadière Against the Jesuit Girard (1732).

A Catalogue of the Most Eminently Venerable Relics of the Roman Catholic Church (1818).

Cazes, A., "Un adversaire de Diderot et des philosophes," in *Mélanges offerts par ses amis et ses élèves à M. Gustave Lanson* (Paris, 1922), 235–49.

Ceyssens, L., "Que penser finalement de l'histoire du jansénisme et de l'antijansénisme," *Revue d'Histoire Ecclésiastique* 88 (1993): 108–30.

————, "L'antijansénisme a la cour de Madrid au tournant des 17e–18e siècles," *Revue d'Histoire Ecclésiastique* 94 (1999): 15–29.

Chapple, C., ed., *The Jesuit Tradition in Education and Missions* (Toronto, 1993).

*Châtellier, L., *The Europe of the Devout: The Catholic Reformation and the Formation of a New Society* (Cambridge, 1989).

*————, *The Religion of the Poor: Rural Missions in Europe and the Foundations of Modern Catholicism, c. 1500–c. 1800* (Cambridge, 1997).

Cheke, M., *Dictator of Portugal* (1938).

Chemnitz, M., *Examination of the Council of Trent, part I,* trans. F. Kramer (St. Louis, Mo., 1971).

Christian, W. A., *Moving Crucifixes in Modern Spain* (Princeton, N.J., 1992).

Cipolla, C., *Clocks and Culture* (1967).

Close, A., *Jesuit Plots from Elizabeth to George V* (1936).

Coffin, E., *A True Relation of the Last Sickness and Death of Cardinall Bellarmine* (St. Omer, 1623).

Cohen, P. A., "The Anti-Christian Tradition in China," *Journal of Asian Studies* 20 (1960): 169–80.

Cohen, T. M., *The Fire of Tongues: Antonio Viera and the Missionary Church in Brazil and Portugal* (Stanford, 1998).

————, "Why the Jesuits Joined, 1540–1600," *Historical Papers* (Canadian Historical Association, 1974), 237–58.

Coleridge, H., ed., *The Life and Letters of Saint Francis Xavier* (2 vols., 1890).

Commissariat, M. S., *Mandelslo's Travels in Western India* (1931).

The Confessor: A Jesuit Tale of the Times (1854).

Conte-Helm, M., *The Japanese and Europe: Economic and Cultural Encounters* (1996).

Conway, J. S., *The Nazi Persecution of the Churches* (1968).

Coppa, F. J., *The Modern Papacy Since 1789* (1998).

Corradini, P., "Italian Jesuit Missionaries and Sino-Western Cultural Exchange," *Canadian Review of Comparative Literature* 24 (1997): 845–55.

Correia-Afonso, J., *Jesuit Letters and Indian History* (Bombay, 1955).

————, *Letters from the Mughal Court: The First Jesuit Mission to Akbar (1580–1583)* (Anand, 1980).

Costa, H. de la, *The Jesuits in the Philippines, 1581–1768* (Cambridge, Mass., 1961).

Courtney, F., "English Jesuit Colleges in the Low Countries 1593–1794," *Heythrop Journal* 4 (1963).

Coyne, G., M. Hoskin, and O. Pederson, eds., *Gregorian Reform of the Calendar* (Vatican City, 1983).

Crashaw, W., *The Bespotted Iesuite* (1641).

————, *Loyola's Disloyalty* (1643).

Crétineau-Joly, J. A. M., *Clément XIV et les jésuites* (Paris, 1847).

Cronin, V., *A Pearl to India: The Life of Roberto de Nobili* (1959).

Crouce, N., *Contribution of the Canadian Jesuits to the Geographic Knowledge of New France* (Ithaca, N.Y., 1924).

*Cubitt, G., *The Jesuit Myth: Conspiracy, Theory and Politics in Nineteenth-Century France* (Oxford, 1993).

Cummins, J. S., *Jesuit and Friar in the Spanish Expansion to the East* (1986).

————, "Two Missionary Methods in China: Mendicants and Jesuits," in Víctor Sánchez, ed., *España en Extremo Oriente* (Madrid, 1979), 33–108.

————, *The Travels and Controversies of Friar Domingo Navarrette, 1618–1686* (Hakluyt Society, 1960).

*Cushner, N., *Lords of the Land: Sugar, Wine, and Jesuit Estates of Coastal Peru, 1600–1767* (Albany, N.Y., 1980).

Dainville, F. de, *L'éducation des jésuites* (Paris, 1978).

D'Alembert, J. Le Rond, *An Account of the Destruction of the Jesuits in France* (1766).

Dallas, R. C., *The New Conspiracy Against the Jesuits* (1815).

Daniel, C., *Une vocation et une disgrâce* (Paris, 1861).

Davies, R. T., *Spain in Decline, 1621–1700* (1957).

Delumeau, J., *Sin and Fear* (New York, 1990).

Demerson, G., B. Dompnier, and A. Regond, eds., *Les jésuites parmi les hommes aux XVIe et XVIIe siècles* (Clermont-Ferrand, 1985).

Dessain, C. S., ed., *The Letters and Diaries of John Henry Newman*, vol. 11 (1961).

The Devotion to the Sacred Heart of Jesus (Bruges, 1767).

Dickens, A. G., and J. Tonkin, *The Reformation in Historical Thought* (Cambridge, Mass., 1985).

Diffie, B., and G. Winius, *Foundations of the Portuguese Empire, 1415–1580* (St. Paul, Minn., 1977).

Dimler. G. R., "The *Imago Primi Saeculi:* Jesuit Emblems and the Secular Tradition," *Thought: A Review of Culture and Ideas* 56 (1981): 433–48.

A Discoverie of the Most Secret and Subtile Practises of the Jesuites (1610).

Disraeli, I., *Despotism, Or the Fall of the Jesuits: A Political Romance* (1811).

The Doctrines and Practices of the Jesuits (1759).

Dominuco, V., ed., *The Jesuit Ratio Studiorum: 400th Anniversary Perspectives* (New York, 2000).

Donne, J., *Pseudo-Martyr: Wherein Out of Certaine Propositions and Gradations, This Conclusion Is Evicted, That Those Which Are of the Romane Religion in This Kingdome, May and Ought to Take the Oath of Allegiance*, ed. A. Raspa (Montreal, 1993).

————, *Ignatius His Conclave: An Edition of the Latin and English Texts*, ed. T. S. Healy (Oxford, 1969).

————, *Biathanatos*, ed. E. W. Sullivan (Newark, 1984).

Donnely, J. P., "The Jesuit College at Padua: Growth, Suppression, Attempts at Restoration: 1552–1606," *AHSI* 51 (1982): 45–79.

————, *Jacques Marquette, S.J., 1637–1675* (Chicago, 1985).

————, "Antonio Possevino's Plan for World Evangelisation," in J. S. Cummins, ed., *Christianity and Missions, 1450–1850* (Aldershot, 1997), 37–56.

Donnelly, P., *Confraternities and Catholic Reform in Italy, France and Spain* (Kirksville, Mo., 1999).

Dorsey, P., "Going to School with Savages: Authorship and Authority Among the Jesuits of New France," *William and Mary Quarterly*, 3rd series 55 (1998): 399–420.

Douarche, A., *L'université de Paris et les jésuites* (Paris, 1888).

Du Jarric, P., *Akbar and the Jesuits* (1926).

Duhr, B., *Jesuiten-fabeln: Ein Beitrag zur Culturgeschichte* (Freiburg im Breisgau, 1899).

————, *Geschichte der Jesuiten in den Ländern deutscher Zunge* (4 vols., Freiburg im Breisgau, 1907–28).

Duller, E., *The Jesuits as They Were and Are* (1845).

Dunne, G. H., *Generation of Giants* (1962).

Edmundson, G., ed. and trans., *Journal of the Travels and Labours of Samuel Fritz in the River of the Amazons Between 1696 and 1723*, Hakluyt Society Publications, 2nd series 51 (1922).

Edwards, F., ed. and trans., *The Elizabethan Jesuits of Henry More* (1981).

————, "Sir Robert Cecil, Edward Squier and the Poisoned Pommel," *Recusant History* 25 (2001), 377–414.

Bibliography

Elia, P. M. d', *Galileo in China: Relations Through the Roman College Between Galileo and the Jesuit-Scientist Missionaries* (Cambridge, Mass., 1960).

*Elison, G., *Deus Destroyed: The Image of Christianity in Early Modern Japan* (Cambridge, Mass., 1973).

Elliot, I. H., *Russia, Poland and the Jesuits* (1863).

Emmett, C, R., ed., *American Jesuit Spirituality: The Maryland Tradition, 1634–1900* (New York, 1988).

Evennett, H. O., *The Cardinal of Lorraine and the Council of Trent* (Cambridge, 1930).

An Exposure of the Jesuits (Cheltenham, 1826).

Fairplay, J., *Notes of the Wandering Jew* (Dublin, 1873).

A Faithful and Exact Narrative of the Horrid Tragedy Lately Acted Out at Thorn, in Polish Prussia (1725).

Farrell, A. P., *The Jesuit Code of Liberal Education* (Milwaukee, 1938).

*Feldhay, R., *Galileo and the Church: Political Inquisition or Critical Dialogue* (Cambridge, 1995).

Findlen, P., *Possessing Nature: Museums, Collecting and Scientific Culture in Early Modern Italy* (Berkeley, Calif., 1994).

Fisher, A. L., "A Study in Early Jesuit Government: The Nature and Origins of the Dissent of Nicolas Bobadilla," *Viator: Medieval and Renaissance Studies* 10 (1979): 397–431.

Flynn, M., *Sacred Charity: Confraternities and Social Welfare in Spain, 1400–1700* (1989).

Foley, H., *Records of the English Province of the Society of Jesus* (7 vols., 1877–84).

Ford, T. R., "Stranger in a Foreign Land: José de Acosta's Scientific Realizations in Sixteenth-Century Peru," *Sixteenth Century Journal* 29 (1998): 19–33.

Forster, M., *The Counter-Reformation in the Villages: Religion and Reform in the Bishopric of Speyer, 1560–1720* (Ithaca, N.Y., 1992).

———, *Catholic Revival in the Age of the Baroque: Religious Identity in Southwest Germany, 1550–1750* (Cambridge, 2001).

Foss, M., *The Founding of the Jesuits, 1540* (1969).

Fouqueray, H., *Histoire de la Compagnie de Jésus en France, 1528–1762* (5 vols., Paris, 1910–25).

———, "Une victime des journées de septembre: Le père Lanfant," *Etudes* 105 (1905): 50–75.

Francis, D., *Portugal 1715–1808: Joanine, Pombaline and Rococo Portugal as Seen by British Diplomats and Traders* (1985).

Freemantle, A., ed., *The Papal Encyclicals in Their Historical Context* (New York, 1956).

Frogier de Ponlevoy, A., *Acts of the Captivity and Death of the Fathers P. Olivaint, L. Ducoudray . . . and A. de Bengy* (1871).

Fülop-Miller, R., *The Power and Secrets of the Jesuits* (1929).

Fumaroli, M., *L'école du silence: Le sentiment des images au XVIIe siècle* (Paris, 1994).

———, *L'âge de l'éloquence: Rhétorique et "res literaria" de la Renaissance au seuil de l'époque classique* (Paris, 1994).

Funkenstein, A., *Theology and the Scientific Imagination* (Princeton, N.J., 1986).

A Further Discovery of the Mystery of Jesuitisme (1658).

Galilei, G., *Dialogue Concerning the Two World Systems*, trans. S. Drake (Berkeley, Calif., 1953).

Gallagher, L. J., "How We Rescued the Relics of the Blessed Andrew Bobola," *The Month* 143 (1924): 116–29.

Ganss, G. E., *The Constitutions of the Society of Jesus* (St. Louis, Missouri, 1970).

———, *Saint Ignatius' Idea of a Jesuit University* (Milwaukee, 1954).

Garraghan, G., *The Jesuits of the Middle United States* (3 vols., New York, 1938).

———, "Some Newly Discovered Marquette and La Salle Letters," *AHSI* 4 (1935): 268–90.

Gaubil, A., *Correspondence de Pékin 1722–59*, ed. R. Simon (Geneva, 1970).

Bibliography

Geddes, M., *The History of the Church of Malabar, from the Time of Its Being First Discover'd by the Portuguezes in the Year 1501* (1694).

Gee, J., *The Foot Out of the Snare: With a Detection of Sundry Late Practices and Impostures of the Priests and Iesuits in England* (1624).

George, J., "The Lincoln Writings of Charles P. T. Chiniquy," *Journal of the Illinois State Historical Society* 69 (1976): 17–25.

Gerard, J., *The Secret Instructions, Monita Secreta, of the Jesuits* (1901).

——, *The Church Versus Science* (1905).

Giard, L., and L. de Vaucelles, eds., *Les jésuites à l'âge baroque, 1540–1640* (Grenoble, 1996).

——, eds., *Les jésuites à la Renaissance: Système éducatif et production du savoir* (Paris, 1995).

Goddard, P. A., "Converting the Sauvage: Jesuit and Montagnais in Seventeenth-Century New France," *Catholic Historical Review* 84 (1998): 219–39.

Godechot, J., *The Counter Revolution: Doctrine and Action 1789–1804* (1972).

Gold, L. J., "Johnson's Translation of Lobo," *Proceedings of the Modern Language Society of America* 80 (1965): 51–61.

Goldie, F., *The First Christian Mission to the Great Mogul; or, The Story of Blessed Rudolf Acquaviva, and of His Four Companions in Martyrdom* (Dublin, 1897).

Goodpasture, H. M., ed., *Cross and Sword: An Eyewitness History of Christianity in Latin America* (Maryknoll, N.Y., 1989).

Goodwin, J., *Athanasius Kircher, Renaissance Man, and the Quest of Knowledge* (1979).

Goodwin, T., *Aggravation of Sinne, and Sinning Against Knowledge and Mercie* (1643).

Grabinski, B., *Das Übersinnliche im Weltkriege* (Hildesheim, 1917).

Gray, E., and N. Fiering, eds., *The Language Encounter in the Americas* (New York, 2000).

Greene, D. J., *The Politics of Samuel Johnson* (New Haven, Conn., 1960).

Greengrass, M., *France in the Age of Henry IV* (1984).

Griesinger, T., *The Jesuits* (1903).

Guettée, F. R., *Histoire des jésuites, composée sur documents authentiques en partie inédits* (3 vols., Paris, 1858–59).

Gwynn, D., *The Action Française Condemnation* (1928).

Haliczer, S., *Sexuality in the Confessional: A Sacrament Profaned* (Oxford, 1996).

Halls, W. D., *Politics, Society and Christianity in Vichy France* (Oxford, 1995).

Hanke, L., *Aristotle and the American Indians* (1959).

Hanley, T. O'Brien, ed., *The John Carroll Papers* (3 vols., Notre Dame, 1976).

Hardy, J., Jr., "French Jesuit Missions and the Enlightenment," *Bucknell Review* 12 (1964): 94–108.

Harney, M. P., *The Jesuits in History: The Society of Jesus Through Four Centuries* (New York, 1941).

Harrington, A., *Japan's Hidden Christians* (Chicago, 1993).

Heilbron, J. L., *Electricity in the Seventeenth and Eighteenth Centuries: A Study of Early Modern Physics* (Berkeley, Calif., 1979).

Heimbucher, M., *Die Orden und Kongregationen der katholische Kirche* (Paderborn, 1965).

Hellman, J., *The Knight-Monks of Vichy France* (Montreal, 1997).

Helmreich, E., *The German Christian Church Under Hitler* (Detroit, 1979).

Hicks, L., ed., *Letters and Memorials of Father Robert Persons, SJ*, vol. I, Catholic Record Society 39 (1968).

Higman, F., ed., *Three French Treatises* (1970).

Hinsch, B., *Passions of the Cut Sleeve* (Berkeley, Calif., 1990).

Hobart Seymour, M., *A Pilgrimage to Rome* (1848).

————, *Mornings Among the Jesuits at Rome* (1850).

Hogan, E. I., *Distinguished Irishmen of the Sixteenth Century* (1894).

Holmes, P., *Resistance and Compromise: The Political Thought of the Elizabethan Catholics* (1982).

————, ed., *Elizabethan Casuistry*, Catholic Record Society 67 (1981).

Hopper, A., " 'The Popish Army of the North': Anti-Catholicism and Parliamentary Allegiance in Civil War Yorkshire, 1642–46," *Recusant History* 25 (2000). 12–28

Hosten, H., "Father Nicholas Pimenta," *Journal and Proceedings of the Asiatic Society of Bengal*, new series 23 (1927). 67–82

Howard, C., *English Travellers of the Renaissance* (London, 1923).

Hsia, R. P.-C., *Society and Religion in Münster, 1535–1618* (New Haven, Conn., 1984).

Hufton, O., "Altruism and Reciprocity: The Early Jesuits and their Female Patrons," *Renaissance Studies* 15 (2001): 328–53.

Hughes, T., *History of the Society of Jesus in North America* (2 vols., New York, 1907–17).

Huppert, G., *Public Schools in Renaissance France* (Urbana, Ill., 1984).

Ingrao, C., *The Habsburg Monarchy 1618–1815* (Cambridge, 1994).

Ishida, M., "A Biographical Study of Giuseppe Castiglione . . . a Jesuit Painter in the Court of Peking," *Memoirs of the Research Department of the Toyo Bunko* 19 (1960): 79–121.

Jaki, S., *The Road of Science and the Ways to God* (Edinburgh, 1978).

The Jesuit Libel Case: Father Bernard Vaughan, SJ, v. "The Rock" (1902).

The Jesuite Discovered; or, A Brief Discourse of the Policies of the Church of Rome (1659).

Jesuitical Policy and Iniquity Exposed: A View of the Constitution and Character of the Society of Jesus (Glasgow, 1831).

The Jesuits Character; or, A Description of the Wonderfull Birth, Wicked Life, and Wretched Death, of a Jesuit (1642).

Jingle, J., *Spiritual Fornication: A Burlesque Poem* (1732).

Jonas, R., "Sacred Mysteries and Holy Memories: Counter-Revolutionary France and the Sacre Coeur," *Canadian Journal of History* 32 (1997): 347–59.

————, "Anxiety, Identity and the Displacement of Violence During the Année Terrible: The Sacred Heart and the Diocese of Nantes, 1870–1871," *French Historical Studies* 9 (1975).

Jonsen, A., and S. Toulmin, *The Abuse of Casuistry: A History of Moral Reasoning* (Berkeley, Calif., 1988).

A Journal of All the Proceedings Between the Jansenists and the Jesuits (1659).

Kafker, F. A., *The Encyclopedists as a Group*, Studies in Voltaire and the Eighteenth Century 345 (Oxford, 1996).

Kaiser, T. E., "Madame de Pompadour and the Theatres of Power," *French History* 19 (1996). 172–81

Karant-Nunn, S., *The Reformation of Ritual* (1997).

Keller, J. A., *The Sacred Heart* (1898).

Kelter, I., "The Refusal to Accommodate: Jesuit Exegetes and the Copernican System," *Sixteenth Century Journal* 26 (1995): 273–83.

Keyssler, J. G., *Journey through Germany . . . and Italy* (1759).

Kingdon, R., *Myths About the Saint Bartholomew Massacres* (1988).

Kircher, A., *China Illustrata*, ed. and trans. C. D. Van Tuyl (Muskogee, Okla., 1987).

Kloczowski, J., *A History of Polish Christianity* (Cambridge, 2000).

Knecht, R., *Francis I* (Cambridge, 1982).

Kolakowski, L., *God Owes Us Nothing: A Brief Remark on Pascal's Religion and on the Spirit of Jansenism* (Chicago, 1995).

Kondrad, H., *A Jesuit Hacienda in Colonial Mexico* (Stanford, Calif., 1980).

Kuhn, T., *The Structure of Scientific Revolutions* (Chicago, 1962).

Kurtz, L., *The Politics of Heresy: The Modernist Crisis in Roman Catholicism* (Berkeley, Calif., 1986).

La Pillonière, F. de, *An Answer to the Reverend Dr Snape's Accusation, by F. de La Pillonière, Formerly a Jesuit, Now Living with the Bishop of Bangor: Containing an Account of His Behaviour . . . Amongst the Jesuits, of His Leaving Their Society, and Afterwards Turning Protestant (1717)*.

Lach, D., *Asia in the Making of Europe*, vol. 1 (Chicago, 1965).

Lacouture, *Jesuits: A Multibiography* (1996).

Lafitau, J.-F., *Customs of the American Indians Compared with the Customs of Primitive Times* (1724).

Langdon, H., *Caravaggio: A Life* (1998).

Lapide, P., *The Last Three Popes and the Jews* (1967).

Lapomarda V. A., "The Jesuits and the Holocaust," *Journal of Church and State* 23 (1981): 241–58.

Larkin, M., *Church and State After the Dreyfus Affair* (1974).

Lattis, J. M., *Between Copernicus and Galileo: Christoph Clavius and the Collapse of Ptolemaic Cosmology* (Chicago, 1994).

Lavin, I., *Bernini and the Unity of the Visual Arts* (1980).

Lazar, L., "The First Jesuit Confraternities and Marginalised Groups in Sixteenth Century Rome," in Nicholas Terpstra, ed., *The Politics of Ritual Kinship: Confraternities and Social Order in Early Modern Italy* (Cambridge, 2000), 132–49.

Le Comte, L., *Memoirs and Observations Topographical, Physical, Mathematical, Mechanical, Natural, Civil, and Ecclesiastical: Made in a Late Journey Through the Empire of China, and Published in Several Letters* (1697).

Lea, H. C., *A History of Sacerdotal Celibacy* (New York, 1957).

Leahey, M., " 'Comment peut un muet prescher l'évangile?': Jesuit Missionaries and the Native Languages of New France," *French Historical Studies* 19 (1995): 105–31.

Leith, W. F., *Narratives of the Scottish Catholics* (Edinburgh, 1885).

Leonard, E., *George Tyrrel and Catholic Tradition* (New York, 1982).

Leroy, M., *Le mythe jésuite: De Béranger à Michelet* (Paris, 1992).

Lettres édifiantes et curieuses (34 vols., Paris, 1702–76).

Lewy, G., "The Struggle for Constitutional Government in the Early Years of the Society of Jesus," *Church History* 29 (1960): 141–60.

Lockhart, J., and S. Schwartz, *Early Latin America: A History of Colonial Spanish America and Brazil* (Cambridge, 1983).

Lockman, J., *Travels of the Jesuits into Various Parts of the World* (2 vols., 1743).

Loriquet, J. N., *Pombal, Choiseul et D'Aranda, ou L'intrigue des trois cabinets* (Paris, 1830).

Lough, J., *France Observed in the Seventeenth Century by British Travellers* (Stocksfield, 1984).

———, "Reflections on Enlightenment and Lumières," *British Journal for Eighteenth Century Studies* 8 (1985): 1–15.

Lynch, J., *The Hispanic World in Crisis and Change* (Oxford, 1992).

Lynde, H., *Via Tuta* (1630).

Lualdi, K., and A. Thayer, eds., *Penitence in the Age of Reformations* (Aldershot, 2000).

Mabry, D. J., "Mexican Anticlericals, Bishops, Cristeros, and the Devout During the 1920s: A Scholarly Debate," *Journal of Church and State* 20 (1978): 81–92.

MacCormack, S., *Religion in the Andes: Vision and Imagination in Early Colonial Peru* (Princeton, N.J., 1991).

MacDonald, T. L., "Riccioli and Lunar Nomenclature," *Journal of the British Astronomical Society* 27 (1967): 112–17.

MacDonnell, Joseph, *Jesuit Geometers* (St. Louis, 1989).

Bibliography

Maclagan, E., *The Jesuits and the Great Mogul* (1932).

Maron, G., *Ignatius von Loyola: Mystik—Theologie—Kirche* (Göttingen, 2001).

Martin, A. L., *Henry III and the Jesuit Plots* (1973).

———, *Plague? Jesuit Accounts of Epidemic Disease in the Sixteenth Century* (Kirksville, 1996).

*———, *The Jesuit Mind: The Mentality of an Elite in Early-Modern France* (Ithaca, N.Y., 1988).

———, "The Jesuit Mystique," *Sixteenth Century Journal* 4 (1973): 31–40.

Maxwell, K., *Pombal: Paradox of the Enlightenment* (Cambridge, 1995).

McBrien, R., *Lives of the Popes: The Pontiffs from St. Peter to John Paul II* (New York, 1997).

McCabe, W., *An Introduction to the Jesuit Theater* (St. Louis, 1983).

McCoog, T., *The Society of Jesus in Ireland, Scotland and England* (Leiden, 1996).

———, " 'Laid up Treasure': The Finances of the English Jesuits in the Seventeenth Century," in W. J. Sheils and D. Wood, eds., *The Church and Wealth*, Studies in Church History 24 (Oxford, 1987), 257–66.

McCullough, P., *Sermons at Court: Politics and Religion in Elizabethan and Jacobean Preaching* (Cambridge, 1998).

McGinness, F., *Right Thinking and Sacred Oratory in Counter-Reformation Rome* (Princeton, N.J., 1995).

McManners, J., *Church and Society in Eighteenth-Century France* (2 vols., Oxford, 1988–98).

Mellon Jr., K., "Christian Priber's Cherokee Kingdom of Paradise," *Georgia Historical Quarterly* 57 (1973): 319–33.

Meskens, A., "The Jesuit Maths School in Antwerp in the Early Seventeenth Century," *Seventeenth Century* 12 (1997): 11–22.

Métraux, A., "Jesuit Missions in South America," in J. H. Steward, ed., *Handbook of South American Indians*, vol. 5 (New York, 1963), 645–54.

Metzler, J., "Foundation of the Congregation de Propaganda Fide by Gregory XV," in Metzler, ed., *Sacrae Congregationis de Propaganda Fide memoria rerum*, vol. 1.1, *1622–1700* (Rome, 1971), 79–111.

Middleton, T., *A Game at Chess*, ed. T. H. Howard-Hill (Manchester, 1993).

Minamiki, G., *The Chinese Rites Controversy from Its Beginning to Modern Times* (Chicago, 1985).

Monaci, P., *The Life and Martyrdom of the Blessed Andrew Bobola* (London, 1855).

Moote, A., *Louis XIII, the Just* (Berkeley, Calif., 1989).

Moran, J. F., *The Japanese and the Jesuits: Alessandro Valignano in Sixteenth-Century Japan* (1993).

Mörner, M., ed., *The Expulsion of the Jesuits from Latin America* (New York, 1965).

Morton, T., *A Full Satisfaction Concerning a Double Romish Iniquitie: Hainous Rebellion, and More Than Heathenish Aequivocation* (1606).

Mousnier, R., *The Assassination of Henry IV: The Tyrannicide Problem and the Consolidation of the French Absolute Monarchy in the Early Seventeenth Century*, trans. J. Spencer (1973).

Mungello, D., *Curious Land: Jesuit Accommodation and the Origins of Sinology* (Stuttgart, 1985).

———, ed., *The Chinese Rites Controversy: Its History and Meaning* (Nettetal, 1994).

———, *The Forgotten Christians of Hangzhou* (Honolulu, 1994).

*———, *The Great Encounter of China and the West, 1500–1800* (Lanham, Md., 1999).

Munitz, J. A., and P. Endean, eds., *St. Ignatius of Loyola: Personal Writings* (1996).

Murphy, M., *St. George's College, Seville, 1592–1767*, Catholic Record Society 73 (1992).

Murray, J., *Antwerp in the Age of Plantin and Brueghel* (Norman, Okla., 1970).

Murray, J., "St. Andrew Bobola and Poland," *The Month* 172 (1938): 22–29.

*Neill, S., *A History of Christianity in India: The Beginnings to AD 1707* (Cambridge, 1984).

News from Heaven: or a Dialogue Between St. Peter and the Five Jesuits Last Hang'd (1679).

Nicholls, D., *God and Government in an "Age of Reason"* (1995).

Nida, E., *Message and Mission* (New York, 1960).

Noble, D., *A World Without Women: The Christian Clerical Culture of Western Science* (New York, 1992).

Noreen, K., "Ecclesiae Militantis Triumphi: Jesuit Iconography and the Counter-Reformation," *Sixteenth Century Journal* 29 (1998): 689–715.

Northeast, C. M., *The Parisian Jesuits and the Enlightenment* (1991).

Notes on the Wandering Jew, or the Jesuits and their Opponents (Dublin, 1873).

Occasional Letters of the Present Affairs of the Jesuits in France (1763).

O'Connell, M. R., *Thomas Stapleton and the Counter-Reformation* (New Haven, Conn., 1964).

Olearius, A., *The Voyages and Travels of the Ambassadors Sent by Frederick Duke of Holstein, to the Great Duke of Muscovy, and the King of Persia . . . Whereto Are Added the Travels of John A. de Mandelslo . . . from Persia, into the East-Indies* (1662).

*O'Malley, J., *The First Jesuits* (Cambridge, Mass., (1993).

———, *Trent and All That: Renaming Catholicism in the Early Modern Era* (Cambridge, Mass., 2000).

*———, et al., eds., *The Jesuits: Cultures, Sciences, and the Arts, 1540–1773* (Toronto, 1999).

O'Reilly, F., "Stonyhurst and Angelo Secchi," *Stonyhurst Magazine* (2000): 28–34.

O'Reilly, T., "Ignatius of Loyola and the Counter Reformation: The Hagiographic Tradition," *Heythrop Journal* 31 (1990): 439–70.

———, *From Ignatius Loyola to John of the Cross: Spirituality and Literature in Sixteenth Century Spain* (Norfolk, 1995).

O'Rourke Boyle, M., *Loyola's Acts: The Rhetoric of Self* (Berkeley, Calif, 1997).

Owen, D., *The Puritan Turn'd Jesuit* (1652).

Owen, L., *Speculum Jesuiticum* (1632).

A Packet from Rome: Containing an Account of Some Extraordinary Transactions of the Jesuits at the Court (1745).

Padberg, J. W., et al., *For Matters of Greater Moment: The First Thirty Jesuit General Congregations* (1994).

———, *Colleges in Controversy: The Jesuit Schools in France from Revival to Suppression 1815–1880* (1969).

Pagani, C., " 'One Continous Symphony': Automata and the Jesuit Missions in Qing China," in B. H. K. Luk, ed., *Contacts Between Cultures: Eastern Asia* (Lampeter, 1992), 279–84.

Pagden, A., *The Fall of Natural Man* (Cambridge, 1986).

The Palme of Christian Fortitude, or The Glorious Combats of Christians in Japonia (St. Omer, 1630).

Palmer, R. R., "The French Jesuits in the Age of Enlightenment: A Statistical Study of the *Journal de Trévoux*," *American Historical Review* 45 (1939–40), 44–58.

Parker, G., *The Thirty Years War* (1987).

Parry, J. H., *The Spanish Theory of Empire in the Sixteenth Century* (Cambridge, 1940).

Pasquier, E., *Le catéchisme des jésuites* (1592).

Passelecq, G., *The Hidden Encyclical of Pius XI* (New York, 1997).

Pastor, L. von, *The History of the Popes from the Close of the Middle Ages* (40 vols., 1923–53).

Paterson, W., *The Great Jesuit Plot of the Nineteenth Century* (Edinburgh, 1894).

Paul, H. W., *The Edge of Contingency; French Catholic Reaction to Scientific Change from Darwin to Duhem* (1979).

Pearson, M. N., *The New Cambridge History of India*, I.i (Cambridge, 1987).

Phillips, H., *Church and Culture in Seventeenth-Century France* (1997).

Picón-Salas, M., *A Cultural History of Spanish America from Conquest to Independence* (Berkeley, Calif., 1962).

Pilbeam, P., *The 1830 Revolution in France* (1991).

Pilkington, J., *Works*, ed. J. Scholefield (Cambridge, 1842).

Pinkney, D., *The French Revolution of 1830* (Princeton, N.J., 1972).

Pitrat, J. C., *Americans Warned of Jesuitism* (New York, 1851).

Plattner, F. A., *Jesuits Go East* (Dublin, 1950).

Pollen, J. H., ed., "The Memoirs of Father Robert Persons'," *CRS Miscellanea 2*, Catholic Record Society (1906).

————, "The Memoirs of Father Persons Continues," *CRS Miscellanea 4*, Catholic Record Society (1907).

Poncelet, A., *Histoire de la Compagnie de Jésus dans les anciens Pays-Bas* (1926).

The Popish Courant (1714).

Pörtner, R., *The Counter Reformation in Central Europe* (2001).

The Proceedings and Sentence of the Spiritual Court of Inquisition of Portugal, Against G. Malagrida, Jesuit, for Heresy, Hypocrisy, False Prophecies, Impostures, and Various Other Heinous Crimes: Together with the Sentence of the Lay Court of Justice (1762).

Purchas, S., *Purchas His pilgrimage, or Relations of the World and the Religions Observed in All Ages and Places Discovered, from the Creation unto This Present (1617).*

Pyrotechnica Loyolana: Ignatian Fire-Works, or the Fiery Jesuit's Temper and Behaviour (1667).

Quynn, D. M., "The Art Confiscations of the Napoleonic Wars," *American Historical Review* 50 (1944–45): 437–60.

Rahner, H., "Der Tod des Ignatius," *Stimmen der Zeit* 158 (1955–56): 241–53.

————, "Der kranke Ignatius," *Stimmen der Zeit* 158 (1955–56): 81–90.

Rajamanickam, X., "The Newly Discovered 'Informatio' of Robert de Nobili," *Archivum Historicum Societatis Iesu* 39 (1970): 224–46.

Ranchetti, M., *The Catholic Modernists* (Oxford, 1969).

Randles, W. G. L., *The Unmaking of the Medieval Christian Cosmos* (Aldershot, 1999).

Rapin, R., *Mémoires*, ed. L. Aubinau (Paris, 1865).

Reef, D. T., "In the Shadow of the Saints: Jesuit Missionaries and their New World Narratives," *Romance Philology* 53 (1999): 165–81.

Reilly, C., *Athanasius Kircher: A Master of a Hundred Arts* (Wiesbaden, 1974).

Reinerman, A. J., "Metternich Versus Chateubriand: Austria, France and the Conclave of 1829," *Austrian History Yearbook* 12 (1976): 155–80.

Relation de ce qui s'est passé entre l'un des éditeurs des documents . . . concernant la Compagnie de Jésus, et MM les rédacteurs du Journal des Débats (Paris, 1827).

A Relation of the Strange Apparition of the Five Jesuits Lately Executed at Tyburn (1680).

Richeome, L., *Discours sur les saintes reliques* (1605).

————, *Defence des pèlerinages* (1605).

Robertson, C., *"Il Gran Cardinale": Alessandro Farnese, Patron of the Arts* (1992).

Rodén, M.-L., "Queen Christina of Sweden, Spain and the Politics of the Seventeenth-Century Papal Court," in E. M. Ruiz and M. de Pazzis Pi Corrales, eds., *Spain and Sweden in the Baroque Era, 1600–1660* (Puertollano, 2000), 783–800.

Ronan, C. E., and B. B. C. Oh, eds., *East Meets West: The Jesuits in China 1582–1773* (Chicago, 1988).

Ronda, J. P., "We Are Well As We Are: An Indian Critique of Seventeenth Century Christian Missions," *William and Mary Quarterly* 34 (1977): 66–82.

————, "The European Indian: Jesuit Civilisation Planning in New France," *Church History* 41 (1972): 385–95.

Root, J. D., "English Catholic Modernism and Science: The Case of George Tyrrell," *Heythrop Journal* 18 (1977): 271–88.

Roper, H. I., *The Jesuits* (1848).

*Ross, A., *A Vision Betrayed: The Jesuits in Japan and China, 1542–1742* (Edinburgh, 1994).

Ross, R. J., "The Kulturkampf and the Limitations of Power in Bismarck's Germany," *Journal of Ecclesiastical History* 46 (1995): 602–16.

Rowbotham, A., *Missionary and Mandarin: The Jesuits at the Court of China* (Berkeley, Calif., 1942).

Royer, F., *Father Miguel Pro* (Dublin, 1955).

Rule, P. A., "The Confucian Interpretation of the Jesuits," *Papers on Far Eastern History* 6 (1972): 1–61.

Russell-Wood, A. J. R., *The Portuguese Empire, 1415–1808: A World on the Move* (Baltimore, 1998).

Sanceau, E., *Knight of the Renaissance: D. João de Castro, Soldier, Sailor, Scientist, and Vice-Roy of India 1500–1548* (1949).

Sánchez, M., *The Empress, the Queen and the Nun: Women and Power at the Court of Philip III of Spain* (Baltimore, 1998).

*Sanneh, L., *Translating the Message* (Maryknoll, 1992).

Scaglione, A., *The Liberal Arts and the Jesuit College System* (1986).

Schilling, B. N., *Conservative England and the Case Against Voltaire* (New York, 1950).

Schurhammer, G., *Francis Xavier: His Life and His Times* (4 vols., Rome, 1973–82).

———, "Xaveriuslegenden und Wunder: Kritisch Untersucht," *Archivum Historicum Societatis Iesu* 32 (1963): 179–92.

Schütte, J. F., ed., *Valignano's Mission Principles for Japan* (2 vols., St. Louis, 1980–95).

Schutz, K., *Papal Primacy, from Its Origins to the Present* (Collegeville, Minn., 1996).

Scribner, R., and T. Johnson, eds., *Popular Religion in Germany and Central Europe 1400–1800* (1996).

Sebes, J., *The Jesuits and the Sino-Russian Treaty of Nerchinsk* (1961).

Seed, P., *Ceremonies of Possession: Europe's Conquest of the New World, 1492–1640* (Cambridge, 1995).

Sharp, S., *Letters from Italy, Describing the Customs and Manners of That Country, in the Years 1765 and 1766: To Which Is Annexed an Admonition to Gentlemen Who Pass the Alps in Their Tour Through Italy* (London, 1767).

Shea, J. G., *History of the Catholic Church in the United States*, vol. I, *Colonial Days* (New York, 1886).

———, *Discovery and Exploration of the Mississippi Valley* (Redfield, N.Y., 1852).

Shore, P., *The Eagle and the Cross: Jesuits in Late Baroque Prague* (St. Louis, 2002).

Sievernich, M., and G. Switek, eds., *Ignatianisch: Eigenart und Methode der Gesellschaft Jesu* (Freiburg, Basel, and Vienna, 1990).

Smith, B. M., "Anti-Catholicism, Indian Education and Thomas Jefferson Morgan, Commissioner of Indian Affairs," *Canadian Journal of History* 23 (1988): 213–33.

The Solemn Mock-Procession: or, The Tryal & Execution of the Pope and His Ministers (1680).

Sorkin, D., "Reform Catholicism and Religious Enlightenment," *Austrian History Yearbook* 30 (1999): 187–219.

Sousa, T. R. de, "Why Cuncolim Martyrs? An Historical Reassessment," in T. R. de Sousa and Charles J. Borges, eds., *Jesuits in India in Historical Perspective* (Macao, 1992), 35–47.

Southern, D., *John La Farge and the Limits of Catholic Interracialism 1911–1963* (Baton Rouge, 1996).

*Spence, J. D., *The Memory Palace of Matteo Ricci* (1985).

———, *The China Helpers: Western Advisers in China, 1620–1960* (1969).

Bibliography

Squire, E., *Authentic Memoirs of that Exquisitely Villainous Jesuit, Father Richard Walpole* (1733).

St. Ignatius' Ghost, Appearing to the Jesuits (1700).

Stegemüller, F., *Geschichte des Molinismus* (Münster, 1935).

Sutcliffe, A., *Paris: An Architectural History* (New Haven, Conn., 1993).

Swann, J., *Politics in the Parlement of Paris Under Louis XV, 1754–1774* (Cambridge, 1995).

Szcześniak, B., "Notes on the Penetration of Copernican Thought in China," *Journal of the Royal Asiatic Society* (1945): 30–38.

Szilas, L., "Konklave und Papstwahl Clemens XIV," *Zeitschrift für Katholische Theologie* 96 (1974): 287–99.

Tacchi Venturi, P., *Storia della Compagnia di Gesù in Italia* (2 vols., Rome, 1910–51).

Tachard, G., *A Relation of the Voyage to Siam Performed by Six Jesuits* (1685).

Taylor, L., *Soldiers of Christ: Preaching in Late Medieval and Reformation France* (Oxford, 1992).

———, *Heresy and Orthodoxy in Sixteenth Century Paris* (Leiden, 1999).

Thoman, M., *Der Ex-Jesuit* (1774).

Thompson, D. G., "The Lavalette Affair and the Jesuit Superiors," *French History* 10 (1996): 206–39.

———, "General Ricci and the Suppression of the Jesuit Order in France, 1760–64," *Journal of Ecclesiastical History* 37 (1986): 426–41.

Thorndike, L., *A History of Magic and Experimental Science* (8 vols., 1923–58).

Thorpe, J., "Notes on Passing Events in Rome," Jesuit English Province Archives.

Thwaites, R. G., ed., *The Jesuit Relations and Allied Documents* (73 vols., Cleveland, 1896–1901).

Tierney, B., *Origins of Papal Infallibility 1150–1350*, Studies in the History of Christian Thought 6 (Leiden, 1972).

Tinker, G., *Missionary Conquest: The Gospel and Native American Cultural Genocide* (1993).

Torbarina, J., "The Meeting of Bošković with Dr. Johnson," *Studia Romanica et Anglica Zagrabiensia* 13–14 (1967).

Towers, E., "The Opening Years of the Venerable English College, Rome," *Ushaw Magazine* 20 (1910): 14–53.

A Translation of the Bull for Effectual Suppression of the Order of Jesuits (1774).

The Travels of Several Learned Missionaries of the Society of Jesus into Divers Parts of the Archipelago, India, China and America (1713).

Trigger, B., *The Children of Aataensic: A History of the Huron People to 1660* (Montreal, 1987).

Trousson, R., "Deux lettres du P. Castel à propos du 'Discours sur les Science et les Arts,' " in John Pappas, ed., *Essays on Diderot and the Enlightenment in Honor of Otis Fellows* (Geneva, 1974), 292–301.

Trudel, M., *The Beginnings of New France, 1524–1663* (Toronto, 1973).

A True Relation of the Proceedings Against John Ogilivie (Edinburgh, 1615).

Trust a Papist and Trust the Devil (1642).

Turlerus, H., *The Traveiler of Jerome Turler* (1575).

Turnbull, *The Kakure Kirishitan of Japan* (1998).

Tylenda, N., *Jesuit Saints and Martyrs* (Chicago, 1998).

Udia, A., "Jesuits' Contribution to Meteorology," *Bulletin of the American Meteorological Society* (1996): 2307–15.

Valentin, J. M., *Le théâtre des jésuites dans les pays de langue allemande* (Bern, 1978).

Valtierra, A., *Peter Claver* (1960).

Van Dyke, P., *Ignatius Loyola: The Founder of the Jesuits* (Port Washington, N.Y., 1986).

*Van Kley, D., *The Religious Origins of the French Revolution: From Calvin to the Civil Constitution, 1560–1791* (New Haven, Conn., 1996).

Bibliography

*————, *The Jansenists and the Expulsion of the Jesuits from France, 1757–1765* (New Haven, Conn., 1975).

Vaticanism as Seen from the Banks of the Tiber (1884).

Vauchez, A., *Sainthood in the Late Middle Ages* (Berkeley, Calif., 1997).

Viner, J., "Secularizing Tendencies in Catholic Social Thought from the Renaissance to the Jansenist-Jesuit Controversy," *History of Political Economy* 10, no. 1 (1978): 114–50.

Vissière, I. and J. L., *Lettres édifiantes et curieuses de Chine par les missionaires jésuites* (Paris, 1979).

Wadsworth, J., *The Memoires of Mr. James Wadswort, a Jesuit That Recanted* (1679).

Waele, M. de, "Pour la sauvegarde du roi et du royaume: L'expulsion des jésuites de France à la fin des guerres de religion," *Canadian Journal of History* 29 (1994): 267–80.

Waley-Cohen, J., "God and Guns in Eighteenth-Century China: Jesuit Missionaries and the Military Campaigns of the Qianlong Emperor (1736–1795)," in B. H. K. Luk, ed., *Contacts Between Cultures: Eastern Asia: History and Social Sciences* (Lampeter, 1992), 94–99.

*Wallace, W., *Galileo and His Sources: The Heritage of the Collegio Romano in Galileo's Science* (Princeton, N.J., 1984).

The Wanton Jesuit (1731).

Waterworth, J., ed., *The Canons and Decrees of the Sacred and Oecumenical Council of Trent* (1848).

Watson, W., *A Sparing Discoverie of Our English Iesuits* (1601).

Webster, R. A., *The Cross and the Fasces* (1960).

Weld, A., *Suppression of the Jesuits in the Portuguese Dominions* (1877).

Wessels, C., *Early Jesuit Travellers* (The Hague, 1924).

Whitfield, T., *Paying the Price: Ignacio Ellacuría and the Murdered Jesuits of El Salvador* (Philadelphia, 1994).

Whyte, L. L., ed., *Roger John Boscovich S.J., F.R.S., 1711–1787: Studies of His Life and Work* (1961).

Wicki, J., "Die Chiffre in der Ordenskorrespondenz der Gesselschaft Jesu von Ignatius bis General Oliva," *AHSI* 32 (1963): 133–78.

Wiest, J.-P., "Bringing Christ to the Nations: Shifting Models of Mission Among Jesuits in China," *Catholic Historical Review* 83 (1997): 654–81.

Williams, M. E., *The Venerable English College Rome* (1979).

Wilson, A. T., ed., *History of the Missions of the Fathers of the Society of Jesus Established in Persia* (Hertford, 1925).

Witek, J., ed., *Ferdinand Verbiest (1623–1688): Jesuit Missionary, Scientist, Engineer, and Diplomat* (Nettetal, 1994).

Wittkower, R., and I. B. Jaffe, eds., *Baroque Art: The Jesuit Contribution* (New York, 1972).

Woolf, H., *The Transits of Venus: A Study of Eighteenth Century Science* (Princeton, N.J., 1959).

Worcester, T., *Seventeenth Century Cultural Discourse: France and the Preaching of Bishop Camus* (New York, 1999).

Wright, A. D., *The Counter Reformation* (1982).

Wright, W., *A Briefe Relation of the Persecution Lately Made Against the Catholike Christians in the Kingdome of Japonia* (St. Omer, 1619).

Young, W. J., ed., *The Letters of Ignatius Loyola* (Chicago, 1959).

Ziggelaar, A., *François de Aguilon SJ (1567–1617), Scientist and Architect* (Rome, 1983).

Index

About the Author

The British historian Jonathan Wright was born in Hartlepool in 1969. He was educated at the universities of St. Andrews, Pennsylvania, and Oxford, where he earned his doctorate in 1998. He has published on various aspects of early modern religious history and is a contributor to Oxford University Press's *New Dictionary of National Biography* and Scribner's revised *Dictionary of American History*.